	SUMMARY OF DOS C		
COMMAND	**DESCRIPTION**	**FORMAT**	
DEBUG	Invokes the assembly-language debugging program	[*D:Path*]DEBUG [*FileSpec*] [*Param1*] [*Param2*]	
DEL	Removes a file from the disk	DEL *FileSpec*	572
DIR	Lists files on a disk or in a directory	DIR [*FileSpec*][/P][/W]	574
DISKCOMP	Compares two diskettes	[*D:Path*]DISKCOMP [*D1*:[*D2*:]][/1][/8]	575
DISKCOPY	Duplicates complete diskette	[*D:Path*]DISKCOPY [*SourceD:DestD:*][/1]	576
EDLIN	Line editor supplied with DOS	[*D:Path*]EDLIN *FileSpec* [/B]	578
ERASE	Removes a file from a disk	ERASE *FileSpec*	579
EXE2BIN	Converts an .EXE file to a .COM file	[*D:Path*]EXE2BIN *SourceFile* [*DestFile*]	580
FASTOPEN	Speeds up file opening	[*D:Path*]FASTOPEN *D1*:[= *Size*] ...	581
FDISK	Partitions a hard disk	[*D:Path*]FDISK	583
FIND	Finds strings in files	[*D:Path*]FIND [/V][/C][/N]"*String*" [*FileSpec*...]	584
FORMAT	Prepares a disk to accept data	[*D:Path*]FORMAT *D1*:[/S][/1][/8][/V][/B][/4][/N:*xx*][/T:*yy*]	586
GRAFTABL	Displays ASCII characters on CGA	[*D:Path*]GRAFTABL [437 ¦ 860 ¦ 863 ¦ 865 ¦ /STATUS]	588
GRAPHICS	Enables PrtSc to print graphics screens	[*D:Path*]GRAPHICS [*PrinterType*] [/R][/B][/LCD]	589
JOIN	Merges two disks into one	[*D:Path*]JOIN [*Drive2*[*Drive1*]][/D]	591

*See Part 6, "DOS Command Reference," for a complete description of subcommands and their parameters.

This summary of DOS commands, plus summaries of EDLIN commands, configuration file commands, and batch-file subcommands, continues at the back of this book.

UNDERSTANDING DOS 3.3

UNDERSTANDING DOS 3.3®

JUDD ROBBINS

San Francisco • Paris • Düsseldorf • London

Cover design by Thomas Ingalls + Associates
Cover photograph by Michael Lamotte
Illustrations by van Genderen Studio
Screen reproductions produced by XenoFont.

To the Sennin Foundation of El Cerrito, California, and the Way of the Universe.

ACKNOWLEDGMENTS

Thanks to all the people at SYBEX who made this book much better than I ever could have alone: Fran Grimble editor; Kay Luthin, copyeditor; Robert Campbell, technical reviewer; Paul Erickson, word processor; Elizabeth Newman, typesetter; Aidan Wylde, proofreader; Anne Leach, indexer; Julie Bilski and Lucie Živny, graphic artists; Rick van Genderen, illustrator; and Michelle Hoffman, screen shot producer.

CONTENTS AT A GLANCE

TABLE OF CONTENTS

P A R T 1 GETTING STARTED

P A R T 2   *MAKING DOS DO MORE*

P A R T   3   *REVVING IT UP* ━━━━━━━━━━

P A R T 5   GOING BEYOND

INTRODUCTION

You and I probably select our software based on what each package offers, and whether we need it for our business. DOS is usually a required part of your system. Just as surely as you need a printer to produce hard-copy reports and a screen to display intermediate results, you need a disk operating system (DOS) to provide the key management capabilities for your hardware. This allows each software package to deal only with its own application needs.

You may have bought DOS because you were told you had to, or simply to run your application software (Lotus 1-2-3, dBASE III PLUS, WordPerfect, and so on). The great wealth of software being advertised, sold, and used in the business world today requires that MS-DOS, PC-DOS, or another DOS manage the overall hardware and operating environment. You will find that using DOS can be remarkably easy.

NECESSARY HARDWARE AND SOFTWARE FOR THIS BOOK

This book assumes that you have an MS-DOS or PC-DOS microcomputer. Although most of the fundamental capabilities are available in earlier versions of DOS, many of the more advanced features seen later in this book are only available to you in the most recent versions. This book uses DOS 3.3, although you will be told when a particular feature is unavailable in earlier versions. In fact, this book will be useful if you are using any version of DOS from 2.X upward; version 2.X introduced the key feature of hierarchical directories.

HOW TO USE THIS BOOK

You may have a computer with diskette drives only, or you may have a hard-disk machine. This book is appropriate for you in either case. Many examples are provided for either situation, and commands are explained in terms of what they can do on *any* disk drive. While you read through the book, you should stop as often as possible to try the commands and features on your computer. Seeing them work immediately will give you the reinforcement necessary for quickly sharpening your skills.

HOW THIS BOOK IS ORGANIZED

You don't need any background at all to get the most out of this book. As in all things, however, experience will help you to learn some things more easily, and to skip other things that you already know. *Understanding DOS 3.3* is structured so that you can jump to the section or chapter that's right for you.

The first 16 chapters of *Understanding DOS 3.3* emphasize the power available to you within DOS itself, and Chapter 17 presents the additional power available in the software marketplace. Although additional utility programs are often worth spending money for, this book can save you such expense by showing you how to implement utility capabilities with DOS commands alone. A well-written DOS command can often take the place of a piece of additional software. You'll learn how to use DOS to set up your own menu system, file-sorting capability, diskette-cataloging mechanism, backup procedure, text-searching facility, and much more.

This book has five parts. Part 1, "Getting Started," presents the strong foundation necessary for any user. Chapter 1 presents the fundamental pieces of hardware and software used when working with a disk operating system. Chapter 2 focuses on your first steps with the DOS diskettes, in preparation for running programs. Beginners must read and become comfortable with the information presented in Part 1. Those with some experience are urged to read this part to review fundamentals and to learn basic skills that might have been overlooked before.

Part 2, "Making DOS Do More," is a self-contained tutorial on how DOS stores and uses information in files on disks. Chapter 3 concentrates on the commands and features used to manipulate files in a host of ways. You then learn in Chapter 4 how a directory structure is created and maintained, as well as the commands necessary to create, name, modify, and manipulate your files. Chapter 5 takes a special look at the elements of a directory system as they pertain to application programs. If you intend to set up your hard disk for running a word processor, a database management system, a spreadsheet program, or almost any other application package, you should read this chapter carefully.

Chapter 6 prepares you to create and modify text files using the DOS line editor, EDLIN. You will need this skill throughout the rest of the book to properly generate and update certain system files, as well as to write your own simple programs with the DOS batch-file mechanism. Finally, in Chapter 7 you will examine the ways you can produce printed output with your system.

Part 3, "Revving It Up," picks up the pace quite a bit. Some advanced capabilities are discussed for those of you who want to learn more than the basics. The general arena of DOS communications is explored in Chapter 8. The flow of data between the central processor and peripheral devices is critical to any successful computer system; you will learn in this chapter the terminology and technology for data transmission, and you will see how certain DOS commands give you complete control over the flow of information.

An important, but often neglected, capability of DOS is its ability to back up and restore all or portions of your hard disk. Chapter 9 introduces the appropriate backup commands and discusses effective techniques for using them. In Chapter 10, you will also learn how to customize your system by means of DOS configuration and startup options. They can significantly improve the performance of your DOS system, as well as its ease of use.

Unique features for the international use of your computer are presented in Chapter 11. These tools enable you to initialize your keyboard layout, printer, and screen for a foreign flair. Chapter 12 examines advanced features—pipes and filters—that give you precise control over the flow of information throughout your entire system.

Part 4, "Life in the Fast Lane," deals primarily with advanced commands and features. It focuses on the sophisticated arena of batch files. You will learn of the possibilities and limitations of these files in Chapter 13, and in Chapter 14, you will extend this knowledge with subcommands and parameters. You'll learn how to combine all of the elements of batch files in creative and powerful ways.

Many actual batch files and techniques are presented in Chapter 15.

You can type in any of these batch files and run them immediately on your system, or you can send for a companion diskette that contains all of the batch files in this book. An order form for this purpose is included at the end of this book.

Chapter 16 deals with the commands available to an advanced DOS user. These powerful commands can connect multiple disk drives into directory superstructures, simulate nonexistent drives with subdirectories, and reroute disk requests from one drive to another. You'll also see uncommon commands that influence the command processor itself and modify the DOS environment. In addition, you'll study a group of specialized commands that provide you with advanced file-manipulation capabilities.

The last chapter in Part 4, Chapter 17, explores the best of the add-on and add-in utility software, which can give you and your DOS a boost. I suggest that you seriously consider buying some of these products. Some will be useful on a daily basis; others will be critical only once in a while. When that time comes, however, you won't want to be without the right piece of software.

Part 5 is truly designed for those of you "Going Beyond" the constraints of DOS, now or in the future. Chapter 17 presents simple steps you can take to increase the power of your DOS system with additional utility software. The three chapters in this section cover the giant steps available to make major advances in your computing environment. Chapter 18 shows the multitasking capabilties available to you within your standard 640K DOS system if you select the Windows program from Microsoft. Chapter 19 explains how a variety of manufacturers have surmounted the 640K barrier using expanded and extended memory techniques. Lastly, Chapter 20 introduces you to OS/2, the exciting new operating system from IBM and Microsoft that provides both multitasking and enhanced memory addressing. Specifically, you will learn how to run your current DOS programs within the framework of the new operating system.

Part 6, the "DOS Command Reference" (Chapter 21), has been included for easy access to all of DOS's commands. The text of *Understanding DOS 3.3* presents the most important DOS commands. You won't find your learning impeded by a blind presentation of all commands and all of their parameters and switches, some of which are not essential. Chapter 21 fills in the gaps by providing you with a quick, alphabetized reference to all commands, all parameters, and all possible switches. You are encouraged to return to this reference chapter over and over as you use DOS. A quick overview of both the usage and format of each command may be all you'll need to speed you on your way with DOS applications.

Three appendices are also included to make your use of DOS a little easier. Appendix A is a complete glossary of relevant computer terms. Appendix B is an extended table of ASCII codes, with an explanation of character sets and numbering systems. Appendix C will come in handy when you need to configure or reconfigure fixed disks.

DOS is now a stable product; it is expected to be a principal operating system for years to come. This book will be a useful companion as you work toward your goal of making effective use of the software available.

ICONS USED IN THIS BOOK

Three visual icons are used in this book. The Note icon

indicates a note that augments the material in the text. The Tip icon

represents a practical hint or special technique. When you see the Warning icon

pay particular attention—it represents an alert or warning about a possible problem or offers a way to avoid the problem.

PART 1

GETTING STARTED

In Part 1, you will get a sense of what DOS is and what it can do. If you're just beginning to use DOS, you should read and become comfortable with the information presented here. Even if you have some experience, you should read Part 1 to refresh your memory and perhaps learn some basics you missed elsewhere.

Chapter 1 explains the fundamental pieces of hardware you will use with DOS: the central processing unit, the disk drives, hard disks and floppy diskettes, and other devices such as printers. It introduces the two types of DOS commands, resident and transient. It also explains how DOS stores data on disks.

In Chapter 2, you will get down to work with DOS. You'll load and start up DOS, and you'll learn how to give commands, set the system date and time, and prepare your disks for use. You'll also learn how to back up diskettes, starting with your DOS master diskettes.

THE FUNDAMENTALS OF DOS

EVERY COMPUTER THAT USES DISKS (HARD OR floppy) must have a master program that coordinates the flow of information from computer to disk and from disk to computer. This is called the *disk operating system,* or *DOS.* In this book, you'll learn about the operating system used on the IBM PC and compatible microcomputers. This operating system is manufactured by Microsoft Corporation and licensed to IBM and other microcomputer manufacturers. The name of this system, when purchased from Microsoft, is *MS-DOS*—that is, *M*icrosoft *D*isk *O*perating *S*ystem. When it is purchased from IBM, it is called *PC-DOS.*

What does all this mean? Simply that the terms *DOS, MS-DOS,* and *PC-DOS* really refer to the same thing, and in fact are often used interchangeably. In this book, the term *DOS* refers to the disk operating system used on IBM microcomputers and the wide range of IBM-compatible microcomputers.

This chapter will teach you how DOS is used and what useful functions it can perform. You will also learn about the fundamental parts of the computer sitting on your desk and about a number of computer devices (peripherals) that you might not own yet but might be interested in acquiring. You'll learn the differences between input and output devices, as well as their purpose.

Most importantly, you'll acquire an understanding of what disks and diskettes are, how they're set up, and how DOS provides you with commands to manage them. You'll see how data is organized on them, so you can make better decisions later about which disks are appropriate for your use. You'll learn a host of good techniques for caring for your disks, so you can significantly reduce the odds of losing critical data through disk failure.

Since the manufacturer of each new computer may make minor adjustments to DOS before releasing it for that machine, you may occasionally notice slight differences between your DOS's messages and those in this book. However, since DOS is virtually the same from machine to machine, you will probably never see any variation other than in the startup message.

WHAT DOS DOES

The disk operating system is assigned the task of integrating the various devices that make up a computer system. There are three major tasks the operating system must carry out. It must

- Coordinate the input and output devices, such as monitors, printers, disk drives, and modems;

- Enable the user to load and execute programs; and

- Maintain an orderly system of files on the disk.

Computer memory has one basic drawback. The area of memory in which your programs and data are stored, called *random-access memory* (*RAM*), cannot store information after the electricity has been turned off, even for a fraction of a second. To store information in the computer, you must have some means of recording it. The most common devices for this task are *disk drives,* which are devices that can read or write to magnetic disks.

Magnetic disks divide generally into two categories: *hard disks* and *floppy disks,* or *diskettes.* On a hard disk the magnetic storage medium is rigid, or hard. Hard disks are called *fixed* or *nonremovable* disks if they are built into the drive itself; they are called *removable cartridges* if they can be inserted into and removed from the disk drive. Information is stored on a disk as a collection of characters. Hard disks usually hold at least 10 million characters, and larger models that hold 70 million characters are now available on the newest IBM Personal

System/2 line of microcomputers. Each 10Mb is roughly equivalent to 5000 pages of typed text.

Diskettes usually store less information. The most flexible and common type, the 5¼'' diskette, can store several hundred thousand characters of information, depending on the density of the magnetic material on the disk's surface. A high-capacity 5¼'' diskette can actually store 1.2 million characters. A less common but increasingly popular type, the 3½'' diskette, is often called a *microfloppy* diskette. It owes its growing popularity to higher storage densities, holding as many as 1.44 million characters. This is the largest storage capacity of any diskette; in addition, the microfloppy's small size makes it easier to store and transport.

By now you understand that different types of disks store different amounts of information. However, all disks share information in the same way—as a collection of characters. You may have heard the term *byte;* it is interchangeable with the term *character.* Any keyboard character can be stored and represented by DOS as a series of eight bits (of binary 0's and 1's), which together make a byte. Approximately one thousand (actually 1024, or $2**10$) of these bytes are together called a *kilobyte,* while approximately one million (actually 1,048,576, or $2**10$) of them are known as a *megabyte.* The eight bits can be arranged in 256 different ways, thereby representing 256 different characters. Some of these characters are the ones you can type in (A–Z, 0–9, and so on), and others are simply interpreted by DOS as *control* characters. This classification includes all special character codes that control special operations, like sounding a bell on a video monitor or performing a carriage return on a printer. See Appendix B for more details on character sets and numbering methods.

Each complete collection of related characters is called a *file.* A disk can have many files that contain either instructions for the computer (*program files*) or data stored by the user (*data files*). A disk can contain both program files and data files. Each file must be given a unique name so that the computer can later refer to the file and load it from the disk into the computer's memory again.

DOS is responsible for managing this flow of information. As you will learn, DOS contains a host of commands and programs that enable it to store information on any disks connected to your computer. It also has full responsibility for arranging your files on these disks in ways that will contribute to easy and efficient retrieval when you need them.

WHAT YOU NEED TO KNOW ABOUT DOS

What does the average user need to know about DOS? This is a hotly debated question. Some people contend that as little time as possible should be spent on DOS. However, since DOS defines the basic structure of the computer system, you must be able to command DOS effectively to exercise full control over the computer. Knowing DOS is especially useful when something goes wrong. In this book, you will learn much about DOS that will help you to deal with both the expected and the unexpected.

THE FUNDAMENTAL HARDWARE

DOS is designed to manage the details of a variety of hardware connections and combinations. You should understand a bit about the hardware before you ever open up the DOS box and use the diskettes.

A microcomputer system is composed of a *central system unit* and a variety of *peripheral devices* (see Figure 1.1). The central system unit usually contains the primary processing chip (the *CPU,* or *central processing unit*), the main system memory (RAM), and usually one or more disk drives. The CPU is the brain of the computer. It performs the various arithmetic operations, as well as controlling the flow of data to and from the additional peripheral devices. The main memory of the computer is the place in which instructions and data are stored during program execution. Keep in mind that the amount of available and required RAM always increases as the sophistication of the programs that are run on your computer increases.

The disk drives in the minimum *configuration* (the arrangement of system components) are usually diskette drives, although a hard-disk drive is included more and more often as hardware prices continue to drop. As Figure 1.1 shows, systems that use diskettes refer to the drives as A: and B:. Systems that use one diskette drive and one hard-disk drive refer to them as A: and C:. This book will refer to these drives simply as A, B, and C.

The peripheral devices in the minimum configuration are the video monitor and the keyboard. The keyboard usually has one of

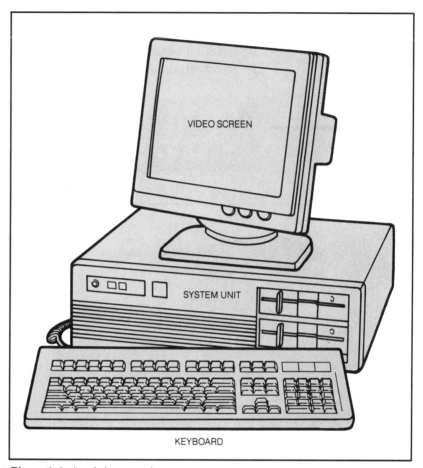

VIDEO SCREEN

SYSTEM UNIT

KEYBOARD

Figure 1.1: A minimum microcomputer system

four layouts, depending upon whether it is designed to be compatible with an IBM PC-XT, the IBM PC-AT, the IBM Personal System/2, or the IBM Convertible. There are several possible choices for a video monitor—monochrome, color graphics, or enhanced graphics are the most common. Higher-resolution monitors, although more expensive, are becoming more common in businesses using desktop-publishing and computer-aided design (CAD) software.

There is virtually no limit to the range of additional devices that can be connected to a microcomputer. Most business microcomputer systems contain more than the minimum, as Figure 1.2 shows. The various *connector ports* in the back of the computer, such as the *parallel* and *serial* ports, allow the straightforward (although not necessarily easy) connection of printers, plotters, digitizers, extra disk drives, and so on. The task of starting DOS so that it manages this hardware is consistent, no matter what hardware configuration you have.

INPUT AND OUTPUT DEVICES

As you have seen, the computer you are working on is really not one machine but a group of related devices. Devices can be attached to the

Figure 1.2: A more standard microcomputer system

Disk drives can be both input and output devices. Most DOS commands deal with the complex process of input from and output to the disk drives.

computer internally (inside the system unit) or externally (in separate boxes attached by cables). Some of these devices deal with the information that is input into the computer system, while other devices manage the output of information from the computer system. Some devices do both (see Table 1.1).

HOW DISKS ARE SET UP

When you buy a box of diskettes, the diskettes in that box are *not* ready to be used with your computer. In order to use them, you must prepare the diskettes with some of the special programs provided with your disk operating system. Even hard disks must be prepared. Most people never get a chance to format and set up their hard-disk drives because the dealers usually do this for them. This is not altogether an advantage, since you never learn the basics of disk setup.

This section explains how and why disk-preparation programs are used. The ideas and techniques presented here are some of the first actions you take with a new computer system. The section not only shows you what to do, it also helps you understand what is really going on when you issue these commands.

THE DISK COMMANDS

The concept of DOS is confusing for two reasons:

1. A large part of DOS is invisible to the user. DOS has two parts, one of which (the *hidden files* part) is stored on the disk but does not appear on the disk directory. The other part is a

DEVICE	FUNCTION
Keyboard	Input only
Screen	Output only
Printer	Output only
Disks	Input and output

Table 1.1: Typical purposes of DOS devices

file called COMMAND.COM, which is visible on every diskette used to start up (or *boot*) the system. In DOS 3.3, COMMAND.COM occupies 25,307 bytes, while the two hidden system files together occupy another 52,259 bytes. This 50K (kilobytes) is a price you will pay on every system (boot) disk you create.

2. The actions performed by DOS are divided into two types. *Resident commands* are actions that DOS can always perform, no matter what disk happens to be in the computer. These commands are always resident in memory, and so they execute immediately when you want. *Transient commands* are really small programs for special purposes. If you want to perform any of these actions, you must have the correct disk in the computer, or (as you'll see in Chapter 4) you must tell DOS where these programs are located on your disks. Since transient commands are only brought into memory from a disk when you request them, it is your responsibility to ensure that they are available when needed.

On floppy-diskette systems, the DOS command files must be accessible through one of the drives. Otherwise, DOS will display an error message indicating that it can't find the requested command.

Table 1.2 shows the resident and transient DOS commands. You will learn more about these commands throughout this book. For now, you will be concerned only with the fundamental disk structure that stores these commands for you and makes them available whenever you need them.

DISK ORGANIZATION

When a floppy diskette is taken out of the box, it is totally blank. So, too, is a hard disk. The primary difference between diskettes and hard disks lies only in the arrangement of the magnetic material. This material can be arranged on one or both sides of a diskette, depending on whether the diskette is single-sided or double-sided. Diskettes can also have differing densities. The more densely the magnetic material is written onto a diskette, the more information it can hold. Hard disks, on the other hand, can have several layers of magnetic material, each with two sides, which means they can store even more information.

In order for the computer system to use any disk as a medium for storing information, the entire disk must be divided into sections organized so that every physical location on the disk has a

RESIDENT COMMANDS		
BREAK	DEL	RMDIR
CHCP	DIR	SET
CHDIR	ERASE	TIME
CLS	MKDIR	TYPE
COPY	PATH	VER
CTTY	PROMPT	VERIFY
DATE	RENAME	VOL
TRANSIENT COMMANDS		
APPEND	FIND	RECOVER
ASSIGN	FORMAT	REPLACE
ATTRIB	GRAFTABL	RESTORE
BACKUP	GRAPHICS	SELECT
CHKDSK	JOIN	SHARE
COMP	KEYB	SORT
DISKCOMP	LABEL	SUBST
DISKCOPY	MODE	SYS
EXE2BIN	MORE	TREE
FASTOPEN	NLSFUNC	XCOPY
FDISK	PRINT	

Table 1.2: Classification of DOS commands

unique address. This is the same concept as assigning ZIP code numbers to various towns and cities. When DOS assigns addresses, it then has an orderly way in which to store and then find various pieces of information.

The system of magnetic storage used by DOS is one of concentric rings (see Figure 1.3). Each ring is called a *track*. For example, there are 40 tracks (numbered 0 to 39) on each double-sided, double-density diskette, while there are twice as many tracks (numbered 0

The "hub hole" in Figure 1.3 is merely the center hole in a disk or diskette, which fits onto the spindle of a disk drive. Like the hole in a record and the spindle on a turntable, this hole and spindle ensure that the disk spins in a true circular path. Data can then be read from and written to consistent places on the tracks of the disk.

Figure 1.3: Tracks laid out on a disk

to 79) on a high-capacity diskette. Each track is divided into smaller parts called *sectors*. Tracks and sectors are created when a disk is formatted. It is DOS's job to assign the necessary addresses for each track and sector. You needn't be concerned about this addressing mechanism, since it is really only for DOS's benefit. DOS needs to know the actual disk location of your files; you only have to know their names. That's what makes the operating system such a valuable ally in running application software.

The exact number of sectors depends on what type of diskette is being formatted (see Table 1.3). Standard double-sided, double-density diskettes have 9 sectors per track, while the high-capacity

Disk Structure	5¹/₄" Double Density	5¹/₄" High Density	3¹/₂" Double Density	3¹/₂" High Density
Number of tracks	40	80	80	80
Sectors per track	9	15	9	18
Characters per sector	512	512	512	512
Total number of sectors	720	2400	1440	2880
Total number of characters	360 K	1.2 M	720 K	1.44 M

Table 1.3: Diskette organization

diskettes available for the IBM PC-AT and compatibles have 15 sectors per track. Each sector can hold 512 bytes. The newest 3¹/₂" diskettes containing 1.44Mb have 80 tracks per side, each track holding 18 standard 512-byte sectors.

Standard double-density diskettes can have a maximum of 112 uniquely named files, while high-capacity diskettes can store 224 files. Hard disks can store significantly more individual files, depending on their size (10Mb, 20Mb, and so on).

Some of the formatted disk space is not available to you for storing data—about 6K on a 5¹/₄" diskette to about 18K on a 3¹/₂" diskette. When a disk is formatted, some of the sectors are set aside for keeping track of the information stored on that disk. Every formatted disk has these areas. Together, they serve as a catalog of the contents of that disk. These areas are called the *file allocation table* (*FAT*), the *boot record,* and the *directory table.* The details of their use are beyond the scope of this book, but their impact on disk-space usage should be considered.

TAKING CARE OF YOUR DISKETTES

If you have never dealt with diskettes before, they may look and feel flimsy. They are not as flimsy as they appear, but they are also not as durable as many users believe. In many offices, computer users seem to use their diskettes as paperweights on their desks. Sometimes people don't even keep the diskettes in the jackets they originally came in. These are usually the ones who complain most vocally about their diskettes failing several times a year.

A well-maintained diskette can easily last for years. Mishandling diskettes can have serious consequences. An accident can destroy the contents of a diskette in only seconds.

Here are some suggestions for diskette handling. Keep in mind that experience and knowledge lie behind every one of them:

- Keep your diskettes in their jackets when not in use. You never know when they may fall on the floor or when something might fall or spill on them. It's simple risk reduction.

- Don't leave your diskettes in the disk drives, especially if the computer is going to be moved. Remember, others who clean around your computer may move it to clean the table tops.

- Don't leave your diskettes in your car, where the temperature often gets high enough to warp them, making them unreadable for your computer. Also keep them away from any sources of magnetic fields, such as motors, telephone bells, and magnetic card keys.

- Don't touch the magnetic surface of the diskettes—hold them by their jackets. Fingerprints have their place, but it's not on a diskette.

- Make backup copies of all original diskettes, and keep current copies of all diskettes with important, newly created program or data files.

- Keep your backup diskette copies in a different location from the original diskette (for example, at home if your computer is at the office; at work if your computer is at home).

- Label all your diskettes, both electronically with a DOS command and with a printed, gummed label. Write on the label before you attach it to the diskette, or use a soft felt-tipped pen to write carefully on an existing label.

- Don't squeeze the last bit of space out of your diskettes. Always leave them a little empty. In the first place, you may later want to add some new files to that very diskette. Later, you may also want to expand the size of some of the files on the diskette.

SUMMARY

This chapter introduced you to DOS—what it is, what it does, and how it is used. The chapter included the following topics:

- You learned about the fundamental pieces of hardware that make up a typical microcomputer system. This hardware constitutes the environment within which the disk operating system and all of your selected application software perform their tasks. The components are

  The central processing unit, or CPU, which performs analytic or computational tasks.

  The disk drives, which work with disks to store your data and program files.

  Disks and diskettes. There are two types of hard disks, fixed and removable, each storing from 10 to 70 megabytes of data. There are two classes of floppy diskettes, 5¼'' (which can store from 180K to 1.2Mb of data) and 3½'' microfloppy diskettes (which can store from 720K to 1.44Mb of data).

  The system console, consisting of a video monitor for output displays and a keyboard for the input of data and commands.

  Other devices such as modems, mice, digitizers, plotters, and a wide range of printers.

- You learned that the primary means of communicating with your computer is with input and output devices. The principal input device is your keyboard, and the principal output device is the video screen. Most printed copy (hard copy) is generated on a printing device, such as a dot-matrix, letter-quality, or laser printer.

- You learned that DOS has two types of commands, resident and transient. Resident commands reside in a portion of memory reserved by DOS and are always available. Transient commands reside in files on your system disk and must be read into memory before being executed.

- You learned that information is stored on a disk in circular patterns called tracks, which are broken up into easily addressable, 512-byte portions called sectors.

- You learned that DOS arranges and maintains the physical and logical arrangement of information stored on the disks. Your programs and data are stored on the disk in collections of bytes called files.

- You learned that you must treat your diskettes with care.

Now that you've learned the fundamentals of DOS, Chapter 2 will help you begin to actually use your computer. Get ready to take those important first steps with DOS disks and DOS commands.

YOUR FIRST STEPS WITH DOS

CHAPTER 2

YOUR FIRST ACTUAL STEPS WITH DOS HAVE LITTLE
to do with the software itself. They involve acquiring the right pieces
of hardware, turning the computer on, and preparing the disks for
use. Your individual application programs may require additional
preparation of certain system parts, such as printers and plotters.

Virtually every piece of peripheral hardware that can be connected
to your computer can be initialized, configured, or set up in a way
that will be helpful for individual application programs. Such possibilities will be discussed later in this book, but for now, you will concentrate on the basic hardware that goes into a typical
microcomputer system.

You will learn in this chapter how to get your DOS system going,
and, consequently, how to get going with any application program
you will be running. You'll learn how to set the time and date correctly if your system doesn't have a built-in clock/calendar. When
Daylight Savings Time comes around, you'll know how to make the
necessary adjustments to your system.

In this chapter you'll also begin to learn more and more DOS commands. You'll learn how to correct the errors you'll make quickly
and efficiently. Since you may change your mind about a command you've given to DOS, you'll learn how to let DOS know about
your changes.

You'll also learn to prepare disks for storing your valuable data
and file information, as well as for booting up your system. Backing
up your disks and exploring the status of a disk are necessary skills
you'll also acquire here. In short, this chapter will start ''teaching
you the ropes'' of DOS.

GETTING STARTED

Your first task after turning on the power is to load DOS into the computer. Place your DOS system diskette into drive A and close the door. (This drive is usually on the left side of most computers; however, some computers place it at the top when the drives are located one on top of the other.) If you have already loaded DOS onto a hard disk, all you need to do is turn the power on at this point. If you haven't prepared your hard disk or loaded DOS onto it, you should refer to your individual disk and DOS manuals for the proper procedure on your computer. Appendix C also offers instructions for this task.

The computer will go through a process called *booting* or *bootstrapping*. This process loads DOS into the memory of the computer and is necessary before the computer can actually be used. Once DOS is in memory, you can begin to work.

SETTING THE DATE AND TIME AT STARTUP

Regardless of whether you have hard disks or floppy diskettes, you should begin by placing the DOS system diskette in drive A. Then turn on the power to the computer. After the computer tests its internal hardware, it will display the following message:

```
Current date is Tue 1-01-1980
Enter new date (mm-dd-yy):_
```

January 1, 1980, is the default startup date each time you bring DOS up on your system. Assuming you do not have an automatic clock in your system, you will see this message each time DOS starts up. You'll be expected to enter the correct date at this point. However, if your system is configured with additional hardware that includes a battery-backed clock, you won't have to enter this date each time. The additional hardware will come with instructions on avoiding the standard DOS request for correcting the date, as well as on dealing with the subsequent request for the time of day:

```
Current time is 0:02:47.82
Enter new time:_
```

DOS keeps track of time in standard military format, so if you wanted to enter a time of 10:30 A.M., you could simply enter 10:30. However, if you wanted to enter 3:30 P.M., you would have to enter 15:30.

After you've entered the correct date and time, you're on your way. DOS will display a version of the following prompt, although the actual wording will vary slightly from computer to computer. In some versions of DOS, you will receive these copyright notices *before* the date and time request:

```
DOS version 3.3
Copyright Matsushita Electric Industrial Co., Ltd 1987
Copyright Microsoft Corporation 1981, 1987
A>_
```

Since in this example the system diskette has been loaded in drive A, the DOS A> prompt now appears. As you will see through much of the rest of the book, when DOS is installed on a hard disk, the typical "DOS is ready" prompt is C>, indicating that DOS is installed and operative on drive C and is waiting for your instructions.

HOW THE DOS SYSTEM GETS GOING

You may wonder how DOS gets into the computer. A small part of it is already in the computer memory. Intelligent bootstrapping logic ensures that the rest of the disk operating system is loaded automatically from the disk when you turn on the computer. That is why *a diskette must always be present in drive A before you turn on the computer.* If you have a hard disk, then that disk is always ready and takes the place of the diskette in drive A. After loading, DOS shares the computer memory with the programs you run and the data those programs use (see Figure 2.1).

To let you know that DOS is active, the computer displays a prompt that looks like this:

A>

This DOS prompt (usually A> or C>) is a simple way of asking you for your instructions. Unless you deliberately change this prompt (as you will see in Chapter 5), it always has two characters: a letter and a

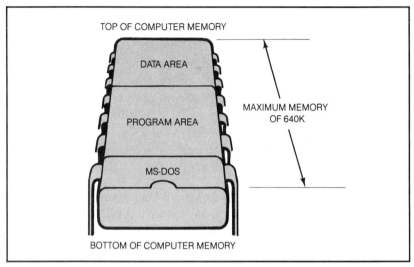

Figure 2.1: Memory map

greater-than sign (>). The letter indicates the current active drive; unless otherwise specified, all commands will affect data on that drive only. If you are using a two-drive system, the letter will be A (for the left drive) or B (for the right drive). Hard-disk users will usually see the letter C, indicating a standard hard-disk drive.

Whenever you see the A> (or C> for hard-disk users), it means that DOS is ready to accept a command from you. It also tells you that you are not working in any other program. Later, you will learn how to change an A to a B or a C.

GIVING COMMANDS TO DOS

You can exercise complete control over what DOS will do for you and when DOS will do it. In this book, you will learn many instructions—commands—that you can give to DOS. Nearly all of the commands must be entered at the DOS prompt. Unless DOS is prompting you for a command entry, you will be unable to enter any commands.

When the blinking cursor is positioned at the DOS prompt, all you need to do is type in a valid DOS command and press the Return key. (The cursor always indicates the position of the next character to be typed.) Some DOS computers label the Return key RETURN;

You must press the Return key after almost every command in DOS. This book will not specify so after each command; instead, you should learn to use the key as an automatic end to each of your commands. Should you *not* be required to press Return for a command, this book will clearly state so at the appropriate point.

Modifying a DOS command with a parameter or a switch is analogous to modifying a verb in a sentence with an adverb. By learning to use these modifiers well in the DOS environment, you can produce results that are as aesthetically pleasing as a well-formed turn of phrase in your native language.

others label it ENTER; still others only label it with the ⬅ symbol. All are equivalent. This book will use the term *Return key* to indicate the key that you should press on your keyboard to do this job.

Pressing the Return key is necessary because some DOS commands require more entry information than the command word itself. Simple commands like DIR (to obtain a directory listing) require only that you type the letters (D, I, and R) followed by the Return key. Since even this simple command may be followed by additional specifications, such as the format of the resultant listing or the disk drive you're interested in, DOS does not process your request until it determines that you have actually pressed the Return key. Only then can it assume that you have completed your request.

The additional qualifications for command requests are called *parameters* or *arguments*. (We'll use the term *parameter* in this book.) In general, parameters can be thought of as placeholders for the data that will be typed in when you execute the actual command. The specific data is called the *value* of the parameter. Later, when you actually run those commands, you'll be expected to supply the values for the variable parameters. Parameters in this book will be represented as descriptive terms in italic type—for example, *FileName*. You'll learn the most important examples of all of these modifiers in the context of the appropriate commands.

Many DOS commands permit the specification of *switches*. A switch slightly changes how the command executes. *What* the command does remains the same; only *how* the command executes its task changes because of the addition of a switch. As you learn new commands in this book, you'll also learn the most important and useful switches available with each command. In some cases, other switches exist, but their purpose is either obscure or not frequently needed. Your DOS user's manual can provide you with an exhaustive list of additional switches.

EDITING CONTROLS

Several keys on the keyboard perform special tasks. The location of these keys differs, depending on whether you are using a keyboard that is compatible with the IBM PC-XT, the PC-AT, the Personal System/2, or the PC Convertible. Figures 2.2 through 2.5 show the complete layouts of these keyboards. Several key combinations also are interpreted in special ways by programs like DOS. The following sections show you how to save energy and time by using these keys.

CORRECTING MISTAKES

What happens if you make a mistake? There are a few editing controls in DOS that you may find handy. The most common one is the Backspace key, often seen as a large ← on your keyboard just above the Return key. If you type

DIR B:*.COM

Figure 2.2: Keyboard layout for the IBM PC-XT and compatible computers

Figure 2.3: Keyboard layout for the IBM PC-AT and compatible computers

but do not press Return, your cursor will be on the space just beyond the last character you typed. To erase that character, you press the Backspace key. The M disappears and the cursor moves one space to the left. To erase the next character, the O, you would again press the Backspace key. Continuing to press this key would remove the entire command, keystroke by keystroke.

Figure 2.4: Keyboard layout for the IBM Personal System/2 and compatible computers

Figure 2.5: Keyboard layout for the IBM PC Convertible and compatible computers

CANCELING A COMMAND

Suppose that you entered a command and decided before you pressed the Return key that you wanted to cancel it. You may have changed your mind, or you may have realized that you simply entered the wrong request; you may even have become confused and need to reconstruct the request completely. One way would be to use the Backspace key to remove all the characters.

A better way, however, is to use the Esc key (short for Escape) to cancel the entire line with a single keystroke. If you entered a typical command like

    DIR B:*.EXE

you could cancel the entire command by pressing Esc. A backslash mark (\) appears on the line you typed, and the cursor moves to the next line. This indicates that the entire command will be ignored:

    DIR B:*.EXE\

    —

Note that the command is not erased from the screen—it is only ignored. The cursor moves to the next line, awaiting entry of your next DOS command.

REPEATING A COMMAND

DOS holds the last command you issued in a special place in its memory. If you press one of the special function keys, located usually on the left side or top of your keyboard, your last command will automatically be retyped for you.

Suppose you needed to locate a particular file called 88BUDGET.WK1 on one of several diskettes. You could place the first possible diskette in drive A or B and enter the command

    DIR 88BUDGET.WK1

If you don't see the file listed, you could remove the first diskette, place the second possible diskette in the drive, and press function key number 3, referred to as F3. Your original DIR command is retyped for you on the line. Pressing Return again will execute this DOS request for the second diskette.

Whenever you have to perform the same DOS request multiple times (whether for several diskettes, several files, or several directories), using the F3 key can often save you much time by retyping the command line for you.

CORRECTING PART OF A COMMAND

Suppose you have entered the command

    DOR B:*.COM

DOS responds with the message "Bad command or file name." This makes sense—the command should have been entered as DIR, not DOR. You might think that the only way to correct this mistake is to retype the entire command. However, DOS provides a better way to edit the most recently entered command. The F1 key will recall one letter at a time from the previous command. With this example, pressing F1 will make the D appear. Now you can type the correct letter, I. To recall the rest of the command line, which was entered correctly, you press F3. The entire corrected command is then ready to be executed. Pressing Return will execute the line as if you had retyped the entire line.

The F1 and F3 keys are handy tools to learn how to use. Although other function-key capabilities exist, you won't use them very often; you can later explore their usage on your own. Table 2.1 summarizes the editing keys and their functions for DOS.

CLEARING THE DISPLAY

As you proceed with various DOS commands, you may at times want to clear the current screen display and begin again with a clean screen. DOS contains a command to do this. Entering

    CLS

and pressing Return will clear the screen and then redisplay the current DOS prompt at the top of the screen with the cursor beside it,

KEY NAME	FUNCTION
F1	Retypes one character at a time from the last command entry
F2	Retypes all characters from the last command entry up to the one identical to your next keystroke
F3	Retypes all remaining characters from the last command entry
F4	Retypes all characters beginning at the first match with your next keystroke, and ending with the last character from the last command entry
F5	Permits direct editing of all the characters from the entire last command
F6	Places a special end-of-file code at the end of the currently open file; sometimes referred to as a CTRL-Z or ˆZ end-of-file code
Ins	Permits insertion of characters at the cursor
Del	Permits deletion of the character to the left of the cursor
Esc	Abandons the currently constructed command without executing it

Table 2.1: DOS editing keys

awaiting your next command. Note that clearing the screen has no effect on either disk files or programs in computer memory. It simply clears the display of text or output left over from previous commands.

CHANGING THE SYSTEM DATE AND TIME

If your system does not have a built-in, battery-backed clock, you will automatically be prompted by DOS to enter the correct date and time each time you power up. However, even if your system does have the hardware for keeping track of the date and time, there may be times when you need to correct one or the other. For instance, twice a year in most of the United States, Daylight Savings Time requires you to adjust all clocks by one hour. You can enter the TIME command at the DOS prompt anytime you want to see the current system time or change it:

```
C>TIME
Current time is 11:09:14.05
Enter new time:_
```

At this point, you could press Return, which would make no changes to the current time, or you could enter a corrected time in the standard format of hours:minutes:seconds.

Occasionally, you may want to run a program that is date-stamped for some day other than the actual day it is run. As an example, consider the case of the paymaster of a large computer company who wanted to run an end-of-quarter report two days early. The quarter ended on Sunday, and he wanted to be off skiing that weekend. He changed the system date with the DATE command like this:

```
C>DATE
Current date is Wed 4-08-1987
Enter new date (mm-dd-yy):
```

Then, after running the report dated for that coming Sunday, he changed the date back for the remainder of the Friday work. (His assumption was that no other transactions would be received and processed in the remaining days of the quarter.) Although his approach is not necessarily advisable, having the command around does give you this capability.

In a more serious vein, the testing of newly developed financial programs, for example, often requires data to be 30, 60, or more than 90 days old. In lieu of creating different data all the time, you could use the same test data and change the system date. This would allow you to make your data *appear to be* 30, 60, and more than 90 days old so you could test the program.

Unless you are running DOS 3.3, the changed time of day or date is only retained until DOS is rebooted or the system shuts down. DOS 3.3 improved the TIME and DATE commands so that they change the actual time on almost any permanent system clock calendar whenever they are used. Earlier versions of DOS require the Diagnostics program from the Utilities disk to do so. Systems containing add-on clock/calendar cards or boards also require you to run special utility programs supplied with the card or board.

PREPARING YOUR DISKS FOR USE

As you learned in Chapter 1, all disks must be prepared correctly before you can use them. This goes for hard disks, regular and high-density diskettes, and microfloppy diskettes. All disks, once formatted, can store any information you like. If you also want a disk to be able to start your system (in other words, boot it), then you must include on that disk special DOS files, and you must prepare the disk in a special way. Once you've done these steps, the disk is called a *system disk*. However, there is now less room remaining on the disk to store data for or from your application programs.

There are three main types of disk preparations:

If you don't need to boot your system from a disk, make your disk a *data disk*. All possible disk space is then available for your program and data storage, and none is consumed for DOS purposes.

- *Formatting a diskette.* This process is used to create a diskette that will operate in the computer but contain no information initially. Such diskettes are used to receive and store data.

- *Creating a blank system diskette.* This process is most often used when you receive a new software package. Most programs are not ready to run when purchased; you must usually perform this process in order to get a working copy of the program.

- *Backing up an existing diskette.* This process makes an exact copy of another diskette. The DISKCOPY command is used; it is the fastest way for DOS to copy a complete diskette.

The next sections will teach you how to perform these three processes. The FORMAT command is the primary means of preparing disks. As you'll see, you simply use different switches to tell DOS whether you want to create a blank data diskette or a system diskette. A number of other switches allow you to specify different diskette densities and layouts, as you will see in Chapter 18. They are less frequently needed, so you won't go over them here.

FORMATTING A DISKETTE

Use a *scratch diskette* to try the following preparation commands—that is, a diskette that is fresh out of the box from your local computer store, or any old diskette that contains information you don't care about. If you do not have one, you should get one before you continue.

Your computer screen should have the A> prompt on the screen (or C> if you are a hard-disk user); as you learned before, this prompt is the computer's way of telling you that it is ready to accept a valid DOS command. Place the scratch diskette into drive B (or drive A, often the only diskette drive on a typical hard-disk system). Now you are ready to format the diskette. Enter the command

FORMAT B:

for a dual-diskette system, or enter

FORMAT A:

for a hard-disk system.

When you format a disk, any information that might have been stored on that disk is destroyed. Make sure that the disk you format does not contain any valuable information.

The computer will then ask you to place a diskette in the drive you've specified. If you had not done so already, you could place the diskette in at this point. When you are ready to begin the formatting process, you press Return. DOS will take over and wipe your diskette completely clean of any data. It electronically lays down a pattern of marks, which makes up the tracks and sectors you learned about in Chapter 1.

Diskettes can be formatted as many times as you like. You can even format some diskettes that were used previously by another computer. Of course, any information stored by the other computer on that diskette will be wiped out.

The number of seconds it takes to format the diskette is variable, depending on the size of the diskette (double-density, high-capacity, or otherwise). When the process is done, the diskette is ready to accept information. The computer will then show you how much room for your files is available on the diskette you have just formatted. This will be 362,496 bytes on a double-sided, double-density diskette or 1,213,952 bytes on a high-capacity diskette.

If a number of beginning users have access to your computer system, you might consider renaming your FORMAT command (see Chapter 3) so that unauthorized users can't accidentally do any disk formatting. This helps guarantee that disks with valid data will not accidentally be formatted (and zapped) by beginners who are experimenting with DOS commands for the first time.

The computer will then ask you if you want to format another diskette. If you enter a Y, the process will begin again, and you will have a chance to insert another diskette into your selected drive. If you are done, you enter an N. The FORMAT command will end, returning you to the DOS prompt. DOS is now ready for your next command.

MAKING A SYSTEM DISKETTE

You come now to the last type of disk setup procedure. This technique requires you to understand the difference between a system disk and a nonsystem disk. A system disk is one that contains three special files. Their most common names are listed in Table 2.2. If you want to boot up the DOS system with a disk, that disk must have these system files stored in reserved sectors at the beginning of the first track. Only if this is true can the DOS bootup program find them, load them, and bring up DOS properly.

Only COMMAND.COM is visible to the user; the other two files, IO.SYS and MSDOS.SYS, are hidden. This does not mean that they do not take up space on the disk—they do. It means that their names do not appear on any directory listing. These hidden files contain most of the information that you have been calling DOS. When you turn on the computer, one of the first things it does is seek the information in these files and read it into memory. The A> or C> prompt is an indicator that these files have been read and stored in the internal memory of the computer.

What would happen if you turned on the computer and the diskette in drive A did not contain these system files? The computer would not load DOS and would therefore not be capable of using the disk drives. You would then receive a message requesting that a DOS system diskette be placed in the boot drive. To correct the situation, you would need to restart the system with the diskette that had the DOS files on it.

You can see that having DOS on a disk is important. When you used the FORMAT command previously, you created a totally blank diskette. This was not a system diskette, because it did not have the three DOS files on it. Now you will learn how to format a diskette and copy the system's files onto it at the same time.

If you enter the following command:

FORMAT B:/S

The IO.SYS file contains the software programs that understand how to send data to and receive data from peripheral devices like printers and disks. The MSDOS.SYS file contains the logic and routines for managing the data organization itself. In essence, the file system is controlled by logic in MSDOS.SYS, and the more nitty-gritty signal and data communications are handled by routines in IO.SYS.

MS-DOS SYSTEMS	PC-DOS SYSTEMS
IO.SYS	IBMBIO.COM
MSDOS.SYS	IBMDOS.COM
COMMAND.COM	COMMAND.COM

Table 2.2: DOS system file names

the /S (the System switch) tells the computer to add the DOS files to the diskette in drive B when the formatting process completes. To begin this formatting process, you simply press Return after making sure you have the right diskette in drive B.

When the process is done, the computer tells you how much space is used by the DOS system and how much remains available for your use. The diskette in B is now a system disk. It is capable of getting the computer started.

Why bother to set up a diskette with only the DOS files? The answer is that you can now transfer files from another disk onto this one. This is usually what you must do when you buy a new software program; most programs do not come on a system diskette. Although you can sometimes put a DOS system onto your newly purchased application program diskette, it is usually preferable to follow these steps:

1. Format a system disk.

2. Transfer your new program files onto that disk.

3. Use the resulting disk both to boot the computer and to run the application program itself.

4. Put your application software's original diskettes in a safe place.

Here's an example of a situation in which you might need to prepare a system disk. Imagine that you want to place BASICA.COM from your DOS supplementary diskette onto a self-booting disk. The ultimate goal will be to automatically initiate the BASICA program when the system powers up (see Chapter 13). Feel free to follow the steps below, substituting an alternate application program, if you wish, for BASICA.COM. First, select a scratch diskette and format it. Next, follow the appropriate steps for your own system's needs:

FOR DUAL-DISKETTE SYSTEMS

1. Place the scratch diskette in drive B and use the command

    FORMAT B:/S

2. Then copy the BASICA.COM file from drive A to the new system diskette in drive B by using the COPY command:

    COPY BASICA.COM B:

Your diskette is now prepared to receive any other application programs (through the COPY command) as well as to boot the DOS system at power-up time.

FOR HARD-DISK SYSTEMS

1. Place the scratch diskette in drive A and use the command

   FORMAT A:/S

2. Then copy the BASICA.COM file from drive C to the new system diskette in drive A by using the COPY command:

   COPY BASICA.COM A:

Your diskette is now prepared to receive any other application programs (through the COPY command) as well as to boot the DOS system at power-up time.

In the preceding example, you were only concerned with preparing a diskette that could both hold files and be used to boot up the system. At the beginning of Chapter 4, you'll learn how you can give the entire diskette a name, or label, during this formatting process. You'll also learn how to display this label and change it when the diskette's contents change.

BACKING UP AN EXISTING DISKETTE

The FORMAT command prepares a disk with tracks and sectors laid out in precise patterns. This is required for DOS to be able to store files of information on that disk. Now you will see how the DISKCOPY command can be used to precisely duplicate the contents of one diskette on another.

The DISKCOPY command does not require you to format the "target" diskette before using it—DISKCOPY automatically formats the target diskette if necessary. This is the only time that you can use an unformatted diskette for any DOS operation.

COPY-PROTECTED DISKETTES   Diskettes that are *copy-protected* cannot be copied by DOS accurately. DOS expects all diskettes to have the same basic setup in terms of tracks, sectors,

directories, and so on. If a diskette is organized at all differently, then the DISKCOPY command will not work.

Copy protection was originally designed to prevent users from making inexpensive copies of expensive software. These cheap copies often prevented original manufacturers from receiving all the income from sales that they were due. However, after several legal battles (over the right of users to make legitimate backup copies for themselves) and several marketing battles (over large corporate accounts refusing to buy copy-protected products that could not be placed on hard disks without continued diskette handling), the current trend has been away from copy-protected programs.

It is possible to purchase special programs like COPY II PC, from Central Point Software. These programs can decipher most of the special codes used by copy-protected software, allowing purchasers of protected software to make backup or archival copies of their disks. Since DOS can't do this, such a package is a good investment if your software collection includes copy-protected software.

BACKING UP YOUR DOS DISKETTES

In this section you'll see how to make duplicate (backup) copies of both of the DOS diskettes so that you can employ the backup diskettes, carefully storing and protecting the originals.

The procedure is slightly different if you have a one-diskette or two-diskette system. You may have one diskette drive in your system because that is all you have, or you may have one diskette drive because your system has a hard disk. In either case, you will use the DISKCOPY command to create an exact copy of each DOS diskette. You will need two double-sided, double-density blank diskettes for this purpose.

This section refers to the startup and operating diskettes contained in DOS 3.3. If you are using an earlier version of DOS, your two diskettes are labelled "System" and "Supplementary." The instructions in this section will apply regardless of the DOS version you are using.

DOS produces several prompting messages during the diskcopying operation, in which your original diskette (which you are copying) is referred to as the *source* diskette, and the new blank diskette (onto which you are making your copies) is referred to as the *target* or *destination* diskette (see Figure 2.6).

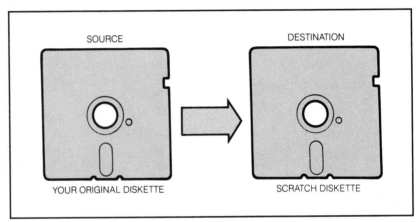

Figure 2.6: Making diskette replicas with DISKCOPY

FOR ONE-DISKETTE SYSTEMS   Assuming you are using drive A, the single diskette drive of your system, you should type the following command:

DISKCOPY

When the DISKCOPY command executes, DOS will prompt you like this:

Insert source diskette in drive A:
Press any key when ready...

In this single-diskette environment, DOS will actually ask you to place both source and destination diskettes, successively, into drive A (see Figure 2.7).

Assuming your DOS diskette is still in drive A, press the Return key to begin the DISKCOPY operation. DOS will give you an informative message as it is copying your diskette. This message will vary according to the diskette's storage density and its number of sides:

Copying 40 tracks
9 Sectors/Track,2 Side(s)

Figure 2.7: Copying diskettes using only one disk drive

When DOS has read as much as it can from the diskette, it will prompt you to

Insert target diskette in drive A:
Press any key when ready...

At this point, take a label and print "DOS Startup Diskette" on it and then place the label on one of the blank diskettes. Place this blank diskette in drive A and press Return. DOS will then copy onto the blank diskette whatever part of the DOS system diskette it was able to read in its first pass. When it has finished copying this information onto your new diskette, it may prompt you to again place the original DOS system diskette in drive A. This will depend on the total size (in bytes) of your source diskette, and whether it can be completely read into memory and then copied in only one pass. If it can't, DOS will prompt you to

Insert source diskette in drive A:
Press any key when ready...

If you receive this message, you should remove your blank diskette and put the original DOS diskette in, so that DOS can continue reading information from the source diskette. At some point it will prompt you to again insert the destination diskette in drive A. This is your cue to take out the original diskette and place your newly labeled diskette in drive A. Depending on the amount of memory you have on your computer and the version of DOS you are using, this juggling of diskettes will continue until all of the information from the original diskette is read, and all of it can be written onto the destination diskette.

At the end of this cycle, DOS asks if you would like to copy another diskette. Since you've just copied the first of the DOS diskettes, you should answer with the letter Y (for Yes), since you now intend to go through the entire cycle a second time for your DOS operating diskette.

Prepare a label that says "DOS Operating Diskette" and place it on your second blank diskette. After answering Y to DOS's question, you will again be prompted to insert a source diskette in drive A. At this point, place your DOS supplementary diskette in drive A and begin the entire process again, this time using your newly labeled "DOS Operating Diskette" blank diskette as the target of the DISKCOPY procedure.

FOR DUAL-DISKETTE SYSTEMS   If your system has two diskette drives, the diskette-copying procedure can go much faster because no juggling is required. Assuming you have your DOS startup diskette in drive A, place your blank diskette, which you should label "DOS Startup Diskette," in drive B. Then type the following command at the DOS prompt:

DISKCOPY A: B:

This tells DOS to read everything from drive A and write it onto the diskette in drive B (see Figure 2.8). DOS will prompt you as follows:

Insert source diskette in drive A:
Insert target diskette in drive B:
Press any key when ready . . .

You should ensure that your DOS startup diskette is in drive A at this point, before you press the Return key, and that your blank diskette, which is to become the copy of the DOS system diskette, is in drive B. Pressing Return will then initiate the operation to completely copy the contents of one diskette onto the other. While DOS makes the copy you will be informed as to what type of diskette it believes it is copying

Figure 2.8: Copying disks using two disk drives

(single- or double-sided, the number of sectors to a track, and so on):

    Copying 40 tracks
    9 Sectors/Track,2 Side(s)

At the end, DOS will ask you if you want to copy another diskette:

    Copy another diskette (Y/N)?

At this point you should answer Y, indicating that you would like to copy another diskette. You will get the same message, indicating that you should place the source diskette (your DOS operating diskette) in drive A and that you should insert the target diskette (your blank, newly labeled operating diskette) in drive B. Then—and only then—should you press the Return key to initiate the new process of copying the operating programs onto your backup diskette.

You can now answer N (for No) to the question about copying another diskette. When the DOS prompt returns, you are ready to begin using DOS in earnest.

The procedure you have just followed to back up the DOS diskettes can also be used to safely back up copies of most of your application software. However, certain copy-protected programs cannot be backed up in this fashion.

CHECKING THE DISK FOR AVAILABLE SPACE

Your DOS system provides a very useful command called CHKDSK. It is used frequently to check the amount of space, both used and unused, on a particular disk. One of DOS's drawbacks is that it does not pack information as densely on the disk as is possible. Files that contain large amounts of information will take up a significant amount of disk space. The CHKDSK command also gives detailed information about the files on your disk.

There are other uses you should know about for the CHKDSK command: finding and fixing file allocation errors. Both have to do with the way DOS stores file information on the disk. DOS actually allocates space for files in groups of sectors called *clusters*. The number of sectors in a cluster varies according to the type of disk and the version of DOS you are using. This explains why you might run out of disk space, even though the sum of all your file sizes is much smaller than the disk you are using.

If the cluster size is four sectors, then any data from 1 byte to 2K will be allocated all four sectors (2048 bytes) on your disk. If the cluster size is eight sectors, then all files will always require at least 4096 bytes. Even larger files may waste a number of bytes, since the last portion of these files will be allocated an entire cluster, even if only one additional byte is needed.

The CHKDSK command will give you a summary of the amount of space available on each disk. For instance, CHKDSK by itself will give you information about the current default disk drive (as shown by the prompt). Typically, this is drive A in a dual-diskette system and C in a hard-disk system, as shown in Figures 2.9 and 2.10. The same results could have been obtained by explicitly telling DOS which drives to check:

CHKDSK A:

or

CHKDSK C:

DOS 3.2 reduced the cluster size for hard disks. If you're still using an earlier version of DOS, this feature in itself may be sufficient reason to upgrade to the latest version. And if you're going to do that, get DOS 3.3; it's faster, offers a number of improved commands, and contains many efficiency features discussed throughout this book. It supports the Personal System/2 series of computers as well.

You might notice after entering the CHKDSK command that the red light on the drive you specified turned on, indicating that the device was activated. Whenever you see the red light, you can assume that the system is reading from or writing to the disk. Unless you are instructed to, you should *never* remove a disk from a drive when the light is on.

```
A>CHKDSK

     362496 bytes total disk space
      45056 bytes in 3 hidden files
     274432 bytes in 43 user files
      43008 bytes available on disk

     524288 bytes total memory
     443136 bytes free

A>
```

Figure 2.9: CHKDSK output for a diskette (no volume label)

CHKDSK gives you the following information about disk space:

- *Bytes total disk space.* This tells you the number of original bytes of storage available on the disk before any files were added.

- *Bytes in hidden files.* This tells you the number of bytes in the special files used by DOS that are usually hidden from the user's view when a directory is listed.

- *Bytes in user files.* This tells you the number of bytes in the files created by you, which appear on a directory listing.

- *Bytes in bad sectors.* This indicates the number of bytes in bad sectors, which are usually sectors that have been blocked off from use because of some defect detected by the computer system. If all sectors are good, then no "bad sector" display will appear.

- *Bytes available on disk.* This tells you the amount of space left for adding new files to the disk.

The last two lines on the CHKDSK display do not deal with the disk drive. They tell you about the internal memory of the computer: how much total memory is installed in your system and how much is still free

```
C>CHKDSK
Volume ROBBINS      created Mar 22, 1987 4:43p

21204992 bytes total disk space
   45056 bytes in 3 hidden files
  124928 bytes in 45 directories
18618368 bytes in 1778 user files
 2416640 bytes available on disk

  524288 bytes total memory
  121920 bytes free

C>_
```

Figure 2.10: CHKDSK output for a hard disk (volume label ROBBINS)

for use. This is usually only an issue to consider if you are using many programs at once, or if you don't have the maximum physical memory available on your machine.

Programs can occasionally create problems in DOS's management area, called the *file allocation table (FAT)*. This is often the result of programs that begin to create files but stop because of some problem.

A special form of the CHKDSK command will list all FAT errors and also tell you if the files are stored in contiguous clusters:

CHKDSK *.*

Contiguous, or adjacent, clusters are desirable since it means the disk heads will travel less distance to read or write the desired sector data; all disk operations will occur faster. The symbol *.* represents a *wildcard* specification. Using the asterisk (*) tells DOS to check all files on the disk. (You'll learn more about wild-card symbols in Chapter 3.) The results of this command might appear as in Figure 2.11, which lets you know that on this disk, at this moment in time, there is only one file, SKN.COM, which is not stored in contiguous sectors.

There is nothing inherently wrong with files in noncontiguous sectors. However, large files in noncontiguous sectors are processed more slowly than are files in contiguous sectors. (Chapter 17 provides more information on this issue and options for improvement.)

```
A>CHKDSK *.*

    362496 bytes total disk space
     45056 bytes in 3 hidden files
    309248 bytes in 44 user files
      8192 bytes available on disk

    524288 bytes total memory
    443136 bytes free

A:\SKN.COM
    Contains 3 non-contiguous blocks.

A>_
```

Figure 2.11: CHKDSK request for file-contiguity information

When possible, it is best not to allow your disk to contain noncontiguous files.

If a CHKDSK command does list file allocation errors, you need to enter a special version of the CHKDSK command to *fix* the errors. The CHKDSK/F command will collect lost or misallocated sectors into a series of files named FILE0000.CHK, FILE0001.CHK, FILE0002.CHK, and so on. These are ASCII text files; you can type their contents from DOS to see the data, or you can use your word processor to try to change the data. (See Appendix B for a more complete description of ASCII codes and files.) You are usually best advised to simply be pleased at recovering the disk space and to erase the "recovered" files. However, if the data they contain represents simple textual data that does not exist any longer in any other form (perhaps it was lost during a power failure), you may use your word processor to try to recover as much as possible. This sometimes saves a good deal of reentry time, especially if the lost data is straight text and there was a good deal of it. See Chapter 17 for information about the Norton Utilities and advanced methods for more complete file-recovery methods.

SUMMARY

This chapter contained specific information to guide your first steps with your new operating system. You discovered many important facts about DOS.

- The DOS system actually gets going automatically at power-up time. The startup procedure reads the first sectors on a system disk to bring the DOS hidden files into memory. This loading process ends with the DOS prompt, which indicates that DOS is waiting for your command request.

- You can set the system date and time at startup with the DATE and TIME commands. If you have a built-in clock/calendar, these commands also allow you to update the date and time values whenever you wish.

- Entering and editing commands at the DOS prompt is as simple as typing the command itself, along with any necessary parameters or switches, and pressing Return. Parameters are merely placeholders for the actual entry values you will type when you give the command. Switches modify the operation of a DOS command, giving you the same sophisticated control over DOS commands as adjectives give you over nouns when you construct a sentence.

- The function keys can provide simple one-keystroke tools to make all your command formulations easier and less time-consuming. DOS uses function keys F1 through F6 for specific command-line editing purposes. The most commonly used function keys are F1, which retypes one character at a time from the last command, and F3, which retypes the entire last command.

- You can correct mistakes immediately by pressing the Backspace key, or cancel a command completely with the Esc key.

- You can erase the entire screen with the CLS command.

- All disks, whether hard, floppy, or microfloppy, must be prepared for use with a required formatting procedure. Disks are set up for different purposes, and you've seen how to prepare a scratch or blank diskette with the FORMAT command. This diskette can be used to boot the system or not, depending on whether you use the /S switch. Using the switch gives the diskette the ability to boot the system, as well as to store files. On the other hand, this does cost you storage space on the diskette; less space is available for your files.

- A working system disk can be created for most software packages by a simple procedure. First, a blank system disk can be prepared; then the appropriate files from your required software can be copied onto it to create a self-booting and complete system disk that contains your application software.

- The DISKCOPY command allows you to make copies of your DOS diskettes. In fact, it can be used to make replicas of any disk that is important enough to back up.

- The CHKDSK command obtains information about how both memory and disk storage are being used. This command can be applied to any disk on your system, and with the /F switch can be used to fix file information (recover lost data) that has gone bad.

In Chapter 3, you'll learn new commands and skills that will enable you to organize your programs and files.

PART 2

MAKING DOS DO MORE

In Part 2, you will learn how to make DOS do much more for you. Chapter 3 will teach you the commands and features you need to manipulate files in a variety of ways. These include listing directories of files, copying files, typing out the contents of text files, renaming files, and erasing files. In Chapter 4, you will then learn how to create and maintain directory structures on floppy diskettes. You will discover how to create, use, and delete directories and subdirectories.

Chapter 5 is a special look at using directory structures on a hard disk. First you will practice formatting your hard disk. You will then set it up for three types of application programs—a spreadsheet, a word processor, and a database management system, or any other programs you plan to use regularly.

Chapter 6 prepares you to create and modify text files using the DOS line editor, EDLIN. You will use EDLIN throughout the rest of the book to generate and update system files, as well as to write your own simple programs (called batch files). Lastly, in Chapter 7, you will learn how to produce printed output of your work with your system.

MANIPULATING FILES

CHAPTER 3

BY NOW, YOU'VE LEARNED THE FUNDAMENTALS OF
DOS, and you've seen what it can do. You've investigated simple
command entry and disk preparation. In this chapter, you will learn
to manipulate files.

When you work with DOS, you will always deal with files of one sort
or another. Program files you purchase must be stored in some portion
of your disk; data files you create must be stored in another portion. The
more practiced you become at defining these disk portions, or directories, the more success you will have with DOS.

You will learn in this chapter how to access files on a disk in a variety of ways. You will also learn how to make backup and secondary
copies of these files for your protection and convenience in making
changes. You will see how DOS deals with external hardware devices
in a manner similar to data files, and how the same commands, once
learned, are doubly valuable.

Manipulating all of your files will give you more confidence and
control over your system. You will learn how to type out the contents
of text files, erase old files that you no longer need or that are occupying too much space, and how to make copies of any files onto 5¼" or
3½" diskettes so you can free disk space for new work.

In order for you to gain the upper hand in the ongoing struggle with
confusion and disorganization, you will see how to easily rename files in
place. And, if simple renaming isn't enough, you will learn to rapidly
copy and regroup files between disk drives with the advanced XCOPY
command.

THE DISK DIRECTORY

How can you tell what files are stored on a disk? On diskettes, at least, you could read the printed disk label, although the label may or may not have the correct information on it. Also, it rarely contains all the information available electronically in DOS. The only way to be sure of what is really on a disk is to have DOS display a *directory* of the files on that disk.

The DIR (Directory) command will display on the screen a listing of all the files stored on a disk. If you enter the command

    DIR

the computer will display a listing of all the files on the current active drive. Figure 3.1 shows a sample directory listing. Because the A> prompt was shown, this directory is for a diskette in drive A. The list of files is scrolled automatically on the screen, since the list has too many lines to be seen at one time on a standard 25-line screen. The bottom of the display shows the amount of space left on the diskette for new files.

Each line that appears in the directory represents a file that is stored on the disk. DOS displays four pieces of information about each file: the file name, the file size, and the date and time of its creation or last update:

    BACKUP   COM   6234   12-30-85 2:00p
    (File Name)   (Size) (Date)   (Time)

Try the DIR command now on each of the drives in your own system:

    DIR A:
    DIR B:
    DIR C:

If you have other drives, try the command on them. If you accidentally try the command with a drive letter that doesn't exist, DOS will tell you so. You'll receive the error message "Invalid drive specification" and then a new DOS prompt will be displayed. However, if

Just before storing each diskette you use, print out a directory listing of its contents using the techniques described in Chapter 7. To add a touch of class, use the techniques in Chapter 12 to print out a sorted listing.

To control the listing of files on the screen, use a *Ctrl-key combination.* The easiest way to do this is to hold the Ctrl key down and then press another key at the same time. For example, the key combination Ctrl-S, or ^S, freezes the screen and stops the scrolling. The same combination will start the screen output going again. This type of key combination is called a *toggle.*

```
Volume in drive A has no label
Directory of  A:\

ANSI     SYS      1651  12-30-85   12:00p
ASSIGN   COM      1536  12-30-85   12:00p
ATTRIB   EXE      8247  12-30-85   12:00p
BACKUP   COM      6234  12-30-85   12:00p
BASIC    COM     19298  12-30-85   12:00p
BASICA   COM     36396  12-30-85   12:00p
CHKDSK   COM      9832  12-30-85   12:00p
COMMAND  COM     23791  12-30-85   12:00p
COMP     COM      4184  12-30-85   12:00p
DISKCOMP COM      5792  12-30-85   12:00p
DISKCOPY COM      6224  12-30-85   12:00p
DRIVER   SYS      1115  12-30-85   12:00p
EDLIN    COM      7508  12-30-85   12:00p
FDISK    COM      8173  12-30-85   12:00p
FIND     EXE      6416  12-30-85   12:00p
FORMAT   COM     11135  12-30-85   12:00p
GRAFTABL COM      1169  12-30-85   12:00p
GRAPHICS COM      3220  12-30-85   12:00p
JOIN     EXE      8955  12-30-85   12:00p
KEYBFR   COM      3291  12-30-85   12:00p
KEYBGR   COM      3274  12-30-85   12:00p
KEYBIT   COM      3060  12-30-85   12:00p
KEYBSP   COM      3187  12-30-85   12:00p
KEYBUK   COM      3036  12-30-85   12:00p
LABEL    COM      2346  12-30-85   12:00p
MODE     COM      6864  12-30-85   12:00p
MORE     COM       295  12-30-85   12:00p
PRINT    COM      8976  12-30-85   12:00p
RECOVER  COM      4297  12-30-85   12:00p
REPLACE  EXE     11650  12-30-85   12:00p
RESTORE  COM      6012  12-30-85   12:00p
SELECT   COM      3826  12-30-85   12:00p
SHARE    EXE      8580  12-30-85   12:00p
SORT     EXE      1911  12-30-85   12:00p
SUBST    EXE      9911  12-30-85   12:00p
SYS      COM      4620  12-30-85   12:00p
TREE     COM      3357  12-30-85   12:00p
VDISK    SYS      3307  12-30-85   12:00p
XCOPY    EXE     11200  12-30-85   12:00p
        39 File(s)      22528 bytes free
```

Figure 3.1: Sample directory listing

you ask for a directory listing on a drive letter that *does* exist on your system, but the drive isn't ready (the drive door isn't closed or the diskette hasn't been inserted), you'll receive the "Abort, Retry, Fail" error message (or "Abort, Retry, Ignore" in versions of DOS earlier than 3.3). If you've really made a mistake, simply type the letter A to abort the request; if the diskette wasn't ready, just prepare it and then type R to retry the DIR request. Only select the FAIL option if you are a DOS programmer and understand the nature of the internal system call that has failed, and how to proceed in the program.

The most important aspect of the resulting directory display is the listing of files. Each entry can have three parts:

1. A drive name (optional)

2. A base name

3. An extension (optional)

The general form of every DOS file name is as follows:

D:BaseName.Ext

where *D* represents an optional one-letter drive identifier (A, B, C, and so on), *BaseName* represents the base name, and *Ext* represents an optional three-character file-name extension. Figure 3.2 illustrates the general form.

The drive name can be any letter from A to Z. However, you must have a device connected to the computer to correspond to the drive designation. For example, two drives allow you to use A or B. Hard disks usually default to a drive identifier of C. The drive name is separated from the base name by a colon.

When you enter a file name, you enter it in a manner different from that in which DOS displays it. In the example line

BACKUP   COM   6234   12-30-85 2:00p

from a directory listing, the name appears as BACKUP   COM, but when you use this name, you must enter it as BACKUP.COM, with a period between the name and the three-character extension.

Figure 3.2: File-name structure in DOS

Note that DOS does not care if the letters are upper- or lowercase. However, you cannot enter spaces as part of a file name, even though that is the way they appear in the directory listing.

A file's base name can be between one and eight characters long. Since DOS checks for invalid characters when you enter a base name, you can use any sequence of characters except the following invalid ones:

.″ / \ [ ]¦ < > + : = ; ,

In addition, all DOS control codes (see Appendix B) are also invalid. For the sake of readability as well as typeability, keep your file names to alphabetic and numeric characters.

The following base name would not be acceptable to DOS because it contains a space:

MY FILE

However, this would be acceptable:

MY_FILE

The space has been replaced with an underscore, which is a legal character. Many people use this character to simulate a space, since it is visually unobtrusive. Use it if you like, but it always slows down the typing of the name; using the name MYFILE with neither a space nor an underscore would be quicker and easier.

An extension is limited to three characters. The same rules on invalid characters in the base name apply to an extension as well. The extension is separated from the base name by a period.

Take a look at the following list of file names:

- A:LETTER.TXT
- SAMPLE DAT
- X
- MY:FILE
- msdos.les
- Sample.File

- C.test.doc

- b:user.fil

Do you know which of these are valid and which are not? If not, reread the preceding sections before going on. The valid file names are A:LETTER.TXT, X, msdos.les, and b:user.fil. The others are all constructed incorrectly.

SAMPLE DAT is not acceptable because it contains a space. MY:FILE is unacceptable because two characters precede the colon. Colons cannot appear in a base name; they can *precede* the base name if a drive identifier begins the file name. However, a drive identifier can only be a single letter. The file name Sample.File is invalid because a file extension can contain only three characters. (In fact, DOS will accept this entry and treat it as if Sample.Fil had been typed; the ending "e" will be ignored.) The last invalid example, C.test.doc, will not work because a drive specification must be followed by a colon. Also, only one period can appear in a file name.

As stated earlier, drive specifications and extensions are optional. The usual purpose of an extension is to group together files with different names of the same type. Traditionally, file extensions such as .BAS (for BASIC language programs), .COM (machine-language command files), and .DAT (data files) have been used to identify the type of information contained within certain files.

Tradition is not the only reason for following conventions—they also make it easier to see, group, and access all files of the same type. When you look at the files contained in any new application package, you can easily understand the usage of many of them simply by noting the extension names (.HLP for help files, .TXT for text files, .OVL or .OVR for overlay files, and so on). See Table 3.1 for commonly used extensions.

LONG DIRECTORY LISTS

There are two alternative ways to list a directory if it is too long to be displayed on a single screen at one time. Enter

DIR/W

The directory might look something like the one in Figure 3.3. This is called a *wide directory,* because the files are listed across instead of

FILE EXTENSION	TYPE OF FILE
.BAK	Backup copies of files
.BAS	BASIC programs
.BAT	Batch files
.BIN	Binary object files
.COM	Simple executable programs (like DOS commands)
.DAT or .DTA	Data files
.DBF	Database files
.DRV	Device driver files
.EXE	Executable programs, usually larger than 64K and more sophisticated than .COM programs
.NDX	Index files
.OVL or .OVR	Overlay files
.PRG	dBASE III PLUS program files
.SYS	DOS device drivers
.TXT	Plain ASCII text files
.WKS or .WK1	Worksheet (spreadsheet) files

Table 3.1: Commonly used file-name extensions

vertically, which means that more names can fit on a single screen. Note that DOS no longer displays the size, date, and time of each file, which saves space on the display. The /W is an example of a switch; it modifies the way the DIR command executes.

Here's another variation on the DIR command. In this case /P is the switch, and it modifies the result of the command in a different way. If you enter

    DIR/P

the screen fills and the list pauses until you press another key. If you then press Return again, the next screenful of file names is displayed.

```
A>DIR/W

  Volume in drive A has no label
  Directory of  A:\

ANSI     SYS    ASSIGN   COM    ATTRIB   EXE    BACKUP   COM    BASIC    COM
BASICA   COM    CHKDSK   COM    COMMAND  COM    COMP     COM    DISKCOMP COM
DISKCOPY COM    DRIVER   SYS    EDLIN    COM    FDISK    COM    FIND     EXE
FORMAT   COM    GRAFTABL COM    GRAPHICS COM    JOIN     EXE    KEYBFR   COM
KEYBGR   COM    KEYBIT   COM    KEYBSP   COM    KEYBUK   COM    LABEL    COM
MODE     COM    MORE     COM    PRINT    COM    RECOVER  COM    REPLACE  EXE
RESTORE  COM    SELECT   COM    SHARE    EXE    SORT     EXE    SUBST    EXE
SYS      COM    TREE     COM    VDISK    SYS    XCOPY    EXE
       39 File(s)     22528 bytes free

A>_
```

Figure 3.3: Wide directory listing

This is somewhat akin to the ^S combination you saw earlier, except the listing breaks at precise places depending on how many directory entries it takes to fill the screen.

In summary, there are three styles of directory listings:

DIR — Full listing of all files, including size, date, and time

DIR/W — Wide directory; file size, date, and time not shown

DIR/P — Directory listing pauses when one screen is filled; size, date, and time shown

REFERRING TO FILES ON OTHER DRIVES

You can specify another drive's directory by following the DIR command with the letter that indicates the drive. On a dual-diskette system with a diskette in the second drive, if you typed

DIR B:

the computer would display the list of files on the diskette in drive B. You could also get a wide display of the list for drive B by entering

DIR B: /W

CHANGING THE DEFAULT DRIVE

The A> prompt indicates that DOS will work with the diskette in drive A unless you specify otherwise. Thus, drive A is considered the *default* drive for all commands. All commands will act on files located on the default drive unless you specifically include another drive name as part of the command or file-name specification. You can change the default drive simply by typing in the letter for the desired new default drive. Entering

B:

would change the A> prompt to B>. (Note that drive names are always followed by a colon.) Entering the DIR command now would cause the red light on drive B to light, since it is now the default drive; DOS would also tell you this by changing its prompt to B>. At this point, you could still get a listing of drive A by entering

DIR A:

LIMITING THE DIRECTORY DISPLAY

While the DIR command is useful in displaying the names of files, some practical problems require other techniques. For example, you might want to know if the disk in the current drive contains a file called ASSIGN.COM. If you simply entered the DIR command, you might be hard pressed to locate visually the file you were interested in, especially if you had scores of files (or hundreds of files, as you might on a hard disk). It might be better to narrow down the display to just the files that begin with the letter A. This would make it much easier to find out whether the file you wanted was on the disk.

DOS allows you a certain degree of ambiguity in asking for files. This means that there are ways to ask for a directory of files that meet certain criteria. The asterisk is used as a wild-card symbol to indicate your criteria. For example, if you want a list of all files that begin with the letter A, you enter

DIR A*

DOS will display a listing that looks something like this:

```
Volume in drive A has no label
Directory of A:\
        ASSIGN      COM    1536  12-30-85 12:00p
        AUTOEXEC    BAT      34   4-01-87  6:27p
               2 File(s) 124928 bytes free
```

It is now a much simpler matter to determine if ASSIGN.COM is on the disk, because DOS has displayed only a couple of specific files.

Suppose you want to see if the disk in drive A contains a file called WS.COM. You can enter

```
DIR W*
```

DOS will display a listing that looks like this:

```
Volume in drive A has no label
Directory of A:\

File not found
```

This tells you that there are no files beginning with the letter W on the disk in drive A; therefore, the file WS.COM is not on the disk.

Wild cards can be used to select listings of files by their extensions as well as by their file names. Suppose you wanted to list all of the files on the disk in drive A that end with a .DAT extension. Since you do not care what the file name is, an asterisk can be used. If you enter

```
DIR *.DAT
```

DOS will list all the files that have the extension .DAT.

Another way to search for names is to use the ? symbol. The question mark is a wild-card symbol for one character, as opposed to the asterisk symbol, which can stand for a number of characters. For example,

```
DIR ????.COM
```

will produce the display seen in Figure 3.4. The ????.COM

```
A>DIR ????.COM

   Volume in drive A has no label
   Directory of  A:\

COMP     COM    4184   12-30-85  12:00p
MODE     COM    6864   12-30-85  12:00p
MORE     COM     295   12-30-85  12:00p
SYS      COM    4620   12-30-85  12:00p
TREE     COM    3357   12-30-85  12:00p
       5 File(s)      22528 bytes free

A>_
```

Figure 3.4: Directory searching with wild cards

specification told DOS to include any files that have names of four characters or less and also have a .COM extension.

The next two commands combine the * and ? wild cards:

> **DIR ??S?????.***
> **DIR ??S*.***

Both of these commands have the same effect: they tell DOS to list only those files that contain the letter S as the third character in their names. (Remember that a DOS base name is limited to a maximum of eight characters plus an extension.)

You can direct DOS to search the disk in drive B by adding B: to the wild card. For example, to list all files on the disk in drive B that begin with F, you would enter

> **DIR B:F***

Look at the following command. What type of files will it list?

> **DIR S???.COM**

Try this command on your DOS master disk. See if your prediction is correct.

Figure out and enter the commands that would elicit the following lists of files:

1. All files on the active drive that begin with M

2. All files on the active drive that end in .COM

3. All files on drive B that begin with S

The solutions are as follows:

1. DIR M*

2. DIR *.COM

3. DIR B:S*

MAKING COPIES OF FILES

Making copies of files is an important ability to have in a computer system, especially a floppy-diskette system. Although a double-density diskette holds about 360 kilobytes and a high-capacity diskette holds 1.2 megabytes, it is often necessary to transfer files from one diskette to another for organizational or backup purposes.

The COPY command will copy files from one device onto another. COPY has many uses. The first one you will learn is how COPY can copy files from one disk to another. (A disk is only one type of device, but it is the most important and commonly used one.)

The general form of the COPY command is

COPY *Source Destination*

or

COPY *OldFile(s) NewFile(s)*

The first name is the name of the file(s) to copy. The second name is the name of the new file(s) to be created. When complete, both files (or sets of files) will contain the same information.

You will find many uses for the COPY command. You might want to make a secondary copy of a file you are working on, or you might want to make a backup copy of a file on another disk for precautionary reasons. You might want to make a replica of several files at the same time, perhaps from someone else's disk to yours. The following sections explore these and other uses of the COPY command.

MAKING SECONDARY COPIES

A second working copy of a file can be made easily with the COPY command. You can retain the original while working on and modifying the copy by entering

COPY BUDGET.TXT BUDGET.BAK

In this situation, a DIR of your disk would show two files where there had previously been only one, as you can see in Figure 3.5.

MAKING BACKUP COPIES

With COPY, you can make a backup copy on another disk. Suppose that you want to place a copy of your PHONES.DAT file onto the diskette in drive B. You could do this by entering

COPY PHONES.DAT B:

```
B>DIR

  Volume in drive B has no label
  Directory of  B:\

BUDGET86 TXT     15999    5-19-86   12:00p
BUDGET   TXT     13888    4-02-87    4:42p
         2 File(s)     286720 bytes free

B>COPY  BUDGET.TXT  BUDGET.BAK
        1 File(s) copied

B>DIR

  Volume in drive B has no label
  Directory of  B:\

BUDGET86 TXT     15999    5-19-86   12:00p
BUDGET   TXT     13888    4-02-87    4:42p
BUDGET   BAK     13888    4-02-87    4:42p
         3 File(s)     272384 bytes free

B>_
```

Figure 3.5: Making a secondary copy of a file

The command will create a copy of PHONES.DAT on the diskette in drive B with the same name. Put this backup diskette away to protect yourself against the time when your original file or disk is inadvertently lost.

MAKING MULTIPLE COPIES

Multiple files can be simultaneously copied by using wild cards with the COPY command. If you needed to copy all files with an .SYM extension to a diskette in drive B, you could enter

COPY *.SYM B:

New users frequently ask if there can be two copies of the same file on a disk if a file is copied twice to the same drive. The answer is no—there is only one copy. DOS will not allow two files to have exactly the same name on the same disk. If a file is copied to a disk that already has a file with that name, DOS erases the old file and then writes the copy of the new file. You receive no warning of this. Thus, it is possible to erase all the information contained in a file by accidentally copying another file of the same name to that disk. When this happens the old file is said to be *overwritten* by the new file, and you are said to be *in big trouble!* (However, as you will see in Chapter 4, when you learn about the possibility of different directories on a disk, there can be two similarly named files on the same disk if the two files are located in different directories.)

Take a moment to practice with the COPY command. If a colleague or friend has some spreadsheet or database files or even games that you've been wanting to take a look at, now's the time. Of course, you should only make copies if there will be no copyright violation involved.

Format a blank diskette, and carefully copy the desired files from the original diskette to your new one. If your system has two diskette drives, you can specify a transfer from A to B by typing

COPY A:*FileNames* B:*FileNames*

If you only have one diskette, you may have to first transfer the files to drive C by typing

COPY A:*FileNames* C:*FileNames*

When you're not completely confident that a wild-card COPY command will copy over only the files you intend, use a DIR command first with the same wild-card specification. This will ensure that no unexpected duplicate file names will be accidentally overwritten. If you discover this possibility, either change the file name on the destination drive or give a unique name as the destination for the COPY command (COPY *OldFile* B:*NewName*).

Then you can switch diskettes and transfer the files onto the new (destination) diskette by entering

COPY C:*FileNames* **A:***FileNames*

MAKING COMPLETE DISK COPIES

One of the most common uses of the COPY command is to copy all the files from one diskette to another. This is necessary because diskettes can become worn out from use over a long period of time. Copying the files onto a new diskette will solve this problem. Also, keeping multiple copies of important files protects you against computer problems, human errors, or accidents such as fires.

You've already been introduced to the DISKCOPY command for making a complete copy of all the files from one disk onto another disk. Why should you consider using a version of the COPY command? The answer is subtle. DISKCOPY copies the original disk exactly, *retaining all noncontiguity*. The following version of the COPY command will usually rewrite files onto contiguous tracks and sectors on the new disk, improving future disk-access speed. The net result is that the performance or responsiveness of all your programs may improve.

To copy all the files from the diskette in drive A to that in drive B, you should enter

COPY *.* B:

COPYING DATA TO OTHER DEVICES

The COPY command can exchange information between the disk and other devices such as the screen and keyboard (CON) or the printer (LPT1). The following command will send the contents of a file named PHONES.DAT to the screen. The destination device CON stands for console device (the monitor):

COPY PHONES.DAT CON:

COPY also allows the user to enter text into a file. If you use CON as the source device, you can use the keyboard to transfer information from the keyboard through the computer to a disk file.

If the destination diskette (in drive B in this example) already contains some files, you may find that there is not enough space to hold all the existing files on B as well as the new files from A. If this occurs, however, DOS will display the message ''Insufficient Space.'' The best solution is to use a freshly formatted diskette or to erase files in advance on the destination diskette to ensure that enough space exists to receive the source diskette's files.

If you enter the following command:

COPY CON: TEXT1.DAT

nothing seems to happen, except that the DOS A > prompt does not appear. This is an indication that you are no longer at the system level. DOS will now allow you to enter text directly from the keyboard, and anything that you type will eventually be stored in the file TEXT1.DAT. You could enter

This is an example of keyboard entry into a text file.

or any other text lines, pressing Return after each line. You would then need to enter the character that DOS uses to mark the end of a file, a Ctrl-Z, which is sometimes shown as ^ Z. You obtain this unusual character by holding down the Ctrl key and pressing the letter Z. The symbol ^ Z will then appear on the screen.

The colon (:) after a device name (as in CON:) is not strictly necessary, since DOS will figure out what you mean. However, it's good form to enter the colon, if only for consistency with the way you enter drive identifiers (such as A: and C:).

To complete the file, press Return. The disk drive will spin and all the lines of text that you typed at the keyboard will be saved as a file. To see the data, you can simply reverse the items in the COPY command and enter

COPY TEXT1.DAT CON:

followed by Return. The text will be displayed just as it was typed in. This is a convenient method for creating small text files quickly. Your alternative is to use a line editor (like EDLIN, which is contained in your DOS software and is described in Chapter 6) or a word processor (which offers much more in the way of text manipulation).

COMBINING FILE COPIES

COPY can also be used to join two or more files together, which allows you to gather up small data files into a single large file. This is sometimes useful when several small documents were created, all of which need to be word processed. To see how this is done, you could enter

COPY CON: TEXT2.DAT
This is additional text that is stored in another text file
 ^Z

and press Return after each line. You would then use the COPY command to join these two files. This is sometimes called *concatenation*. The general form of the command is shown below. The + sign is used to indicate the joining of text from two or more files:

COPY *SourceFile(s) DestinationFile(s)*

or

COPY *FirstFile* + *SecondFile* + *etc. CombinationFile*

If you want to combine two existing files like TEXT1.DAT and TEXT2.DAT, you would enter the following command:

COPY TEXT1.DAT + TEXT2.DAT COMBO.DAT

To see the results, you could enter

COPY COMBO.DAT CON:

The resultant file, COMBO.DAT, would contain all the text lines from both of the two source files:

This is an example of keyboard entry into a text file.
This is additional text that is stored in another text file.

You can even use the wild-card commands to join text files. For example, if you wanted to join together all the text files with a .DAT extension into one file, you would use a command like

COPY *.DAT ALL.TXT

This form is simpler than typing "*file1* + *file2* + *file3* + ..." if all the files have the same extension. It is another example of how wild cards can be helpful; it's also a good example of how to save time and effort by intelligently naming similar files with consistent extensions.

VERIFYING ACCURATE DATA TRANSFERS

Another useful switch is the /V switch. If this switch is specified for disk COPY operations, the entire data transfer is verified for accuracy. With normal, unverified transfers, this validation is not guaranteed.

Figure 3.6 shows the normal COPY mechanism, in which COPY reads data from a source disk file into memory and then writes it into the destination disk file. As the figure shows, a portion of memory acts as a *buffer* between the original source of the data (perhaps a disk file) and the eventual destination of the data (perhaps another disk file). In Chapter 8, you'll learn about DOS buffers in more detail. It's enough to know now that a portion of memory is reserved for the temporary storage of file information on its way to or from disk files.

Normally, DOS will copy file information from a source file to a destination file by successively reading one buffer's worth of data into memory and then writing it to the destination drive. Usually, there's no problem. But if the destination drive has a hardware malfunction (unrecognized bad sectors, for example), the resulting destination file may not be the expected replica of the original source file.

The /V switch will take care of the problem. Adding a /V at the end of the COPY command line will cause DOS to perform the sequence depicted in Figure 3.7. In this verified COPY operation, an extra step is undertaken. Each buffer's worth of information that is written to the destination file is also read back into memory. It is then reread to check for errors that may have occurred; if no errors

Figure 3.6: Unverified COPY operation

are discovered, DOS assumes that the destination file has received the source file's data accurately. If it is different, DOS can try to rewrite the data again or simply report an error.

Since this procedure adds an additional burden on your system, and since hardware malfunctions do not occur very often, you probably don't need to add the /V switch very often. The tradeoff is time versus security. However, if you want the security but don't want the bother of specifying /V all the time, DOS allows you a special command. Entering VERIFY at the DOS prompt with a parameter of ON (or OFF) will have the effect of appending (or not appending) a /V switch on all copies.

VERIFY ON

followed by Return will guarantee that all future COPY commands act like the one in Figure 3.7, with what is sometimes called *read-after-write* verification.

USING THE XCOPY COMMAND TO TRANSFER FILES

A special command called XCOPY (available only in DOS 3.2 or 3.3) allows more sophisticated file transfers between disks and directories. It is preferable for multifile transfers because it is usually faster

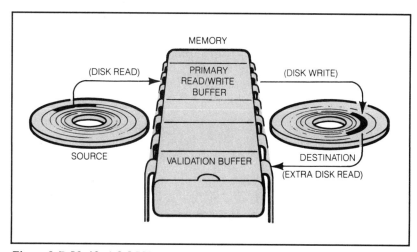

Figure 3.7: Verified COPY operation

than COPY. It is also preferable for transferring files that exist in multiple directories, because XCOPY understands better than COPY how to select files located in remote sections of the disk. You'll learn more about these remote sections, called *subdirectories,* in Chapter 4; they are subdivisions of existing directories on a disk.

The general format of the XCOPY command is

XCOPY *SourceFile(s) DestinationFile(s) /Switches*

where *SourceFile(s)* and *DestinationFile(s)* are specified as they are with the COPY command. Using */Switches* properly can greatly expand the range of files encompassed. Try performing some sample operations using the files contained in three sections of a disk, as shown in Figure 3.8. Conventional directory listings of the files involved are shown in Figures 3.9 and 3.10.

XCOPY cannot be used to transfer multiple files to a printer. It is designed for disk transfers only.

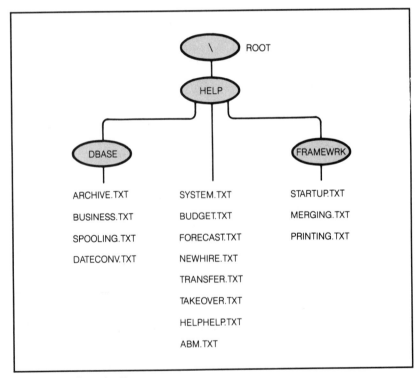

Figure 3.8: Sample directory structure

The simplest example of using the XCOPY command is the following:

XCOPY \HELP*.* A:

will copy all files in the HELP directory to the disk in drive A. As you can see in Figure 3.11, DOS echoes the file names to the screen as they are copied.

```
C>DIR \HELP

 Volume in drive C is ROBBINS
 Directory of  C:\HELP

 .            <DIR>      5-Ø3-87   8:16a
 ..           <DIR>      5-Ø3-87   8:16a
 SYSTEM   TXT     328   1-13-87   7:5Øp
 BUDGET   TXT    2186   1-22-87   6:Ø8p
 FORECAST TXT     256   1-Ø2-87  12:25p
 NEWHIRE  TXT    1781   2-26-87   6:39p
 TRANSFER TXT    4429   1-19-87   2:55p
 TAKEOVER TXT     621   1-Ø1-87  12:16p
 HELPHELP TXT     258   1-14-87   2:41p
 ABM      TXT     383   1-13-87   6:33p
 DBASE        <DIR>      5-Ø3-87   8:24a
 FRAMEWRK     <DIR>      5-Ø3-87   8:24a
       12 File(s)   113Ø496 bytes free

C>_
```

Figure 3.9: The HELP directory

```
 Volume in drive C is ROBBINS
 Directory of  C:\HELP\DBASE

 .            <DIR>      5-Ø3-87   8:24a
 ..           <DIR>      5-Ø3-87   8:24a
 ARCHIVE  TXT    1152  1Ø-25-85   6:46p
 BUSINESS TXT     561   4-16-87  1Ø:Ø4p
 SPOOLING TXT    2816  1Ø-25-85   6:38p
 DATECONV TXT    1536  1Ø-25-85   6:41p
        6 File(s)   1124352 bytes free

C>DIR \HELP\FRAMEWRK

 Volume in drive C is ROBBINS
 Directory of  C:\HELP\FRAMEWRK

 .            <DIR>      5-Ø3-87   8:24a
 ..           <DIR>      5-Ø3-87   8:24a
 STARTUP  TXT     195   3-Ø5-86   9:25a
 MERGING  TXT     638   2-19-86  1Ø:56a
 PRINTING TXT     147   2-19-86  1Ø:58a
        5 File(s)   1124352 bytes free

C>_
```

Figure 3.10: The HELP\DBASE and HELP\FRAMEWRK directories

```
C>XCOPY  \HELP\*.*  A:

Reading source file(s)...
\HELP\SYSTEM.TXT
\HELP\BUDGET.TXT
\HELP\FORECAST.TXT
\HELP\NEWHIRE.TXT
\HELP\TRANSFER.TXT
\HELP\TAKEOVER.TXT
\HELP\HELPHELP.TXT
\HELP\ABM.TXT
        8 File(s) copied

C>_
```

Figure 3.11: XCOPY reading files into memory and writing destination files

The unique aspect of this command is hidden behind the message "Reading source file(s)," which appears first on the screen. The COPY command reads a source file and then writes a destination file. The XCOPY command first reads as many source files as possible into available memory. Only then does it stop to write the destination files. Since memory operations occur much more rapidly than disk operations, the overall operation speed is increased. Simply said, less disk work and more memory work means the entire file is transferred faster.

SWITCHES FOR THE XCOPY COMMAND You should now take a look at the XCOPY command's switches, in the order of their importance. The most powerful switch is /S, which gives you the ability to select files located in the subdirectory structure. Notice in Figure 3.11 that the expected eight .TXT files in HELP were copied. That's the same result as would have been obtained by using the COPY command, but the operation went a little faster.

In Figure 3.12, you can see the direct effect of using the /S switch. It directs DOS to look in all subdirectories of HELP for file names that match the specified *.TXT wild card. As simply as that, the additional four .TXT files in the HELP\DBASE subdirectory are copied, along with the additional three .TXT files in the

```
C>XCOPY  \HELP\*.*  A: /S

Reading source file(s)...
\HELP\SYSTEM.TXT
\HELP\BUDGET.TXT
\HELP\FORECAST.TXT
\HELP\NEWHIRE.TXT
\HELP\TRANSFER.TXT
\HELP\TAKEOVER.TXT
\HELP\HELPHELP.TXT
\HELP\ABM.TXT
\HELP\DBASE\ARCHIVE.TXT
\HELP\DBASE\BUSINESS.TXT
\HELP\DBASE\SPOOLING.TXT
\HELP\DBASE\DATECONV.TXT
\HELP\FRAMEWRK\STARTUP.TXT
\HELP\FRAMEWRK\MERGING.TXT
\HELP\FRAMEWRK\PRINTING.TXT
       15 File(s) copied

C>■
```

Figure 3.12: The /S switch searching all subdirectories for wild-card matches

HELP\FRAMEWRK subdirectory. If the respective directories do not already exist on the destination disk, DOS automatically creates them for you and then copies the files into them.

You can exercise further control over the copying operation by employing the /P switch, which offers another improvement. It asks DOS to prompt you (hence /P) for each file name that matches the wild-card specification, giving you control over whether each file name will be included in the actual copying operation.

Look at the example XCOPY transfer in Figure 3.13, which uses the same /S switch as in the last example but asks you to answer a prompt for each file. In the figure's example, the prompt was answered affirmatively (Y) only four times. The destination drive consequently received copies of the four selected files only. These files were

- HELP\BUDGET.TXT
- HELP\FORECAST.TXT
- HELP\DBASE\BUSINESS.TXT
- HELP\FRAMEWRK\MERGING.TXT

It's important to notice that two of these files are in subdirectories of the HELP directory. The /S switch also ensures that the same

```
C>XCOPY  \HELP\*.*  B:  /S /P
\HELP\SYSTEM.TXT (Y/N)? N
\HELP\BUDGET.TXT (Y/N)? Y
\HELP\FORECAST.TXT (Y/N)? Y
\HELP\NEWHIRE.TXT (Y/N)? N
\HELP\TRANSFER.TXT (Y/N)? N
\HELP\TAKEOVER.TXT (Y/N)? N
\HELP\HELPHELP.TXT (Y/N)? N
\HELP\ABM.TXT (Y/N)? N
\HELP\DBASE\ARCHIVE.TXT (Y/N)? N
\HELP\DBASE\BUSINESS.TXT (Y/N)? Y
\HELP\DBASE\SPOOLING.TXT (Y/N)? N
\HELP\DBASE\DATECONV.TXT (Y/N)? N
\HELP\FRAMEWRK\STARTUP.TXT (Y/N)? N
\HELP\FRAMEWRK\MERGING.TXT (Y/N)? Y
\HELP\FRAMEWRK\PRINTING.TXT (Y/N)? N
       4 File(s) copied

C>_
```

Figure 3.13: The /P switch prompt before copying

subdirectory structure is recreated on the destination disk (if it is not there already), as you can see in Figure 3.14. Figure 3.15 verifies that the specified files are also copied over accurately and into the proper subdirectories.

Another important switch, /D, allows you to specify that all files should be copied if their creation dates are the same as or later than the date specified. The form required is /D:mm-dd-yy unless you have installed a DOS version with a different international date format (see Chapter 11). In that case, you can specify the date in whatever format your system recognizes. As an example, Figure 3.16 demonstrates how all files in the HELP directory that were created on or after January 19, 1987, are copied to drive A.

Remaining switches are of less practical importance. The /A switch selects files that are marked for backup (see Chapter 9 for a discussion of backups). The archive attribute is not changed by this switch. The /M switch copies the same files that are marked for backup, but it does change the archive attribute to indicate that the files have been backed up.

The /V switch performs the same task as it does on the COPY command, requesting the extra read-after-write verification step. The /W switch is hardly worth mentioning, since its only job is to pause briefly, asking you to press any key to begin copying files.

```
C>DIR B:

 Volume in drive B has no label
 Directory of  B:\

BUDGET   TXT     2186   1-22-87   6:08p
FORECAST TXT      256   1-02-87  12:25p
DBASE         <DIR>     5-03-87   9:20a
FRAMEWRK      <DIR>     5-03-87   9:20a
       4 File(s)    173568 bytes free

C>_
```

Figure 3.14: Destination drive after using /S and /P

```
C>DIR B:\DBASE

 Volume in drive B has no label
 Directory of  B:\DBASE

.            <DIR>     5-03-87   9:20a
..           <DIR>     5-03-87   9:20a
BUSINESS TXT      561   4-16-87  10:04p
       3 File(s)    173568 bytes free

C>DIR B:\FRAMEWRK

 Volume in drive B has no label
 Directory of  B:\FRAMEWRK

.            <DIR>     5-03-87   9:20a
..           <DIR>     5-03-87   9:20a
MERGING  TXT      638   2-19-86  10:56a
       3 File(s)    173568 bytes free

C>_
```

Figure 3.15: Accurately created destination subdirectories

OTHER FUNDAMENTAL ACTIVITIES

There are just a few more commands that you should know about to aid your activities at this point. Of course, many other commands do exist, but you'll only need them in more advanced situations, covered later in this book. You should now become comfortable with typing out text files, renaming files, and deleting files.

```
C>XCOPY   \HELP\*.*   A:   /D:1/19/87

Reading source file(s)...
\HELP\BUDGET.TXT
\HELP\NEWHIRE.TXT
\HELP\TRANSFER.TXT
        3 File(s) copied

C>_
```

Figure 3.16: Specifying dates with XCOPY and /D

TYPING OUT A TEXT FILE

The TYPE command is similar to the COPY CON command. It can show the contents of any standard text or ASCII file. TYPE is also the best way to view the contents of *batch files,* which are only simple ASCII text files. In both cases, these files consist solely of letters, numbers, and symbols that can be typed on a standard keyboard. Although you won't learn about DOS batch files in depth until Chapter 13, you should take note of the TYPE command now.

Many business application programs are purchased on diskette. Whether you eventually use the software on diskette or on a hard disk, the manufacturer usually provides a special file called README.TXT or some similar name. Special usage information that arrived too late to be included in the printed user manual usually is included in this file. The TYPE command is the easiest way to read the file. To use it, enter

TYPE README.TXT

> Remember to use the Ctrl-S key combination to stop and start the display of the contents of the README.TXT file. In Chapter 12 you'll learn how to use the MORE command at the DOS prompt to display one screenful of information at a time.

CHANGING THE NAME OF A FILE

You can change the name of a file without affecting the contents of that file. There may be times when you want to change some file names so that you can take advantage of the ? or * wild card to deal with blocks of files.

During the writing of this book, many screen images were captured and a number of text-file figures were created. When screen images are captured, they are given names like SCREEN##.CAP. It is more convenient to rename them according to the chapter and figure name, since then all figures can be managed together using wild-card expressions.

Figure 3.17 shows a wide directory listing of a group of figures prepared for this book. At the bottom of the figure, the listing shows the file containing the most recently captured screen image, SCREEN03.CAP. Using DOS's RENAME command, you can change the SCREEN03 file name without changing the data inside the file, and still retain the extension (see Figure 3.18):

RENAME SCREEN03.CAP FIG8-12.CAP

The command has changed SCREEN03.CAP to FIG8-12.CAP. Notice in Figure 3.18 that DIR SCREEN*.CAP doesn't find any screen files, since the only previously existing .CAP had its name changed to FIG8-12.CAP.

The general form of this command is

RENAME *OldName NewName*

The first file name is the old name you want to change. The file name that follows is the new name the file will receive.

You can also use the * and ? wild cards with the RENAME command. For example, if you want to change all files that have an extension of .CMD to files that end in .PRG, you can do so with one command:

RENAME *.CMD *.PRG

This sort of operation often is required when you switch from one system to another, or when a software manufacturer makes a major change in its naming conventions. For example, if you need to run programs written in Ashton-Tate's dBASE II under the auspices of your dBASE III PLUS, this is exactly the type of renaming task you would perform.

You can only use the RENAME command for a single file on a single disk. You *cannot* use the RENAME command to simultaneously copy a file from one disk to another while renaming it—use the COPY command to do that particular chore. RENAME only changes the name of the file, whereas COPY creates a new file entirely. With COPY, you begin with one file and end up with two; with RENAME, you begin with one file and end up with the same file.

```
C>DIR/W  FIG*.CAP

 Volume in drive C is ROBBINS
 Directory of  C:\PROGRAMS\FW\SYBEX

FIG11-1   CAP      FIG11-2   CAP      FIG11-3   CAP      FIG11-5   CAP      FIG11-6B CAP
FIG2-10   CAP      FIG2-11   CAP      FIG2-12   CAP      FIG2-6    CAP      FIG2-7   CAP
FIG2-8A   CAP      FIG2-8B   CAP      FIG4-10A  CAP      FIG4-10B  CAP      FIG4-10C CAP
FIG4-14   CAP      FIG4-15   CAP      FIG4-2    CAP      FIG4-3    CAP      FIG4-4   CAP
FIG4-5    CAP      FIG4-6    CAP      FIG4-7    CAP      FIG4-8    CAP      FIG4-9   CAP
FIG7-3    CAP      FIG7-4    CAP      FIG7-5    CAP
       28 File(s)   2293760 bytes free

C>DIR SCREEN*.CAP

 Volume in drive C is ROBBINS
 Directory of  C:\PROGRAMS\FW\SYBEX

SCREEN03 CAP     4256   3-30-87   9:38a
        1 File(s)   2287616 bytes free

C>_
```

Figure 3.17: Listing of figure and screen files

```
C>RENAME  SCREEN03.CAP  FIG8-12.CAP

C>DIR/W FIG*.CAP

 Volume in drive C is ROBBINS
 Directory of  C:\PROGRAMS\FW\SYBEX

FIG11-1   CAP      FIG11-2   CAP      FIG11-3   CAP      FIG11-5   CAP      FIG11-6B CAP
FIG2-10   CAP      FIG2-11   CAP      FIG2-12   CAP      FIG2-6    CAP      FIG2-7   CAP
FIG2-8A   CAP      FIG2-8B   CAP      FIG4-10A  CAP      FIG4-10B  CAP      FIG4-10C CAP
FIG4-14   CAP      FIG4-15   CAP      FIG4-2    CAP      FIG4-3    CAP      FIG4-4   CAP
FIG4-5    CAP      FIG4-6    CAP      FIG4-7    CAP      FIG4-8    CAP      FIG4-9   CAP
FIG7-3    CAP      FIG7-4    CAP      FIG7-5    CAP      FIG8-12   CAP
        29 File(s)   2281472 bytes free

C>DIR SCREEN*.CAP

 Volume in drive C is ROBBINS
 Directory of  C:\PROGRAMS\FW\SYBEX

File not found

C>_
```

Figure 3.18: Using the RENAME command

The RENAME command also offers a limited degree of protection. You may not be the only person with access to your computer and disks. In that case, you may desire a measure of security for some of your data files. You can rename an obvious file like BUDGET.WK1 to TEMP.NDX, a clearly misleading name. Prying eyes are not as likely to come to rest on the renamed file.

Take a moment now to try this renaming technique on any files for which you'd like to restrict access. But be careful: first, don't forget the new file name you choose; second, don't select a dispensable name (like TEMP.NDX) if anyone else using your disk is at all likely to delete files.

ERASING A FILE

From time to time you will want to get rid of a file on a disk. The ERASE command will do this for you. The general form of the command is

> ERASE *FileName(s)*

The following command will erase the file PHONES.DAT from drive A:

> ERASE phones.dat

The ? and * wild-card operators also work with ERASE, so you can erase groups of related files with a single command. Be careful with ERASE—it will erase files without asking for confirmation. The following command will erase all .TXT files:

> ERASE *.TXT

As you were advised in the section on the COPY command, *be certain* when you issue a command with wild cards that it will affect only the files you intend.

The only time DOS will ask you if you really meant what you said is when you specify

> ERASE *.*

This command includes all files. Be sure of yourself if you answer yes to that question. If you make a mistake and accidentally erase any files you didn't mean to—or all of them—stop immediately. Do nothing else until you buy a file recovery program. See Chapter 17 for more information.

Another command exists that works exactly the same as ERASE: the DEL command. However, this command should be avoided—it's much closer in appearance to the commonly used DIR command, but devastatingly different in its effect. Too many people have typed DEL *.* when they intended to type DIR *.*; you don't have to make the same mistake. Use the ERASE command when you want to remove files from your disks.

You should always precede an ERASE request that uses wild cards with a DIR command, using the same wild-card specification, to ensure that you know which files will be picked up by the command.

The most common use for the ERASE command is to clean up disks that have been in use for a while. Old versions of data files often proliferate; early copies of memos and other word-processed documents always seem to expand to fill any available space on your disk. If you have a disk that fits this description, now is a good time to use ERASE and clean it up.

SUMMARY

To use your computer effectively, you need to understand how data, programs, and information of any sort is stored in files and how to properly manage these files. This chapter presented the principal commands and mechanisms in DOS for file management. You learned the following:

- The DOS disk directory contains a listing of all base names and extensions for each separate file in it. It also contains the sizes, as well as the dates and times of creation of these files.

- The DIR (Directory) command permits you to obtain listings of each directory's contents.

- Certain switches modify the DIR command request. More files can be listed on the screen with the /W (Wide) switch, and information can be presented one screenful at a time with the /P switch.

- DOS references files only on the current default drive. However, by preceding the file name with a drive identifier, like A: or C:, you can reference files on different drives.

- The DIR listing can be restricted to only some of the files in the directory by using placeholding wild-card symbols. The * and ? symbols can be used to ask DOS to manipulate multiple files at the same time. These symbols can take the place of part or all of a file's base name and extension.

- The powerful COPY command can be used to make secondary copies or backup copies of files by specifying the desired file name as the source file, and the new file name as the destination file.

- COPY can also copy multiple files at a time if you carefully use wild cards as the source and destination file names.

- COPY can transfer data between several different physical devices if you simply specify a device identifier (for example, PRN: for a printer) as either the source or destination for the COPY file transfer.

- Files can be combined if you combine their names with a plus sign as the source specification for a COPY command.

- The XCOPY command, available in DOS 3.2 or 3.3, can provide extended capabilities for transferring files between disks and directories.

- Several other useful and fundamental commands exist for typing out the contents of text files (TYPE), for changing the name of a file (RENAME), and for completely deleting a file (ERASE). In each case, these commands require you to specify the file names you want to use as parameters on the command line.

In the next chapter, you'll take a closer look at what goes on behind the scenes when you make any of these file management requests. You'll see how the disk directory can be organized in special ways for efficiency and clarity. You'll learn how to set up your disk in the best way for your application plans, and you'll see how to quickly maneuver around your sophisticated organizational design.

UNDERSTANDING THE DOS DIRECTORY STRUCTURE

CHAPTER *4*

CHAPTER 3 TAUGHT YOU HOW TO MANAGE AND manipulate your files and introduced the concepts of directories and subdirectories. In this chapter, you'll explore what subdirectories are and how you can use them to organize your data and program files efficiently. If you have DOS version 2.X or higher, every disk in your system can be logically split up into directories and subdirectories. This ability to create and maintain purposeful groupings of files is the most powerful organizational tool in DOS.

Directories are like separate drawers in a file cabinet. Subdirectories are like the further labeled categories within each drawer. Files are stored in subdirectories and isolated from other files. Just as a well-organized file cabinet promotes efficiency in the office, a well-organized set of DOS directories and subdirectories enables you to quickly and easily store and retrieve your program and data files.

As Table 4.1 shows, a hard disk will store many times the amount of data or number of files that can be stored on a floppy diskette. For example, if the average size of your files is 20,000 bytes, then a 10-megabyte hard disk would hold approximately 500 uniquely named files. If the average file is smaller (say, 10,000 bytes), then you could have 1000 different files on the disk. This raises the problem of keeping order among a huge list of files. DOS allows you to create subdirectories—units of organization that divide the hard disk into sections—to solve this problem.

While subdirectories are usually associated with hard disks, DOS can just as easily create subdirectories on floppy diskettes. They will function exactly the same on diskettes as they do on hard disks, and they will differ only in the volume of data they are capable of holding.

The words *directory* and *subdirectory* are often used interchangeably in DOS. Both are correct. *Subdirectory* is a relative term; any directory is a subdirectory of another directory, with the exception of the root directory. In this book, the word *subdirectory* refers to any directory on a disk other than the *root* (main) directory. The word *directory* refers to either the root or any one of the many possible subdirectories extending from it.

TYPE OF DISK	**TOTAL STORAGE (BYTES)**	**NUMBER OF 20K FILES**
5¹/₄'' floppy	360K	18
High-capacity 5¹/₄'' floppy	1.2Mb	60
Double-sided 3¹/₂'' floppy	1.44Mb	72
Hard disk	10Mb	500
Hard disk	20Mb	1000

Table 4.1: Potential files on differently sized disks

In this chapter, you'll explore the directory commands in the context of a diskette. In Chapter 5, you'll apply what you learn to the more spacious realm of the hard disk. Read this chapter even if you have a hard-disk system—it presents many concepts and techniques you'll need for hard disks as well.

A FIRST LOOK AT A DISK'S DIRECTORY STRUCTURE

Figure 4.1 shows the directory listing for a sample user diskette placed in drive B. (Hard-disk users can try these methods on any diskette placed in drive A.) As the directory shows, there are five files stored on the diskette.

Look at the first line of the directory display:

Volume in drive B has no label

This line refers to the *volume label,* an 11-character name. If you have a label for your disk or diskette, it will appear at the top of the directory listing whenever you enter the DIR command. (The disk will also have an additional hidden file entry, which is inaccessible to you, to store the 11 characters in the label.)

The sample diskette in Figure 4.1 has no label because it was prepared according to the instructions in Chapter 2. Unfortunately, most

Always label your disks when formatting them. Use a name that is indicative of the kind of data or files you intend to place on the disk. You can go back with DOS's LABEL command (available on version 3.0 and higher) to modify the volume label whenever you wish.

```
B>DIR

 Volume in drive B has no label
 Directory of  B:\

IMCAP    COM     6114   6-20-85    1:09p
IMSHOW   EXE    20090   6-20-85   10:09a
QD2      EXE    74752  11-14-86   12:00p
SKN      COM    34009   8-05-85    6:14p
SR       COM     5356   1-01-85
         5 File(s)    175104 bytes free

B>_
```

Figure 4.1: Directory listing of sample diskette

users don't bother with labels, which were designed for the user's benefit. Labels are a simple but effective method of categorizing the files on a disk. Anyone using that disk can quickly ascertain the nature or purpose of the disk's contents. When no label is entered, DOS displays the message "Volume in drive B has no label."

To prepare a diskette for a volume label, you can use the /V switch with the FORMAT command, which allows you to enter an 11-character name. Spaces are allowed in this label, even though file names do not permit spaces. Figure 4.2 shows a typical sequence used to prepare a completely different diskette, which will be able to boot up the DOS system (/S) with a volume label (/V) that says SYBEX BOOK.

If you decide after you have formatted a diskette to add a volume label, or if you wish to modify an existing volume label, you should use the LABEL command, available on DOS version 3.0 and higher. Figure 4.3 shows how the label BOOK SAMPLE has been placed on the previously unlabeled diskette.

The second line of the initial directory display shown in Figure 4.1 indicates which directory is being listed. It reads

Directory of B:\

A disk with no subdirectories has only a single directory. The back-slash symbol (\) is used to indicate a directory name. When DOS

```
A>FORMAT B: /S /V
Insert new diskette for drive B:
and strike ENTER when ready

Format complete
System transferred

Volume label (11 characters, ENTER for none)? SYBEX BOOK


    362496 bytes total disk space
     69632 bytes used by system
    292864 bytes available on disk

Format another (Y/N)?N
A>■
```

Figure 4.2: Formatting a diskette with a volume label

```
A>LABEL B:

Volume in drive B has no label

Volume label (11 characters, ENTER for none)? BOOK SAMPLE


A>DIR  B:

 Volume in drive B is BOOK SAMPLE
 Directory of  B:\

IMCAP    COM     6114   6-20-85    1:09p
IMSHOW   EXE    20090   6-20-85   10:09a
QD2      EXE    74752  11-14-86   12:00p
SKN      COM    34009   8-05-85    6:14p
SR       COM     5356   1-01-85
         5 File(s)    220160 bytes free

A>■
```

Figure 4.3: DOS's LABEL command

shows B:\, it indicates that you are looking at the main or root directory of the disk. This root directory is created when a disk is formatted. Every disk has one—and only one—root directory. In the next section, you'll see how to subdivide the root directory into smaller but more refined groupings: subdirectories.

CREATING A SUBDIRECTORY

In this section you will create a subdirectory called UTIL to store a group of related files. The UTIL subdirectory will hold some DOS utility programs selected from a DOS master disk. Without subdirectories, you would have to store all the files in the single unorganized root directory.

Before you create this first subdirectory, you should log on to the disk drive with the sample diskette. If your machine has a hard-disk drive and one floppy-diskette drive, your sample diskette should be in drive A and you should log on to that drive by simply typing A: at the DOS C> prompt:

```
C>A:
```

For dual-diskette systems, switch to drive B by typing B: at the DOS A> prompt:

```
A>B:
```

To create a subdirectory you can use the Make Directory command—either MKDIR or MD. Both versions have the same effect, but the MD command is easier to type. The command to create the UTIL subdirectory on your sample diskette is as follows:

```
MD \UTIL
```

This command produces the new directory display seen in Figure 4.4. Note that you use the left-slanting backslash character, not the right-slanting slash character usually used to indicate arithmetic division. This backslash symbol is used in DOS to clarify the hierarchical directory structure. A backslash is a *delimiter* that precedes any subdirectory's name, in part to specify the name as representing a subdirectory, and in part to separate its name from the directory in which it can be found.

The directory in Figure 4.4 has a new type of entry. It is marked with the <DIR> symbol, which tells you that UTIL is not a file but the name of a subdirectory. Remember, directories just contain files (or other directories, as you'll soon see); files actually contain data or programs.

```
B>MD \UTIL

B>DIR

   Volume in drive B is BOOK SAMPLE
   Directory of  B:\

   IMCAP    COM     6114    6-20-85    1:09p
   IMSHOW   EXE    20090    6-20-85   10:09a
   QD2      EXE    74752   11-14-86   12:00p
   SKN      COM    34009    8-05-85    6:14p
   SR       COM     5356    1-01-85
   UTIL         <DIR>       1-01-80   12:46a
        6 File(s)     219136 bytes free

B>_
```

Figure 4.4: Listing of root directory containing new subdirectory

ACCESSING FILES IN A SUBDIRECTORY

You can indicate that a command should work with a subdirectory by using the name of the subdirectory preceded by the \ symbol. Entering the DIR command with a first argument of \UTIL produces the directory listing shown in Figure 4.5. This figure shows the directory of the files stored in the new subdirectory UTIL. There are no files listed because you have not created or copied any files into this subdirectory.

You may wonder about the two entries that do appear, the one-dot and two-dot entries. Ignore them! These obscure references to the "current directory" and the "parent directory" are used so infrequently that they are practically useless to the typical DOS user.

What happened to the two files you had before? They are still on the disk, but they are in the root directory. To see them, you can always explicitly request a directory listing of the root directory like this:

**DIR **

```
B>DIR  \UTIL

 Volume in drive B is BOOK SAMPLE
 Directory of  B:\UTIL

 .           <DIR>      1-Ø1-8Ø  12:46a
 ..          <DIR>      1-Ø1-8Ø  12:46a
        2 File(s)    219136 bytes free

B>_
```

Figure 4.5: Directory listing of new subdirectory

CHANGING THE
DEFAULT DIRECTORY

Just as DOS allows you to select a default drive, it also allows you to select a default directory for a disk. Once you've created a new directory, you can tell the operating system that you want it, rather than the root, to be the default directory. This allows you to work with only the files contained within that subdirectory. Then you won't have to enter the subdirectory name before each DOS command in order to reference files tucked away in some other subdirectory.

The command used to change directories is the CHDIR or CD command. (Again, CD is easier to type.) If you simply enter a DIR command, you see a listing of the root directory; if you enter a DIR command followed by the backslash and a subdirectory name, you see a listing of that subdirectory. The CD command, on the other hand, allows you to enter DOS commands that will then assume that the new default area of the disk (the subdirectory) is the specified one. For example, entering

CD \UTIL

makes the UTIL subdirectory the current DOS default whenever you make references to files on the current disk drive.

Notice in Figure 4.6 that the same DIR command produces a listing of the current default directory, which is different before and after the CD \UTIL command. The directory listing at the bottom of the figure is for the UTIL subdirectory. The CD command has reset the default directory to UTIL, so the DIR command lists only the files contained within that subdirectory.

COPYING FILES INTO A SUBDIRECTORY

Now that you have created a subdirectory, you can use it to store files. The basic DOS commands (COPY, ERASE, RENAME, and so on) will work with subdirectories. Since the default drive is the one you're working with, you'll need to specify the source drive for the files you're going to copy into the new UTIL subdirectory. First copy FORMAT.COM from drive A into this subdirectory by entering

    COPY A:FORMAT.COM

Notice there is no second argument to indicate the destination. When you don't specify a destination, the COPY command assumes that the current drive and the current subdirectory (UTIL) are the defaults, using the same file name for this default destination file name. Copying another file into the UTIL subdirectory with

    COPY A:CHKDSK.COM

and then entering a directory listing request will result in the listing shown in Figure 4.7. This confirms that the files have been copied successfully from your source diskette to the UTIL subdirectory of your sample diskette.

RETURNING TO THE ROOT DIRECTORY

You can reset the default to the root directory at any time by entering the CD command and using the root directory symbol (\)

```
B>DIR

 Volume in drive B is BOOK SAMPLE
 Directory of  B:\

IMCAP    COM     6114   6-20-85   1:09p
IMSHOW   EXE    20090   6-20-85  10:09a
QD2      EXE    74752  11-14-86  12:00p
SKN      COM    34009   8-05-85   6:14p
SR       COM     5356   1-01-85
UTIL          <DIR>     1-01-80  12:46a
        6 File(s)    219136 bytes free

B>CD \UTIL

B>DIR

 Volume in drive B is BOOK SAMPLE
 Directory of  B:\UTIL

.             <DIR>     1-01-80  12:46a
..            <DIR>     1-01-80  12:46a
        2 File(s)    219136 bytes free

B>_
```

Figure 4.6: Changing the current default directory

```
B>COPY  A:FORMAT.COM
        1 File(s) copied

B>COPY  A:CHKDSK.COM
        1 File(s) copied

B>DIR

 Volume in drive B is BOOK SAMPLE
 Directory of  B:\UTIL

.             <DIR>     1-01-80  12:46a
..            <DIR>     1-01-80  12:46a
FORMAT   COM    11135  12-30-85  12:00p
CHKDSK   COM     9832  12-30-85  12:00p
        4 File(s)    197632 bytes free

B>_
```

Figure 4.7: Organizing files in a subdirectory

There can only be one active directory at a time. If you use the CD command to make a directory active, it is implicit that all the other directories are inactive.

all by itself:

CD \

Entering the DIR command now would produce the same results as you saw in Figure 4.4, before you switched defaults to the UTIL subdirectory. Note that the files copied into UTIL do not appear in this directory. They can only be seen now by specifically referring to the UTIL subdirectory.

HOW SUBDIRECTORIES WORK

DOS keeps track of the unique groupings of subdirectories by attaching a prefix or *path name* to every file that is stored in a subdirectory. Normally, the prefix is not displayed when you use the DIR command. However, there is a special form of the CHKDSK command that reveals the prefixes attached to files. Entering

A:CHKDSK/V

results in a detailed display like that in Figure 4.8. This is necessary for discovering the hierarchical grouping of any disk. Once you've created a number of directories and placed various files in them, it becomes harder and harder to remember where everything is. This command can help you to stay in control of your files and the disk structure you've created for them.

Remember that CHKDSK is not a resident DOS command, so if it's not on the current default drive (B), you must specify where it can be found. That explains why you need to preface the name CHKDSK

Full path-name referencing of this type is a convenience available to DOS 3.X users. DOS 2.X can only access commands on the active directory of a particular drive.

```
B>A:CHKDSK /V
Volume BOOK SAMPLE created Jan 1, 1980 12:06a
Directory B:\
        B:\IMCAP.COM
        B:\IMSHOW.EXE
        B:\QD2.EXE
        B:\SKN.COM
        B:\SR.COM
        B:\BOOK SAM.PLE
Directory B:\UTIL
        B:\UTIL\FORMAT.COM
        B:\UTIL\CHKDSK.COM
        B:\UTIL\FIG4-8.CAP

   362496 bytes total disk space
        0 bytes in 1 hidden files
     1024 bytes in 1 directories
   168960 bytes in 8 user files
   192512 bytes available on disk

   524288 bytes total memory
   435136 bytes free

B>_
```

Figure 4.8: Verbose output from the CHKDSK command

with A:, since in this simple dual-diskette configuration, the DOS master files are on the disk in drive A. The /V switch requests a *verbose* listing, which includes complete file names (see Figure 4.8).

The display reveals first the disk-drive prefix, then the directory prefix for every file. The FORMAT.COM file in the UTIL subdirectory may be accessed by using the path name of B:\UTIL, while the SKN.COM in the root may be accessed by preceding its name with the path-name prefix of B:\.

MULTILEVEL DIRECTORIES

The path system in DOS subdirectories allows you to create ever more complex yet organized groupings. Taking advantage of this system, you can create subdirectories of subdirectories. You could create a subdirectory of UTIL called SPECIAL with the following command:

MD \UTIL\SPECIAL

However, if you used the DIR command to look at the entries in the root directory, you would see only the original files and the UTIL subdirectory (see Figure 4.9). Where is the new subdirectory? It does not appear on this listing because it is a subdirectory of UTIL. In order to see a listing of the new subdirectory, you must first log into UTIL with the CD command, as shown in Figure 4.10.

APPLYING DOS COMMANDS TO SUBDIRECTORIES

Many DOS commands allow you to specify the subdirectory in which the files are to be found or placed. The COPY command can accept this type of parameter. For example, suppose that you wanted to copy all the files from drive A that begin with the letter M into the subdirectory UTIL\SPECIAL. You would enter the following:

COPY A:M*.* \UTIL\SPECIAL

However, a directory listing now would not list the resulting files unless you first changed the default directory to the new SPECIAL subdirectory, or unless you specified the complete path name to the desired subdirectory (see Figure 4.11).

UNDERSTANDING THE CONCEPT OF PATHS

In order to get through to the SPECIAL subdirectory, you must first go through the UTIL subdirectory. This requirement to follow a

```
B>MD \UTIL\SPECIAL

B>DIR \

  Volume in drive B is BOOK SAMPLE
  Directory of  B:\

IMCAP    COM     6114   6-20-85    1:09p
IMSHOW   EXE    20090   6-20-85   10:09a
QD2      EXE    74752  11-14-86   12:00p
SKN      COM    34009   8-05-85    6:14p
SR       COM     5356   1-01-85
UTIL          <DIR>     1-01-80   12:46a
       6 File(s)    196608 bytes free

B>_
```

Figure 4.9: Current root directory

```
B>CD \UTIL

B>DIR

  Volume in drive B is BOOK SAMPLE
  Directory of  B:\UTIL

.             <DIR>     1-01-80   12:46a
..            <DIR>     1-01-80   12:46a
FORMAT   COM    11135  12-30-85   12:00p
CHKDSK   COM     9832  12-30-85   12:00p
SPECIAL       <DIR>     1-01-80    4:19a
       5 File(s)    191488 bytes free

B>_
```

Figure 4.10: Display of a subdirectory within a subdirectory path to any particular file can be compared to climbing a tree. All trees have roots, but to get to any particular branch, you have to first climb past the larger branches leading to it. Any branch on the tree is analogous to a DOS directory or subdirectory.

Each branch of a tree can have new branches growing from it. Similarly, each subdirectory can have new subdirectories defined within it. And just as each branch may also have fruit or leaves on it, each subdirectory may have program or data files stored in it.

The series of subdirectories that you link together is the path. You can see by the way the tree is structured that each subdirectory, and each file within it, has a unique path from the root directory. The large arrows shown in Figures 4.12, 4.13, and 4.14 represent the current default directory in each of the three situations that were presented in Figures 4.9, 4.10, and 4.11, respectively. Use these figures to help you understand the concept of paths.

It's helpful to always keep in mind which directory is the DOS default on the disk drive you're using. Otherwise, you could end up like the tree surgeon who forgot where he was while working on a tree. Figure 4.15 shows you what could happen!

Let's make one last subdirectory. Enter the command

MD \UTIL\SPECIAL\FINAL

```
B>COPY  A:M*.*  \UTIL\SPECIAL
A:MODE.COM
A:MORE.COM
        2 File(s) copied

B>DIR \UTIL\SPECIAL

  Volume in drive B is BOOK SAMPLE
  Directory of  B:\UTIL\SPECIAL

  .            <DIR>      1-Ø1-8Ø   4:19a
  ..           <DIR>      1-Ø1-8Ø   4:19a
  MODE    COM      6864  12-3Ø-85  12:ØØp
  MORE    COM       295  12-3Ø-85  12:ØØp
        4 File(s)    178176 bytes free

B>_
```

Figure 4.11: Listing of the SPECIAL subdirectory

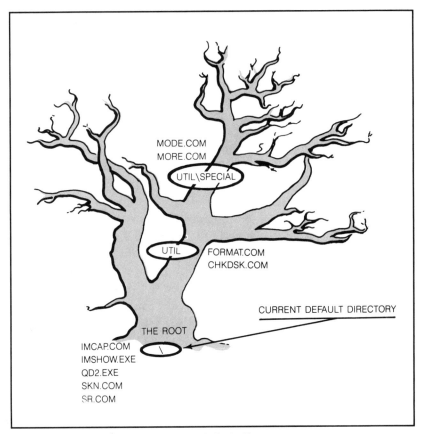

MODE.COM
MORE.COM

UTIL\SPECIAL

UTIL
FORMAT.COM
CHKDSK.COM

CURRENT DEFAULT DIRECTORY

THE ROOT

IMCAP.COM
IMSHOW.EXE
QD2.EXE
SKN.COM
SR.COM

\

Figure 4.12: Root (\) as the current default directory

You have now extended the tree another level. To see how well you've understood the methods and concepts of directories and subdirectories, create the tree of directories described so far in this chapter, ending with the SPECIAL directory. Then copy all the .EXE files from your DOS master disk to the SPECIAL directory.

Verify that your creation and transfer worked properly by listing the contents of the SPECIAL directory. It should list the one- and two-dot entries, along with all the .EXE files from your DOS master disk.

MOVING FILES BETWEEN DIRECTORIES

So far, you've copied files from drive A into subdirectories on drive B. But what if you want to transfer files from one subdirectory to another

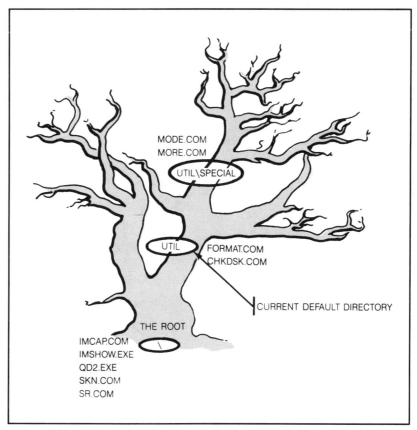

Figure 4.13: UTIL as the current default directory

on the same diskette? For example, you might want to move the two utility programs in the root, IMCAP.COM and IMSHOW.EXE (see Figure 4.1), into the newly created SPECIAL directory. This will require two steps:

1. Use COPY to make a copy of each of the files in the new directory.

2. Use ERASE to erase the original copies of the files after verifying that the transfer took place correctly.

The key is to specify the correct path name when you enter the commands. Remember that you want to copy a file in the root (path

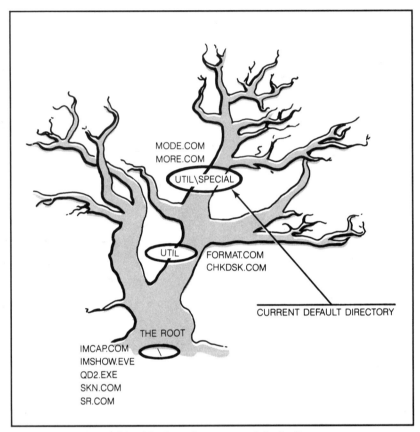

Figure 4.14: UTIL\SPECIAL as the current default directory

name \) to a directory with the full path name \UTIL\SPECIAL.
Type

    COPY \IMSHOW.EXE \UTIL\SPECIAL
    COPY \IMCAP.COM \UTIL\SPECIAL

and press Return after each command. Figure 4.16 shows this
sequence followed by a DIR command to verify the transfer and an
ERASE command to delete the old files from the root.

SOME FINE POINTS ABOUT COPYING FILES   In all of the
cases so far, the new file created in the destination directory received
the same name as the original file. When necessary, you can direct
DOS to assign new names as part of the COPY procedure. For

Figure 4.15: Forgetting where you are in the directory tree

example, the command

    COPY *.DBF \BACKUPS*.BAK

will make backup copies of all .DBF (database) files in the current directory. The new copies will appear in the BACKUP directory with the extension .BAK.

Note that in having a first argument of *.DBF, you are assuming that all the .DBF files are on the current drive and in the current directory. In the second argument, since you specify the desired directory, BACKUPS, you are only making an assumption about the current drive. For anything other than the default, you must specify either the drive, the directory, or both.

```
B>COPY \IMSHOW.EXE  \UTIL\SPECIAL
        1 File(s) copied

B>COPY \IMCAP.COM  \UTIL\SPECIAL
        1 File(s) copied

B>DIR  \UTIL\SPECIAL

 Volume in drive B is BOOK SAMPLE
 Directory of  B:\UTIL\SPECIAL

  .            <DIR>      1-01-80   4:19a
  ..           <DIR>      1-01-80   4:19a
 MODE    COM     6864  12-30-85  12:00p
 MORE    COM      295  12-30-85  12:00p
 IMSHOW  EXE    20090   6-20-85  10:09a
 IMCAP   COM     6114   6-20-85   1:09p
        6 File(s)   151552 bytes free

B>ERASE \IMSHOW.EXE

B>ERASE \IMCAP.COM

B>_
```

Figure 4.16: Copying files between directories on the same disk

MANEUVERING AROUND THE DOS DIRECTORY STRUCTURE

While subdirectories are essential for good organization, they can become confusing very quickly. DOS has some commands that help you navigate through the complex tangle of directories.

VIEWING THE STRUCTURE

The TREE command enables you to get a summary of the directories and subdirectories on a disk. TREE is not a resident command. This means that it will not work at all times or in every circumstance. TREE, like CHKDSK, is really a program file provided in DOS. This file, TREE.COM, must be present on one of the disks in your system, or you cannot execute the TREE command.

Since TREE.COM is in drive A of the dual-diskette example, entering

A:TREE

will list the volume label of the diskette in the current default drive (BOOK SAMPLE) as well as all the directories created on that diskette and any subdirectories created within them. See Figure 4.17.

```
B>A:TREE
DIRECTORY PATH LISTING FOR VOLUME BOOK SAMPLE
Path: \UTIL
Sub-directories:   SPECIAL


Path: \UTIL\SPECIAL
Sub-directories:   None



B>_
```

Figure 4.17: DOS's TREE command

You can also get a more detailed tree display that lists the specific files in each subdirectory. Entering

   A:TREE/F

produces the output seen in Figure 4.18. The /F switch asks DOS to include the file names found in each directory.

It's hard to display a TREE listing on the screen, because it is usually too long for one screen. If you have a printer, you can get a printed copy of the screen display by entering

   A:TREE /F > PRN

This command uses a special feature called *redirection,* which will be presented in much more depth in Chapter 12.

SEARCHING PATHS

The main purpose of the subdirectory system is to separate groups of files. However, there may be instances when you will need to reach a file in a directory other than the one you happen to be in (that is, the default directory). For example, the sample diskette used so far now has some files located in the root directory, others in the UTIL directory,

```
DIRECTORY PATH LISTING FOR VOLUME BOOK SAMPLE

Files:              QD2      .EXE
                    SKN      .COM
                    SR       .COM

Path: \UTIL

Sub-directories:    SPECIAL

Files:              FORMAT   .COM
                    CHKDSK   .COM


Path: \UTIL\SPECIAL

Sub-directories:    None

Files:              MODE     .COM
                    MORE     .COM
                    IMSHOW   .EXE
                    IMCAP    .COM


C>_
```

Figure 4.18: Detailed TREE listing (/F switch)

and still others in UTIL\SPECIAL. A copy of CHKDSK, for example, is located in the UTIL directory.

Assume you are currently back in the root directory (CD \). If you try to execute the CHKDSK command by typing

CHKDSK

and pressing Return, the computer will tell you that you have entered a bad command or file name. Why? The answer is simple. You are currently logged into the root directory, and the CHKDSK file is located in UTIL.

DOS has a command that you can enter to specify where to look for files that are not located in the default directory. When this path is opened, the computer will search the directories to find the command file you are looking for. To create a path from the current working directory to the UTIL directory, you would enter

PATH \UTIL

This command opens a path between the current working directory and the directory containing the desired file. Entering CHKDSK now will produce the desired result; the CHKDSK program will execute because DOS was able to find it along the specified search path in the UTIL directory.

The PATH command does not change the active directory. It simply tells DOS to search another directory if the program requested is not to be found in the active directory.

Test your understanding of the PATH command now. If you have a directory structure set up with a program you normally use, purposely change the current directory (CD) to some other directory. Then set the path properly so you can run the desired program, even though it is not available in the current directory. Also, try setting up the path with multiple directory entries, so you can run several different programs without having to change directories.

If your own system is not set up yet with any usable utility or application programs, look at the structure shown in Figure 4.18. You can see that there is a file named IMSHOW.EXE in the UTIL\SPECIAL directory. How would you set the path in DOS to run this program if your current default directory is still the root? For example, which of these commands would you use?

1. PATH \UTIL;\SPECIAL;\FINAL
2. PATH \UTIL
3. PATH \UTIL\SPECIAL
4. PATH UTIL\SPECIAL

Many people are uncertain about the use of delimiters, which are simply characters that separate one computer term from another. How and when they are used is always very critical. In this example, three delimiters must all be used correctly. The backslash symbol, as you know, separates directory names in a single path. The space symbol separates the PATH command from the list of directory names. The semicolon separates different directory names in the same path listing.

Choice 3 is the correct one. PATH \UTIL\SPECIAL is the full path name from the root to the directory containing the desired program. The semicolons make choice 1 incorrect, since this path specifies the UTIL directory and the nonexistent SPECIAL directory. It does not exist in the root; it exists in the UTIL branch of the directory tree. Choice 2 is wrong, since UTIL is the branch of the directory tree that contains the subdirectory SPECIAL, and not the desired program IMSHOW.EXE.

Choice 4 is going to be wrong *most* of the time. It will be correct only when you try to execute the IMSHOW.EXE program while your current default directory is the root. At all other times, the lack of a leading backslash means that the path branches off the current directory.

SETTING UP A COMPLEX PATH

You can open a path to several directories at once by entering a series of path names separated by semicolons. For example, if DOS can't find the program you ask for in the current default directory, you could ask it to search the UTIL directory first and then UTIL\SPECIAL by entering

PATH \UTIL;\UTIL\SPECIAL

Each directory to be successively searched should be separated by a semicolon (and no space). Multiple paths allow you to access programs in several directories without having to constantly revise the PATH command declaration.

WHEN THE PATH COMMAND ISN'T ENOUGH

The PATH command can only be used to search a directory for files with the extensions .COM, .EXE, and .BAT. The first two types are executable programs, and the last is a DOS batch file. (Batch files are presented in depth in Chapters 13 through 15; they are simple DOS programs that contain sets of DOS commands.) DOS will not search the path directories for files with other extensions, nor will it search those drives for data files not found in the active drive.

Some programs require special *overlay* or *driver* files in order to load properly. These files have extensions like .OVR, .OVL, and .DRV and contain additional program information that usually won't fit into memory all at the same time. The PATH command enables DOS to locate and load the main program, like WS.COM, it but may fail to locate WSOVLY1.OVR, the required overlay program.

Some of the newest programs requiring overlays are able to run because they are smart enough to use DOS's path information themselves to locate any required overlay files. Older programs that need overlay files often cannot be run simply by opening a path to the directory in which they are stored. If you are using one of the older programs, you may have to use the Change Directory command to run the program from within the directory that contains the main and overlay files. DOS 3.3 contains a new command, APPEND, which also provides a solution. This command is presented in depth in Chapter 16. In essence, APPEND provides you with the ability to set up a path to overlay files and data files, effectively closing up the former gap in DOS's ability to locate these files. You'll look at this issue again in the next chapter.

CHECKING THE PATH

There will be times when you have worked in different directories of your hard disk and may not be sure which is the current directory. You may also not be sure which path DOS will take to search for files not found in the current directory. If this is the case, you can make DOS show you the current path. To see what the current defined path is, you can enter

> PATH

To close the path, enter the PATH command with the semicolon (;) alone. This indicates that the path is once again reset to the current working directory:

> PATH;

After you've entered this, asking DOS for the current path will produce the message "No Path."

PRUNING THE TREE

There comes a time on many disks, as on many trees, when a branch must be cut back or cut off. It's a good idea to use the ERASE command regularly to limit uncontrolled use of space on your diskette. Once in a while, you may also want to put files together and collapse two directories into one. Or, if all the files in a directory are no longer needed, you may want to completely remove the directory they're in.

Performing the following sequence will move all the files from UTIL\SPECIAL into the UTIL directory. Keep in mind that the directory tree looks somewhat like Figure 4.19.

```
Directory B:\

        B:\QD2.EXE
        B:\SKN.COM
        B:\SR.COM
        B:\BOOK SAM.PLE

Directory B:\UTIL

        B:\UTIL\FORMAT.COM
        B:\UTIL\CHKDSK.COM

Directory B:\UTIL\SPECIAL

        B:\UTIL\SPECIAL\MODE.COM
        B:\UTIL\SPECIAL\MORE.COM
        B:\UTIL\SPECIAL\IMSHOW.EXE
        B:\UTIL\SPECIAL\IMCAP.COM


C>_
```

Figure 4.19: Current directory tree

First you need to copy the files from UTIL\SPECIAL to the UTIL directory:

COPY \UTIL\SPECIAL*.* \UTIL

DOS will display the file names as they are copied:

B:\UTIL\SPECIAL\MODE.COM
B:\UTIL\SPECIAL\MORE.COM
B:\UTIL\SPECIAL\IMSHOW.EXE
B:\UTIL\SPECIAL\IMCAP.COM
            4 File(s) copied

You should always verify that your new copies are in place before erasing the old copies (see Figure 4.20).

Since the files have been copied successfully, you can now use the RD (Remove Directory) command to remove the old directory:

RD \UTIL\SPECIAL

DOS will immediately respond with

Invalid path, not directory, or directory not empty

```
DIR \UTIL

Volume in drive B is BOOK SAMPLE
Directory of  B:\UTIL

    .            <DIR>      1-01-80  12:46a
    ..           <DIR>      1-01-80  12:46a
FORMAT   COM    11135   12-30-85  12:00p
CHKDSK   COM     9832   12-30-85  12:00p
SPECIAL          <DIR>      1-01-80   4:19a
MODE     COM     6864   12-30-85  12:00p
MORE     COM      295   12-30-85  12:00p
IMSHOW   EXE    20090    6-20-85  10:09a
IMCAP    COM     6114    6-20-85   1:09p
         9 File(s)    149504 bytes free




C>_
```

Figure 4.20: Directory status of UTIL

This is DOS's way of protecting you from a major catastrophe—namely, the removal of an entire directory when there may still be useful but forgotten programs stored within it. In this case, you haven't made a mistake. You just need to erase the old files before removing the directory from the DOS tree with the RD command:

ERASE \UTIL\SPECIAL*.*
Are you sure (Y/N)?Y

RD \UTIL\SPECIAL

Figure 4.21 reveals the new directory structure.

SUMMARY

In this chapter you have examined the treelike directory structure of DOS and worked with directories and subdirectories on floppy diskettes. You learned the following things:

- Each diskette can be given a unique name, called a volume label, with the LABEL command. This name can be as long as 11 characters. It is used to identify either the contents or the ownership of a disk.

```
Directory B:\

        B:\JUNK1.TXT
        B:\QD2.EXE
        B:\SKN.COM
        B:\SR.COM
        B:\BOOK SAM.PLE

Directory B:\UTIL

        B:\UTIL\FORMAT.COM
        B:\UTIL\CHKDSK.COM
        B:\UTIL\MODE.COM
        B:\UTIL\MORE.COM
        B:\UTIL\IMSHOW.EXE
        B:\UTIL\IMCAP.COM








    C>_
```

Figure 4.21: Revised directory tree structure

- The MD (Make Directory) command creates new areas on your disk. Each new area becomes a separately named portion of your disk, and can be used to effectively group your files for easy storage and retrieval.

- Files can be easily moved into and among various disk directories with the COPY command.

- You can make any disk directory into the current working directory with the CD (Change Directory) command. All program or DOS command references to files will look in this default directory first, before looking elsewhere.

- The CHKDSK/V and the TREE/F commands offer two ways to list all the files by directory group. CHKDSK/V is more concise, more readable, and therefore more desirable.

- The PATH command allows you to specify a list of other directories on your disk where you want DOS to look whenever you or your programs refer to .EXE (executable), .COM (command), or .BAT (batch) files. The APPEND command allows you to direct DOS to look in directories beyond the current working one for any other type of file. This includes overlay files, data files, and all possible application files.

- DOS commands apply to files in the current directory unless you have set up a PATH or APPEND sequence. However, even if these are not set up, you can still refer to files or commands in other directories by simply using the full path name as a prefix in front of the file name.

- The RD (Remove Directory) command removes empty directories from your hierarchical structure. However, DOS will only do this if there are no other directories or files of any sort remaining in the directory you are trying to remove.

In the next chapter you will continue your study of DOS directories, but in the context of the more complex and eminently more useful environment of a hard disk.

WORKING WITH HARD-DISK DIRECTORY STRUCTURES

CHAPTER 5

WORKING WITH HARD DISKS REQUIRES GOOD organization and planning. This chapter takes you through some pragmatic examples that will give you that organizational ability. In Chapter 4, you learned about the DOS directory structure and the commands necessary to set up and use that structure on your floppy diskettes. This chapter focuses on the directory structure of hard disks.

As the price of hard disks decreases, their availability on typical computer systems increases. Knowledge of DOS directory structures becomes even more important as the amount of hardware under your control grows. Knowing how to successfully manage all that disk space will make you more efficient and save you time; the manipulation of diskettes to run your application programs can then be replaced by the knowledgeable manipulation of DOS directories.

In this chapter, you'll format your hard disk, or review the formatting process if your disk is already formatted. Then you'll use the appropriate directory commands to set up the hard disk for three common and very popular types of programs: a spreadsheet, a word processor, and a database management system. The techniques you learn will be directly applicable to setting up a hard disk for using any application software.

This chapter describes how to create new directories, copy files between disks and directories, list subdirectories, and change the active directory. It also tells you how to include directory information in the DOS prompt and how to view the hard-disk structure.

FORMATTING THE DISK

Just like floppy diskettes, hard disks must be prepared or formatted before information can be stored on them. If your machine is brand new, you should follow any instructions from the manufacturer to prepare it (this usually involves running an FDISK program; see your DOS user's manual).

Place the DOS master diskette into drive A and close the door. Then enter the proper format command at the A> prompt. Remember that you want to create a system disk out of the hard disk; therefore, you must use the following form of the FORMAT command. It will format the disk and copy the system information files at the same time. Since the hard-disk drive is usually drive C, type

A>FORMAT C: /S

When the formatting is complete, change the active drive to C:

A>C:

Follow these formatting instructions only if your hard disk is totally unprepared, or if you purposely intend to erase everything on it.

For the rest of this chapter, the default drive will be C, and you'll be moving around the directory tree on the hard disk.

A PLACE FOR THE DOS FILES

The DOS prompt on your screen now indicates that drive C is the active drive. The first command you should enter is the Directory command, DIR. Entering it reveals that you have one file on your drive, COMMAND.COM, and that you have over 10 million bytes of free space (or 20 or 30 million bytes, depending on the size of your hard disk). The display also tells you that COMMAND.COM is in the root directory, indicated by the backslash (C:\). The COMMAND.COM file is part of the computer's basic operating system and must always appear in the root directory.

The DOS system has a number of special utility programs that will be helpful to the proper operation of your system. Right now these programs are stored on the DOS master diskettes, but they can be copied to your hard disk. If you have 5¼'' floppy-diskette drives, these utility files are separated on two 360K floppies; if you have the appropriate 3½'' microfloppy drive, all the DOS utility files are included on one diskette also included with your DOS 3.3 package. These files include all of the disk-resident DOS commands, from CHKDSK, to FORMAT, to support for international-type keyboards. Performing any of these utility operations requires that the appropriate DOS support files be available on your hard disk. However, before the copies are made, you need to take an organizational step.

CREATING NEW DIRECTORIES

When adding files to a hard disk, it is always a good idea to create a special directory for all files that are related to one another. Having similar and related files together will make it easier and faster to find them and use them later. In this example, all of the DOS files will be copied to a directory called DOS so that they are all grouped together.

To create the directory, you enter the Make Directory command, MD:

MD \DOS

You can see that on the screen, nothing has happened, but in fact the computer has recorded a change. Entering a DIR request produces this information:

```
Volume in drive C is JUDDROBBINS
Directory of C:\

COMMAND COM 23791 12-30-85 12:00p
DOS       <DIR>        1-01-80 12:05a
     1 File(s) 10565240 bytes free
```

The <DIR> symbol next to the name DOS indicates that DOS is not a file, but a directory. You can now store information in that directory.

COPYING FILES BETWEEN DISKS AND DIRECTORIES

The COPY command transfers copies of files from one disk to another and to subdirectories on the same or different disks. The next

When entering commands, remember that you should always follow drive names with a colon, as in A:, B:, or C:, while subdirectory names should always be preceded by a backslash character, such as \DOS, \LOTUS, or \DBASE.

step will transfer the DOS support files from the source diskette in drive A to the destination hard disk directory, C:\DOS (drive C, subdirectory DOS). Enter

COPY A:*.* C:\DOS

DOS will list the files as they are copied. However, a directory listing now will still show only one file, COMMAND.COM. This is because the current directory listing is for the root directory; the files that were just copied were stored in the DOS directory.

To see the contents of this subdirectory, one of two methods can be used:

1. Specify the subdirectory name in the DIR command.

2. Change the default directory to the desired directory and enter the DIR command.

The following sections employ both methods.

LISTING A SUBDIRECTORY

To list the contents of a directory other than the current default directory, you can add the name of the subdirectory to the DIR command:

DIR \DOS

If your current default disk were in a drive other than C, you could even explicitly ask for the DOS directory on drive C by typing

DIR C:\DOS

CHANGING THE ACTIVE DIRECTORY

The second method used to list the contents of a subdirectory requires you to tell the operating system that you want to work in a directory other than the root. When you issue a command to change the directory, you are telling the computer to assume that all succeeding commands should affect the files in that directory, and not in the root directory.

If you enter a command that tells the computer to change the directory to DOS, and then enter DIR, only the files in the DOS subdirectory will be listed. The advantage of changing the directory is that you do not have to bother to type the prefix \DOS after each command and before each file name.

As you saw in Chapter 4, entering the Change Directory command (CD) allows you to ask for a DIR operation without specifying any directory. Type

```
CD \DOS
DIR
```

and press Return after each line. The desired directory is now the current default directory. All names for files in the DOS subdirectory will now be listed.

RETURNING TO THE ROOT DIRECTORY

The CD command can be used to return the default to the root directory. If you enter the backslash character alone as

```
CD \
```

the default directory will be reset to the root directory. A request for a directory listing will now produce a listing for the root directory.

You may need to use the CD command often. Each time you switch directories in order to run a special program like 1-2-3 or dBASE, it's a good idea to reset to the root directory afterward. This will avoid trouble—it's good hard-disk management.

CHANGING THE PROMPT

As you know, the DOS prompt usually consists of two characters: a letter indicating the active drive and the > character. The > character is not required, but it makes the display easier to read by separating the drive letter from any command you might type in.

When you are working on a disk with more than one directory, it is useful to expand the prompt to include the directory name along with the drive identifier. The PROMPT command can be used to change the prompt displayed whenever DOS is active.

To change the prompt, you should enter

PROMPT pg

after the > character. PROMPT recognizes the argument $p as a command to display the directory and the argument $g as a command to tell DOS to display the > character. (The letters p and g can be entered in either upper- or lowercase.) This command changes the DOS prompt from the default C> to C:\>, which shows both the drive identifier (C:) and the current directory (the root \) followed by the > character. The DOS prompt will now always reflect the current default directory. For example, entering a Change Directory command like

CD \DOS

after the C:\ prompt will cause DOS to change the prompt to

C:\DOS>

The prompt tells you that the active directory is now C:\DOS.

You can ask DOS to return to its normal prompt at any time by reentering the PROMPT command by itself:

C:\DOS>PROMPT

The prompt will return to

C>

You will explore more advanced uses of the PROMPT command in Chapter 10.

LOADING YOUR WORD PROCESSOR ONTO THE HARD DISK

In this section, you'll set up your hard disk to store all your word-processing files in a particular directory. To do this, you must have a copy of the program already on a floppy diskette. It is assumed that your word processor is *not* copy-protected. If it is, you'll need to follow the special instructions in its user's manual.

Although your word processor may be different from the example given here, the process of setting up your hard disk will be similar. You'll still need to take the following steps:

1. Create a subdirectory for word processing.

2. Copy the word-processing files from the floppy diskette onto the correct subdirectory of the hard disk.

3. Change the default directory to the word-processing directory.

4. Run the program.

CREATING YOUR WORD-PROCESSING DIRECTORY

To create a word-processing directory, enter the MD (Make Directory) command:

MD \WP

To check that all went well, you could enter a DIR command. The root directory would show two entries with the <DIR> indicator, DOS and WP. There are now two directories branching off from the root directory (see Figure 5.1). The next step is to copy the files from your word-processing diskette(s) to the new WP directory.

COPYING WORD-PROCESSING PROGRAMS TO THE NEW DIRECTORY

Sometimes, your new word-processing program diskette will have a prewritten installation program to do all of the following steps. Use it. You can always redo things in your own way later, after you've become more comfortable with directory structures. In any case, the next step that either you or the installation program should follow is to place the word-processing master diskette into drive A and use the COPY command:

COPY A:*.* C:\WP

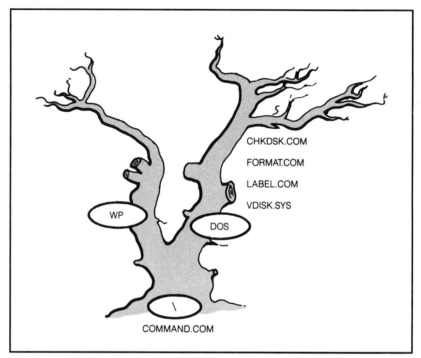

Figure 5.1: DOS and WP directory structure

When you press Return, the computer lists the names of the files as they are copied. If your word processor is on more than one diskette, repeat this step for each diskette.

RUNNING YOUR WORD PROCESSOR FROM THE NEW DIRECTORY

If you want to run your word processor, you must change the default directory to WP and type the name of the main program. To do so, you enter

    CD \WP

Then enter

    WS

for WordStar,

    WP

for WordPerfect, or the name of whatever other program you use.

The opening screen of your word processor will appear. Now it's time to open up your word processor's user's manual and proceed to create and edit documents. When you finally exit the program, remember to return to the root directory with

**CD **

Now that your word processor has been copied to the hard disk, remember that you must change the default to the WP directory each time you want to run the program again. The root directory now only lists the COMMAND.COM file and the primary DOS and WP directories, which themselves contain the bulk of your files. Keeping the root directory uncluttered makes finding your way around the hard disk much easier. If you did not have subdirectories, the root directory would be a virtually unreadable list of hundreds of files.

LOADING YOUR SPREADSHEET PROGRAM ONTO THE HARD DISK

When entering commands, remember that you should always follow drive names with a colon, as in A:, B:, or C:, while subdirectory names should always be preceded by a backslash character, such as \\DOS, \\LOTUS, or \\DBASE.

Loading a popular spreadsheet like Lotus 1-2-3 onto a hard disk is not much different from working with a word processor like WordStar or WordPerfect. Although the procedure will be similar if you have a different spreadsheet program, the example presented here uses 1-2-3 because it contains a copy-protection mechanism (unlike the word-processing example of the previous section). This special situation requires some discussion.

All the information necessary to run some copy-protected programs like 1-2-3 cannot be straightforwardly transferred to the hard disk. Lotus employs a copy-protection scheme on its program disks; thus, if you simply transfer all the Lotus files to the hard disk with the COPY command, 1-2-3 still needs to access the original floppy diskette in order to run.

The most recent versions of 1-2-3 allow you to install the software onto the hard disk permanently. Even though the program is copy protected, it is still worthwhile to copy the files to the hard disk for two reasons:

- The program will load more quickly.

- All of the Lotus 1-2-3 system files can be placed in a single
  subdirectory, thus requiring no future juggling of all the
  Lotus diskettes.

SUBDIRECTORIES FOR DATA

Most newer software packages like 1-2-3 allow you to store work
and access files in one of several directories. With earlier and still
popular versions of programs like WordStar, all of the data files you
create occupy the same subdirectory as the program.

1-2-3 can switch from one data subdirectory to another while
the program is operating. This allows you to group together related
1-2-3 program files and separate them from worksheet files. As you'll
soon see, you can use the DOS directory structure more effectively
by maintaining directories for groups of worksheets, separate from
the main LOTUS directory of program files.

The first step is to create a directory for all of the Lotus system
files. Enter

    MD \LOTUS

Then, for each of the original diskettes in the Lotus package, copy the
necessary programs into that directory by entering

    COPY A:*.* C:\LOTUS

Now that the 1-2-3 files have been copied, you can run the program. First change the default directory to the LOTUS directory
and then enter the name of the main program, pressing Return after
each command:

    CD \LOTUS
    LOTUS

The screen will then prompt you to select a program. If you select the
main 1-2-3 spreadsheet program, 1-2-3 will spin the diskette in drive

A to check the copy-protection scheme if you have not installed it permanently according to the manufacturer's instructions. In either case, you no longer need to have the floppy diskette in drive A.

CONFIGURING PROGRAMS

When you copy a program to a hard disk from a floppy diskette, the program is not necessarily *configured.* Configuration refers to those special settings in the software that give the program all of the information unique to your system, such as what type of screen display and printer are being used. In addition, some programs require you to specify the default data drive and directory. 1-2-3 is one of those programs.

Just because the program was copied to the hard disk, it does not follow that 1-2-3 knows what actual drive you want to use for data. Many times when 1-2-3 is copied onto a hard-disk drive, it still attempts to store data on drive B. To change the default disk and directory for any program like this, there is usually some command in the software that can be invoked. You should refer to your application software's user's guide to discover it. In 1-2-3, it is the /wgdd command.

CREATING MULTIPLE SUBDIRECTORIES FOR YOUR DATA FILES

Since 1-2-3 allows you to change the subdirectory used to store program data, you can create a separate directory for your spreadsheet files. In fact, if you work in an office where more than one person uses the computer, each person's work can be stored in a different subdirectory. The same concept can be used to store work related to different projects in separate subdirectories.

To see how this works, you must return to the operating system level. As you know, subdirectories are organized in a heirarchical order. The root directory is the parent of all subdirectories. Each directory created in the root can in turn have its own children; for example, LOTUS is a subdirectory of the root. LOTUS can also have subdirectories of its own.

Suppose that in your office, three people, Sue, Harry, and Alice, will be working with 1-2-3. To keep their work from getting confused, it might be useful to separate and store their files into unique sub-directories. Create individual directories for each of these people by entering the following:

```
MD \LOTUS\SUE
MD \LOTUS\HARRY
MD \LOTUS\ALICE
```

Drive C will then be structured as shown in Figure 5.2. Figure 5.3 shows another way to visualize the directory structure. In the remainder of this chapter, you'll use this line view.

Figure 5.2: DOS directory structure (tree view)

RUNNING PROGRAMS FROM WITHIN SUBDIRECTORIES

At this point you have set up a directory that contains the main program files (the Lotus programs in this example, but it could just as well be the word-processing programs of the last section). To run the program, you would change the main directory to LOTUS with CD, bring up the program, and then tell the program in which subdirectory you wish it to work. This type of request from within a program varies with each program, but the concept remains the same.

In 1-2-3, the command to change default subdirectories is the File Directory command (/FD). The program will first display the current directory setting. Because you started 1-2-3 when you were in the main LOTUS directory, 1-2-3 automatically sets the default to C:\LOTUS. To change directories, you would enter the full path name of the subdirectory that you want to use. If you were Alice, for instance, you would specify to 1-2-3 that you want it to use your specific directory. Including the drive as well, you would enter

C:\LOTUS\ALICE

All files would be saved in or retrieved from the subdirectory LOTUS\ALICE. In this way, Alice can have her work separated

Because every program has different assumptions about default directories, you may at times try to retrieve a file and not find it. Check the default directory. The solution is often as easy as resetting it to the directory that you usually use for file work.

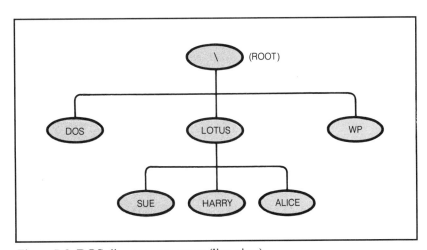

Figure 5.3: DOS directory structure (line view)

from Harry's and Sue's. If Harry or Sue later logged on, they could go through the same sequence to ensure that they had access to the files in their different subdirectories.

RUNNING YOUR DATABASE MANAGEMENT SYSTEM

As a last example, let's create a directory for a DBMS (database management system). Suppose you intend to use a package like dBASE III PLUS for several purposes. You may plan to write your own custom accounting program to manage your entire inventory system; you may even plan to manage your company's personnel records with the software.

With the following commands you can quickly visualize and then create the new directory structure:

```
MD \DBMS
MD \DBMS\ACCOUNTS
MD \DBMS\INVNTORY
MD \DBMS\PRSONNEL
```

The results are shown in Figure 5.4. As you can see, you've set up a directory structure that is organized by application purpose. Similarly, in the last section, you set up several subdirectories, one for the data files for each user of the spreadsheet program. It's always up to you to decide on the grouping of your files.

Of course, now you probably want to run your DBMS program. If you are a dBASE III PLUS user, you could simply use the CD \DBMS command and then enter the program name:

```
DBASE
```

You could then change the default directory from within the program. However, the default file directory can be conveniently set *before* you execute the main program. The next section will describe this useful method.

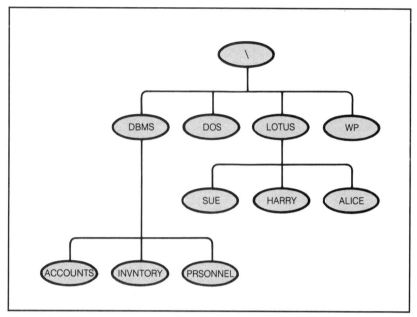

Figure 5.4: Directory structure for DBMS applications

RUNNING ANY PROGRAM ON YOUR HARD DISK

There will be many times when you have set the working directory to the one you want to be in; related files will be read from and written into that directory. Sometimes, you will then want to run a utility program that is in another directory. For instance, you may want to run the CHKDSK program in the DOS directory, or a special hard-disk management program like QDOS II, located in the UTILITY\MISC directory.

Most of the time, you do not want to leave the current directory and go through the hassle of resetting to another directory. In fact, since more and more programs are allowing you to run other programs while they are still active, you will purposely want to maintain the current working directory. The PATH and APPEND commands are your best solution. (APPEND, however, is only available to DOS 3.3 users.)

Assuming that you've copied all the necessary database programs onto the hard disk, suppose you wanted to see how much space was left on it. If you entered CHKDSK now to analyze the disk, you would probably get the message "Bad command or file name." This means that DOS is unable to run the CHKDSK program. DOS looks only in the current directory for that program. You are probably logged into the DBMS directory, so DOS reports that it cannot find the program you requested.

The CHKDSK program *is* on the hard disk, but it is stored in the DOS subdirectory. How can you tell DOS to check the DOS subdirectory if it can't find the requested program in the current directory? You can use the PATH command. It tells DOS what subdirectories, in addition to the current one, it should check when you enter a program to run.

To open a path to the DOS subdirectory, you would enter

PATH \DOS

The CHKDSK command would now execute properly, because the path to the correct subdirectory is open.

As you saw in Chapter 4, you can open a more complex path by using a semicolon to separate a list of directory names. For this example, enter

PATH \DOS;\WP;\LOTUS;\DBMS

Do not leave any spaces between the entries on the path list. DOS stops reading the line when it comes across the first space on the list.

If the program name you enter can't be found in the current default directory, DOS will first look for that program in the DOS subdirectory. If it isn't there, DOS will then successively look in the WP, LOTUS, and DBMS subdirectories. Only if it doesn't find it in any of these directories will it return the "Bad command or file name" message to you.

What this all means to you is that you can anticipate setting the default directory before you start up your main program. You can have the path set to enable DOS to find the requested program. Whenever your program reads or writes files, it will use the default directory. To do database work with the accounting files, you could set the DOS default to the DBMS\ACCOUNTS directory and the path to DBMS, and then invoke the database management program (in this case, dBASE III PLUS) by entering

```
CD \DBMS\ACCOUNTS
PATH \DBMS
DBASE
```

Preface all entries in a path with a drive designator for that directory. Then you can execute the program in that directory from any logged drive.

and pressing Return after each line. The default directory is now ACCOUNTS, so dBASE will expect to find all databases and program (.PRG) files in that directory. It will hunt for its own management programs along the directories specified on the path, and it will find them in DBMS.

LIMITATIONS OF THE PATH COMMAND

PATH opens a searching channel for programs and batch files only—it can't be used to access data files in other subdirectories. In fact, some main programs like WordStar (through version 3.3) can't even run properly if you use the PATH command. The reason is that WordStar, dBASE, 1-2-3, and most other sophisticated microcomputer programs need to occasionally load overlay files in addition to the main .COM or .EXE file. (Remember, overlay files contain additional program information that usually just can't fit into memory all at the same time as the main .COM or .EXE file.) The PATH command will only search the designated directories for files that end with .COM, .EXE or .BAT. The result is that while DOS may find WS.COM in the WP subdirectory, WordStar can't find the .OVR files that it needs to run.

The SMARTPATH program is only one of many utility programs you can buy to significantly extend the power of DOS. In the likely event you begin to collect these add-on tools, it is a good idea to place them in their own utility directory. You can create this directory once and then copy your new utility programs to it. You can then add the UTIL directory name to the main path so that DOS can find the SMARTPATH program and any other utility programs when you ask for them.

Some programs like dBASE III PLUS are smart enough to search the operating system path themselves. In such cases, you can set up a useful partitioned directory structure like the one seen in Figure 5.4. However, when the main program is *not* smart enough to use path information, you may have to put up with the limitation, placing all your data files along with the main program files in one large directory.

There is a better solution that still allows you the flexibility of using DOS's directory organization. If your DOS is version 3.2 or earlier, you can use a separately purchasable utility program called SMARTPATH, which extends the path concept to include other types of files besides .EXE, .COM, and .BAT files. In Chapter 17, you will read about several other useful utility programs that you should seriously consider acquiring to enable you to both extend and more easily harness the capabilities of your operating system.

For now, you should consider using a single PATH command that enables DOS to hunt for and find all of your main programs:

PATH \DOS;\UTIL;\LOTUS;\DBMS;\WP

As an alternative, DOS 3.3 users can use the APPEND command, whose syntax is similar to PATH. Just list the directory names containing the files you want DOS to find, after the command name itself. For instance,

APPEND \WP;\DBMS\DATA

will establish another searching path that DOS will follow when the need arises to locate overlay files for a word processor or command and database files for your database management system.

Consider redefining the directory path for certain applications. The more often DOS has to resort to the path to find files, the longer it will take and the slower the system's response time will be. In addition, since DOS searches the path in the order in which you list directory names, you should list the directories in the order most likely to succeed.

MAPPING YOUR HARD DISK

When you work with floppy diskettes, the DIR command is usually a sufficient way to get a map of each diskette. That's because you probably don't have anything but a root directory on most or all of your floppy diskettes. When you are working with a hard disk that contains many directories, however, DIR is no longer adequate—it will operate only on one directory at a time. The TREE and CHKDSK commands will allow you to get information about the hard disk as a whole.

As you saw in Chapter 4, TREE is used to list all the directories and subdirectories on a disk. Figure 5.5 shows a TREE listing for the hard-disk directory structure created in this chapter. In Chapter 4, you also saw another option—the CHKDSK/V command. This command will list not only all directories but the file names within them, as well as information about disk and memory usage. If this information is unneeded, you should stick to the TREE command. If you like the format of the TREE command but also want the file names listed (but not the disk and memory status information), you can use the /F switch with TREE.

```
DIRECTORY PATH LISTING FOR VOLUME SYBEX_BOOK

Path: \DBMS
Sub-directories:   ACCOUNTS
                   INVNTORY
                   PRSONNEL

Path: \DBMS\ACCOUNTS
Sub-directories:   None

Path: \DBMS\INVNTORY
Sub-directories:   None

Path: \DBMS\PRSONNEL
Sub-directories:   None

Path: \DOS
Sub-directories:   None

Path: \LOTUS
Sub-directories:   SUE
                   HARRY
                   ALICE

Path: \LOTUS\SUE
Sub-directories:   None

Path: \LOTUS\HARRY
Sub-directories:   None

Path: \LOTUS\ALICE
Sub-directories:   None

Path: \WP
Sub-directories:   None
```

Figure 5.5: Output from the TREE command

With either CHKDSK/V or TREE/F, the resultant listing is usually much longer than one screenful of data. Since the information displayed by TREE is very valuable to have, you might want to print the TREE display. You can do this by using the >PRN redirection command with the TREE command:

TREE/F > PRN

You will now get a complete printed listing of all the files on your hard disk. (You will learn more about this interesting redirection capability in Chapter 12.) Like the TREE/F command, the CHKDSK/V command can also generate a printed copy if you use the redirection command:

CHKDSK/V > PRN

You have now seen two methods by which you can produce a complete listing of all the files on the hard disk. With these lists, you can figure out where on the hard disk various programs and files are stored. They can also help you to find lost files and identify which files should be erased.

SUMMARY

In this chapter, you have explored the DOS capability for setting up a complex but highly usable structure of directories on any hard disk. You learned how to set up your hard disk for a word processor, a spreadsheet, and a database management system. Using these examples, you should be able to set up a functioning directory structure for any application software system.

The chapter has presented a number of commands that allow you to create and maneuver around any desired hard-disk structure:

- You can use the Make Directory (MD) command to create a new subdirectory in any existing directory.

- You can use the Change Directory (CD) command to reset the default directory pointer to any chosen disk directory.

- You can use the PROMPT command to automatically display the current default directory when you enter DOS commands for your hard-disk system.

- You can use the PATH command to direct DOS to search through a specified series of selected directories for .EXE, .COM, and .BAT files that are not located in the current working directory.

- With DOS 3.3, you can use the APPEND command to tell DOS to search through a specified series of directories for data and overlay files not located in the current working directory.

- You can use the TREE/F or CHKDSK/V command to view the hard-disk map or structure.

The next two chapters, on the DOS editor and DOS printing, will teach you how to manage the output of information created and manipulated by your particular applications. You will be able to make textual changes to standard text files, which will be crucial to effective management of certain DOS configuration and control features to be discussed later in this book. You will soon learn how to control the flow of information to the screen (Chapter 6), to the printed page (Chapter 7), and even to other devices through the DOS communications ports (Chapter 8).

USING THE DOS EDITOR

CHAPTER 6

IN ADDITION TO THEIR ABILITY TO PROCESS NUMBERS and large amounts of data, computers are exceptionally good at manipulating text. It comes as no surprise, then, that there are so many different programs available to do this.

The advantages of using a computer instead of a typewriter are many. Text can be manipulated on the screen, changed, and corrected before it is printed out. Also, whole documents and reports can be stored on disk for later use. This means you can type in half a report, go away for a week, and then come back and finish it. You can also create a rough draft and later make corrections to it in minutes, without having to retype everything.

There are two primary kinds of programs that allow you to create and manipulate text. The first kind is a line editor like the DOS EDLIN editor. With a line editor, you work with a line of text at a time. Line editors number each line and reference each line by these numbers. You can make corrections to only one line at a time.

The second kind of program, a word processor, shows you a full screen of text. You can move the screen cursor to any character position on any line and make changes anywhere on the screen. Word processors usually support such features as multiple fonts, boldfacing, and underlining.

Naturally, it's up to you to choose the kind of program you want. You may want to use both, at different times. The DOS line editor is very small (only 7526 bytes), and it can comfortably fit on most application diskettes in diskette-based systems. This means that you won't need to juggle diskettes often. On the other hand, you may feel much more comfortable using the more extensive set of commands available with most word processors. You might also prefer to edit any character on any line in the full-screen mode of a typical word processor. However, word processors usually require tens of thousands of bytes of disk space merely to contain them, and they have more extensive RAM requirements than line editors. In addition, you must usually purchase them, whereas EDLIN is available in your DOS system at no additional charge.

DOS provides the EDLIN.COM program as part of your system. It is disk-resident and acts like any other transient command. You can use EDLIN to create and edit text files, which are files that contain standard letters, numbers, and punctuation symbols. Except for the special codes indicating carriage returns, line feeds, and the end of a file (Ctrl-Z), these files have no control codes for such features as underlining on a printer or high intensity on a display. (A text file can be displayed easily onscreen with the TYPE command.) In short, EDLIN works with whole lines of text, but you cannot use it to change fonts or to produce boldface or underlined text. EDLIN can, however, manipulate text files, and it contains search and replace functions and standard text-editing features.

The EDLIN program is so small that you can keep a copy of it on each of several diskettes for rapid and easy file editing. Most advanced word processors are too large to fit on diskettes that contain any other sophisticated software.

GETTING EDLIN STARTED

EDLIN is started from the DOS prompt with the command

EDLIN *FileSpec*

The optional /B switch (short for Binary) can be used with this EDLIN command when the file you will be working on contains Ctrl-Z markers other than the end-of-file marker. As you'll learn later in this chapter, you can use EDLIN to incorporate and then edit control characters in a text file.

where *FileSpec* is the drive, path, file name, and extension of the file to be edited. You must use the full file name, including any extension. As always, EDLIN must either be resident on the disk you are using, in the current default directory, or on the path to be searched by DOS.

STARTING A NEW FILE

If EDLIN is invoked with a *FileSpec* value for a file that does not currently exist, it will respond with the following message and prompt:

New file
*_

EDLIN is giving you a clean slate, awaiting your commands. Table 6.1 summarizes the commands you can use with EDLIN, their actions, and their general formats. You will learn about each of these as you work through this chapter.

CHANGING AN EXISTING FILE

Invoking EDLIN with the *FileSpec* of an existing file will yield the following:

```
End of input file
*_
```

EDLIN tries to load your entire text file into available memory

COMMAND	ACTION	GENERAL FORMAT
A	Appends lines	[*Num*]A
C	Copies lines	[*Line*],[*Line*],*Line*[,*Count*] C
D	Deletes lines	[*Line*][,*Line*] D
—	Edits line	[*Line*]
E	Updates and exits	E
I	Inserts lines	[*Line*]I
L	Lists lines	[*Line*][,*Line*] L
M	Moves lines	[*Line*],[*Line*],*Line*M
P	Displays full page	[*Line*][,*Line*] P
Q	Aborts and exits	Q
R	Replaces globally	[*Line*][,*Line*] [?] R[*String*][^ ZNewString]
S	Searches globally	[*Line*][,*Line*] [?] S[*String*]
T	Merges files	[*Line*] T [*FileSpec*]
W	Writes lines	[*Num*] W

Table 6.1: Summary of EDLIN commands

(RAM). When it tries to load a file that is longer than 75 percent of the currently available RAM, it will load only the first part of that file and will use only 75 percent of the available memory. The message just shown will not appear, but the prompt will. You may then edit the lines that were loaded. When you are done editing these lines, you can use EDLIN commands to write the edited lines out to a diskette and then bring in additional text lines to edit.

BRINGING NEW TEXT INTO MEMORY

The command needed to add new, unedited lines of text from a disk file is the Append command, abbreviated as the single character A. This command is only used when you have loaded a file that is larger than 75 percent of current memory. Entered at the EDLIN * prompt, its general format is

   [*Num*]A

The brackets around parameters in this chapter indicate that these EDLIN parameters are optional for a command. The brackets themselves are not entered as part of the command.

This command loads *Num* lines from the rest of the file (where *Num* is the number of lines to load), provided there is room. If there is insufficient room to load any more lines from your file, the command will not load anything. You must then use the W command (described shortly) to write some of your edited lines from EDLIN to disk.

If you successfully load the rest of the file into memory, the following message will appear:

   End of input file

You can then continue editing using any of the EDLIN commands.

COMBINING SEPARATE TEXT FILES

The Transfer command (T) is used to combine two text files: one in memory and another somewhere else. When you specify the file to be transferred into the middle of your current file (*FileSpec*), the whole file is read in and inserted before the line number specified by *Line:*

   [*Line*] T *FileSpec*

If *Line* is not specified, the file's contents are inserted before the current line.

This command can be quite useful. For example, suppose you have the following two files:

```
File1                 File2
1: Line 1, File 1      1: Line 1, File 2
2: Line 2, File 1      2: Line 2, File 2
3: Line 3, File 1      3: Line 3, File 2
4: Line 4, File 1      4: Line 4, File 2
```

If File1 is the current file being edited in memory, and you enter the following command:

```
3 T FILE2
```

the result is a new combined file, which looks like this:

```
1:  Line 1, File 1
2:  Line 2, File 1
3:*Line 1, File 2
4:  Line 2, File 2
5:  Line 3, File 2
6:  Line 4, File 2
7:  Line 3, File 1
8:  Line 4, File 1
```

Note that the current line is now the first line of the transferred file, as indicated by the EDLIN * prompt.

MAKING SPACE FOR LARGE FILES

The Write command (W), like the Append command, is only needed when your file is too large to fit in 75 percent of available memory. In that situation, only 75 percent of your file will have been loaded. If you want to edit the rest of the file, you need to make some room. You must transfer lines from the file in memory to disk, thus freeing up enough space to let more if not all of the rest of the file be loaded. The general format of this command is

[Num] W

where *Num* is the number of lines to be written. After you execute this command, you can load the rest of the file with the A command.

If you do not specify the number of lines to be written, the W command will keep writing lines to the disk, starting with line 1, until 75 percent of available memory is free. If there is already 75 percent of available RAM freed for EDLIN text lines, then no lines will be written to disk. If, for example, the first 200 lines were written to disk, then line 201 of the total file would become line 1 of the memory portion being worked on by EDLIN. For example, the command

200 W

would cause the first 200 lines of the current file to be transferred to disk, and line 201 would be numbered line 1. You could then read in additional text lines from the disk file with the A command.

DISPLAYING EDLIN FILES

Perhaps the most common activity you'll ask your line editor to perform will be to show you the text in your file. EDLIN offers two commands for this purpose: the L command for listing any range of lines, and the P command for rapidly looking at complete screenfuls of your file.

LISTING YOUR TEXT FILE

Since line numbers change each time you add or delete a line, the List command (L) will probably be your most frequently used command. You will always want to see the new numbers assigned to each of your text lines before you execute new line-oriented commands.

You can list a block of lines in a variety of ways. If you don't provide explicit line numbers for starting and stopping, EDLIN will attempt to display 23 text lines—a screenful. The size of the display range can extend from 11 lines before the current line to 11 lines after the current line.

Perhaps the most common format for this command is to specify the precise line numbers at which to begin and end the listing. For example,

6,19L

displays lines 6 through 19 on your screen and then redisplays EDLIN's prompt.

Simply typing L with no line-number specification will display the 11 lines preceding the current line, then the current line, and then the 11 lines after the current line. If your file does not have 23 lines, the entire file will be listed.

LISTING YOUR TEXT FILE RAPIDLY

The Page command (P) is like the L command, except that it redefines the current line number to whatever line has been displayed last on the screen. This command provides you with a rapid way to list all the lines in your text file, a screenful at a time.

Entering a line number alone, as in

    17 P

will display up to 23 lines starting with line 17. The last line listed becomes the current line. You can also display a specified range of lines and make the last line the current line, as in

    14,28 P

If you simply enter P, EDLIN will make its standard assumptions, giving you a 23-line display, starting with the line after the current line and making the last line displayed the new current line.

EDITING EDLIN FILES

As you have worked through the previous sections on getting EDLIN started, you have seen that EDLIN is *command-oriented;* that is, it does not display menus, but rather expects you to enter individual commands, just as DOS does. Because of this, you can move around and do things in EDLIN much more quickly than you could with a menu system, but you must know the commands in order to execute them quickly.

You have also seen the EDLIN prompt, the asterisk symbol. Whenever you see this on the screen with a blinking cursor next to it, EDLIN is prompting you for a command. This prompt also shows you the current line of the file being edited, which is the default line being worked on. Any EDLIN command you enter will deal with the text on this particular line (and possibly others as well). You can move a certain number of lines forward or backward from the current line, and you can insert, edit, or delete in relation to it.

Here are some useful tips to keep in mind as you work with EDLIN:

- Most commands can be entered using just the first letter of the command. When you are performing an operation on a specific line or group of lines, specify the line numbers first.

- The EDLIN letter commands can be entered in uppercase, lowercase, or a combination of the two.

- Line numbers can be specified in a number of ways; however, they must be whole numbers between 1 and 65529. When you enter more than one line number, you must separate them with commas. If you enter a line number higher than the highest line number in memory and you are going to add a line, the line will be added after the highest line number.

- You can use the number sign (#) to refer to the as-yet-nonexistent line following the highest line number in memory.

- You can use a period to specify the current line.

- The Plus and Minus keys can be used to specify lines *relative* to the current line number. For example,

    −20, + 5D

    will delete the 20 lines preceding the current line number, the current line number, and 5 lines after the current line number. If the current line number was 50, lines 30 through 55 would be deleted.

- You can enter more than one command on a line. If you do this, separate each complete command by a semicolon (;).

- It is possible (although not often necessary) to enter a control character into your file. To do this, you must press Ctrl-V first and then the desired control character (in uppercase).

• If you are displaying a lot of data, you can pause the screen output by pressing the Break key, Ctrl-ScrollLock. Press Ctrl-ScrollLock again to restart the output. Note that the processing of the command will have stopped also.

Now let's take a look at the editing tasks you'll want to do with EDLIN, and the commands that perform these tasks.

INSERTING NEW LINES

The Insert command (I) is used to insert lines. Its general format is

   [*Line*]I

Again, *Line* may be specified as either a specific or a relative line number. Not including *Line* will result in lines being added before the current line. If you created a new file called LINCOLN.TXT by calling up EDLIN, you would use the I command to insert text for the first time at line 1. Entering 1I at the EDLIN * prompt like this:

   *1I

would yield

   1:*_

which places you in insert mode. As you can see in Figure 6.1, EDLIN shows you each line number as you type it.

Notice the ^C on line 4. This is EDLIN's response when you press Ctrl-C during text insertion. Use the Ctrl-C key combination to exit from text insertion and return to the EDLIN prompt.

The I command can also be used to insert new text before any existing text line in the file. Simply specify the line number in the file before which you want the new text to be placed.

CHANGING EXISTING LINES

Editing a line merely means that you are changing the information on the line, *not* adding or deleting a line. If no line number is specified (in other words, you have simply pressed Return), then you will start

Inserting lines will change all line numbers after the insertion. For example, if you insert new text at line 3, remember that all line numbers after 3 have been changed. It's best to do a new listing (L) to discover the new numbering before issuing any new commands.

editing the line after the current line. If the current line is the last line in the file, pressing Return will do nothing but produce another * prompt. Usually, however, you can enter any line number to put you into edit mode for that line. You may also use relative line numbers to edit a line.

When you are put into edit mode (for example, by entering 3 and pressing Return), the display looks something like this:

```
3:*a new operating system (more or less).
3:*_
```

The arrow keys or any of the function keys will work as they do at the DOS prompt. For example, pressing F3 will do the following:

```
3:*a new operating system (more or less).
3:*a new operating system (more or less)._
```

The original line 3 is completely retyped, with the cursor waiting at the end of the line for additional input.

While editing any line, pressing the Right Arrow key will move the cursor one character to the right and display the character it was on (or under). Pressing Esc-Return or the Break key combination anywhere on the line will take you out of edit mode and leave the line unchanged.

If you want to add something to the end of the line, simply press F3 and start typing. You will automatically be put into insert mode. If your cursor is located anywhere else on the line, you must press the Ins key to enter insert mode, and press it again to leave that mode. In Figure 6.2, you can see how line 3 of our example was changed. F3 was pressed, the Backspace key was used to erase the period, and then the new characters ", dedicated" were typed. Both before and after the change, the L command was used to list the current contents of the file.

The edit to line 3 is only the first step in a common sequence, as shown in Figure 6.3. A change is made, followed by a listing of the file. Then another editing command follows (in this case, a new text insertion at the end of the file), and yet another L command is used to verify the results of the last edit. Continuing this process and adding still more text (with a correction to line 10 along the way) results in the 12-line text file shown in Figure 6.4.

```
C>EDLIN  LINCOLN.TXT
New file
*1I
        1:*Four score and seven months ago (approximately),
        2:*DOS's forefathers brought forth upon this nation
        3:*a new operating system (more or less).
        4:*^C

*_
```

Figure 6.1: Inserting text for the first time

```
C>EDLIN LINCOLN.TXT
End of input file
*L
        1:*Four score and seven months ago (approximately),
        2: DOS's forefathers brought forth upon this nation
        3: a new operating system (more or less).
*3
        3:*a new operating system (more or less).
        3:*a new operating system (more or less), dedicated
*L
        1: Four score and seven months ago (approximately),
        2: DOS's forefathers brought forth upon this nation
        3:*a new operating system (more or less), dedicated
*_
```

Figure 6.2: Making corrections to a line

MOVING LINES (CUTTING AND PASTING)

The Move command (M) allows you to move one line or a body of lines in a file to a new location in the file. (A group of lines to be moved is called a *block*.) For example, entering

9,12,6M
L

```
C>EDLIN LINCOLN.TXT
End of input file
*L
        1:*Four score and seven months ago (approximately),
        2: DOS's forefathers brought forth upon this nation
        3: a new operating system (more or less).
*3
        3:*a new operating system (more or less).
        3:*a new operating system (more or less), dedicated
*L
        1: Four score and seven months ago (approximately),
        2: DOS's forefathers brought forth upon this nation
        3:*a new operating system (more or less), dedicated
*4I
        4:*to the proposition that all computers (with the same
        5:*microcomputer chip) are created equal.
        6:*^C

*L
        1: Four score and seven months ago (approximately),
        2: DOS's forefathers brought forth upon this nation
        3: a new operating system (more or less), dedicated
        4: to the proposition that all computers (with the same
        5: microcomputer chip) are created equal.
*▪
```

Figure 6.3: Adding new lines at the end of a file

```
        5: microcomputer chip) are created equal.
        6: We are met today to chronicle a part of these DOS
        7: wars.  It is altogether fitting and proper (some may
        8: disagree) that we should do this.
        9: Now, we are engaged in a great computer war (more
       10: have fallen than have risen), testing whether this DOS
       11: or any other DOS so conceived and so dedicated, can
       12: long endure.
*10
       10:*have fallen than have risen), testing whether this DOS
       10:*have fallen than have risen), testing whether this DOS,
*L
        1: Four score and seven months ago (approximately),
        2: DOS's forefathers brought forth upon this nation
        3: a new operating system (more or less), dedicated
        4: to the proposition that all computers (with the same
        5: microcomputer chip) are created equal.
        6: We are met today to chronicle a part of these DOS
        7: wars.  It is altogether fitting and proper (some may
        8: disagree) that we should do this.
        9: Now, we are engaged in a great computer war (more
       10:*have fallen than have risen), testing whether this DOS,
       11: or any other DOS so conceived and so dedicated, can
       12: long endure.
*▪
```

Figure 6.4: Intermediate version of the text file

at the EDLIN prompt will move lines 9 through 12 in the file shown
in Figure 6.4 to a new position—in front of line 6, as shown in Figure
6.5. This is commonly called *cutting and pasting*. Naturally, when the
operation is completed, all affected lines are renumbered. Notice that
the current line has moved to the new sixth line, since this was the
first line in the block that was moved.

```
        3: a new operating system (more or less), dedicated
        4: to the proposition that all computers (with the same
        5: microcomputer chip) are created equal.
        6: We are met today to chronicle a part of these DOS
        7: wars.  It is altogether fitting and proper (some may
        8: disagree) that we should do this.
        9: Now, we are engaged in a great computer war (more
       10:*have fallen than have risen), testing whether this DOS,
       11: or any other DOS so conceived and so dedicated, can
       12: long endure.
   *9,12,6M
   *L
        1: Four score and seven months ago (approximately),
        2: DOS's forefathers brought forth upon this nation
        3: a new operating system (more or less), dedicated
        4: to the proposition that all computers (with the same
        5: microcomputer chip) are created equal.
        6:*Now, we are engaged in a great computer war (more
        7: have fallen than have risen), testing whether this DOS,
        8: or any other DOS so conceived and so dedicated, can
        9: long endure.
       10: We are met today to chronicle a part of these DOS
       11: wars.  It is altogether fitting and proper (some may
       12: disagree) that we should do this.
    *_
```

Figure 6.5: Cutting and pasting text

COPYING LINES

The Copy command (C) is used to copy blocks of lines to other places in a file. It is similar to the M command, although not as frequently used. When you use the C command, the original lines are not bodily moved to a new place in the file; instead, they are replicated in the new place, leaving the original lines intact. After the copy has been made, all line numbers will be recalculated, and the first line that was copied will become the new current line.

There are three versions of the C command. In the first, you can make a replica of the current text line anywhere else in the file. The copy of the current line will be inserted in front of the line specified by *Line:*

,,*Line*[,*Count*] C

The commas represent placeholders for values that haven't been entered by you; the default (that is, the current line) is used. The optional *Count* parameter can be used to specify the number of times the operations should be repeated.

You can also copy multiple lines at once using the C command. The following format causes all of the lines from *Line1* through the current line to be copied to the position before *Line2*:

> *Line1,,Line2[,Count]* C

The third possible format of the C command allows you to explicitly specify the range to be copied:

> *Range,Line3[,count]* C

Range represents a pair of delimited line numbers. This version of the C command is similar to the previous version, except that in *Range* you specify the last line number to be copied, instead of defaulting to the current line number.

Here's an example of using the *Count* parameter with the C command. If you were editing any text file of at least five lines and executed the following:

> *1,4,5,3 C

you would be telling EDLIN to make a copy of lines 1 through 4 in your file at a point just before line 5, and then to repeat this operation twice more (a total of 3 for *Count*).

SEARCHING FOR TEXT STRINGS

The Search command (S) locates lines. You can ask EDLIN to carry out the search over a variety of ranges. The general format of this command is

> *[Scope] [?] S[String]*

Scope can be defined as any of the following parameters:

- *Line* causes the search to start at *Line* and stop at the end of the file;
- *,Line* causes the search to start at the line after the current line and end at *Line;*
- *Line1,Line2* causes the search to cover only the lines within the block between *Line1* and *Line2.*

In any EDLIN command that allows the specification of multiple lines, the beginning line number must be less than or equal to the ending line number. EDLIN cannot work backwards.

• Not using the *Scope* parameter results in the search starting at the line after the current line and ending at the last line in the file.

The *String* parameter specifies the text that you are looking for. The first character of this text should immediately follow the S. If *String* is not included on the command line, the search string last used in a Search or Replace command is used. If no Search or Replace command has yet been used in the session, then the message "Not found" will be displayed.

If you specify ? in this command, EDLIN will stop each time it locates the specified string, and it will ask you for confirmation that the string is the correct one.

As an example of using the Search command, let's look for all occurrences of the word *is* in the following file:

```
1: This is the first line
2: of a test file to demonstrate
3: the use of the Search command.
4: It is included for your own
5: information.
```

You would enter the following command:

```
*1,5 ? Sis
```

You would then see

```
 1: This is the first line
O.K.? n
 4: It is included for your own
O.K.? n
 Not found
*_
```

The Search and Replace commands are case-sensitive—they will look for *exactly* what you type. For example, the S command will consider *Judd* and *judd* to be two different words because of the different capitalization.

You can see that line 4 has become the current line, as it was the last line to contain a match with *String*. Notice that line 1 only came up once in the search. This is because the search finds a whole line with a match on it. If there is more than one match, it's a waste of time to successively redisplay the same line.

SEARCH AND REPLACE CAPABILITIES

R is the Replace command. It gives you the ability to search through any specified range of lines and replace every occurrence of specific text (*String*) with new replacement text (*NewString*).

The general format for the R command is

[*Scope*] [?] R[*String*][Ctrl-Z*NewString*]

The *Scope* and *String* parameters are the same as those for the Search command. If you are going to enter replacement text (*NewString*), end *String* by pressing Ctrl-Z. (This is optional, since you may only want to search for and remove the specified string wherever it is found.)

NewString is the text that will replace *String*. It does not need to be the same size as *String,* since it will be inserted after *String* has been deleted. If *NewString* is left out, then *String* will be deleted in the specified block. If *String* is left out as well, EDLIN will use the *String* value from the last Search or Replace command, and the *NewString* value from the last Replace command. If Search and Replace have not been used during the current session, you will get the message "Not found."

When ? is specified in this command, EDLIN will display the replaced or modified line and ask whether you wish to confirm the changes that were made ("O.K.?"). You should answer Y or press Return if you want the changes to become permanent.

> Once an occurrence of *String* has been found and you have accepted or not accepted the change, the search will continue in the specified block. Multiple occurrences on the same line are included in the replacements.

Let's try this command with the example you worked with earlier in this chapter. You can quickly ask EDLIN to search in the file for each occurrence of the text string *DOS*. When found, the command will replace *DOS* with *MS-DOS* (see Figure 6.6).

In this example, you specified that all occurrences in lines 1 through 12 are to be acted upon. You can see by the EDLIN prompt that line 10 has become the current line, since it was the last line changed. Notice also that each line that contained the sought-after string of characters was displayed after the change was made (lines 2, 7, 8, and 10). As shown in the figure, you usually execute the L command to verify the results of your command request.

```
         7: have fallen than have risen), testing whether this DOS,
         8: or any other DOS so conceived and so dedicated, can
         9: long endure.
        10: We are met today to chronicle a part of these DOS
        11: wars.  It is altogether fitting and proper (some may
        12:*disagree) that we should do this.
*1,12RDOS^ZMS-DOS
         2: MS-DOS's forefathers brought forth upon this nation
         7: have fallen than have risen), testing whether this MS-DOS,
         8: or any other MS-DOS so conceived and so dedicated, can
        10: We are met today to chronicle a part of these MS-DOS
    *L
         1: Four score and seven months ago (approximately),
         2: MS-DOS's forefathers brought forth upon this nation
         3: a new operating system (more or less), dedicated
         4: to the proposition that all computers (with the same
         5: microcomputer chip) are created equal.
         6: Now, we are engaged in a great computer war (more
         7: have fallen than have risen), testing whether this MS-DOS,
         8: or any other MS-DOS so conceived and so dedicated, can
         9: long endure.
        10:*We are met today to chronicle a part of these MS-DOS
        11: wars.  It is altogether fitting and proper (some may
        12: disagree) that we should do this.
    *_
```

Figure 6.6: Search and replace operation

DELETING LINES

The Delete command (D) is used to delete one or more lines from the file. Its general format is

[*Line*],[*Line*]D

The *Line* parameters specify the line or lines that you want to delete.

Suppose you had written some new text and added it to the current file beginning at line 13 (see Figure 6.7). Then you decided (either immediately or later) that this new text was not appropriate, so you needed to delete it with the D command. Figure 6.8 shows the results of deleting the lines and then listing the remaining file.

Deleting lines causes all lines after the deletion to be renumbered. Even if you do not request a listing of the lines (with L), they are still renumbered. For example, if you execute the command 1D twice, you will have deleted lines 1 and 2.

ENDING THE EDITING SESSION

There are two ways to exit EDLIN, depending on whether you want to save the changes you've made to the file or not. You can abort the entire editing operation and restore the file to its original condition, or you can save all your edits to the disk file, permanently engraving those changes in the original file.

QUITTING THE EDITING
SESSION WITHOUT SAVING

Entering the Quit command (Q) all by itself is one way of getting
out of EDLIN and back to DOS without saving all of the work you
have just done. EDLIN will ask you if you are sure you wish to leave
without saving your file. Anything other than an answer of Y will
abort the Q command, and you will be back at the EDLIN prompt.

```
          8: or any other MS-DOS so conceived and so dedicated, can
          9: long endure.
         10: We are met today to chronicle a part of these MS-DOS
         11: wars.  It is altogether fitting and proper (some may
         12: disagree) that we should do this.
   *13I
         13:*The world will little note (not counting book reviewers,
         14:*of course) nor long remember what we say here, but you
         15:*can never forget what you learn here (who could possibly
         16:*forget such drama, not to mention irreverence?).
         17:*^C

   *L
          6: Now, we are engaged in a great computer war (more
          7: have fallen than have risen), testing whether this MS-DOS,
          8: or any other MS-DOS so conceived and so dedicated, can
          9: long endure.
         10: We are met today to chronicle a part of these MS-DOS
         11: wars.  It is altogether fitting and proper (some may
         12: disagree) that we should do this.
         13: The world will little note (not counting book reviewers,
         14: of course) nor long remember what we say here, but you
         15: can never forget what you learn here (who could possibly
         16: forget such drama, not to mention irreverence?).

   *_
```

Figure 6.7: Additional text entries

```
          7: have fallen than have risen), testing whether this MS-DOS,
          8: or any other MS-DOS so conceived and so dedicated, can
          9: long endure.
         10: We are met today to chronicle a part of these MS-DOS
         11: wars.  It is altogether fitting and proper (some may
         12: disagree) that we should do this.
         13: The world will little note (not counting book reviewers,
         14: of course) nor long remember what we say here, but you
         15: can never forget what you learn here (who could possibly
         16: forget such drama, not to mention irreverence?).
   *13,16D
   *1L
          1: Four score and seven months ago (approximately),
          2: MS-DOS's forefathers brought forth upon this nation
          3: a new operating system (more or less), dedicated
          4: to the proposition that all computers (with the same
          5: microcomputer chip) are created equal.
          6: Now, we are engaged in a great computer war (more
          7: have fallen than have risen), testing whether this MS-DOS,
          8: or any other MS-DOS so conceived and so dedicated, can
          9: long endure.
         10: We are met today to chronicle a part of these MS-DOS
         11: wars.  It is altogether fitting and proper (some may
         12: disagree) that we should do this.

   *_
```

Figure 6.8: Multiple lines deleted

This exit path usually is used when you have made a mistake. Suppose, for example, that you changed your mind about the deletion of lines 13 to 16 done in the last section. You've decided to keep those lines in the text after all. You could type them in all over again; or, if there are no other edits at stake, you could abort the entire editing process, go back to DOS, and then call up the text file for editing once again. Figure 6.9 demonstrates this process. Using Q to abort the editing process, returning to DOS, and then immediately recalling the LINCOLN.TXT file returns the unchanged text file to you.

SAVING YOUR WORK AND EXITING TO DOS

The usual way to exit EDLIN and save your changes is to use the End command (E). With this command, the file you originally named when you started EDLIN will be given a .BAK extension; the edited file will retain the original extension. If you created a completely new file, no .BAK file would be created.

At the end of the file, EDLIN will insert a carriage return and line feed if they are not already there. It will also insert a Ctrl-Z code to be used for an end-of-file marker.

EDLIN will *not* prompt you to make sure you want to leave. Entering E followed by a press of the Return key is all you need to save all of your editing changes and return to DOS (see Figure 6.10).

Make sure that there is enough room on your disk for the file to be saved. If there is not, the part of the file that *can* fit will be saved with an extension of .$$$. The original file will be retained on the disk, no new .BAK file will be created, and the part of the edited file not saved will be lost.

```
        10: We are met today to chronicle a part of these MS-DOS
        11: wars.  It is altogether fitting and proper (some may
        12: disagree) that we should do this.
*Q
Abort edit (Y/N)? Y
C>EDLIN LINCOLN.TXT
End of input file
*L
         1:*Four score and seven months ago (approximately),
         2: MS-DOS's forefathers brought forth upon this nation
         3: a new operating system (more or less), dedicated
         4: to the proposition that all computers (with the same
         5: microcomputer chip) are created equal.
         6: Now, we are engaged in a great computer war (more
         7: have fallen than have risen), testing whether this MS-DOS,
         8: or any other MS-DOS so conceived and so dedicated, can
         9: long endure.
        10: We are met today to chronicle a part of these MS-DOS
        11: wars.  It is altogether fitting and proper (some may
        12: disagree) that we should do this.
        13: The world will little note (not counting book reviewers,
        14: of course) nor long remember what we say here, but you
        15: can never forget what you learn here (who could possibly
        16: forget such drama, not to mention irreverence?).
*_
```

Figure 6.9: Aborting the editing process

```
        12: disagree) that we should do this.
*Q
Abort edit (Y/N)? Y
C>EDLIN LINCOLN.TXT
End of input file
*L
         1:*Four score and seven months ago (approximately),
         2: MS-DOS's forefathers brought forth upon this nation
         3: a new operating system (more or less), dedicated
         4: to the proposition that all computers (with the same
         5: microcomputer chip) are created equal.
         6: Now, we are engaged in a great computer war (more
         7: have fallen than have risen), testing whether this MS-DOS,
         8: or any other MS-DOS so conceived and so dedicated, can
         9: long endure.
        10: We are met today to chronicle a part of these MS-DOS
        11: wars.  It is altogether fitting and proper (some may
        12: disagree) that we should do this.
        13: The world will little note (not counting book reviewers,
        14: of course) nor long remember what we say here, but you
        15: can never forget what you learn here (who could possibly
        16: forget such drama, not to mention irreverence?).
*E

C>■
```

Figure 6.10: Normal EDLIN termination sequence

SUMMARY

In this chapter, you've learned about the commands available in DOS's line editor, EDLIN, for creating and manipulating text files, as well as for modifying the text within them. Here is a brief review:

- All of EDLIN's capabilities are accessible with simple one-letter commands. These commands act on one or more lines within the text file, and act on the text within those lines.

- You can create a new file simply by typing EDLIN *FileName*. The file will be created and you can execute any of EDLIN's editing commands by typing in the appropriate command at the asterisk prompt.

- If the available memory in your system is not sufficient to hold your entire text file, you can use the Write command with the Append command to write edited lines to disk and then add unedited lines to memory.

- You can enter new text with the Insert command. The Break key allows you to terminate the data entry.

- You can list any or all text lines with the Line command. You can also list the entire file, a screenful at a time, with the Page command.

- Once entered, text can be modified in a variety of ways. The DOS function keys can be used to modify any line once you've brought up that line by typing its number.

- You can move one or more lines around in the file with the Move command. You can also leave those lines in place, while making a complete copy of them elsewhere with the Copy command.

- Besides the Move and Copy commands, which manipulate large blocks of text, the Transfer command can insert one complete text file into another.

- What goes in can always come out. The Delete command can remove one or more text lines—permanently.

- Any text string can be searched for with the Search command. The even more powerful Replace command can search for any text string and replace it with another string. If you like, the Replace command can be used to replace one string with *nothing,* effectively creating a large-scale (global) deletion capability.

- You can end your EDLIN editing session with the End command, which saves your edited work under the original file name and then returns you to the DOS prompt. Or you can abort the entire editing session with the Quit command, which, after confirming that you really mean to do it, restores your file to its original condition.

Now that you know how to create and modify text files with EDLIN, you should turn to Chapter 7. Having beautifully sculpted text on a disk may be satisfying, but printing it out on paper is even better. You will find that it's much better to read the entire file from a printed manuscript than from one 23-line display at a time.

PRINTING

CHAPTER 7

COMPUTERS CAN DO MANY MARVELOUS THINGS, AND do them all at lightning speeds. Cardiac simulations, missile interception analyses, genetic and chemical modeling are just a few of the tasks that would be tedious or even impossible without computers. However, the magic of the computer would be all for naught if there were no way to see the results.

We often take output for granted. Yet, you know by now that without a DIR, TYPE, or COPY command, you'd never be able to see the results of your work. In this chapter, you'll learn a wide range of output capabilities in DOS. You'll discover some easy methods, some "quick-and-dirty" techniques, and some sophisticated commands for controlling when output will occur, where it will go, and what it will look like. You'll also learn why these alternatives work as they do.

Printing simple screen images of both text and graphics screens is the easiest kind of output to master quickly, so you'll learn that right away. Since printing onto paper is unquestionably the standard method for obtaining hard-copy results from programs, the principal focus of this chapter will be on producing printed output.

Indirect printing plays a very important role in more and more systems. The last section in this chapter will take an in-depth look at this feature. With indirect printing, you can continue to work on your computer while it sends output to a printer. This is DOS's first step into the world of multitasking and multiprocessing, where more than one program can execute at one time and more than one user can share the system's capabilities. The full potential of this power will not be realized until the next generation of hardware and software becomes available. For now, however, it can provide a significant improvement in system performance, allowing printing to occur simultaneously with other computing tasks.

PRINTING SCREEN IMAGES

A Color Graphics Adapter (CGA) monitor can generate graphics images using an array of pixels (dots) that is 640 pixels wide by 200 high. This density—128,000 pixels—is acceptable for most applications, although many programs produce more pleasing and detailed results using denser output screens. An Enhanced Graphics Adapter (EGA) monitor has a density that is twice that of the CGA. Its graphics mode produces an array of 640 × 350 pixels, while its successors, the Professional Graphics Adapter (PGA) and the Video Graphics Array (VGA), produce 640 × 480. The VGA has several additional display modes, a popular one being 720 × 400 resolution for increasing the number of text lines displayed. The top of the line in graphics capabilities on the new Personal System/2 machines features a 1024 × 768 pixel addressability.

It's often easier to generate results on the video screen than on any other output device. However, as you'll learn in this chapter, anything that can be displayed on your video screen can also be transferred to your printer.

All printers can create an exact replica of any text that appears on a screen. With DOS commands, you can easily obtain hard copies of any important data that is being displayed on your monitor. This may be all you ever need to be satisfied with printed output from your computer system. In fact, many users never need to print anything with DOS commands—their application programs have built-in commands for managing output printing. To accurately replicate an image on the screen that was created in graphics mode instead of text mode, however, you must have a printer capable of creating graphics.

If neither you nor your dealer has yet connected your printer, you should do so now. If you need to do more than simply connect your printer and cable to the appropriate ports, consult Chapter 8, which covers communications in detail.

DOS requires you to press the keystroke combination Shift-PrtSc to print a copy of whatever is on the screen. The Shift-PrtSc key combination will work on any video monitor if the information being displayed is in standard text characters. To see how it works, turn on your computer and bring up any program at all; or just try a simple DOS directory command. Turn on your printer, and press Shift-PrtSc. It's as simple as that to obtain hard copy.

Assuming you have a printer capable of generating graphics images, you can also create printed images of graphics by following a simple preparatory procedure. The GRAPHICS command in DOS is a disk-resident program that enables the same Shift-PrtSc combination to capture a graphics screen image for printing if you have an IBM- or Epson-compatible printer. You must invoke this command *before* attempting to print a graphics screen.

The simplest form of the command is invoked by typing

GRAPHICS

This causes future presses of the Shift-PrtSc combination to reproduce on your printer all screen images, including graphics images. Graphics images cannot be printed without taking this crucial step.

If you have a graphics program or an integrated package that includes graphics, try running it now and printing one of the resulting graphics images. First try it without executing GRAPHICS. Then go back to DOS and run the GRAPHICS command. Return to your program, and try Shift-PrtSc with the same graphics image.

The GRAPHICS command has some flexibility when it comes to output appearance. Its general form is

GRAPHICS *PrinterType* /R /B

where *PrinterType* is one of the possible parameter values defining printer type, as shown in Table 7.1. /R and /B are switches you can use for background color and reverse video, as you will see shortly. As always, if the GRAPHICS.COM file is not in the current directory,

PARAMETER	PRINTER TYPE
COLOR1	For a color printer with a black ribbon (prints up to four shades of grey)
COLOR4	For a color printer with a red/green/blue ribbon
COLOR8	For a color printer with a cyan/magenta/yellow ribbon
COMPACT	For the IBM Personal Computer Compact printer
GRAPHICS	For the IBM Personal Graphics printer, or the IBM Proprinter (this is the default)
THERMAL	For the IBM PC Convertible printer

Table 7.1: PrinterType parameters for the GRAPHICS command

you should precede the GRAPHICS command with the drive and directory where it can be found.

Figure 7.1 shows a typical graphics screen. If you do not run the GRAPHICS command, and simply try to print this screen with the Shift-PrtSc combination, the result will be unsatisfactory, as you see in Figure 7.2. However, if you use the GRAPHICS command with the default graphics *PrinterType* by first typing

GRAPHICS

then pressing Return, and *then* using Shift-PrtSc, the printed result will be what you want to see, as shown in Figure 7.3.

If you specify *PrinterType* as COLOR4 or COLOR8, you have the option of printing the background screen color. You then use the /B switch when you invoke the command by typing, for example,

GRAPHICS COLOR4 /B

As an alternative, the /R switch with this command produces a striking *reverse-video* image (white letters on a black background). For example, typing

GRAPHICS COLOR4 /R

Printing a screen that contains only text with Shift-PrtSc is reasonably quick (under a minute for most microcomputer printers). Printing a screen containing graphics will take several minutes, depending on the graphics resolution and screen contents, as well as the speed of your printer.

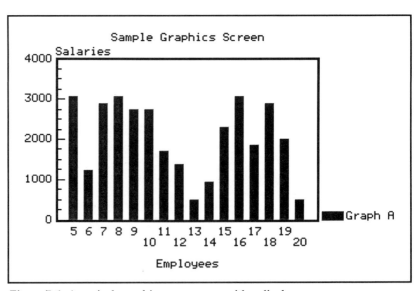

Figure 7.1: A typical graphics screen on a video display

would produce the reverse-video printing shown in Figure 7.4.

Finally, you should know that the graphics mode of your video display will affect the printed image. If your screen is in high-resolution

Figure 7.2: Figure 7.1 printed with the Shift-PrtSc combination

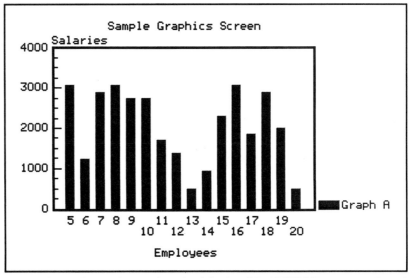

Figure 7.3: Figure 7.1 printed with the GRAPHICS command and Shift-PrtSc

Figure 7.4: Reverse-video printout of Figure 7.1

mode (640 columns by 200 rows), then the printed image will be rotated 90 degrees on the paper. This is often called a *horizontal landscape* image. If the screen is in medium-resolution mode (320 columns by 200 rows), the printed image will be printed as you see it. This is called a *vertical portrait* image. The resolution affects color printouts as well as displays; it is possible to obtain four colors in medium-resolution mode, but only two different colors in high-resolution mode.

PRINTING FILES

Creating exact replicas of displayed data with the Shift-PrtSc command and the GRAPHICS command is easy, but it is limited to one screenful of information at a time. There will be many times when you need a printed copy of an entire data file. Most files are created as standard ASCII files, which usually contain standard letters, numbers, and punctuation. In addition, each line of an ASCII file has a carriage return and line feed (CR/LF) at the end of it, but no other special control characters are embedded within the file. An ASCII file can be printed in several ways, as you will see in the following sections.

PRINTING FILES WITH THE COPY COMMAND

Keep in mind that if a file is stored in some special format (as it is for spreadsheet programs, database programs, and many word-processing programs), you will need to use a special output printing sequence for the appropriate program to obtain a printed copy.

The most straightforward way to print one or more data files is to use the COPY command. The general form of the COPY command is

COPY *FileName(s) DeviceName*

where *FileName(s)* is the name of the file (or files) and the destination, *DeviceName,* is the printer's *reserved device name.* (You will learn about these names in Chapter 8.) DOS reserves several special names like LPT1 or COM1 for the hardware ports to which printers are connected.

If the file you want to print is called KEYS.DTA, then it can be printed simply by specifying either of the following two commands:

COPY KEYS.DTA LPT1:
COPY KEYS.DTA PRN:

In these commands, LPT1 is a name for the first parallel printer port (see Chapter 8) and PRN is the standard default device name for the first connected printer. The printer will be engaged immediately, and the entire file will be printed. You will now have to wait until the printout is completed before the DOS prompt will return. Nothing else can be done by your DOS system or by you until the printing terminates.

As you learned in Chapter 3, you can copy multiple files with one command by using a wild-card specification. In this situation, you can also initiate the printing of multiple text files with one statement. For instance, you could initiate the printing of all the .TXT files in the HELP directory by entering

COPY \HELP*.TXT PRN:

DOS will respond to this request by successively echoing on the screen the name of each .TXT file. After echoing a name, it will transmit all the contents of that file to the printer and move on to the next file in the HELP directory that meets the .TXT file specification. Once again, you will not regain control at the DOS prompt until all of the specified files have been printed.

INDIRECT PRINTING AND SPOOLING ▬

In the previous section, the COPY command allowed you to transfer files to a printer. However, COPY will not relinquish control of the system until the print transfer is complete. Since the DOS prompt does not reappear, you are unable to enter any other DOS command or do anything else while the printing proceeds.

The PRINT command is DOS's solution. Unlike the COPY command, which directly prints to your printer, the PRINT command causes printing to occur indirectly. PRINT sends information out to a disk file to indicate which data files are to be printed. Then, later, while you are doing other work, DOS will independently read this disk file to discover which data files should be printed. The printing will occur simultaneously with other work you may then be doing with DOS and your computer system.

Indirect printing is often called *spooling,* an acronym for "*s*imultaneous *p*eripheral *o*perations *on-l*ine." Spooling is the only form of limited multitasking available in the current DOS operating system. (Multitasking is the apparent simultaneous operation of different programs or computer tasks.)

Switches and wild cards, when used intelligently, can also help you control the flow of information and files from one place to another—in this case, from a disk to a printer. The biggest complaint about system performance centers is the long waiting time for slow peripheral devices like printers and plotters, and the PRINT command and switches help to address that complaint.

Use the directory of .PRG text files seen in the DBASE\ADMIN\EXPERT directory of Figure 7.5 as you work through the following sections.

PRINTING FILES WITH THE PRINT COMMAND

The PRINT command is functionally similar to COPY. You could enter the following to print a file name or names on a standard system printer:

COPY *FileName(s)* **PRN:**

You could also enter just

PRINT *FileName(s)*

```
C:\DIR/W \DBASE\ADMIN\EXPERT\*.PRG

 Volume in drive C is ROBBINS
 Directory of  C:\DBASE\ADMIN\EXPERT

ARCHIVE  PRG    COLPRINT PRG    COMM     PRG    DATE     PRG    DELAY    PRG
DIR      PRG    DISKRPT  PRG    DUPLICAT PRG    GETSPACE PRG    LOWER    PRG
MAIL     PRG    MENU     PRG    MESSAGE  PRG    MODIFY   PRG    PRINT    PRG
PRINTER1 PRG    PRINTER2 PRG    PRINTER3 PRG    RUNDIR   PRG    SBENTRY  PRG
SBREPORT PRG    SBUPDAT2 PRG    SBUPDATE PRG    SNAP     PRG    STATS    PRG
STRIP    PRG    TIME     PRG    VALIDATE PRG    WASH     PRG    WINDEMO  PRG
WINDOW   PRG
       31 File(s)   1212416 bytes free

C>_
```

Figure 7.5: The DBASE\ADMIN\EXPERT directory

Unlike the COPY command, which has to be told a printing destination such as PRN, PRINT *knows* that its job is to send the specified file names to a printer. You can use one of the special switches, discussed later in this section, to indicate which printing device the files are to be printed on, but it's not really necessary. If you haven't specified the switch, DOS will ask you for a destination the very first time you invoke the PRINT command:

Name of list device [PRN]:

At this point, you could just press Return to accept the displayed default device name of PRN, or you could enter a specific reserved device name (like COM2) for your system.

Stop now briefly and try the PRINT command to print any text files (.TXT, .BAT, .DTA, and so on) you have on your system. Just enter the PRINT command at the DOS prompt, followed by a list of the file names you want to print. Use two or three names the first time; then, when DOS asks you for the name of the list device (the destination), just press Return.

DUAL TASKING WITH PRINT

The major difference between PRINT and COPY is apparent immediately after you specify the file names to print and answer any questions PRINT may ask you the first time you use it. The DOS prompt returns right after PRINT begins its work. You can invoke other programs or commands while PRINT prints your files. The effect is apparently simultaneous action: the CPU seems to be managing the printing job at the same time it is responding to your new requests at the DOS prompt for nonprinting work. The indirect printing, or spooling, is called a *background task,* while your principal new work (if any) is called the *foreground task.*

This dual-tasking technique is actually electronic chicanery—a silicon sleight-of-hand. A DOS computer has only one central processing chip (CPU), and it can really only do one thing at a time. However, it *can* do things very quickly. In any given period of time, a CPU can rapidly shift its processing attention from a slow printer to a slow typist to a not-really-so-fast disk drive.

If an operating system were advanced enough to manage all this shifting of attention from one operation to another and from one device to another, you would see a true multitasking environment. However, DOS is only advanced enough to play this juggling game between two things: printing and, at most, one other activity.

Figure 7.6 shows a request for the printing of a single text file, MAIL.PRG, as a background task. In this example the PRINT command has been invoked for the first time since DOS was brought

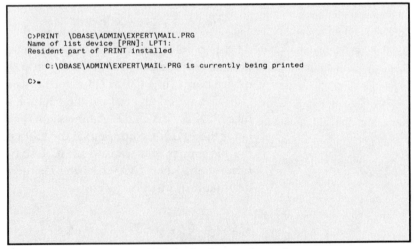

```
C>PRINT  \DBASE\ADMIN\EXPERT\MAIL.PRG
Name of list device [PRN]: LPT1:
Resident part of PRINT installed

    C:\DBASE\ADMIN\EXPERT\MAIL.PRG is currently being printed

C>_
```

Figure 7.6: First use of PRINT for background printing

up. The name of the desired printer was solicited (with DOS using the formal specification ''list device''), and LPT1 was explicitly entered.

Notice that a message appears informing you that the resident part of PRINT has been installed. PRINT expands the resident memory requirements of DOS when it runs. Although the extra memory requirement reduces the memory remaining for your primary application program, this cost is a small price to pay for the ability to continue using your computer while printing proceeds. PRINT also displays a message stating that the requested file is currently being printed. Then the standard DOS prompt reappears. If you now initiate any other command or program, DOS will simply shift its processing power back and forth between the new job and the currently running print job.

Depending on how much slack time exists in your new program (for example, keyboard or disk waiting), the new program may not get held up to any noticeable extent. Usually, however, the print job can never run as fast as it could if it were not contending with a foreground task for the processor's attention. DOS will do its best to efficiently juggle the time-sharing between tasks.

USING SWITCHES WITH PRINT

DOS provides you with certain switches that give you performance controls for indirect printing. Detailed analysis of these switches is beyond the scope of this book. In fact, using these switches at all may be unnecessary for the average user. When future versions of DOS permit multitasking, these parameters will be more useful for fine-tuning advanced DOS.

In the example seen in Figure 7.6, no switches were specified. DOS set its own intelligent initial values for the performance parameters. However, you can specify other values for these parameters. The memory-resident setup will follow defaults unless you specify other values by switches. Some of these switches can only be used the first time PRINT is invoked. These switches and their parameters are shown in Table 7.2.

The only one of the six initialization switches that you might want to consider setting consistently is /Q, the Queue switch, which indicates how many separately named files can be managed by the

PRINT command. A *queue* is just a waiting line, like a line of people waiting for a bus or bank service. In this context, a queue is a list of files to be printed. DOS allows ten file names in the queue as a default

SWITCH AND PARAMETER	EFFECT
/D:*Device*	Specifies the device to which print output is to be sent (COM1, LPT2, and so on)
/Q:*QueueSize*	Specifies how many files can be accepted by the PRINT command at one time for background printing. Maximum number is 32, and the default value is 10
/M:*MaxTicks*	Specifies the maximum of CPU clock ticks to be used by the PRINT command each time it is given control by the CPU. Range of allowable values is 1 to 255, with a default value of 2
/B:*BufferSize*	Specifies the number of bytes in memory to be used for data to be printed. 512 bytes is standard, but it can be increased in 512-byte increments
/U:*BusyTicks*	Specifies how many clock ticks to wait for a printer that is still busy with earlier printing. Allowable range is 1 to 255, with a default value of 1
/S:*TimeSlice*	Specifies how long PRINT waits prior to getting its share of the CPU. Range is 1 to 255, with a default value of 8

Table 7.2: Switches and parameters for the first PRINT command

maximum, but you can adjust that value with the /Q switch.

Figure 7.7 shows what will happen if you try to ask DOS to queue more than 10 files under normal conditions. Even though there are 31 files that match the wild-card specification (*.PRG), only the first 10 are accepted for printing into the queue. Since the /Q switch has not been used, the default assumption of ten slots was taken by PRINT.

In this situation, DOS displays several messages. It first indicates that the PRINT queue is full. Next, it indicates that the first file, ARCHIVE.PRG, is currently being printed. Messages also appear indicating that each of the other nine files is currently in the queue. Figure 7.8 portrays how this queueing works.

The remaining 21 .PRG files that were not accepted into the queue for printing will have to be queued up with other PRINT commands after these 10 finish printing. At best, other PRINT commands that are issued when some of the ten slots open up will fill the open slots. However, the total number of queued files can never exceed the maximum queue size. If you know that you will frequently need to queue up more than ten files at a time, you can type your very first PRINT request as

PRINT *FileName(s)* **/Q:32**

```
C>PRINT   \DBASE\ADMIN\EXPERT\*.PRG
PRINT queue is full

    C:\DBASE\ADMIN\EXPERT\ARCHIVE.PRG is currently being printed
    C:\DBASE\ADMIN\EXPERT\COLPRINT.PRG is in queue
    C:\DBASE\ADMIN\EXPERT\COMM.PRG is in queue
    C:\DBASE\ADMIN\EXPERT\DATE.PRG is in queue
    C:\DBASE\ADMIN\EXPERT\DELAY.PRG is in queue
    C:\DBASE\ADMIN\EXPERT\DIR.PRG is in queue
    C:\DBASE\ADMIN\EXPERT\DISKRPT.PRG is in queue
    C:\DBASE\ADMIN\EXPERT\DUPLICAT.PRG is in queue
    C:\DBASE\ADMIN\EXPERT\GETSPACE.PRG is in queue
    C:\DBASE\ADMIN\EXPERT\LOWER.PRG is in queue

C>PRINT /T
PRINT queue is empty

C>_
```

Figure 7.7: Partial PRINT queue

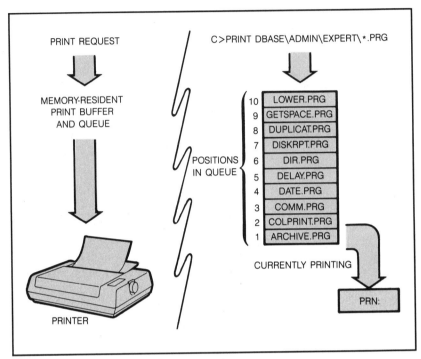

PRINT REQUEST

C>PRINT DBASE\ADMIN\EXPERT*.PRG

MEMORY-RESIDENT
PRINT BUFFER
AND QUEUE

10	LOWER.PRG
9	GETSPACE.PRG
8	DUPLICAT.PRG
7	DISKRPT.PRG
6	DIR.PRG
5	DELAY.PRG
4	DATE.PRG
3	COMM.PRG
2	COLPRINT.PRG
1	ARCHIVE.PRG

POSITIONS
IN QUEUE

CURRENTLY PRINTING

PRN:

PRINTER

Figure 7.8: How the PRINT queue works

Although each increase in queue size takes up additional memory, you should use this command if you frequently need to print many files.

Three other switches are always available to you for management of the queue and its entries. As you can see in Table 7.3, they are /P (Print), /C, (Cancel printing), and /T (Terminate all spooling). These can be used each time PRINT is invoked, although you'll usually prefer to simply list the files you want to print.

You'll probably use /P least often, since it is already the system default. If you enter

```
CD  \DBASE\ADMIN\EXPERT
PRINT  STRIP.PRG  SNAP.PRG  WASH.PRG
```

DOS will queue the three text files specified, assuming that there are at least three available slots in the queue. The /P switch was assumed by DOS; it was not necessary to enter it specifically. You will only need to use it when you construct more complicated PRINT requests.

SWITCH AND PARAMETER	EFFECT
/P:*FileName(s)*	Prints the file(s) specified; this is the default
/C:*FileName(s)*	Cancels the printing of the file(s) specified
/T:*FileName(s)*	Terminates the printing of all specified file(s) in the PRINT queue

Table 7.3: Switches and parameters for any PRINT command

When specifying file names in a PRINT command, you can list several separately named files on the same PRINT request line.

If you want to cancel the printing of one or more files already in the queue, you can do so with the /C switch. For instance, to remove the DIR.PRG and DATE.PRG entries from the queue, effectively canceling the former print request for those two files, enter

PRINT DIR.PRG /C DATE.PRG

Notice that the /C switch applies to the file name immediately preceding the switch in the command line and all files listed after it (up until the next switch). This allows a complex but useful construction in which you simultaneously add and remove queue entries. In the next example, LOWER.PRG and DUPLICAT.PRG are removed from the queue with /C, while STATS.PRG is added with /P:

PRINT LOWER.PRG /C DUPLICAT.PRG STATS.PRG /P

Like the /C switch, the /P switch applies to the file name immediately preceding it on the command line.

If the file you wish to cancel is currently printing, the printing will stop and you will receive a message to that effect. If the file you cancel is elsewhere in the queue, it will be removed, and the new status of the PRINT queue will be displayed on your monitor. In fact, you can always see the current queue status by simply entering the PRINT command at the DOS prompt with no parameters or switches. Figure 7.9 demonstrates a status request issued partway through the printing of the .PRG files.

```
C>PRINT

    C:\DBASE\ADMIN\EXPERT\DISKRPT.PRG is currently being printed
    C:\DBASE\ADMIN\EXPERT\DUPLICAT.PRG is in queue
    C:\DBASE\ADMIN\EXPERT\GETSPACE.PRG is in queue
    C:\DBASE\ADMIN\EXPERT\LOWER.PRG is in queue

C>_
```

Figure 7.9: Current status of the PRINT queue

Finally, the /T switch will cancel all file names in the queue. Perhaps the paper has jammed, or an ink-jet cartridge has run dry while the printing continues. In these cases, you may like to cancel all outstanding print requests and then restart the output spool, naming specific files in your desired order. Simply enter the command

PRINT /T

DOS will print the message ''All files canceled by operator'' on the printer. It will also display on the screen a message stating that the PRINT queue is empty.

If you use a plotter and your software allows off-line plotting (that is, the software doesn't have to control the plotting process directly), you can use the PRINT command to queue several plots at once. Refer to your plotting program's documentation for further details.

SUMMARY

Printed output from your system is fundamental for nearly all software applications. This chapter has presented a variety of methods for obtaining printed output for both simple screen images and files:

- You can easily obtain hard-copy printouts of screen images consisting solely of text characters by using the Shift-PrtSc key combination.

- You can generate printed images of graphics screen images with the same Shift-PrtSc combination, provided that you first run the GRAPHICS command.

- You can use the GRAPHICS command with two useful switches for "special effects." The /B switch prints a separate background screen color if you are using multicolor printer ribbons. The /R switch produces the dramatic effect of white letters on a solid black background.

- You can use COPY to print larger text files that don't fit on one screen, by simply copying the files to a printer instead of to another file.

- You can use PRINT to print files indirectly while you work at the same time with other DOS programs or commands. This works for plotters as well as printers.

- You can control the files placed into the PRINT queue for output spooling by means of switches. You can initially configure the queue to hold up to 32 files with the /Q switch, and you can control how much time and memory DOS will reserve for spooling operations with the /M, /B, /U, and /S switches.

- You can add more files to the PRINT queue with the /P switch, remove files from the queue with the /C switch, and terminating all spooling operations by removing all files from the queue with the /T switch.

Now that you've learned several methods of printing with DOS, you can extend these techniques with the information in the next chapter. Printing is only one form of data communications. Chapter 8 will take you on an extended tour of other DOS communications capabilities, which permit information to be transferred to many other output devices besides printers.

This concludes the second major section of this book, "Making DOS Do More." You have acquired all the principal skills necessary to use DOS effectively, both on its own and with other application programs. The next section of this book, "Revving It Up," will speed you on your way to becoming a DOS power user. It will address the more advanced techniques available in DOS.

PART 3

REVVING IT UP

In Part 3, you will learn advanced techniques that are normally overlooked by beginning and by many intermediate DOS users. Chapter 8 describes communications terminology and technology, and shows you how to control data transmission with DOS commands. Chapter 9 tells you how to protect your files by backing them up and how to restore backed-up files if the originals are lost.

In Chapter 10, you will start learning how to customize your disk operating system. You will find out how to specify the number of active files and buffers, create and use a RAM disk, control the screen display, and redefine keys. Chapter 11 describes specialized customization methods for using your computer in a foreign country or for working with a foreign language. These include adapting your keyboard, screen display, and printer.

Finally, Chapter 12 teaches you how to use pipes, filters, and redirection to control input and ouput in your computer system.

COMMUNICATIONS

PRINTING IS ONE FORM OF SYSTEM COMMUNICATIONS; you learned about it first in Chapter 7 because of its central role in any computer system. This chapter concentrates on the speaking and listening that goes on between computer devices. As you'll see, there are many other devices to understand besides printers in any complete computer system. Beyond simply connecting these devices, you will learn in this chapter how to get them started and how to transfer information to and from them. Learn this information well, and you will no longer be at anybody else's mercy when it comes to buying and hooking up new equipment.

This chapter will help you understand the differences between parallel and serial communications, so you can make intelligent decisions about which is right for you. You will also learn enough about the various aspects of these two kinds of communications to use the DOS communications setup commands properly.

One major DOS command in particular, the MODE command, is central to an understanding of data transfer to printers, serial ports, and the video display. You'll learn what it can do for you and when to use it. It will give you control over

- Your printer (for improving the appearance of your hard-copy output),

- Your video screen (for enhancing all displayed information),

- Your keyboard (for getting more out of each key than simply what is printed on the key), and

- Just about any additional device at all that connects to one of the communications ports (plugs) in the back of your computer. This includes such devices as plotters, modems, and digitizers.

SYSTEM COMMUNICATIONS IN GENERAL

To understand computer communications, you need to understand the concept of data structure and storage. When you enter keyboard characters into programs, either as data or instructions, you enter them as numbers, letters, or punctuation marks, as represented on the face of the key. Each of these keystrokes is interpreted by the computer as a well-defined string of *binary digits,* the 0's and 1's you may already know about.

A computer and all its connected devices (*peripheral* devices) can be thought of simply as a large collection of very tiny electronic parts. Each of those parts can receive—or *not* receive—a small voltage, according to the logic built into the computer. The voltages affect the bits of magnetic material that store data for you or store instructions for the computer itself. If a bit is energized with a small voltage, it has a value of 1. If it receives no voltage, it has a value of 0. The word *binary* means two; as you see, a single bit has two possible values, 0 or 1.

You may not realize it, but in communicating with others, you usually perform a variety of tasks based on simple yes/no answers or simple directives. Everything can be broken down into smaller and smaller components, from hitting a baseball properly, to conducting an interview, to carrying out a superior's orders. Similarly, in a computer system, everything can be broken down into component bits. Complex logic and decision making are broken down into sequences of bits that either receive voltage or do not receive voltage—values of 1 or 0. Perhaps this is not as rich an alphabet as A through Z, but it serves the same purpose.

Communication between people is a sequence of sentences, which consist of a sequence of words, which in turn consist of a sequence of letters. These sequences are broken up by verbal pauses or inflections, or written punctuation marks, intended to help the listener (or reader) better understand the speaker (or writer). Pauses and punctuation, therefore, help to *synchronize* the communication of information. To synchronize computer communications, a sequence of 0's and 1's is grouped into seven or eight data bits, each group representing a character. Characters can be letters (A–Z), numbers (0–9), or special symbols or codes (* # % " : > ? and so on).

To understand why some communications use seven data bits while others use eight, let's briefly look at the binary number system. One bit can have the value 0 or 1. Therefore, two bits in a row have four possible combinations of values, since each bit has two possible values:

- 0 followed by 0, or 00
- 0 followed by 1, or 01
- 1 followed by 0, or 10
- 1 followed by 1, or 11

Taking this a step further, three bits in a row can have eight possibilities:

- 0 followed by 00, or 000
- 0 followed by 01, or 001
- 0 followed by 10, or 010
- 0 followed by 11, or 011
- 1 followed by 00, or 100
- 1 followed by 01, or 101
- 1 followed by 10, or 110
- 1 followed by 11, or 111

As you can see, the binary system is based on powers of the number 2. With one data bit, there are two possibilities (2^1); with two data bits, there are four possibilities (2^2); and with three data bits, there are eight possibilities (2^3). Continuing this progression will result in the following:

- Four data bits = 16 possibilities (2^4)
- Five data bits = 32 possibilities (2^5)

- Six data bits = 64 possibilities (2^6)
- Seven data bits = 128 possibilities (2^7)
- Eight data bits = 256 possibilities (2^8)

The standard keyboard and ASCII character set is more than covered by the 128 possibilities contained in seven data bits. However, there are additional characters (graphics characters, foreign-language characters, and so on) that constitute what is called the *extended ASCII set*. When these additional characters must be transmitted, the eight-bit form of data communications is used. Appendix B covers this issue more fully. You will usually see characters represented as eight bits, and communicated as such. This conventional eight-bit unit is a byte, the fundamental storage and data unit you deal with throughout DOS.

The groups of bits we have been examining represent either data or controlling information. In a conversation, you gain someone's attention by saying their name or saying something like "Hey, you." Computer communications use special groups of bits to gain the attention of another device. Once the attention is obtained with this *control code,* or special sequence of bits, the actual data transmission can begin.

Computers also use additional bits to ensure synchronization. *Stop bits* follow each unique character code (string of bits) to set it off from other transmitted information. In order to minimize sending or receiving errors, a *parity bit* is also sent after the data bits. This bit is used by both the transmitting and receiving equipment, but how it is computed and used is beyond the scope of this book.

PARALLEL VERSUS SERIAL COMMUNICATIONS

When you type a capital J from the keyboard, a code is sent to the computer's input routines, which translate it into the binary digits 01001010. The letter itself is echoed back to the video screen to confirm what you typed (see Figure 8.1). Remember that the video screen is part of what the system calls its console; the keyboard is the input part of the console and the video screen is the output part.

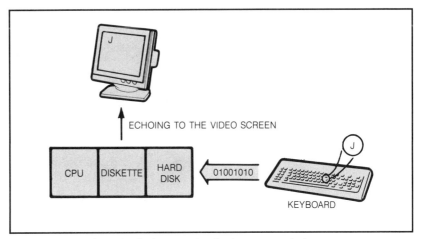

Figure 8.1: Keyboard echoing—a simple data transmission

The passing of information between these parts is called data transmission.

There are two methods of data transmission: parallel and serial. Nearly all DOS microcomputers are connected with peripheral devices using one of these two communication techniques. Although most printers use the parallel method of data transmission, some use the serial method. Other peripheral devices like plotters, digitizers, modems, and mice usually transmit data serially.

If a peripheral device is connected to a serial port and is designed for serial transmission, each bit will be sent to or received from the central processing unit one bit at a time, and only one transmission wire will be used. If the peripheral device is connected to a parallel port and is designed for parallel transmission, then eight separate bits will be transmitted simultaneously over eight separate wires. (In both cases, other wires are used for additional purposes, such as the synchronization of signals or grounding; however, it's sufficient in this context to understand the concept in terms of one wire versus eight.)

Consider a simple analogy. In Figure 8.2 an airport's baggage terminal has eight conveyor belts, and passengers' suitcases are unloaded from eight flights simultaneously. In Figure 8.3, however, the airport has only one conveyor belt. The baggage from all eight flights is unloaded onto it. The passengers in this situation have to wait eight times as long as those in the first airport, and they probably

Figure 8.2: Unloading luggage with multiple conveyor belts

Figure 8.3: Unloading luggage with one conveyor belt

won't be happy about it. Then again, the airline officials may not mind, since they spent one-eighth the amount of money on the conveyor mechanism and the ongoing expenses for maintenance and terminal space rental. It's a tradeoff of time versus money. In this analogy, you are the airline officials. You make the decision about what equipment you buy and use, deciding whether to spend more money on parallel connections or less money on serial connections, which require more waiting time for certain peripheral devices.

Let's return to the example of keyboard data transmission. Say you type in the word JUDD and you want the CPU to send it to a peripheral device. Your keystrokes will be translated into the ASCII character codes shown in Table 8.1.

Figure 8.4 shows a parallel transmission of these characters. As you can see, eight wires are used. A serial transmission of the same characters would require only one wire, as you can see in Figure 8.5. However, the transmission of data would be much slower. This explains why virtually all printers that print faster than several hundred characters per second *must* use parallel transmission and be connected to a computer correctly for parallel transmission.

Serial communications are often referred to as asynchronous communications, because the sending and receiving devices do not send and receive simultaneously, or synchronously. Instead, each uses an agreed set of electrical signals to indicate when to stop and start actual data transmission (see the MODE command later in this chapter).

DOS DEVICES VERSUS FILES

Operating systems treat devices that represent either the source of data or the destination for data in a consistent manner. As you've seen many times already, you specify the source and destination of the data in your software commands. The consistency with which you can reference hardware devices (like the console) or software

LETTER	BINARY DIGITS
J	01001010
U	01010101
D	01000100
D	01000100

Table 8.1: ASCII codes for the letters J, U, D, and D

"devices" (like a disk file) makes it easy to learn both new commands and new concepts. As you saw in Chapter 3, commands like COPY work in precisely the same way for a data transfer from a CPU to a disk file or a data transfer from a CPU to a peripheral device (a printer).

DOS is designed to understand and permit the referencing of certain typical peripheral devices. Unlike file names, which you can make up yourself (as long as you obey certain rules), device names

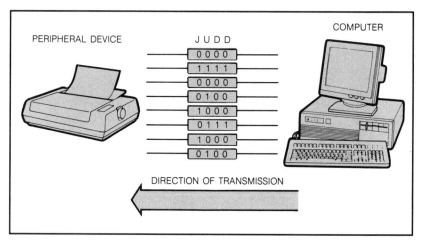

Figure 8.4: Parallel data transmission

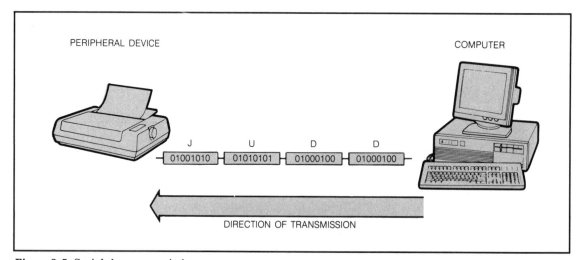

Figure 8.5: Serial data transmission

are restricted to certain reserved names, shown in Figure 8.6. DOS allows only three specific parallel device names (LPT1, LPT2, and LPT3) and four serial device names (COM1, COM2, COM3, and COM4). Versions of DOS earlier than 3.3 only allowed two serial device names, COM1 and COM2.

The additional device names in Figure 8.6, AUX and PRN, are called standard device names. They are used to communicate with the first connected serial and parallel ports, respectively. You can use these nonspecific device names if you don't want to be bothered with the details of which communications port is connected to your printer or device. Programs don't necessarily have to know which device is connected to which port. They can simply reference PRN, and the output will be routed to the first connected parallel port; or they can reference AUX, and the output will be routed to the first connected auxiliary communications (serial) port.

Keep in mind that you must purchase the actual hardware to make the proper connections. In other words, DOS may understand what it means to send data to a serial port called COM1, but you must have a serial connector on your system, and it must be connected to a serial device, or the request is meaningless.

Even if you have purchased various pieces of peripheral equipment and sufficient add-in boards to connect them, DOS may not be able to address all of them. For instance, if your setup is like that in Table 8.2, there are no more reserved names available if you decide

> Like the drive names in previous chapters (A, B, C, and so on), reserved device names should be followed by a colon in your commands. This lets DOS know when the device name ends and the sequence of parameter values begins.

> You can improve the flexibility of your system design by using PRN and AUX as port device names. AUX can refer to any one of the four serial ports, COM1 to COM4. Later, you can easily change your hardware connections without having to make any changes to your software references.

Figure 8.6: Reserved device names in DOS

DOS RESERVED NAME	DEFINITION	EXAMPLE CONNECTION
LPT1	First parallel port	Fast draft printer
LPT2	Second parallel port	Letter-quality printer
LPT3	Third parallel port	Laser printer
COM1	First serial port	Modem
COM2	Second serial port	Plotter
COM3	Third serial port	Mouse
COM4	Fourth serial port	Digitizer

Table 8.2: An example port configuration

to buy another serial device (perhaps an inexpensive networking alternative). In this case, you would have to buy some form of switch. You would need to connect the switch to one port (say, COM1) and then connect the two peripherals (the mouse and the modem, for example) to the switch.

> When you are using the same serial line for two purposes, one operation must wait for the other to finish. If you are plotting, you cannot throw the switch to activate the mouse until all the plotting data has been transmitted to the plotter. When you are using the mouse to control cursor movement and menu selections, you cannot switch over to the plotter for output until all mouse movements have been completed.

Once all this hardware has been connected, you still must exercise great care to ensure that your software will work. The key to this is to make sure that two or more devices connected to the same switch do not try to transmit data at the same time. Your first reaction may be that this isn't a complication you expect to run into very often. On the other hand, you may have a computer with only one serial port (COM1), and you might want to use a graphics package that requires a mouse for input and a plotter for output. In this case, short of buying another serial-port connector, you can run your software by using a switch for the two devices. You might not think that there will be any problem with both devices trying to use the same serial line simultaneously, but what actually happens is that you become impatient with the slowness of the plotter, and long to regain control of the computer while the plot progresses independently.

INITIALIZING DEVICES AND PORTS

Different peripheral devices, when connected to the computer, require special setup sequences. The MODE command permits you to initialize aspects of your printers and your serial-port devices, as well as to redirect output between parallel and serial ports, and even to control some features of your video display. Other capabilities of MODE for the support of foreign-language characters will be discussed in Chapter 10. Figure 8.7 depicts the four capabilities of the MODE command that you'll explore in this section.

In all four situations, the MODE command is invoked like any other disk-resident external DOS command. Simply typing MODE at the DOS prompt, preceded by any drive or path-name specification, will initiate the MODE operations. Assuming MODE is either in the current drive and directory or on the path you have specified, you would enter

MODE *Parameters*

Depending on what parameters you specify, one of the four versions of this command will be activated. The four major versions of this command almost act as four separate commands.

CONTROLLING THE PRINTER

An operation that is often desired by users is to turn on *compressed print*. Wide spreadsheets and database records are often hard to read when the number of characters per line exceeds the standard 80 characters. Most printers assume a normal default of 80 characters, because most programs generate data using an 80-column video screen. Printers also assume a default value of 6 lines per vertical inch, but you can control that as well.

This version of the MODE command assumes you are using the most common kind of printer: an EPSON MX series, an IBM graphics printer, or a compatible. Any other printer may require different control codes, making this DOS command useless to you.

Programs that can scroll left and right, like spreadsheets and database management programs, can generate more than 80 columns on a line. The following version of MODE gives you a simple way to instruct DOS to send the printer the necessary control codes requesting it to squeeze up to 132 characters on a line, or to squeeze up to 8 lines of output per vertical inch on the paper. The general form of this MODE command is

MODE *PrinterPort CharsPerLine LinesPerInch*

Filling in the parameters with values, you could issue the following command to initialize the printer port to LPT1, the characters per

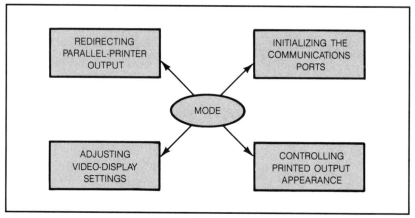

Figure 8.7: Four capabilities of the MODE command

line to 132, and the lines per inch to 8:

MODE LPT1: 132, 8

Figure 8.8 demonstrates what a sample text file would look like if it was printed after this command was executed. Figures 8.9 through 8.11 show the other variations on the two parameters controlling characters per line and lines per inch.

With these MODE commands for compressed print, DOS will respond to your command entry with statements similar to the following:

> **LPT1: not rerouted**
> **LPT1: set for 132**
> **Printer lines per inch set**
> **No retry on parallel printer time-out**

The first and fourth lines of these DOS messages refer to other versions of the MODE command, which you'll see shortly. The second and third lines indicate the horizontal and vertical printer settings, respectively.

Dot-matrix printers make the horizontal compression occur by printing the dots closer together. Letter-quality printers create the same effect by leaving less space between characters. Compressing the print on letter-quality printers usually requires you to change the print wheel or thimble so the resulting squeezed printout is readable.

The MODE command has limited capability for sending control codes to printers. Some applications like Lotus 1-2-3 and Framework II offer you the convenience of sending control codes directly to a printer. In fact, you can use EDLIN or your own word processor to include a sequence of control codes in a file (say, CTRLCODE.TXT), and then send the file and the control codes directly to a printer with the simple instruction COPY CTRLCODE.TXT PRN.

```
↑   This line and the next are limited to 80 characters or less.
|   ........10........20........30........40........50........60........70........80
|   This next line typifies wide spreadsheet rows or data base records (and 'wraps around' in 80 column mode)
1"  ........10........20........30........40........50........60........70........80........90........100.......120.......132..
|   These next four lines take up 1/2" vertically
|   when lines per inch (LPI) is set to 8,
|   and take up 2/3" when LPI = 6,
↓   regardless of how the characters per line is set.
```

Figure 8.8: Output of MODE LPT1: 132,8

```
↑   This line and the next are limited to 80 characters or less.
|   ........10........20........30........40........50........60........70........80
|   This next line typifies wide spreadsheet rows or data base records (and 'wraps a
1"  round' in 80 column mode)
|   ........10........20........30........40........50........60........70........80
↓   ........90.......100.......120.......132..
    These next four lines take up 1/2" vertically
    when lines per inch (LPI) is set to 8,
    and take up 2/3" when LPI = 6,
    regardless of how the characters per line is set.
```

Figure 8.9: Output of MODE LPT1: 80,6 (the DOS default)

```
↑   This line and the next are limited to 80 characters or less.
|   ........10........20........30........40........50........60........70........80
|   This next line typifies wide spreadsheet rows or data base records (and 'wraps around' in 80 column mode)
1"  ........10........20........30........40........50........60........70........80........90........100.......120.......132..
|   These next four lines take up 1/2" vertically
|   when lines per inch (LPI) is set to 8,
↓   and take up 2/3" when LPI = 6,
    regardless of how the characters per line is set.
```

Figure 8.10: Output of MODE LPT1: 132,6

```
↑   This line and the next are limited to 80 characters or less.
|   ........10........20........30........40........50........60........70........80
|   This next line typifies wide spreadsheet rows or data base records (and 'wraps a
1"  round' in 80 column mode)
|   ........10........20........30........40........50........60........70........80
|   ........90.......100.......120.......132..
↓   These next four lines take up 1/2" vertically
    when lines per inch (LPI) is set to 8,
    and take up 2/3" when LPI = 6,
    regardless of how the characters per line is set.
```

Figure 8.11: Output of MODE LPT1: 80,8

INITIALIZING THE SERIAL COMMUNICATIONS PORT

Synchronization is a difficult problem when serial devices are connected to computers. For example, if a computer sends data out to the serial port at a rate of 1200 bits per second, any printer connected

Don't bother initially with this version of the MODE command; follow the initialization instructions in your software program's manual or in your serial device's instruction book. This usually is all you need for success—only if this fails will you need to understand these MODE parameters more fully.

to that port must be set (by means of hardware switches or software initialization) to receive this information at the same rate. This requirement also works in reverse.

A second version of the MODE command allows you to correctly set a number of parameters for this and other aspects of serial communications. The general form of this MODE command is

> MODE *SerialPort BaudRate, Parity, DataBits, StopBits, DeviceType*

The parameters have the following meanings:

- *SerialPort* indicates which one of the four possible peripheral connectors is being used by DOS for a particular device.

- *BaudRate* sets the speed at which data bits will be transmitted through the serial port.

- *Parity* represents the number of binary 1's, if any, that are used in a data transmission; this is used for error detection.

- *DataBits* specifies the number of bits used to represent actual transmitted data.

- *StopBits* represents the one or two bits used at the end of the data bits to indicate that end.

- *DeviceType* indicates whether or not the port is being used by a serial printer.

Table 8.3 contains the allowable values for these parameters.

As an example, the following command issued at the DOS prompt would set the second serial port to transmit at 1200 baud, with no parity, using eight data bits with one stop bit:

> MODE COM2: 1200, N, 8, 1, P

The last parameter value, P, requests that DOS automatically try again to send data to a busy communications port. This is necessary when the first request is met by a control signal indicating that the device is still busy processing the last transmission. The P value is particularly useful with printers, which process data significantly slower than the computer's central processing unit.

PARAMETER	POSSIBLE VALUES
SerialPort	COM1, COM2, COM3, or COM4
BaudRate	110, 150, 300, 600, 1200, 2400, 4800, 9600, or 19200
Parity	N, O, or E (none, odd, or even)
DataBits	7 or 8
StopBits	1 or 2
DeviceType	P (if a serial printer); otherwise blank

Table 8.3: Allowable parameter values for serial communications

This version of the MODE command is disk-resident, but it does require that a permanent part of physical memory be reserved for its processing and buffering chores. This means that when you run the command for the first time, it will take up a small additional amount of memory, extending the memory requirements of your DOS's memory-resident portion. A message to that effect is issued by DOS at the same time as confirmation is made of the port settings:

```
Resident portion of MODE loaded
COM2: 1200,n,8,1,p
```

Normally, serial devices are accompanied by instruction manuals that describe the required settings. The best advice is to follow scrupulously the suggested settings for connection. Switches often have to be set on or in the printer, as well as on the board that is controlling your serial port itself. In addition, the software product you are using might need to be initialized as well, since it may send its data directly to the port.

All of these locations and parameters are opportunities for error or frustration in connecting serial devices to computers. Unfortunately, there is no consistent standard for serial communications as there is for parallel communications. You must determine the characteristics of your serial device and issue the proper MODE command *before* using the port in any way. Good luck!

CONNECTING A SERIAL PRINTER TO A COM PORT

In the specific case where the serial device you have connected to a COM port is a printer, an additional version of the MODE command is required. Printed output usually goes to a PRN device (usually a parallel port like LPT1), so you must redirect that output to a COM port with the command

MODE LPT*Number:* = COM*Number*

The *Number* parameter should hold the specific number of your chosen port.

Assuming that you have first initialized the communications parameters for the port so that the device and the CPU are synchronized, as in the last section, you can redirect the LPT1 port to the COM2 port with

MODE LPT1: = COM2

DOS will confirm the redirection for all succeeding print output requests with the following:

LPT1: rerouted to COM2:

CONTROLLING THE MODE OF THE VIDEO DISPLAY

Certain video characteristics can be controlled with the final version of the MODE command. This version is used most often when you purchase nonstandard equipment and when you connect multiple monitors to your computer. The command is used to tell DOS which monitor is receiving the video-display request; it also allows you to adjust the video image in a horizontal direction.

The command has at most three parameters, of which the first is the most often used:

MODE *VideoType, Direction, TestPattern*

The three parameters can take on the values shown in Table 8.4.

PARAMETER	POSSIBLE VALUES
VideoType	MONO (for IBM monochrome display)
	CO80 (for color 80-column display)
	CO40 (for color 40-column display)
	BW80 (for black-and-white, 80-column display; this disables color on a normal color monitor)
	BW40 (for black-and-white, 40-column display)
	80 (adjusts to 80-column display; does not change the color status)
	40 (adjusts to 40-column display; does not change the color status)
Direction	R or L (for right or left)
TestPattern	T (if a test pattern is to be shown)

Table 8.4: Video-display values for MODE parameters

The simplest form of this version of the MODE command only involves the *VideoType* parameter. Setting the display mode to 40 or 80 characters is as simple as entering

MODE 80

or

MODE 40

80-column mode is the standard for business applications, although some games reset the mode to 40 columns. Naturally, 40-column mode produces larger, more legible characters on the video monitor. Figures 8.12 and 8.13 demonstrate the same directory display in 80- and 40-column modes.

Entering a parameter value of 40 or 80 for *VideoType* will not affect the current status of the monitor's color. Assuming the monitor is controlled by a CGA (color graphics adapter) or an EGA (extended graphics adapter), you can explicitly enable or disable color by preceding the column number by CO (to enable color) or BW (to disable color, leaving a black-and-white image). If you have an IBM mono-chrome display, the proper parameter value is MONO. In fact, if your system has both a monochrome *and* a color graphics monitor, you can switch output between them by simply entering

MODE MONO

```
C>DIR

 Volume in drive C is ROBBINS
 Directory of  C:\UTILITY\XENO

 .              <DIR>       5-02-86   1:17p
 ..             <DIR>       5-02-86   1:17p
 XENOCOPY EXE   83968       8-17-87   6:18p
 README          5067       8-21-87  12:35p
 XDEF     OPT    1221       8-25-87  10:06a
 SYBEX    OPT    1221       8-25-87  10:07a
         6 File(s)    634880 bytes free

 C>_
```

Figure 8.12: Directory display after a MODE 80 command

```
C>DIR

 Volume in drive C is ROBBINS
 Directory of  C:\UTILITY\XENO

 .              <DIR>       5-02-86   1:17p
 ..             <DIR>       5-02-86   1:17p
 XENOCOPY EXE   83968       8-17-87   6:18p
 README          5067       8-21-87  12:35p
 XDEF     OPT    1221       8-25-87  10:06a
 SYBEX    OPT    1221       8-25-87  10:07a
         6 File(s)    634880 bytes free

 C>_
```

Figure 8.13: Directory display after a MODE 40 command

to switch output to the monochrome monitor, or

MODE CO80

to switch output to the color monitor, using 80 columns with color enabled.

Some monitors need a certain amount of horizontal adjustment. You may not need to adjust yours very often, but if you do, the *Direction* and *TestPattern* parameters will come in hardy. You can shift the display to the right or to the left by entering an R or an L as the *Direction* parameter. In either case, you can display a test pattern on the screen to help with the adjustments by entering a T as the *TestPattern* parameter. Entering

MODE 80, L, T

produces the screen shown in Figure 8.14.

If you answer N (for No) to the question on seeing the rightmost 9, DOS will shift the entire screen image to the left by one character (if the display mode is 40 columns) or by two characters (if it is 80 columns). You will then be asked the same question, and you can shift the display until all 80 characters are visible—when the rightmost 9 can be seen.

Figure 8.14: Shifting the video image left with MODE

SUMMARY

This chapter covered important communications aspects of DOS. Output from your system is fundamental to effectiveness, and in this chapter, you learned quite a bit about data transfer and system output in general. Here is a brief review:

- Files and hardware devices share certain similarities, which permits you to use them interchangeably in a number of commands.

- Devices communicate with the central processing unit of your computer in one of two ways: by parallel or serial data transmission. Parallel communications send data bits out to a device on separate wires simultaneously. Serial communications send the same data bits out to a device on a single wire successively, using additional control characters and bits to help distinguish when and where the transmission and characters begin and end.

- Each bit of magnetic memory—data bit—can be either energized with a voltage or not energized, with a value of 1 or 0, respectively. Eight bits make up the proverbial byte, and each byte can represent up to 256 different codes. These codes can represent either standard letters, numbers, and punctuation, or special control codes, foreign-language characters, and graphics characters.

- DOS can send and receive bytes of information to and from three parallel devices connected to hardware ports. These devices and their parts are addressed by programs as LPT1, LPT2, and LPT3.

- DOS 3.3 also can send data to and accept data from as many as four separate devices connected to four communications ports. These serial ports are addressed by the names COM1, COM2, COM3, and COM4. Earlier versions of DOS only allowed the first two COM ports to be referenced.

- The MODE command is the principal DOS command for controlling serial communications. It handles both the setup and status of certain serial and parallel output devices. It is also required to properly initialize the communications between a computer and a printer or plotter. Several parameters defining the command must be carefully set in order to synchronize the CPU and the device, or the data transfer may not work at all. The parameters include the baud rate, the parity of the transmission, the number of data bits and stop bits, and the type of device.

- Other versions of the MODE command allow you to control multiple display monitors, which can be either color or black-and-white and can display either 40 or 80 columns across.

By now you've certainly learned many new things about DOS and have no doubt begun to use your disk and hardware capabilities more efficiently. This is a good time to step back and consider the work invested in your system. The next chapter emphasizes the protection of this investment—it shows you how to make copies of any and all of your important files.

BACKUPS AND RESTORATIONS

CHAPTER *9*

ONE OF THE DISADVANTAGES OF HARD DISKS IS THAT
when and if they fail, or crash, all the information stored on them can
be lost. Much more is at stake than just one floppy diskette's worth of
contents. Back up your hard disk regularly or run the constant risk of
losing your data!

Of course, you can also rewrite backed-up versions of files back
onto your hard disk; this is usually done when the hard-disk version
has been deleted, destroyed, or corrupted. You may never need to
restore a file, but your backup files will provide you with some inexpensive protection against either hardware or software failure.

This chapter describes in depth how to protect your programs—
and more importantly, your data—from loss due to operator error or
hardware failure. However, you must remember to back up your
files on a regular basis to keep the backup floppy diskettes up-to-date
with the changes you've made on your hard disk. Depending on how
frequently you generate new data files or update old ones, you may
want to back up your disk every week or every month (or more or less
frequently).

In fact, other than the regular backups you are going to make,
there are three times when you should back up your hard disk:

1. Your computer is going to be moved. Especially if your computer will be traveling long distances in airplane cargo holds
   or in shipper's trucks, you should back up your data before
   the trip. Your hard disk may not survive the physical handling (or occasional abuse).

Experience seems to
be the best teacher
in all things, and most
people who back up files
regularly do so because
they have experienced an
uncomfortable loss of
data at some point. The
more data they lost, the
more frequently they now
back up.

2. You are running out of space on your hard disk, and you decide to take an hour or two to delete some files, consolidate some directories, and create new branches in your directory tree since you now feel much more comfortable using the DOS directory structure. With such a massive project, you should protect yourself against your own enthusiasm and fatigue by doing a backup.

3. You are going to run a fragmentation elimination program like Hard Disk Tuneup. You will learn more in Chapter 17 about how programs like this can reorganize all the files on your disk, providing improved system performance afterwards. During the reorganization, your entire hard-disk contents are liable to loss in the event of a power failure. Do a complete disk backup just prior to running such a program.

SPECIAL COMMANDS FOR YOUR DISKS

If you're using a dual-diskette system, you can easily use DISKCOPY, COPY, or XCOPY to back up diskette files onto another diskette. Protecting yourself from the major trauma of losing an entire hard disk, however, requires more effort than that. DISKCOPY is designed for diskette copies, and the COPY and XCOPY commands have a fundamental weakness: the destination for your copied files is limited to what can be stored on that one drive. If the directory you're in contains more files than can fit on one destination diskette, or even if it contains one extremely large file that exceeds the capacity of the backup floppy, the COPY and XCOPY commands simply can't handle the job.

In order to allow you to back up files onto a series of floppy diskettes or another fixed (hard) disk, DOS provides a special command called BACKUP. With BACKUP you can make copies of the files on any of your disks. This command is usually used to back up the files from a hard disk and spread them, if necessary, over a series of floppy diskettes.

The BACKUP command does not work for copy-protected diskettes. As you will learn in Chapter 17, utility programs like COPY II PC allow you to back up diskettes that are copy-protected.

HOW BACKUP FILES ARE STORED

The files placed on a diskette by the BACKUP command are not stored as standard DOS files. Figure 9.1 shows the directory listing of the original files from the hard disk. Figure 9.2 shows the directory listing of the first backup diskette in drive A after the backup procedure has been completed. Compare these two figures. You'll see that

```
     Volume in drive C is ROBBINS
     Directory of  C:\DBASE\ADMIN

   DB3BOOK   PRG      449  11-26-86    2:41a
   START     PRG     2532  11-26-86    2:21a
   INVOICE   PRG     3010   3-12-86    7:40a
   CERTIF    PRG     1981  11-26-86    2:38a
   RECOMM1   PRG      463  11-26-86    2:40a
   RECOMM2   PRG      422  11-26-86    2:42a
   PAYROLL   PRG     4224   4-28-86   12:57p
   PAYROLL2  PRG     1792   3-12-86    9:17p
   EXPERT    PRG     2432  10-24-85    6:48p
   EXPERT1   PRG     2146   6-13-85    9:57p
   EXPERT2   PRG     2944  10-18-85    8:11p
   EXPERT3   PRG     3689  10-25-85   10:59a
   EXPERT4   PRG     2176   7-30-86    9:08p
   MESSAGE   PRG     1280   4-09-85    3:41p
   LEDGER    PRG     2688  11-26-86   10:53a
   INVOICE2  PRG     3200  11-26-86   11:16a
   BOOKS2    PRG     2048  11-26-86   11:20a
   DISKPREP  PRG      905  11-26-86    2:00a
          18 File(s)    880640 bytes free

   C>_
```

Figure 9.1: Directory of original files before backup

```
   C>DIR A:

     Volume in drive A is BACKUP  001
     Directory of  A:\

   BACKUP   001    38381   7-09-87   10:23a
   CONTROL  001      821   7-09-87   10:23a
          2 File(s)    322560 bytes free

   C>_
```

Figure 9.2: First backup diskette after completion

your original files have not been backed up in their original format.

Figure 9.3 shows you the manner in which your files have been backed up. Your original files have been combined efficiently into one single file, called BACKUP.001, which contains only the original data. A separate control file, called CONTROL.001, contains the actual file names and their lengths, as well as the source directory from which these files were obtained. You could add up the file lengths seen in Figure 9.3 to verify that BACKUP.001 has efficiently combined all the bytes from each of the original files.

This procedure is new with DOS 3.3. If you have an earlier DOS version, your backup diskette will be quite different. It will have *file versions* (not replicas) of each of your original files, as well as an additional entry in the directory listing called BACKUP.@@@, with a length of 128 bytes. If you have a disk with this entry, it indicates that the files stored on that disk have been put there with an earlier DOS version of the BACKUP command.

Files stored with earlier versions of BACKUP *appear* to be independently accessible, but they cannot be read meaningfully with any of DOS's other commands, like the COPY command. In earlier versions of DOS, BACKUP changes the actual file contents, whereas in Version 3.3, it compacts the files into one file. You can only use these

The DOS 3.3 version of BACKUP is faster than previous versions, while requiring less disk space to store the original files. The primary reason for this is that each file does not waste extra disk cluster space during the storage process. The compaction technique uses both space and time more efficiently.

Figure 9.3: The BACKUP command compacts files

files again by restoring them to their original condition with the
RESTORE command.

MAKING BACKUP
COPIES OF YOUR FILES

You can back up a hard disk either onto diskettes or onto another
hard disk. When you back up a hard disk onto diskettes, you also
need to format enough diskettes before you begin. If you are using
DOS 3.3, you will be able to format them during the backup process.
If you are using an earlier version of DOS, however, you should prepare in advance enough formatted destination diskettes to hold all of
your data, since you cannot back up onto unformatted disks. (Only
the DISKCOPY command can do that.) You will have to stop the
backup process (or borrow someone else's computer) if you run out
of formatted disks in the middle of backing up your files.

Backing up files from one hard disk to another is much faster than
backing them up onto a collection of diskettes. It is also easier, since
you don't have to insert and remove successive diskettes; the backup
process between hard disks can proceed unattended.

Before you start backing up files, you should learn how to use the
DOS VERIFY command. VERIFY controls the degree of error
checking performed by DOS after all disk write operations. When
you execute the command

VERIFY ON

the verification mode is turned on. Each disk write will be followed by
a confirmation procedure verifying that the data just written can be
read without error. It is a good idea to execute this command just
prior to running a backup; it increases the likelihood that your
backup files will be written accurately. Although data errors occur
infrequently, a backup file is the worst place for such an error to
occur. After your backup operation, you can execute VERIFY OFF
at the DOS prompt to restore normal read/write operations. When
the verification mode is on, overall DOS operations are significantly
slowed down.

When you format a
diskette for use
during the backup pro-
cess, it is not necessary to
use the /S switch. In fact,
it is inadvisable: using /S
will make less space
available for the backup
files on floppy diskettes.

If your system has
an extra hard disk
for backup, make sure
that it has enough space
to hold all the backup
files. If it doesn't, the
entire process will terminate, and you'll have to
make space on the
backup disk by deleting
some files.

BACKING UP A COMPLETE DIRECTORY

The general form of the BACKUP command has two parameters:

> BACKUP *SourceFile(s) DestinationDrive*

SourceFile(s) is the standard path name plus any specific file names you wish to select for backup. *DestinationDrive* is the letter identifier of the disk drive that will receive the file copies.

Suppose that you wanted to back up all the files in your DBASE\ADMIN directory. You would simply specify the name of the desired directory as the first parameter. When you do not specify any specific files, DOS selects and copies all files in the directory to the backup drive (A).

> BACKUP C:\DBASE\ADMIN A:

DOS displays the message

> Insert backup diskette 01 in drive A:
>
> Warning! Files in the target drive
> A:\ root directory will be erased
> Strike any key when ready

This warning gives you a chance to verify that you put the correct diskette into drive A, before DOS overwrites everything on it. Presumably, you are placing a blank diskette into the destination drive to receive the source files. You could, of course, be reusing a previously used diskette containing files you don't mind writing over.

Pressing Return at this point will begin the backup process. All the files in the named directory will now be copied over to your backup diskette (or your backup hard disk, if your destination drive is another hard disk). DOS will list all the files in this directory as they are being backed up to the specified disk drive.

BACKING UP A PARTIAL DIRECTORY

You can also perform selective backups—for example, backing up only the .PRG files from the DBASE\ADMIN directory. Simply specify the names of the files you wish to back up. To back up all .PRG files in the DBASE\ADMIN directory, enter

BACKUP C:\DBASE\ADMIN*.PRG A:

As always, DOS will list the files while it writes the backup copies (see Figure 9.4). You *must* enter the leading drive identifier (in this example, C:). Otherwise, DOS will display the message "Invalid drive specification."

If DOS runs out of room on your first diskette, you will be prompted like this:

Insert backup diskette 02 in drive A:

Warning! Files in the target drive
A:\ root directory will be erased
Strike any key when ready

DOS will continue to copy backup versions of your files onto this second diskette. The process will continue with additional diskettes, as necessary, until all your requested files have been copied.

Files created by the BACKUP command may not be deleted; they are created with an attribute indicating that they are read-only, which means that you cannot erase them (see the ATTRIB command in Chapter 16). In order to regain the disk space on this diskette, you will have to reformat it with the FORMAT command.

```
    Strike any key when ready

    *** Backing up files to drive A: ***
    Diskette Number: 01

    \DBASE\ADMIN\DB3BOOK.PRG
    \DBASE\ADMIN\START.PRG
    \DBASE\ADMIN\INVOICE.PRG
    \DBASE\ADMIN\CERTIF.PRG
    \DBASE\ADMIN\RECOMM1.PRG
    \DBASE\ADMIN\RECOMM2.PRG
    \DBASE\ADMIN\PAYROLL.PRG
    \DBASE\ADMIN\PAYROLL2.PRG
    \DBASE\ADMIN\EXPERT.PRG
    \DBASE\ADMIN\EXPERT1.PRG
    \DBASE\ADMIN\EXPERT2.PRG
    \DBASE\ADMIN\EXPERT3.PRG
    \DBASE\ADMIN\EXPERT4.PRG
    \DBASE\ADMIN\MESSAGE.PRG
    \DBASE\ADMIN\LEDGER.PRG
    \DBASE\ADMIN\INVOICE2.PRG
    \DBASE\ADMIN\BOOKS2.PRG
    \DBASE\ADMIN\DISKPREP.PRG

    C>_
```

Figure 9.4: DOS lists file names as files are backed up

OTHER TYPES OF BACKUP PROCESSING

You may often need to do more than back up to a blank diskette all or some of the files in a DOS directory. For example, you might want to add additional files to a backup set to maintain some grouping and organization in your backups. You might also want to include files in the directory tree *below* the main directory you've just specified. Then again, you might want to combine these possibilities with selection criteria that go beyond simple wild-card specifications. You might want to back up files that have changed since your last backup, and not want to spend time backing up unchanged files when they are already on a perfectly good backup disk. Or, you might want to back up only those files created or modified since a certain date or even after a certain time on a certain day.

All of these options can be invoked by using one or more of the DOS switches for the BACKUP command (see Table 9.1). These switches are described in the following sections. You will concentrate in this chapter on the most important ones; the others are presented more fully in Part V, the command-reference section of this book.

ADDING FILES TO AN EXISTING BACKUP

The /A switch tells DOS not to erase (write over) any existing files stored on the floppy diskette, but to add the newly backed-up files to

⊙ If you already know how to use some advanced commands like SUBST, JOIN, APPEND, or ASSIGN (see Chapter 16), do not have these commands active when you issue the BACKUP command. They're difficult enough to use properly; it would not be possible for DOS to later restore files properly if these commands were active in a different way when you ran the BACKUP command.

SWITCH	RESULT
/A	Adds files to a backup disk
/S	Backs up subdirectories
/M	Backs up modified files only
/D	Backs up files by date
/T	Backs up files by time on the date specified by /D
/F	Formats the destination diskette if necessary
/L	Creates a log file for the files contained in the compacted backup file

Table 9.1: Switches for the BACKUP command

that disk. For example, Figure 9.5 shows the selective file backup of all the files in the CHAP07 subdirectory. The resulting backup-diskette directory would look like the one in Figure 9.6, with BACKUP.001 and CONTROL.001 files.

At some point, you might also want to back up the files in another directory (in this example, the CHAP09 directory). Although you could back them up to a separate diskette, you might logically want to

```
C>BACKUP C:\PROGRAMS\FW\CHAP07 A:

Insert backup diskette 01 in drive A:

Warning! Files in the target drive
A:\ root directory will be erased
Strike any key when ready

*** Backing up files to drive A: ***
Diskette Number: 01

\PROGRAMS\FW\CHAP07\CHAP07.FW2
\PROGRAMS\FW\CHAP07\FIG7-14.CAP
\PROGRAMS\FW\CHAP07\FIG7-15.CAP
\PROGRAMS\FW\CHAP07\FIG7-16.CAP
\PROGRAMS\FW\CHAP07\SAMPLE.DTA
\PROGRAMS\FW\CHAP07\TBL7-1.TXT
\PROGRAMS\FW\CHAP07\TBL7-2.TXT
\PROGRAMS\FW\CHAP07\TBL7-3.TXT
\PROGRAMS\FW\CHAP07\TBL7-4.TXT
\PROGRAMS\FW\CHAP07\PART-3.FW2
\PROGRAMS\FW\CHAP07\TOC7.TXT

C>_
```

Figure 9.5: Backup requiring only a partial diskette

```
C>DIR A:

 Volume in drive A is BACKUP   001
 Directory of  A:\

BACKUP   001    52050   7-09-87  12:23p
CONTROL  001      583   7-09-87  12:23p
        2 File(s)    309248 bytes free

C>_
```

Figure 9.6: Resultant directory listing after backup

add these additional files to the same backup set. You could do this—even if more than one diskette is required—by using the /A switch. Figure 9.7 shows the CHAP09 directory and the four files within it. It also shows the necessary form of the BACKUP command:

BACKUP C:\PROGRAMS\FW\CHAP09 A: /A

This adds the new files to the BACKUP.001 file on the diskette in drive A. It also updates the CONTROL.001 file with information about the newly added files. Figure 9.8 portrays this process. Compare it to the original portrayal in Figure 9.3.

The resulting backup diskette (see Figure 9.9) now contains all the originally backed-up files, as well as the newly added ones. Notice the increase in size of the two files. As before, this increase represents the augmentation of the BACKUP.001 file with the contents of the four CHAP09 files, and the addition of information about the files to the CONTROL.001 file.

If the existing backup required multiple diskettes, you would be prompted to insert the last backup diskette before the actual backup copies would be written to the backup set:

Insert last backup diskette in drive A:
Strike any key when ready

```
C>BACKUP C:\PROGRAMS\FW\CHAP09 A: /A

Insert last backup diskette in drive A:
Strike any key when ready

*** Backing up files to drive A: ***
Diskette Number: 01

\PROGRAMS\FW\CHAP09\TBL9-1.TXT
\PROGRAMS\FW\CHAP09\FIG9-1.CAP
\PROGRAMS\FW\CHAP09\FIG9-14.TXT
\PROGRAMS\FW\CHAP09\CHAP09.FW2

C>_
```

Figure 9.7: Adding files to an existing backup set

Let's put some of these skills to work on your system. First, select two separate sets of files on your disk that need to be backed up. Try choosing files in two separate but important directories. Next, prepare several formatted diskettes to receive your selected files.

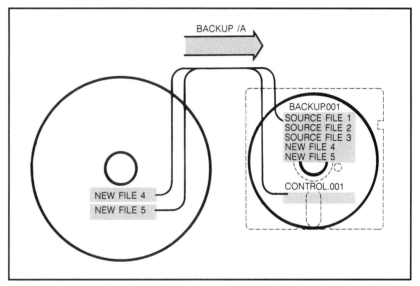

Figure 9.8: Adding files updates BACKUP and CONTROL files

```
C>DIR A:

 Volume in drive A is BACKUP  ØØ1
 Directory of  A:\

BACKUP   ØØ1    77655   7-Ø9-87  12:13p
CONTROL  ØØ1      789   7-Ø9-87  12:13p
        2 File(s)    283648 bytes free

C>_
```

Figure 9.9: Augmented disk directory after successive backups

DOS 3.3 makes it easy for you to back up a variable amount of file information. If you add an /F switch to a BACKUP command, DOS will automatically format any diskette being used that is not already formatted. This relieves you from the obligations of calculating how many diskettes you'll need and preparing sufficient formatted diskettes. Using this switch requires that the FORMAT.COM command file be available either in the current default directory or somewhere along the DOS path.

In order to decide how many diskettes you need, use the DIR command to display the names of all the files you plan to back up. Add up all the file sizes for your selected diskettes, and then divide by the number of bytes on each of your backup diskettes. This number represents how many diskettes you'll need. For example, if you were backing up onto double-density, double-sided diskettes (360K), your calculations might go like this:

1. Total size of all selected files: 3Mb

2. Number of bytes per diskette: 360K

3. 3,000,000 divided by 360,000: 9 diskettes

This calculation is only approximate for two reasons. First, 360K is really not 360,000 bytes. (Since a kilobyte equals 1024 bytes, 360K equals 360 × 1024, or 368,640 bytes.) The approximation is close enough, however, since the CONTROL.001 file takes up a variable number of bytes, depending largely on how many files are backed up. Performing the same type of calculation for the other types of diskettes supported by DOS 3.3 would give the results seen in Table 9.2.

Once you have calculated the correct number of diskettes and formatted them, issue the correct BACKUP command to back up all

DESCRIPTION	CAPACITY	REQUIRED DISKETTES TO BACK UP 10M
5¼" single-sided	160K	63
5¼" single-sided	180K	56
5¼" double-sided	320K	32
5¼" double-sided	360K	28
5¼" high-capacity	1.2Mb	9
3½" double-sided	720K	14
3½" double-sided	1.44Mb	7

Table 9.2: Calculating the number of required backup diskettes

the files in your first selected directory. Then issue a second BACKUP command to append the files from the second directory you chose onto the first backup-diskette set. Use the /A switch.

Finally, issue one or more DIR commands for the backup diskettes to verify that all the original files were successfully copied. You'll have to add up the sizes of the original files to be sure of the backup diskette's completeness.

BACKING UP SUBDIRECTORIES

The /S switch tells DOS to copy the files contained in any sub-directories of the directory being backed up. This switch is extremely powerful with the BACKUP command, on par with the ability of the XCOPY command to move automatically through the directory tree structure. For example, if you started the backup in the root directory (C:\) and you used the /S option:

    BACKUP C:\ A: /S

DOS would attempt to back up the entire hard disk.

The /S switch tells DOS first to back up all data and program files in the root directory and then to go to each subdirectory in the root. DOS backs up all files in each subdirectory and then proceeds to do the same for each subdirectory of that subdirectory.

If you wanted to back up just a portion of your hard-disk tree structure, you would just specify the main branch to begin with. Assuming a tree structure like the one in Figure 9.10, you could back up all the files in the DBASE branch by entering

    BACKUP C:\DBASE A: /S

DOS would first back up the files in the DBASE directory. Then it would proceed to the next directory in that portion of the tree (DB3PLUS) and copy the files located there. It would then continue on through each of the other subdirectories (CLASSES and ADMIN) in the tree structure, copying all the files in them. DOS will prompt you to enter additional backup diskettes as each one fills up.

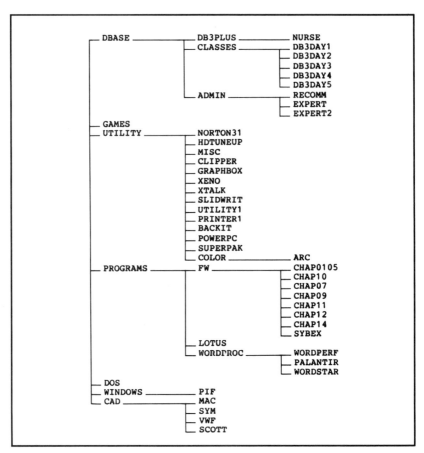

Figure 9.10: Sample directory structure

PERFORMING MULTIPLE OPERATIONS WITH ONE COMMAND

As in most DOS commands, multiple switches can be used simultaneously as long as it makes sense to do so. The /A and /S switches can work together for some useful purposes. You might be interested in locating and backing up all the BASIC program files (*.BAS) on your entire disk. Using the /S switch will allow the BACKUP command to look successively into each subdirectory you specify.

The following command will locate and back up all .BAS files anywhere on the disk:

```
BACKUP C:\*.BAS A: /S
```

This works because you've specified the root directory with which to begin (C:\), the wild card for finding BASIC files only (*.BAS), and the subdirectory search switch (/S).

As you know, changing the starting directory can limit the portion of the directory tree that is searched. The following command will find only .BAS files located in the UTILITY subdirectory and in all subdirectories located below it in the directory structure (see Figure 9.11):

BACKUP C:\UTILITY*.BAS A: /S

The addition of an /A switch to the preceding examples will add all the files found to the existing backup disk:

BACKUP C:\UTILITY*.BAS A: /S /A

BACKING UP MODIFIED OR NEW FILES

The /M option tells DOS to back up only files that have not already been backed up or that have been modified since the last backup. DOS is able to do this because it marks each file on the disk as it is backed up. This mark—actually a bit stored by DOS for every file—is called the *archive bit.* Whenever a file is modified or a new file is created, DOS changes the mark to indicate that the file will need to be backed up later. This archiving feature allows the backup process to skip files that have not been changed since the last backup. When any file is newly created in DOS, its archive bit is set to indicate that it should be treated like any other existing file that has undergone some changes.

As an example, suppose that you have a GAMES directory in which you keep your children's favorite computer games. Naturally, you need to safeguard your sanity in the event of a disk crash. You may suffer more if all these games are lost than you would if your business files were lost. Of course, neither situation will faze you if you've been conscientiously backing up your files.

Assume that you recently backed up all your files in this example directory. Your children then bring home two new games, HEADROOM.COM and MADMAX.EXE. You can add these to your existing GAMES backup set with the /M and /A switches (see Figure 9.12). The /A switch tells DOS to add all selected files to an existing

```
C>BACKUP C:\UTILITY\*.BAS A: /S

Insert backup diskette 01 in drive A:

Warning! Files in the target drive
A:\ root directory will be erased
Strike any key when ready

*** Backing up files to drive A: ***
Diskette Number: 01

\UTILITY\MISC\POUNDS.BAS
\UTILITY\MISC\TREETOP.BAS
\UTILITY\MISC\OKIDATA.BAS
\UTILITY\BASMAIN\PARKIT.BAS
\UTILITY\BASMAIN\MENUONE.BAS
\UTILITY\BASMAIN\GAMESMNU.BAS

C>_
```

Figure 9.11: Subdirectory search for files to add to backup

```
C>BACKUP C:\GAMES  A:  /M /A

Insert last backup diskette in drive A:
Strike any key when ready

*** Backing up files to drive A: ***
Diskette Number: 01

\GAMES\MADMAX.EXE
\GAMES\HEADROOM.EXE

C>BACKUP C:\GAMES  A:  /M /A

Warning! No files were found to back up

C>_
```

Figure 9.12: Backing up recently created or modified files

backup, while the /M switch selects only the two new files from the much larger collection of unchanged files.

Immediately attempting to back up the very same files again would result in a message stating that no files were found to back up. This is because the archive bit was changed to indicate that the two files had already been backed up. Figure 9.12 also demonstrates this situation.

BACKING UP BY DATE AND TIME

DOS allows you to specify by date, and by time on that date, the files to be backed up. When you enter a date, DOS will back up only files that possess the same date or a more recent date.

Let's look at an example. In the word-processing directory named PALANTIR, there are 37 files (see Figure 9.13). Some of these are the word processor's system files, some are old document files, and others are more recent work. Assume that all the files dated earlier than February 4, 1987, are either on backup disks or on the original system disks. You can selectively back up only the 11 files created in this directory since February 4 by using the /D switch:

> **BACKUP C:\PROGRAMS\WORDPROC\PALANTIR A:**
> **/D:2/4/87**

As usual, the first argument selects the directory or the set of desired files, the second argument indicates the destination drive, and the final entry on the line is the switch (see Figure 9.14). Notice that the /D switch is followed by a colon, which is followed immediately by the specific date on or after which you want the new and updated files to be selected for backup.

CREATING A LOG FILE
OF THE FILES BACKED UP

Since all the files you back up are compacted into a single backup file, it's a good idea to simultaneously ask DOS to create a log file for you. This file will store the date and time of the backup, as well as the full path and file name of each backed-up file. It will have the extension .LOG. Also, DOS will indicate which of the possible backup diskettes each particular file was stored on.

To use this feature you need to add another switch to your BACKUP command. The /L switch alone will cause DOS to create the log file under the name BACKUP.LOG; it will store this file in the root directory of your source drive. If you would like to give the log file another name, the switch format to use is

/L:LogFileName

If you are using a date format for a different country, as discussed in Chapter 11, you should revise the form of the date used here. For example, European countries usually use dates in the form *day/month/year,* so a selection of files on or after February 4, 1987, would require /D:4/2/87 to be entered for the switch.

As an example, if you wanted to generate a log file for the previous presented backup of word-processing files, you would add an /L switch to the complete BACKUP command:

BACKUP C:\PROGRAMS\WORDPROC\PALANTIR A:
/D:2/4/87 /L

```
C>DIR/W \PROGRAMS\WORDPROC\PALANTIR

  Volume in drive C is ROBBINS
  Directory of  C:\PROGRAMS\WORDPROC\PALANTIR

  .                            STUDY5    WP    PALANTIR WPO    STANDARD WPF
WPINSTAL EXE    SPELL    HLP    WP        COM   LEX      4      LEX      3
SPELL    COM    LEX      1      LEX       2     DEFAULT  WP     STUDY1   WP
STUDY2   WP     CAD2     WP     CAD1      WP    CADBOOK1 WP     CADBOOK2 WP
QUELETT  WP     CADEXERS WP     CADBOOK3  WP    STUDY4   WP     STUDY3   WP
WORK     BLK    VISITYPE BAS    VISITYPE  COM   SYBEX    WPB    WKSHPS   WP
NEWBOOK  WPB    LASTPAGE TXT    UCSC      WP    STUFF    WP     SYBEX    WP
NEWBOOK  WP     CHICAGO  WP
        37 File(s)    768000 bytes free

C>_
```

Figure 9.13: All files in the sample PALANTIR directory

```
C>BACKUP C:\PROGRAMS\WORDPROC\PALANTIR A: /D:2/4/87

Insert backup diskette 01 in drive A:

Warning! Files in the target drive
A:\ root directory will be erased
Strike any key when ready

*** Backing up files to drive A: ***
Diskette Number: 01

\PROGRAMS\WORDPROC\PALANTIR\VISITYPE.BAS
\PROGRAMS\WORDPROC\PALANTIR\VISITYPE.COM
\PROGRAMS\WORDPROC\PALANTIR\SYBEX.WP
\PROGRAMS\WORDPROC\PALANTIR\SCREEN04.CAP
\PROGRAMS\WORDPROC\PALANTIR\SCREEN05.CAP
\PROGRAMS\WORDPROC\PALANTIR\WKSHPS.WP
\PROGRAMS\WORDPROC\PALANTIR\NEWBOOK.WP
\PROGRAMS\WORDPROC\PALANTIR\LASTPAGE.TXT
\PROGRAMS\WORDPROC\PALANTIR\UCSC.WP
\PROGRAMS\WORDPROC\PALANTIR\STUFF.WP
\PROGRAMS\WORDPROC\PALANTIR\CHICAGO.WP

C>_
```

Figure 9.14: Backing up files by date of last update

If you preferred to store the log-file information in a file in the original source directory, you could do so by making the /L switch more specific:

BACKUP C:\PROGRAMS\WORDPROC\PALANTIR A: /D:2/4/87
/L:\PROGRAMS\WORDPROC\PALANTIR\FEB4.LOG

The results of running this BACKUP command switch can be seen in Figure 9.15, which represents what DOS displays on the screen during the logging operation.

Figure 9.16 shows the contents of the log file (FEB4.LOG) itself. Using logging again during file-adding operations (/A) will add the newly backed-up files, along with their full path names, to this log file. This parallels the adding of file data and controlling information to the BACKUP and CONTROL files on the backup disk.

RESTORING FILES FROM A BACKUP DISK

The RESTORE command is used to bring files from a backup-diskette set (or a fixed disk) back onto a hard drive. It can be the original source hard-disk drive for the files, or it can be another hard-disk drive onto which you want to place the files.

```
Logging to file \PROGRAMS\WORDPROC\PALANTIR\FEB4.LOG

Insert backup diskette Ø1 in drive A:

Warning! Files in the target drive
A:\ root directory will be erased
Strike any key when ready

*** Backing up files to drive A: ***
Diskette Number: Ø1

\PROGRAMS\WORDPROC\PALANTIR\VISITYPE.BAS
\PROGRAMS\WORDPROC\PALANTIR\VISITYPE.COM
\PROGRAMS\WORDPROC\PALANTIR\SYBEX.WPB
\PROGRAMS\WORDPROC\PALANTIR\FEB4.LOG
\PROGRAMS\WORDPROC\PALANTIR\WKSHPS.WP
\PROGRAMS\WORDPROC\PALANTIR\NEWBOOK.WPB
\PROGRAMS\WORDPROC\PALANTIR\LASTPAGE.TXT
\PROGRAMS\WORDPROC\PALANTIR\UCSC.WP
\PROGRAMS\WORDPROC\PALANTIR\STUFF.WP
\PROGRAMS\WORDPROC\PALANTIR\SYBEX.WP
\PROGRAMS\WORDPROC\PALANTIR\NEWBOOK.WP
\PROGRAMS\WORDPROC\PALANTIR\CHICAGO.WP

C>_
```

Figure 9.15: DOS messages during logging operation

```
C>TYPE \PROGRAMS\WORDPROC\PALANTIR\FEB4.LOG

7-9-1987  23:11:13
001   \PROGRAMS\WORDPROC\PALANTIR\VISITYPE.BAS
001   \PROGRAMS\WORDPROC\PALANTIR\VISITYPE.COM
001   \PROGRAMS\WORDPROC\PALANTIR\SYBEX.WPB
001   \PROGRAMS\WORDPROC\PALANTIR\FEB4.LOG
001   \PROGRAMS\WORDPROC\PALANTIR\WKSHPS.WP
001   \PROGRAMS\WORDPROC\PALANTIR\NEWBOOK.WPB
001   \PROGRAMS\WORDPROC\PALANTIR\LASTPAGE.TXT
001   \PROGRAMS\WORDPROC\PALANTIR\UCSC.WP
001   \PROGRAMS\WORDPROC\PALANTIR\STUFF.WP
001   \PROGRAMS\WORDPROC\PALANTIR\SYBEX.WP
001   \PROGRAMS\WORDPROC\PALANTIR\NEWBOOK.WP
001   \PROGRAMS\WORDPROC\PALANTIR\CHICAGO.WP
C>_
```

Figure 9.16: Contents of the FEB4.LOG file

The RESTORE command is the only way to properly copy files from a backup diskette. Neither the COPY nor the XCOPY command will accomplish this task correctly.

The general form of the RESTORE command is

RESTORE *BackupDrive Destination*

Restoring files is almost the reverse of backing them up, with fewer switches and options for restoration. Unfortunately, there is one point of potential confusion. Contrary to what you might expect, RESTORE does not work in exact reverse of the BACKUP command. With BACKUP, you can specify a directory name alone, indicating you want to back up all files in the directory. With RESTORE, it's a little trickier. The second parameter, *Destination*, is the problem. If you do not specify a destination at all, the restoration is made to the current directory. However, in such a case, the current directory must be the same directory as the original source of the files on the backup disk. Otherwise, you'll receive the possibly misleading message "No files were found to restore." And, as Figure 9.17 shows, it isn't even enough to specify the correct directory as an argument to the RESTORE command.

The additional requirement for the *Destination* parameter is that you explicitly specify a file name, as in Figure 9.18, which simply adds the wild-card *.* specifier. Perhaps the simplest way to solve this problem is shown in Figure 9.19, which requires the CD

```
C>RESTORE  A:   \PROGRAMS\WORDPROC\PALANTIR

Insert backup diskette 01 in drive A:
Strike any key when ready

*** Files were backed up 07-09-1987 ***

*** Restoring files from drive A: ***
Diskette: 01

Warning! No files were found to restore

C>
```

Figure 9.17: Incorrectly formed RESTORE command

```
C>RESTORE  A:   \PROGRAMS\WORDPROC\PALANTIR\*.*

Insert backup diskette 01 in drive A:
Strike any key when ready

*** Files were backed up 07-09-1987 ***

*** Restoring files from drive A: ***
Diskette: 01
\PROGRAMS\WORDPROC\PALANTIR\VISITYPE.BAS
\PROGRAMS\WORDPROC\PALANTIR\VISITYPE.COM
\PROGRAMS\WORDPROC\PALANTIR\SYBEX.WPB
\PROGRAMS\WORDPROC\PALANTIR\FEB4.LOG
\PROGRAMS\WORDPROC\PALANTIR\WKSHPS.WP
\PROGRAMS\WORDPROC\PALANTIR\NEWBOOK.WPB
\PROGRAMS\WORDPROC\PALANTIR\LASTPAGE.TXT
\PROGRAMS\WORDPROC\PALANTIR\UCSC.WP
\PROGRAMS\WORDPROC\PALANTIR\STUFF.WP
\PROGRAMS\WORDPROC\PALANTIR\SYBEX.WP
\PROGRAMS\WORDPROC\PALANTIR\NEWBOOK.WP
\PROGRAMS\WORDPROC\PALANTIR\CHICAGO.WP

C>
```

Figure 9.18: RESTORE requires a complete path name

command to be issued prior to RESTORE. In that case, specifying only drive C as the destination is sufficient, since the default directory is now the proper one—the one from which the files were originally backed up. Naturally, as with all DOS commands, the drive specifier C: is not strictly necessary since, in its absence, the current directory would be used by default anyway.

```
C>CD   \PROGRAMS\WORDPROC\PALANTIR

C>RESTORE  A:  C:

Insert backup diskette Ø1 in drive A:
Strike any key when ready


*** Files were backed up Ø7-Ø9-1987 ***

*** Restoring files from drive A: ***
Diskette: Ø1
\PROGRAMS\WORDPROC\PALANTIR\VISITYPE.BAS
\PROGRAMS\WORDPROC\PALANTIR\VISITYPE.COM
\PROGRAMS\WORDPROC\PALANTIR\SYBEX.WP
\PROGRAMS\WORDPROC\PALANTIR\SCREENØ4.CAP
\PROGRAMS\WORDPROC\PALANTIR\SCREENØ5.CAP
\PROGRAMS\WORDPROC\PALANTIR\WKSHPS.WP
\PROGRAMS\WORDPROC\PALANTIR\NEWBOOK.WP
\PROGRAMS\WORDPROC\PALANTIR\LASTPAGE.TXT
\PROGRAMS\WORDPROC\PALANTIR\UCSC.WP
\PROGRAMS\WORDPROC\PALANTIR\STUFF.WP
\PROGRAMS\WORDPROC\PALANTIR\CHICAGO.WP

C>_
```

Figure 9.19: Restoring the current directory

RESTORING ONLY SOME OF YOUR BACKED-UP FILES

As always, DOS provides a variety of very useful switches for commands like RESTORE. There are two principal switches presented here that will be quite useful to you at various times. Other possible switches are presented in Part V.

> The ability to select the files you want restored can be very useful. It can also cut down on the time required to restore files by restoring only those files you actually need.

If you have backed up an entire directory tree or any subdirectory tree, you will need to use the /S switch to restore the subdirectory tree structure. Also, if you have made changes to any of the previously backed-up files, you should use the /P switch to ensure that the old version does not overwrite the new version.

RESTORING DIRECTORY STRUCTURES   The /S switch on the RESTORE command is the exact reverse of the /S switch on the BACKUP command. When used with BACKUP, /S allows you to search through a directory and all of its subdirectories for files to back up. When used with RESTORE, /S ensures that the backed-up files are restored to their proper subdirectories.

In fact, if DOS discovers that a subdirectory is missing during the restoration process, it will automatically recreate that subdirectory before copying the backed-up files to it. Your destination directory may be missing for a variety of reasons. Your entire disk may have crashed or have been erased inadvertently. More likely, you may have erased the directory and file contents, after backing them up, in order to reclaim the disk space for other purposes. Or you may simply be restoring the directory structure and files to a different computer and hard disk.

PROTECTING AGAINST ACCIDENTAL OVERWRITING The /P switch is extremely useful if you're not completely sure of yourself or if a good deal of time has elapsed between the backup and restoration. When this switch is specified, DOS will ask you during the restoration if you really mean to restore an old version and overwrite an existing disk file. It will do this when the existing disk file has been updated since the earlier backup version, or if the disk file has been marked as read-only. (The latter situation almost never occurs, so you needn't worry about it; you will learn about read-only files in Chapter 15.)

As a last example of RESTORE, let's use DOS's selective restoration capability to redo the example shown Figure 9.13. Instead of restoring all the files from the diskette in drive A, let's select only the document files (.WP):

RESTORE A: C:\PROGRAMS\WORDPROC\PALANTIR*.WP

Since the files UCSC.WP and STUFF.WP have been changed since the backup, let's make sure that they aren't accidentally overwritten:

RESTORE A: C:\PROGRAMS\WORDPROC\PALANTIR*.WP /P

The resultant protective sequence is shown in Figure 9.20.

The /P switch enabled RESTORE to note that two of the .WP files had been changed since they were backed up. The prompt allows you to inhibit overwriting and protect the changed version. Unfortunately, the display is somewhat confusing, since some but not all of the other restored files are interspersed between the warnings.

Now test your understanding of the RESTORE process. First back up any selected set of text files. If you completed the earlier exercises using BACKUP, you can use the resulting diskette if it contained text files. Otherwise, choose some files from your word processing (or other text-oriented) directory.

```
C>RESTORE  A: \PROGRAMS\WORDPROC\PALANTIR\*.WP /P

Insert backup diskette Ø1 in drive A:
Strike any key when ready


*** Files were backed up Ø7-Ø9-1987 ***

*** Restoring files from drive A: ***
Diskette: Ø1
Warning! File SYBEX.WP
was changed after it was backed up
Replace the file (Y/N)?
N

\PROGRAMS\WORDPROC\PALANTIR\WKSHPS.WP
Warning! File NEWBOOK.WP
was changed after it was backed up
Replace the file (Y/N)?
N

\PROGRAMS\WORDPROC\PALANTIR\UCSC.WP
\PROGRAMS\WORDPROC\PALANTIR\STUFF.WP
\PROGRAMS\WORDPROC\PALANTIR\CHICAGO.WP
-
```

Figure 9.20: Protecting against file overwriting with /P

Make some textual change to one of the text files by using your word processor or DOS's EDLIN (see Chapter 6). Next, restore the backed-up files to their original directory. Use the /P switch so you do not overwrite the newly changed text files. Use your text-editing program to verify that the old versions of the changed files were not rewritten onto your disk.

SUMMARY

This chapter has taught you how to back up your disks. Power failures do occur in businesses, brownouts occur even more frequently, and a multitude of other incidents can cause the intermittent loss or corruption of important files. Therefore, making backups is of critical importance for avoiding disaster. This chapter has presented the following backup information:

- You should back up your files before moving your computer, when you are close to filling up your hard disk, and just before running a fragmentation reduction program.

- The BACKUP command can make a complete copy of all the files in a directory when you simply specify the directory name and the disk drive to receive the backup copies.

- Backup copies of files are written into a compacted file on each backup diskette. The compacted file is called BACK-UP.*xxx,* where *xxx* is the number of the backup disk.

- Each BACKUP.*xxx* file is accompanied by a file called CONTROL.*xxx* (again, *xxx* is the disk number). This file contains such controlling information as the names and lengths of the files compacted into the BACKUP.*xxx* file.

- With the BACKUP command you can make selective backups of some of the files in a directory by using appropriate switches. For instance, you can make backups of files that have changed since the last backup was performed by using the /M switch.

- The /D switch permits the backup of files that have changed or that have been created since a certain date.

- The /T switch permits the backup of files based on the time of creation or modification.

- Adding a new set of files to a backup set is easily done by using the /A switch.

- The powerful /S switch allows you to back up files located deep within the directory tree.

- Automatic formatting of the destination diskettes for the BACKUP command will be done by DOS whenever you specify the /F switch.

- All backup processing can be recorded in a log file by using the /L switch. You can specify your own path and file name to receive the logging information; otherwise, a BACKUP.LOG file is created in the root directory of the source drive.

- The RESTORE command allows you to write files and directories from the backup-diskette set back to a hard disk—either the original or a new one. The /S switch permits restoration of the treelike directory structure. The /P switch allows you to complete this process safely in the event that existing disk versions of any files are newer and should not be overwritten.

In Chapter 17, you'll learn about several additional utility programs that you can purchase for backing up your files; they go
beyond the power and flexibility of the DOS BACKUP command.
For example, hard-disk backup programs like BACK-IT give you
much more flexibility and convenience in including and excluding
sets of files during the backup process. Naturally, these programs cost
extra money, while DOS's BACKUP and RESTORE commands
are free.

In the next two chapters, you'll look at more precise control over
DOS's internal setup and system configuration. In Chapter 10,
you'll learn how to initialize several key DOS parameters and how to
exploit the power of DOS drivers. In Chapter 11, you'll revisit the
MODE command in yet another one of its significant roles—support
for foreign-language characters, graphics characters, and multiple
keyboard layouts.

CUSTOM CONFIGURATIONS
OF DOS

CHAPTER *10* _____

SO FAR, EVERYTHING YOU'VE SEEN ABOUT DOS HAS
been clearly defined. Every feature has had a concrete definition and
strict limits on how it could be used and what results you could
expect. Behind the scenes, however, there are several additional
aspects to DOS itself which have considerable flexibility, and which
you can control.

DOS is like your home: you can walk in and accept everything as it
is, or you can adjust the environment to your liking. In your home,
you can open some windows or close others; you can turn the lights
on or off; you can set the thermostat to a different temperature; you
can even rearrange the furniture. DOS, too, also has a certain way in
which it appears when you "walk in," or start it up. This internal
configuration, and how you can adjust it, is the subject of this
chapter.

In DOS, you can customize your system in many ways. Chapters
13, 14, and 15 concentrate on the batch-file mechanism for complete
on-line adjustments. Here, you'll focus on customizing some of the
inner workings of DOS itself.

Two principal mechanisms exist for the internal setups: the
CONFIG.SYS file and the PROMPT command. Using the CON-
FIG.SYS file, you can specify the number of internal DOS buffers.
You can also use CONFIG.SYS to load additional drivers such as
ANSI.SYS, which enables you to redefine keys and control the dis-
play. DOS has another driver you can load to create a RAM disk. In
this chapter, you'll learn all these customization methods.

USING THE CONFIG.SYS FILE

When a microcomputer is turned on, it runs through a built-in bootstrap program. The time-consuming part of a typical bootstrap is a memory test. The more memory you have, the longer the test will take; if you ever expand the memory of your system, you will probably notice the difference.

Following the memory test, the bootstrap attempts to find the disk-resident portion of DOS on one of the drives in the system, usually beginning with drive A. That is why the light on drive A comes on before the hard drive is accessed, even if you have a hard disk. It is also why anyone can circumvent a menu system set up on your hard disk—one can always place a DOS system disk in drive A, boot the system from that disk, and then access any files on the hard disk.

When the system drive is found (the one that has a copy of the DOS files on it), the computer reads the information into its memory. The next thing DOS does is to scan the root directory of the drive from which it has read the DOS files for a special file called CONFIG.SYS. If this file is not present, DOS initializes your system according to built-in default values. If a file called AUTOEXEC-.BAT exists (see Chapter 15 for a detailed explanation of this file), DOS then proceeds with the instructions in that file and displays the DOS prompt (usually A> or C>, depending on which drive contained the system files).

If a CONFIG.SYS file is present in the root directory DOS scans, it will contain a list of special statements that define a nonstandard system configuration. Figure 10.1 shows a sample CONFIG.SYS file actually used on a typical 640K DOS system. You'll learn in this chapter what each line of this file represents.

CONFIG.SYS is unique in the following ways:

- It can alter the internal setup of DOS itself.

- It can only be activated by booting or rebooting the computer.

```
FILES=20
BUFFERS=15
DEVICE=C:\DOS\ANSI.SYS
DEVICE=C:\DOS\VDISK.SYS 120
```

Figure 10.1: A typical CONFIG.SYS file

• It can contain only a limited set of commands.

Since the CONFIG.SYS file is a standard ASCII text file, you can create and modify it with a text editor like EDLIN (see Chapter 6) or your own word processor. Each line in this file has the form

Command = Value

The commands you'll learn about in this chapter are the most important and useful ones. They are FILES, BUFFERS, and DEVICE. (You can refer to the Part V command reference for other possibilities.) Let's look at each of these.

SPECIFYING THE NUMBER OF ACTIVE FILES

More and more frequently, users are running sophisticated programs like WordStar 4.0, dBASE III PLUS, and Framework II. These programs can work with several files at the same time, so they require the installation of a special CONFIG.SYS file. This usually requires you to change the normal DOS default value for FILES.

The default value set by DOS is only eight files. This means there are eight places reserved by DOS inside its own memory space to track information about open files. DOS itself uses three of these, and every running application program, overlay file, RAM-resident program, and so on, may use additional places out of the eight.

Most popular application programs recommend that you set the FILES value to 20 in your CONFIG.SYS file, although some programs recommend higher or lower settings. Unless you're willing to run extensive performance tests in your system environment, just follow the software manufacturer's instructions for setting the value of FILES. However, you might be using several different software application packages. For example, you may be using a computer-aided design package that recommends the setting FILES = 20, and you may also be using a database management package that recommends FILES = 15. Take the larger value. Although it will cost you some additional memory space when DOS boots up, it won't be much (48 bytes per open file), and at least you'll be guaranteed that your software will run.

SPECIFYING THE NUMBER
OF INTERNAL DOS BUFFERS

The BUFFERS command refers to the way DOS manages the input and output of data to and from the disk drives. When a command is issued by a program to read information from a file, DOS really serves the role of an intermediary by loading the information into a reserved buffer area. Figure 10.2 presents a visual interpretation of this activity.

Efficiency is the primary reason that operating systems use buffers. Imagine yourself in the role of an operating system. Then imagine that someone (an application program) wants to give you something, while someone else (a disk file) wants to get that same thing. If you act as a buffer by accepting the object with one hand and then hold it until you can locate the receiving person, the transaction will be fairly straightforward. However, if you try to do this procedure without using your hands or moving around, getting the giver together with the receiver in the same room, you've made your job much more difficult. In addition, you would not be able to do much else until the two-person operation was completed. DOS uses buffering to make transactions efficient.

When a disk request is made, DOS checks the information in its buffer before it tries to read the disk. This can sometimes eliminate the need to actually read the disk; DOS may find that the requested

Figure 10.2: Disk data passing through DOS buffers

file data is already in the buffer—if, for instance, the file has recently been called up by another program or DOS request. (This is, in part, the principle behind disk-buffering programs like Lightning, discussed in Chapter 17.) The result is that some programs will perform certain operations faster.

Each buffer in DOS can hold 528 bytes. If you increase the number of buffers, the memory-resident requirements for DOS itself will increase. This will decrease the available memory for any application program, as well as for any memory-resident program you wish to use during your main program's execution. Sophisticated programs like Framework II, which has its own buffer management and configuration file and therefore uses memory intensively, will suffer greatly from too large of a BUFFERS value.

A law of diminishing returns is at work here. Up to a point, more DOS buffers means faster performance for your system. On the other hand, too many buffers means DOS may spend more time looking through its buffers than it would spend to just go to the disk and read the necessary data. Unless you have a good reason, use the software manufacturer's recommended setting for BUFFERS. A common setting is a value of 15.

USING DEVICE DRIVERS TO CUSTOMIZE DOS

The CONFIG.SYS file is also used to load additional software drivers into DOS. Software drivers are special-purpose programs whose only responsibility is to control specific peripheral devices (see Chapter 11 for an additional discussion of device drivers). DOS can't be responsible for knowing all the control codes for all possible external devices; operating systems in general leave the details of communicating with and controlling these devices to the special driver programs.

Device drivers extend the command range of DOS. Naturally, they also take up more memory, which is one reason why they are optional. A special driver called ANSI.SYS extends the functions of DOS to include reprogramming or redefinition of keys and screen colors in DOS. You'll look at that feature more closely in the following section.

Memory reserved for use as a RAM disk is no longer available for internal use by programs like Framework II or Symphony. If you take up too much space with a RAM disk or any other memory-resident software, there may not even be enough remaining memory to load your main application software. You can make more memory space available by using extended or expanded memory, discussed below.

DOS also has a driver that is used to create a *RAM disk* (sometimes called a *virtual disk*). The RAM disk is not really a disk—it is an area in memory that simulates the operations of an additional disk drive. A critical aspect of this mechanism is that any files placed on the RAM disk are really memory-resident. They can therefore be retrieved at the speed of memory, which is usually microseconds or nanoseconds. Files on actual mechanical disk drives are slower, usually in the millisecond range.

You must do a bit of calculating to figure out how much memory is available for your RAM disk. Simply subtract the memory required by your version of DOS from your total physical memory (640K, 512K, or whatever). Then subtract the memory requirements of your particular application program (for example, 378K for dBASE III PLUS or 512K for CADVANCE) from the remaining number. This tells you the maximum remaining memory that could be allocated for a RAM disk. For example, if the total physical memory of your system is 640K, the space required by your DOS 3.3 is 45K, and the space required by your application program is 384K, you have 211K remaining for your RAM disk (640 − 45 − 384 = 211).

There are a few other things you must consider. The size of your version of DOS varies according to the values of FILES, BUFFERS, and any other CONFIG.SYS parameters. It also varies according to how many additional DOS programs you've run, which requires extra memory (like the MODE command of Chapter 7 and the KEYB command of Chapter 9). Naturally, if you run any memory-resident programs like Sidekick, you need to subtract their memory requirements as well.

Use only as much memory for your RAM disk as you need. You should know in advance how you plan to use this space.

CREATING A RAM DISK

You know that DOS maintains a directory and a file allocation table (a DAT and an FAT) on each disk, along with the actual data and program files. In order to simulate this structure in memory, a special piece of software is required. This software is included in your DOS in a file called either VDISK.SYS (for PC-DOS) or RAM-DRIVE.SYS (for MS-DOS).

The simulated RAM disk seen in Figure 10.3 can be implemented simply by including the following values in your DEVICE

Figure 10.3: RAM disk simulation using physical memory

specification:

DEVICE = C:\DOS\VDISK.SYS 120

This DEVICE setting brings into memory the VDISK (virtual or RAM disk) driver.

In this example, the VDISK.SYS file itself is located on drive C in the DOS directory. The parameter value of 120 indicates that a total simulated disk of size 120K should be created from the available physical memory (640K or whatever you have in your system).

If you have an IBM PC-AT or a compatible computer, you should know about a switch you can use when you set up a RAM disk. The /E switch will use *extended memory*—extra memory above the conventional 1Mb of addressable memory—if your machine has this additional memory installed. The previous example could be modified to generate a 120K RAM disk in extended memory like this:

DEVICE = C:\DOS\VDISK.SYS 120 /E

DOS also allows you to have multiple RAM disks simultaneously. Just as you can use different physical devices to protect files from one another by separating them on different drives, you can do the same

If you are using a version of DOS for any machine other than an actual IBM computer, you will need to substitute RAMDRIVE.SYS wherever you read VDISK.SYS in this text.

If you don't have AT extended memory, you can place your RAM disk in *expanded* memory, such as Intel's Above Board. Expanded memory, specially configured according to the "LIM standard," works in regular PCs and XTs, as well as ATs. It actually overcomes the DOS 640K limit, so many programs are written to use it for data just like regular memory.

If you intend to create and use disk drives with drive identifiers beyond the letter E, DOS 3.2 and 3.3 will permit you to do so but will require another statement in your configuration file. This additional statement must be of the form LASTDRIVE = x, where x is the last valid alphabetic character DOS will use for a drive identifier.

with the much faster RAM disks. Each RAM disk will be given a new single-character drive identifier by DOS.

All you need to do to create multiple RAM disks is have multiple copies of the DEVICE command. DOS knows what physical drives exist in your system, and it creates the additional drives using the next available letters. For instance, if your system had one or two diskette drives and one hard-disk drive, then adding the following two statements to your CONFIG.SYS file would create the RAM disks D and E with sizes of 120K and 184K (see Figure 10.4):

```
DEVICE = C:\DOS\VDISK.SYS 120
DEVICE = C:\DOS\VDISK.SYS 184
```

There are other methods for creating RAM disks. These usually require software that comes with enhancement boards like AST's Six-Pak Plus or Quadram's Quadboard, or they require add-on boards that act as dedicated RAM disks. Some of these have their own power supplies and battery backups, which means no data loss will occur during power outages. Another benefit of this type of add-on is that no system memory is used up by the device driver that manages the RAM disk. Installing a RAM disk with software packages or add-on boards requires a different procedure; you should follow the manufacturer's instructions.

```
C>CHKDSK D:
Volume VDISK   V3.3 created Dec 6, 1984 12:00p

    119168 bytes total disk space
         0 bytes in 1 hidden files
    119168 bytes available on disk

    524288 bytes total memory
    132208 bytes free
C>CHKDSK E:
Volume VDISK   V3.3 created Dec 6, 1984 12:00p

    183936 bytes total disk space
         0 bytes in 1 hidden files
    183936 bytes available on disk

    524288 bytes total memory
    132208 bytes free

C>_
```

Figure 10.4: Multiple RAM disks

None of the
CONFIG.SYS file's
settings take effect until
the DOS system is booted
up. Remember this if you
make any changes to
your CONFIG.SYS
file—you must reboot
before the changes take
effect.

An advantage of these other methods is that the RAM disk doesn't have to be carved out of memory at bootup time. Instead, you can first run your own programs, making use of all available memory. Then, at your convenience, you can run the special software to set up the RAM disk. Only then will you need to confront the problem of memory requirements. In Figure 10.4, the 512K machine with two RAM disks has only 152,912 bytes free in which to run programs. Having consumed so much memory with the two RAM disks, you would have to change the CONFIG.SYS file and reboot before you could reuse that memory space in any other way.

USING A RAM DISK

Now that you know how to create a RAM disk, you should also know how to use what you've created to its best advantage. Here are some suggestions for using your RAM disk.

Place a copy of your DOS system's primary disk-resident program, COMMAND.COM, on your RAM disk. Then employ the following special instructions to inform DOS that all future references to COMMAND.COM can locate it on the RAM disk, not on the boot disk. Assuming your RAM disk is on drive D (substitute the appropriate letter on your system), you should enter the following command at the DOS prompt:

```
SET COMSPEC = D:\COMMAND.COM
```

This will speed up all programs that invoke DOS from within themselves, such as Framework II or QDOS II. These programs work by loading a second copy of the command processor (COMMAND-.COM) from a RAM disk. This command will also speed up application software that overwrites the command-processor portion of DOS and then requires its reloading before the software can restore DOS and its prompt.

Load the files for frequently referenced DOS commands, like CHKDSK.COM and FORMAT.COM, onto your RAM disk; also load EDLIN.COM if you use EDLIN often to edit small text files (see Chapter 6). In fact, load any text files that are run frequently, like batch files.

Load any large support files (like spelling dictionaries or a thesaurus file) that your word processor or integrated software may need. Also place index-type files (generated by many database management systems) on the RAM disk for much more rapid accessing of data records, especially if you must search through many records in large data files.

Place your favorite disk-resident utility programs (shareware, public domain, or purchased, like the Norton Utilities) on the RAM disk if you use them frequently. Also place overlay files on your RAM disk for improved execution of your software. These overlays contain the portion of your application program that couldn't fit into memory and is normally read into a special part of memory only when needed. The overlay features of your software will operate at rapid RAM speeds if you place them on your RAM disk. Note that you will need to make your RAM disk into the default DOS disk before invoking your application program so it will look for the overlay file on the RAM disk and not on the standard drive.

Remember to set your path properly so DOS can find main programs. Set the RAM disk near or at the front of the PATH specification so that the file copies on the RAM drive are accessed first, not the original files that may also be accessible from directories on the path.

Before you follow these suggestions for using your RAM disk effectively, you should learn how to use it safely. As you know, using a RAM disk is much faster than using real disks. Programs that formerly took hours to run may take minutes, minutes can become seconds, and waiting time can disappear. When RAM disks are used improperly, however, hours of work can disappear in seconds.

Since a RAM disk is created in memory, any information stored on it will vanish when the computer is turned off. You gain great advantage by storing and accessing the right files on a RAM disk, but you must remember that these files are destroyed when you turn off the power or a power failure occurs, if there's a brownout in your building, if your computer plug comes out of the wall, or if you reboot your system with Ctrl-Alt-Del.

If you place and update important data files on a RAM disk for the sake of rapid access, save copies of them to a real disk before you turn off the power. Also back up copies of them to a real disk at frequent intervals to avoid losing all your work.

ADDING POWER
WITH THE ANSI SYSTEM DRIVER

The ANSI (American National Standards Institute) system allows you to modify the default setup of your screen and keyboard. For example, you can change the characteristics of the screen, including both the cursor position and screen colors (with a color monitor, of course). You can also redefine the expected value of keys on your keyboard, so you can customize the use of your function keys, as well as how the Ctrl, Shift, or Alt key affects them.

In order to obtain any of these customizing capabilities, you must have the ANSI.SYS driver installed in your system. The third line of CONFIG.SYS (see Figure 10.1) does just that:

DEVICE = C:\DOS\ANSI.SYS

Some special-purpose application programs like PreCursor, a hard-disk management program, and SuperKey, a keyboard redefinition program, require that you include this type of command in your CONFIG.SYS specification. Of course, you should specify the full path name to the ANSI.SYS file; in this example, ANSI.SYS is located in directory DOS on drive C.

Even if you are not yet using application software that requires the ANSI.SYS driver, the possibilities in the next section will probably inspire you to include this line in your CONFIG.SYS specification all the time.

ANSI.SYS AND
THE PROMPT COMMAND

The PROMPT command is used to enter ANSI commands. For example, the form of the PROMPT command used to change the color of the screen is

PROMPT $e[aaaam

The letter m in the PROMPT escape sequence signifies the end of your sequence of attribute settings. It must be lowercase.

where *aaaa* represents screen attributes or colors (shown in Table 10.1). Separate these values with semicolons if you use more than one. $e is a special symbol combination (the dollar sign $ followed by the letter e),

recognized by DOS as an equivalent of the Esc key. The ANSI driver
is invoked when an escape sequence is received, which is any series of
keystrokes begun with the Esc key; therefore, $e invokes the ANSI
driver. There is no limit to the number of attributes you can enter
between the left bracket [and the letter m.

CONTROLLING THE SCREEN DISPLAY

It's up to you to decide if you like the standard white letters on a
black background (even if you've bought a color monitor), or if you
prefer something flashier. Using the attribute and color codes shown
in Table 10.1, along with the PROMPT command, you can customize things as you like.

ATTRIBUTES	
0	All attributes off
1	Bold
4	Underline (on IBM-compatible monochrome monitors only)
5	Blinking
7	Reverse video

COLORS	FOREGROUND	BACKGROUND
Black	30	40
Red	31	41
Green	32	42
Yellow	33	43
Blue	34	44
Magenta	35	45
Cyan	36	46
White	37	47

Table 10.1: Video-screen color and attribute codes

To switch the display to dark letters on a light background (see Figure 10.5), you would use an attribute value of 7 for reverse video:

PROMPT $e[7m

All future output on your screen will now appear as reverse video—black on white. Notice that in Figure 10.5, the DIR/W itself is displayed in reverse video after the PROMPT command has been executed.

To return to normal video (see Figure 10.6), you would use an attribute value of 0, which turns off all special attributes:

PROMPT $e[0m

USING META SYMBOLS

Notice that there appears to be no visible prompt at the bottom of the screens just shown. This is because the PROMPT command was used to set video attributes only. Various other possibilities can be combined with these attributes by stringing them together. You can create a wide range of output possibilities by using symbolic replacements, called *meta symbols,* for the desired output result. Table 10.2

Figure 10.5: Setting reverse video with PROMPT and ANSI.SYS

Figure 10.6: Resetting to default video attributes

SYMBOL	MEANING
e	The Esc key
p	Current directory of the default drive
g	The > character
n	Default drive identifier
d	System date
t	System time
v	Version number
l	The < character
b	The ¦ character
q	The = character
h	A backspace
_	The carriage-return/line-feed sequence

Table 10.2: Meta symbols for the PROMPT command

lists the single-character meta symbols that can be used in conjunction with the $ character to influence the output of the PROMPT command.

For instance, to display the current directory, you would enter

PROMPT $p

To display the current directory and the > symbol, you would enter

PROMPT pg

To display the current directory and the > symbol, *and* to set to bold-face all future video output, you would enter

PROMPT pg$e[1m

The results of this command are shown in Figure 10.7.

COMBINING MULTIPLE ATTRIBUTES

All of the preceding possibilities can be combined to create more complex prompt effects. The simplest combinations only involve two attributes at once. For example, to create a reverse-video display that blinks, you can combine the codes for blinking (5) and reverse video (7):

PROMPT $e[5;7m

Future output will be seen as black characters that blink on a light background. To set things back to normal again, you would enter

PROMPT $e[0m

You can enter text into your prompt by simply typing it with no special meta symbols; text can also be embedded between any special-purpose meta symbols. For example, you can change the prompting message to "Your Command?" and display it in high intensity with the following:

PROMPT $e[1mYour Command?$e[0m

The beginning $e[1m turns high intensity on for the phrase "Your Command?" and the ending $e[0m turns it off.

```
SYS       COM    TREE      COM    VDISK     SYS   XCOPY     EXE    DEMO      BAK
AUTOEXEC  BAK    S-SAVE    COM    IMCAP     COM   SR        COM    VTREE     COM
DEMO      BAT    LOCATE    BAT    HELP      BAK   AUTOEXEC  BAT    CONFIG    SYS
        50 File(s)         2048 bytes free

A>PROMPT $P$G$E[1m

A:\>DIR/W

    Volume in drive A has no label
    Directory of  A:\

ANSI      SYS    ASSIGN    COM    ATTRIB    EXE   BACKUP    COM    IMSHOW    EXE
SKN       COM    CHKDSK    COM    COMMAND   COM   COMP      COM    DISKCOMP  COM
DISKCOPY  COM    DRIVER    SYS    EDLIN     COM   FDISK     COM    FIND      EXE
FORMAT    COM    GRAFTABL  COM    GRAPHICS  COM   JOIN      EXE    KEYBFR    COM
KEYBGR    COM    KEYBIT    COM    KEYBSP    COM   KEYBUK    COM    LABEL     COM
MODE      COM    MORE      COM    PRINT     COM   RECOVER   COM    REPLACE   EXE
RESTORE   COM    SELECT    COM    SHARE     EXE   SORT      EXE    SUBST     EXE
SYS       COM    TREE      COM    VDISK     SYS   XCOPY     EXE    DEMO      BAK
AUTOEXEC  BAK    S-SAVE    COM    IMCAP     COM   SR        COM    VTREE     COM
DEMO      BAT    LOCATE    BAT    HELP      BAK   AUTOEXEC  BAT    CONFIG    SYS
        50 File(s)         2048 bytes free

A:\>_
```

Figure 10.7: Combinations in the PROMPT command

> Complicated or long screen prompts can wrap around to a second screen line as you type them in, but you should not press the Return key to get to the second line. The Return key terminates your prompt-string input; DOS will wrap a multiple-line command request on its own.

Color monitors present other interesting alternatives. Using the color codes of Table 10.1 and the meta symbols of Table 10.2, it's easy to set any desired combination for foreground and background colors. For example, the following command will set a three-line prompt. The first line will contain the current directory (p). The carriage-return/line-feed sequence (_) ensures that the system date (d) appears on the next line. The time (t) and the > character (g) will be on the third line, and all succeeding text (including the future prompting strings) will be displayed as blue characters on a yellow background:

PROMPT p_d_tg$e[34;43m

A slight change to this command could give you similar information, while using reverse video for the special information only. In this way, the same PROMPT command could be used for both color and monochrome monitors. Notice in Figure 10.8 that the display of commands and output is in normal video, since the reverse-video code is reset immediately after the > symbol is output:

PROMPT $e[7m$p$_$d$_$tge[0m

You may not like the multiline appearance of this information. You could just as easily put the same information on one line with the

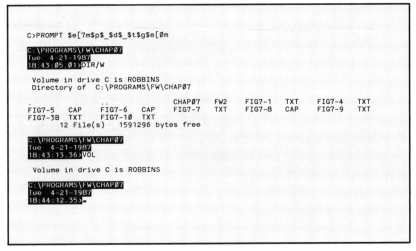

```
C>PROMPT $e[7m$p$_$d$_$t$g$e[Øm

C:\PROGRAMS\FW\CHAPØ7
Tue  4-21-1987
18:43:05.Ø1>DIR/W

Volume in drive C is ROBBINS
Directory of  C:\PROGRAMS\FW\CHAPØ7

  .             ..                CHAPØ7   FW2      FIG7-1   TXT     FIG7-4   TXT
FIG7-5   CAP    FIG7-6   CAP     FIG7-7   TXT      FIG7-8   CAP     FIG7-9   TXT
FIG7-3B  TXT    FIG7-1Ø  TXT
       12 File(s)   1591296 bytes free

C:\PROGRAMS\FW\CHAPØ7
Tue  4-21-1987
18:43:13.36>VOL

Volume in drive C is ROBBINS

C:\PROGRAMS\FW\CHAPØ7
Tue  4-21-1987
18:44:12.35>_
```

Figure 10.8: A three-line, reverse-video prompt

following variation:

PROMPT $e[7m$p $d tg$e[0m

The spaces in this command are critical to the separation of the directory name, date, and time. The results are shown in Figure 10.9.

There are many more fanciful things you can do with the PROMPT command to control the video display. The codes required would go well beyond the scope of this book, but you can manipulate the cursor and its location in a variety of ways.

Use the PROMPT command now to redefine your DOS prompt to provide more information. Issue the proper command to display the DOS version number on one line, the system date on the next line, and the current directory on the third line of this multiline prompt. On a fourth line, generate the text string

Enter next command, please :

If you have a monochrome monitor, have this message appear in reverse video. Remember to reset the video attribute so that the rest of the video display appears in normal video. If you have a color monitor, have this message appear as white letters on a red background.

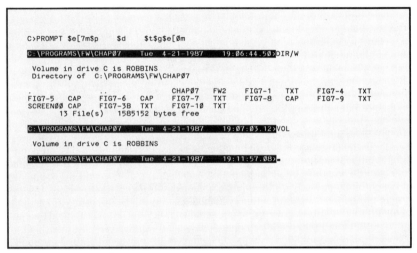

Figure 10.9: A one-line, reverse-video prompt

REDEFINING KEYS

As well as changing screen colors, you can use the ANSI system to reprogram some of your keys to type out commands or phrases. You can define any of the ASCII keys or the extended keyboard keys (F1–F10, Home, End, and so on). Some people have even used this technique to redefine individual keys to represent other individual keys, so that the keyboard assumes a different layout.

Like screen attributes, key reassignment begins with the special symbol for the Esc key ($e) and continues with the left bracket ([). If you want to assign new values to a normal key like the "a" key or the = key, you enter the ASCII value of the key, like 96 for the letter a or 61 for = . However, if you want to reassign values to the special keys on your keyboard (which is a more common goal), you must begin the key assignment with a zero and then follow it with the special code given the key by DOS (see Table 10.3).

For example, F10 has the reassignment code 68. Suppose that you wanted to have the F10 key automatically type the command DIR/W. You would enter

PROMPT $e[0;68;"DIR/W";13p

First, $e[tells DOS that an ANSI command is being entered. Next, 0

FUNCTION KEY	REDEFINITION CODE	FUNCTION KEY	REDEFINITION CODE
F1	59	Ctrl-F1	94
F2	60	Ctrl-F2	95
F3	61	Ctrl-F3	96
F4	62	Ctrl-F4	97
F5	63	Ctrl-F5	98
F6	64	Ctrl-F6	99
F7	65	Ctrl-F7	100
F8	66	Ctrl-F8	101
F9	67	Ctrl-F9	102
F10	68	Ctrl-F10	103
Shift-F1	84	Alt-F1	104
Shift-F2	85	Alt-F2	105
Shift-F3	86	Alt-F3	106
Shift-F4	87	Alt-F4	107
Shift-F5	88	Alt-F5	108
Shift-F6	89	Alt-F6	109
Shift-F7	90	Alt-F7	110
Shift-F8	91	Alt-F8	111
Shift-F9	92	Alt-F9	112
Shift-F10	93	Alt-F10	113

Table 10.3: Function-key redefinition codes

tells DOS that the key to be redefined is part of the extended keyboard. The 68 selects F10 as the key to be redefined. "DIR/W" is the text of the command. (Note that these text characters are enclosed in quotation marks to indicate that they are not codes for ANSI.SYS to interpret.) 13 is the code for the Return key, which is required after the DIR/W command, just as it would be if you typed in DIR/W at the keyboard yourself. The last character in a key redefinition is always p, just as the last character in the video redefinition was an m.

Try out this technique now. Use the ANSI.SYS system to program your F7 function key to perform a CHKDSK command. Don't forget to make sure you have a CONFIG.SYS file in your root directory, and be sure it contains a DEVICE specification that loads the ANSI.SYS driver.

Finally, some very fancy custom menu systems can be set up simply with the PROMPT command and a well-thought-out group of function-key assignments. There are ten function keys (F1–F10), ten shifted function keys, ten Ctrl–function-key combinations, and ten Alt–function-key combinations. These provide 40 assignment possibilities. The extended code numbers for redefining these keys are also shown in Table 10.3.

The following PROMPT commands redefine several keys. The first will cause the shifted F4 key to type FORMAT A:. The second will cause the Ctrl-F6 combination to type CHKDSK, and the third will cause the Alt-F8 combination to type CD \:

```
PROMPT $e[0;87;"FORMAT A:";13p
PROMPT $e[0;99;"CHKDSK";13p
PROMPT $e[0;111;"CD \";13p
```

You must assign a key its original code value in order to reset it. The following sequence will reset all three of the example function-key sequences:

```
PROMPT $e[0;87;0;87p$e[0;99;0;99p$e[0;111;0;111p
```

The nicest thing about all these possibilities is that they are cumulative—that is, you can issue any number of key redefinition requests and they will accumulate. Until you reset each one, they will retain their new definitions while you are at the DOS prompt level.

Some programs reset the function-key definitions when they begin, and you will not be able to use the PROMPT command for key redefinition. When you encounter such a situation, the best solution is to purchase and use a keyboard redefinition program like Keyworks (see Chapter 17), which will allow you to redefine any key while another program is operating.

SUMMARY

In this chapter, you've learned some very powerful methods in DOS to customize your system for both power and convenience:

- The CONFIG.SYS file permits you to initialize several internal DOS system variables at bootup time.

- The BUFFERS command defines precisely how many internal buffers DOS will use.

- The FILES command specifies the maximum allowable number of open files that DOS will understand and support while DOS and your application programs run.

- The DEVICE command allows you to incorporate any number of specialized peripheral device drivers into your DOS configuration.

- A RAM disk is a memory-resident simulation of a typical mechanical disk. It offers you increased system performance and speed.

- The ANSI.SYS device driver provides extraordinary controls over both the video monitor and the keyboard. It provides a number of special codes, which give you the ability to redefine any keys and to control the video output. Using these codes with the PROMPT command allows you to make your system more intelligent, useful, and fun to operate.

In the next chapter, you'll learn about another type of system configuration: initializing your keyboard and monitor to understand and display international character sets.

INTERNATIONAL SETUP
OF DOS

DIFFERENT COUNTRIES USE DIFFERENT SYMBOLS TO represent their own systems. For example, currency symbols differ among countries—the $ in the USA, the DM in Germany, and the F in France. Time formats also vary: the separator symbol between the hour and minutes is a colon in the U.S., but a period in Norway. Decimal numbers are also punctuated differently; in the U.S., they contain a period, but in Spain they contain a comma. You'll learn in this chapter how to set up your version of DOS to understand the default values for symbols used in different countries.

Different countries also employ different keyboard layouts. If you learned to type in the U.S. and then tried typing on a French typewriter or keyboard, you would type the letter A each time you meant to type a Q, and vice versa. This is because the key labeled A on an American keyboard is labeled Q on a French keyboard. You'll also learn in this chapter about the differences between keyboard layouts in different countries and how you can easily ask DOS to redefine all the keys properly. In addition, you'll learn how to rapidly switch between the various possible layouts.

This chapter presents the national language-support features found in DOS 3.3 only. You may need to make some adjustments to your system to improve the display and printout of foreign characters; the required steps will be presented later in this chapter.

If you're a foreigner in the U.S., you can easily switch between the U.S. default key values and your own. In this way, you can avoid learning the U.S. keyboard layout in order to work on computers here. The same is true in reverse for Americans working abroad. This feature is explained in detail later in this chapter.

CHARACTER SETS FOR DIFFERENT COUNTRIES

The group of characters used in a country or on a computer composes the character set of that country or computer. Most countries, like the United States and Great Britain, share a common set of characters. However, some countries have enough different characters and symbols to justify creating a special character set just for them.

Along with the different character sets comes different placement of the characters on a computer keyboard, which makes sense—commonly used elements must be easy to use. For example, on a French keyboard certain keys are reversed, and other keys facilitate the production of accented letters.

ASCII CODES

A computer does not interpret letters as letters per se, but assigns an ASCII code to each letter. These codes range from 0 to 255, representing the 256 possible combinations of binary digits contained in an eight bit byte.

Codes 0 through 31 are usually reserved for control codes, the codes that do not produce a visible character but perform some particular action. For example, printing the code 7 on most computers causes the computer to beep, and code 13 causes a carriage return. These codes control the functions of the hardware.

Codes 32 through 126 are standard characters and symbols (see Table 11.1). The capital alphabet starts at code 65, and the lowercase alphabet starts at code 97. Code 127 represents the deletion symbol. The control codes and the standard character codes together make up an entire set (from 0 to 127) called ASCII codes. The computer translates characters into these codes, and so does any other device using the characters. When a computer sends ASCII 65 to the printer, it expects an A to be printed out, so the printer must also translate from code 65 to A. You can see why it is important for these codes to be standardized; many pieces of equipment rely on the same code.

Codes 128 through 255 are computer/printer specific. IBM uses codes 128 through 255 for some graphics characters, while Epson, on some of its printers, uses them for italics.

The extended ASCII codes also represent certain specialized keys or key combinations, such as Alt-C or F1. These codes are defined by

HEX DIGITS	1st	0-	1-	2-	3-	4-	5-	6-	7-
2nd									
-0					0	@	P	'	p
-1				!	1	A	Q	a	q
-2				"	2	B	R	b	r
-3				#	3	C	S	c	s
-4				$	4	D	T	d	t
-5				%	5	E	U	e	u
-6				&	6	F	V	f	v
-7				'	7	G	W	g	w
-8				(	8	H	X	h	x
-9				)	9	I	Y	i	y
-A				*	:	J	Z	j	z
-B				+	;	K	[	k	{
-C				,	<	L	\	l	|
-D				-	=	M	]	m	}
-E				.	>	N	^	n	~
-F				/	?	O	_	o	△

Table 11.1: Standard ASCII characters and symbols

first sending an ASCII null character (code 0) to the device, and then another code. For example, sending code 0, then code 59 would have the same effect as pressing the F1 key.

The combinations of all these codes produce the complete visual and printed output you are used to seeing. Depending on where you live and work, however, you may have altogether different characters in your language and keys on your keyboard.

WHAT COUNTRY DO YOU CALL HOME?

When DOS boots up, the system date and time are queried. Everybody agrees that any given date has a month, a day, and a year, but not everyone agrees on that order. In the U.S., dates are shown with the month first, the day next, and the year last. In Europe, the day is shown first, the month next, and the year last. In the Far East, the year is first, the month next, and the day last. Hence, 11/04/07 can mean November 4, 1907; April 11, 1907; or April 7, 1911. It depends on who's writing the date *and* who's reading it. Again, that's why standards are so important.

The DATE function in DOS will display the system date according to the accepted custom in a specific country. Table 11.2 shows the countries currently understood by DOS, along with their country and keyboard codes. You'll learn later in this chapter how to set up your version of DOS to understand which country or keyboard is in use.

The order of the month, day, and year fields is only one of many things that differ among countries. Separator symbols between the month, day, and year values also vary from country to country. In fact, there are a host of special symbols that vary among countries: time separators (a colon or a period), list separators (a semicolon or a comma), decimal separators (a period or a comma), thousands separators (a comma or a period), and currency symbols ($, F, Fr, MK, DKR, and others). The U.S. shows time in 12-hour A.M./P.M. format, while most other countries use a 24-hour display. Most countries show two decimal places of accuracy in currency displays, while Italy shows none.

DOS maintains internal tables of these differing values according to which country has been set up as the system default. If you do nothing, the U.S. will be assumed to be the standard. However, if you wish to customize the system for some other country, you can simply use the proper country code from Table 11.2 to add a line to your CONFIG.SYS file:

COUNTRY = *Code*

Figure 11.1 shows the results of DOS date and time requests after the system CONFIG.SYS file was changed to a default of Switzerland (code 041).

Getting the date and time was easy in this example. The real value of the COUNTRY code in CONFIG.SYS can only be realized fully by programmers using specialized assembly-language techniques.

COUNTRY	COUNTRY CODE	KEYBOARD CODE
Arabic	785	
Australia	061	US
Belgium	032	BE
Canada (Eng.)	001	US
Canada (Fr.)	002	CF
Denmark	045	DK
Finland	358	SU
France	033	FR
Germany	049	GR
Hebrew	972	
Italy	039	IT
Latin America	003	LA
Netherlands	031	NL
Norway	047	NO
Portugal	351	PO
Spain	034	SP
Sweden	046	SV
Switzerland (Fr.)	041	SF
Switzerland (Ger.)	041	SG
United Kingdom	044	UK
United States	001	US

Table 11.2: International DOS country and keyboard codes

Thus, only a programmer can really obtain the specialized symbol and separator information necessary to customize an application program to the country it may run in. However, you can make a reasonable amount of adjustment yourself.

UNDERSTANDING CODE PAGES

DOS provides a complex ability to redefine its understanding of the keyboard you use. This is based on the new feature in DOS 3.3

called *code pages*. Code pages represent some complicated concepts, but with a little help and some extra knowledge, they can easily be understood. Let's start with the keyboard.

THE KEYBOARD TRANSLATION TABLE

The keyboard is simply a segregated group of buttons, monitored by a microprocessor that sends a signal to DOS when any key is pressed. The signal that goes to DOS is called a *scan code*. A scan code is not a letter or an ASCII code, but simply a code that tells DOS which key has been pressed. It has nothing to do with what is printed on the physical key, but merely with the physical location of the key.

At any time, whether DOS is busy or not, something will happen inside the computer when you press a key. This ''something'' is called an *interrupt*. One kind of interrupt occurs when a hardware device asks for the attention of the CPU. In the case of a keyboard, a small electrical signal—a scan code—is sent to DOS, indicating which key was pressed. The part of DOS that takes in the interrupt and processes it is called a *device driver* (or sometimes an *interrupt handler*).

When the keyboard device driver receives a signal, it processes the scan code to determine which key was pressed *and* to convert the scan code back into an ASCII code. This translation is done through a

During the entire process of handling each keyboard interrupt, DOS does not treat a scan code as any particular letter or symbol (such as the letter A), but simply as an ASCII code (such as 65).

```
C>TYPE \CONFIG.SYS
FILES=20
BUFFERS=15
DEVICE=C:\DOS\ANSI.SYS
COUNTRY=041

C>DATE
Current date is Thu  7.05.1987
Enter new date (dd-mm-yy):

C>TIME
Current time is 17.36.46.15
Enter new time:

C>_
```

Figure 11.1: Date and time requests for COUNTRY = Switzerland table in memory that compares scan codes and ASCII codes. Figure 11.2 diagrams this process.

Take a look at the two different Personal System/2 keyboards used in the United States and France, shown in Figures 11.3 and 11.4. There are more than fifty other keyboard layouts in use on different computers in different countries. All of these are understood by DOS; the complete layouts for these alternatives are displayed in your DOS user's manual.

On a U.S. keyboard, if you press A, its scan code will be translated into ASCII code 65. However, if you hit the same key on a computer with a French keyboard translation routine embedded in the device driver, the same scan code will be converted to ASCII code 81, or the letter Q.

If a key combination such as Alt-Ctrl-2 is pressed with the U.S. translator installed, not much will happen, because the U.S. keyboard translator does not have an entry in its table for this scan code. However, if you press this key combination on a computer with the French keyboard translator in effect, you will get the @ symbol. The French translator understands this scan code and will match it up. The ASCII code generated will be 64, which is the same code

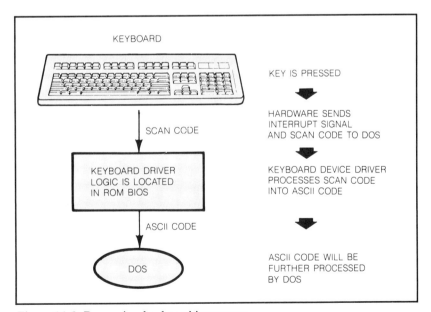

Figure 11.2: Processing keyboard interrupts

generated by pressing Shift-2 with a U.S. keyboard translator. Both yield the same @ symbol. The two keyboard translation tables translate different keyboard scan codes to the same ASCII codes, allowing countries with different keyboards to use all the same characters, even though the keys are labeled differently. Countries that have different keyboard layouts but still use the same character set are grouped into the same code page.

Figure 11.3: U.S. Personal System/2 keyboard

Figure 11.4: French Personal System/2 keyboard

CODE PAGES

After interpreting what key was pressed on the keyboard and converting the scan code into an ASCII code by means of a translation table, DOS next determines where the ASCII code should go. If it goes to a disk drive, it is simply routed there and stored on the disk. If, however, it is destined for a monitor or printer, it is first processed by a code page. A code page is yet another translation table that converts an ASCII code into a printable or displayable character.

There are five code pages available in DOS. The standard code page (numbered 437 in DOS) for the United States can be seen in Table 11.3. (Refer to Appendix B for a complete explanation of the hexadecimal system shown in this table, as well as other number systems.) The other principal code page is the Multilingual code page, numbered 850 (see Table 11.4). It contains a host of international characters.

You'll soon learn how to use and switch between these code pages, as well as the other three code pages also available in DOS (Portugese, Norwegian, and Canadian French). See your DOS user's

HEX DIGITS 1st 2nd	0-	1-	2-	3-	4-	5-	6-	7-	8-	9-	A-	B-	C-	D-	E-	F-
0-		►		0	@	P	`	p	Ç	É	á	▒	└	┴	α	≡
1-	☺	◄	!	1	A	Q	a	q	ü	æ	í	▓	┴	╤	β	±
2-	☻	↕	"	2	B	R	b	r	é	Æ	ó	▓	┬	╥	Γ	≥
3-	♥	‼	#	3	C	S	c	s	â	ô	ú	│	├	╙	π	≤
4-	♦	¶	$	4	D	T	d	t	ä	ö	ñ	┤	─	╘	Σ	⌠
5-	♣	§	%	5	E	U	e	u	à	ò	Ñ	╡	┼	╒	σ	⌡
6-	♠	▬	&	6	F	V	f	v	å	û	ª	╢	╞	╓	μ	÷
7-	•	↨	'	7	G	W	g	w	ç	ù	º	╖	╟	╫	τ	≈
8-	◘	↑	(	8	H	X	h	x	ê	ÿ	¿	╕	╚	╪	Φ	°
9-	○	↓	)	9	I	Y	i	y	ë	Ö	⌐	╣	╔	┘	Θ	∙
A-	◙	→	*	:	J	Z	j	z	è	Ü	¬	║	╩	┌	Ω	·
B-	♂	←	+	;	K	[	k	{	ï	¢	½	╗	╦	▓	δ	√
C-	♀	∟	,	<	L	\	l			î	£	¼	╝	╠	▬	∞	ⁿ
D-	♪	↔	-	=	M	]	m	}	ì	¥	¡	╜	═	▌	φ	²
E-	♫	▲	.	>	N	^	n	~	Ä	Pt	«	╛	╬	▐	ε	■
F-	☼	▼	/	?	O	_	o	⌂	Å	ƒ	»	┐	╧	▄	∩	

Table 11.3: Code page 437 for the United States

Hex Digits 1st / 2nd	0-	1-	2-	3-	4-	5-	6-	7-	8-	9-	A-	B-	C-	D-	E-	F-
0-		►		0	@	P	`	p	Ç	É	á	▓	└	ð	Ó	-
1-	☺	◄	!	1	A	Q	a	q	ü	æ	í	▒	┴	Ð	β	±
2-	☻	↕	"	2	B	R	b	r	é	Æ	ó	▓	┬	Ê	Ô	=
3-	♥	‼	#	3	C	S	c	s	â	ô	ú	│	├	Ë	Ò	¾
4-	♦	¶	$	4	D	T	d	t	ä	ö	ñ	┤	─	È	õ	¶
5-	♣	§	%	5	E	U	e	u	à	ò	Ñ	Á	┼	ı	Õ	§
6-	♠	▬	&	6	F	V	f	v	å	û	ª	Â	ã	Í	µ	÷
7-	•	↨	'	7	G	W	g	w	ç	ù	º	À	Ã	Î	þ	¸
8-	◘	↑	(	8	H	X	h	x	ê	ÿ	¿	©	└	Ï	Þ	°
9-	○	↓	)	9	I	Y	i	y	ë	Ö	®	╣	╒	┘	Ú	¨
A-	◎	→	*	:	J	Z	j	z	è	Ü	¬	║	╧	┌	Û	·
B-	♂	←	+	;	K	[	k	{	ï	ø	½	╗	╤	█	Ù	¹
C-	♀	∟	,	<	L	\	l			î	£	¼	╝	╟	▄	ý	³
D-	♪	↔	-	=	M	]	m	}	ì	Ø	¡	¢	─	¦	Ý	²
E-	♫	▲	.	>	N	^	n	~	Ä	×	«	¥	╪	Ì	´	■
F-	☼	▼	/	?	O	_	o	△	Å	ƒ	»	┐	□	▀	´	

Table 11.4: Code page 850 for multilingual operations

manual for the precise layouts of these remaining code pages.

Code pages are simply character sets. As you saw in the last section, one character set (code page) can satisfy the needs of several different countries. Countries with significantly different character sets and keyboards are grouped into other code pages. The 21 different country codes (shown in Table 11.2) correlate altogether with, at most, five different character sets, so only five different code pages are needed. Remember, a code page has 256 entries, so even if in the U.S. you rarely use an accented e, it is included in one of the extra spaces in the U.S. character set.

After the scan code has been translated into an ASCII code, it is matched to the currently active code-page translation table. Now you're into the output side of DOS management. The device driver responsible for the output device now uses built-in logic to send a sequence of control instructions to the output device. These instructions describe precisely how to display the character that was represented by the ASCII code. The process by which DOS and the output device drivers convert the ASCII code to visual output is shown in Figure 11.5.

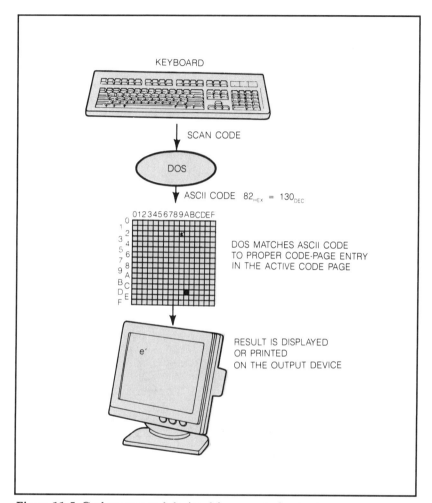

Figure 11.5: Code pages and device drivers control output

DEVICES AND THEIR DRIVERS

All output consists of sequences of codes being sent to an output device like a monitor or printer. Unfortunately, not all monitors or printers act the same, have the same features, or can be controlled by the same device driver. In fact, sometimes the device driver consists of software instructions residing in your computer's main memory, while at other times these instructions reside in special memory built into the output device. Microsoft provides device drivers for two printers, the IBM Proprinter Model 4201 and the IBM Quietwriter III Printer Model 5202, as well as device drivers for the PC Convertible display (LCD) and the Enhanced Graphics Adapter used on the PC-XT, PC-AT, and Personal System/2 displays.

Each output device driver translates the requested output data into the specific commands needed to form the character for each device. Figure 11.6 shows this part of the process. As the figure suggests, you must have one of the special monitors or printers to access any special additional symbols available in DOS 3.3's four code pages other than the U.S. page.

TRANSLATION TABLES AND DEVICE DRIVERS

DOS supports more than 50 different keyboard layouts and 11 languages. Microsoft has supplied all of the necessary keyboard

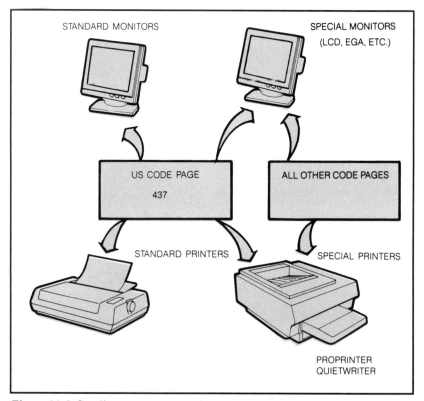

Figure 11.6: Sending output to standard and special devices

Some computers manufactured solely for foreign use have the foreign character set built in, as well as a keyboard with the appropriate key labels in place. These computers will not respond at all when you try to switch keyboard layouts with either the KEYB command or the Ctrl-Alt-function key combinations. No logic has been included to load in additional keyboard tables, since the necessary non-U.S. tables are already there.

translation tables in a file called KEYBOARD.SYS, which is loaded into the computer by using the KEYB command at the DOS prompt.

The output device drivers are loaded into memory from individual files. They are contained on the IBM startup disk in the files 4201.CPI, 5202.CPI, EGA.CPI, and LCD.CPI. CPI stands for code-page information; 4201 and 5202 refer to the IBM Proprinter and the IBM Quietwriter III Printer, respectively. EGA refers to both the standard Enhanced Graphics Adapter and the IBM Personal System/2 display types, while LCD will drive the IBM Convertible's LCD screen.

As you know, a DOS device driver has five different code pages to choose from. Each of these is referred to by a unique number, as shown in Table 11.5. Since code page 437 is the standard U.S. code page that is used with any monitor, 437 is the default when DOS boots up. This is the only code page that can be used with devices other than the two printers and two monitors supported by the drivers included with DOS 3.3 (see Figure 11.6).

Figure 11.7 ties all of the preceding sections together. It shows the entire process of moving information from beginning to end—from the keyboard interrupt to the final display or printed output.

Let's quickly run through a last example of the process. Assume you've loaded the Canadian French keyboard translation table into the computer (you'll learn how to do this in the next section). You've also loaded code page 863 and the 4201.CPI device driver, as you wish to print a character on the Proprinter. The character you want to print is the 3/4 symbol, which is not included in the normal ASCII

LANGUAGE	CODE PAGE
United States	437
Multilingual	850
Portuguese	860
Canadian French	863
Norwegian and Danish	865

Table 11.5: Code-page identification numbers

character set of U.S. computers or printers. The 3/4 symbol on the Canadian keyboard can be printed by using the key combination Alt-Shift- = .

When this key combination is pressed, a scan code is sent to the keyboard device driver, which routes the scan code to the keyboard

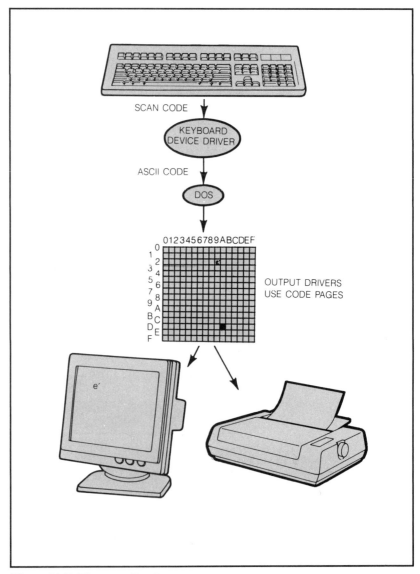

Figure 11.7: The overall code-page process

translation table. Here, the scan code is matched against the ASCII table, and an ASCII code (in this case, 173) is sent back to DOS. DOS sees that this character was destined for the printer and sends it on its way. The code is now processed by the Proprinter, which uses the installed code page. The Proprinter's driver now translates ASCII 173 to a set of hardware instructions that describe how to print a 3/4 symbol.

WORKING WITH CODE PAGES

Now that you understand how code pages are used, you must learn the required sequence of DOS 3.3 commands necessary to implement them. You first need to learn how to tell DOS that you will be using the national language-support scheme (NLS), which is just another name for the code-page mechanism. You also need to learn how to prepare, select, and switch between the various code pages. The following sections will teach you the mechanics of the process. Figure 11.8 provides an overview of the DOS command sequences necessary for a complete international setup, which you will explore in this chapter.

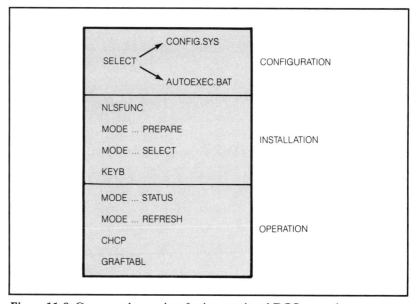

Figure 11.8: Command overview for international DOS operations

LOADING CODE-PAGE SUPPORT ROUTINES

NLSFUNC (short for national language-support functions) is a DOS 3.3 command that allows for the use of the new extended country information provided with DOS 3.3. This command will load in all of the required country-specific information. It must be run *before* you attempt to select any code page other than the default (437). As part of the format for the NLSFUNC command, you must tell DOS where you've placed the COUNTRY.SYS file. This file contains information that defines the country standards, such as the date and time format, the rules of capitalization, and special symbol usage for each of the 21 available country codes (see Table 11.2). U.S. standards will be assumed if you neglect to specify the location of the COUNTRY.SYS file.

Assuming you have created a DOS directory that contains COUNTRY.SYS, the command can be invoked as simply as

    NLSFUNC \DOS\COUNTRY.SYS

The code-page support routines will be loaded into memory. No direct action or messages will be shown on the screen.

LOADING SPECIFIC CODE PAGES

After preparing DOS for national language-support operations, you can select specific code pages to use. The primary command for this purpose is a familiar one: MODE. In DOS 3.3 this command has several versions. They all have a similar format:

    MODE *DeviceName* CODEPAGE *Clause*

DeviceName is any valid DOS output reserved name, such as CON or LPT2. *Clause* represents a parameter you can use with several different values:

- You can load the desired code pages with a PREPARE parameter; you specify that one to five code pages be available for output operations.

- Use the SELECT parameter to choose which of the code pages is to be the active one for a particular output device.

- Use the /STATUS parameter to display the status of all code pages and connected output devices supporting code-page operations.

- For advanced output devices that retain code-page information in memory located within the device itself (as opposed to main memory), use the REFRESH parameter to restore the information in case the device is turned off or loses power.

Let's discuss the processing managed by the MODE command in a bit more depth. You first use the PREPARE parameter to install the code-page information necessary for the output drivers to handle the special international characters. With the SELECT parameter you then select the code page to be activated on the specified device. This means you can have several code pages loaded into the device at once, but only one can be active at any one time. At any time, you can use the /STATUS parameter to display the active code page and all of the other code pages available. Finally, with REFRESH you can reinstall the currently active output driver into the specified device if it was erased due to power loss.

With the PREPARE parameter, you can load one or several code pages for a device with one MODE command. This requires that you specify the device reserved name, the list of allowable code pages (one or more), and the file containing the output driver. Code page 437 is the default code page; it is automatically loaded into the device. 437 is also the only code page that can access a nonspecified device (that is, one that IBM has not specifically written drivers for).

Think of it this way. A small buffer is set up for each device, and into this buffer can go from one to five code-page specifications, one of which is active at a time. For example, entering

```
MODE CON CODEPAGE PREPARE = ((850,437)
C:\DOS\EGA.CPI)
```

will load the code-page information file EGA.CPI, specify that code pages 850 and 437 be selected for possible activation, and attach these code-page values to the EGA display.

In all versions of the MODE command, CODEPAGE can be contracted to CP. In addition, PREPARE can be abbreviated to PREP, SELECT to SEL, REFRESH to REF, and STATUS to STA. You can reduce your typing burden by using these abbreviations, as well as saving time and reducing the likelihood of errors. The full spelling is shown in this chapter for the sake of clarity only.

Suppose that later you decide that you want to replace 850 with 863, and that also you want to make code page 865 available. You would enter

MODE CON CODEPAGE PREPARE = ((863,,865) C:\DOS\EGA.CPI)

The two commas hold the place of the second code page, thereby leaving 437 (the U.S. code page) as the second code page. If you had specified ((,850,437) instead, then the first code page would have been saved and the second and third written over and reset to 850 and 437.

If you execute this command and the requested device is unavailable (not hooked up), you will get the message

Codepage operation not supported on this device

Assuming you really do have a device that supports code-page operations, check to see that it is connected properly to your system, that it is powered up, and that it is on-line.

The next parameter for the international version of the MODE command can only be used after you have properly prepared your code pages with PREPARE; the SELECT parameter will only work if the requested code-page device driver has been loaded. SELECT activates the specified code page on the specified device. For example, entering

MODE CON CODEPAGE SELECT = 850

If the device driver for your output device is resident in hardware, using PRE-PARE is unnecessary, since it will overwrite the hardware page. See your DOS user's manual for more detail on hardware code pages.

will make code page 850 the active code page for the console or the display device. Using this parameter in the previous example would make 850 active for an EGA display.

When you want to see information on the currently active code page, as well as a list of selectable code pages for a specific active device, you only need to enter

MODE CON CODEPAGE /STATUS

DOS will display information about the current code page assigned to the monitor and keyboard.

The last parameter, REFRESH, is very useful if for some reason you need to turn your printer off. The output device drivers stay resident inside the device they drive. The available code pages and their related information are available through DOS, which is resident in your computer. So, when a device driver is installed, a copy is made of the code-page information in the computer and loaded into the memory of the device. If the device is turned off, then its memory is lost, and hence its modified driver. However, the original copy is still in the computer's memory. Instead of having to load the code page again with PREPARE, REFRESH just makes another copy and sends it out to the device's memory.

For example, suppose you've entered the following sequence of commands:

```
MODE LPT1 CODEPAGE PREPARE = ((850,437)
\DOS\4201.CPI)
MODE LPT1 CODEPAGE SELECT = 850
```

This means you have installed code-page information for the IBM 4201 Proprinter and that you have two code pages to choose from, with 850 the currently active code page. Selecting a code page (with SELECT) causes the code-page driver to be copied into the hardware device (in this case, the printer connected to LPT1). Now, if you decide to turn the Proprinter off and then back on (perhaps to reset some switches), it would lose its local memory copy of the code-page information. To reload the code-page driver without spending the system's time to retrieve it from the disk, you would issue the command

```
MODE LPT1 CODEPAGE REFRESH
```

LOADING A KEYBOARD TRANSLATION TABLE

You have properly prepared your system to use national language support with the NLSFUNC command. You have also correctly installed the desired code-page information with MODE's PREPARE parameter, and you have selected a specific code page to use with MODE's SELECT parameter. The next step involves the KEYB command. This command is used to load in a new keyboard translation table for a specific country. In fact, it loads in a complete replacement for the keyboard driver resident in your computer's hardware (ROM BIOS). You can now select from the 21 different country codes you saw in Table 11.2.

If you were using alternate character sets in previous versions of DOS, then you need to use code page 850 in DOS 3.3, since the character sets and keyboard layouts of the previous versions are incompatible with this version (see Table 11.6).

COUNTRY	KEYBOARD CODE	EXISTING CODE PAGE	NEW CODE PAGE
Australia	US	437	850
Belgium	BE	437	850
Canada—English	US	437	850
Canada—French	CF	863	850
Denmark	DK	865	850
Finland	SU	437	850
France	FR	437	850
Germany	GR	437	850
Italy	IT	437	850
Latin America	LA	437	850
Netherlands	NL	437	850
Norway	NO	865	850
Portugal	PO	860	850
Spain	SP	437	850
Sweden	SV	437	850
Switzerland—French	SF	437	850
Switzerland—German	SG	437	850
United Kingdom	UK	437	850
United States	US	437	850

Table 11.6: Old versus new code-page conversion table

The Multilingual code page (850) can support the primary character symbols used by all countries. If you switch between documents from different countries, it would be a good idea to load in code page 850 in addition to your native code page so that you can view these other documents.

The general format for the KEYB command is

KEYB *KeyCode, CodePage, FileSpec*

where *KeyCode* is one of the two-letter country codes in Table 11.2, *CodePage* is one of the five three-digit code-page numbers, and *FileSpec* is the full path name to the keyboard definition file KEYBOARD-.SYS. For example, entering the command

KEYB NL, 850, \DOS\KEYBOARD.SYS

will load the Netherlands keyboard translation table, based on code page 850, which is contained in the KEYBOARD.SYS file. Located in the DOS directory, the KEYBOARD.SYS file contains all of the keyboard translation tables for all possible countries.

Once you complete this initialization, the keys on the keyboard will no longer necessarily result in the letter, number, or character shown on the key. The assumption is that you will be using one of the scores of different keyboard layouts, each with its own key labels. In fact, if you're taking advantage of the keyboard reconfiguration capability but you are still using your original keyboard, it's a good idea to get new key labels, switch the key labels around, or simply to put new labels on the keys that have been changed.

There are often more accented characters than there are possible keys to assign. In this case, DOS understands special two-key sequences to represent the specially accented character. For instance, certain foreign letters require a circumflex over them. On the French keyboard, this symbol looks like the control, or "hat," symbol located over the 6 on the top row of a U.S. keyboard. In order to create this particular language-dependent effect, you must press the lowercase key just to the right of the letter p and *then* press the letter you want to put the circumflex over. In other words, you must employ a two-keystroke sequence to generate the two-part character symbol.

The set of these special keys that initiate a two-part character sequence are referred to as *dead keys* in DOS. If you make a mistake in typing the sequence, DOS will usually beep at you, show the erroneous result, and require you to erase the error and reenter the proper dead-key sequence. In this way, DOS provides yet another time-saving capability with the KEYB command, which saves you from having to touch up your text results with added accents and other special marks after the fact.

You can have up to two keyboard translation tables in memory at one time, but one of these must always be the standard U.S. table. To switch between the U.S. and another translation table, use these key combinations:

- Ctrl-Alt-F1 for the standard U.S. translation table
- Ctrl-Alt-F2 for a non-U.S. translation table

SWITCHING BETWEEN AVAILABLE CODE PAGES

Now that your system is prepared for code pages and you've selected one to be active, there may be times when you'd like to switch to a different code page. You'll need to do this when you are switching between documents written by personnel either in or for different contries. The CHCP command allows you to change the currently loaded code page. It is a very simple command to use. By issuing the command

CHCP 850

If you only want to change the code page on a particular device, use the MODE command with SELECT. Use the CHCP command to change all prepared code-page devices at once.

you can replace the currently active code page with code page 850. Any of the other four possible code-page numbers can be used if they have been properly prepared with the MODE command first.

The CHCP command does not have a parameter indicating which output device is being selected. That's because CHCP works on all prepared output devices, changing the active code page on all of them to the requested number.

DISPLAYING EXTENDED ASCII CODES ON A COLOR GRAPHICS ADAPTER

A CGA monitor shows less detail than EGA, PGA, and VGA monitors because it has fewer pixels. When your CGA monitor is in graphics mode, you must use the GRAFTABL command in order to display the nonstandard characters with ASCII codes above 128. Entering

GRAFTABL 860

will load the Portugese code page and display the following message:

Portugese Version of Graphic Character Set Table has just been Loaded.

This means that the characters—whether graphics symbols or national symbols—that occupy the ASCII codes above code 128 will be accessible, and the ones displayed will be those from the special Portuguese code page.

To dramatize the necessity of this command, Figure 11.9 shows the extended ASCII codes for the U.S. code page when a CGA

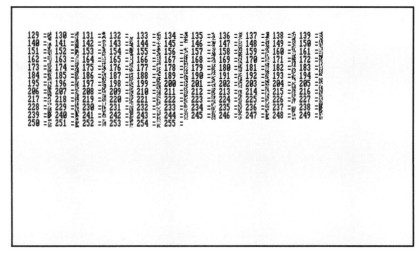

Figure 11.9: Extended ASCII codes before GRAFTABL is used

You should only consider using the GRAFTABL command if you run programs that set the video mode to graphics. Otherwise, you lose the memory occupied by the alternate character set and gain nothing in return.

monitor is in graphics mode. As you can see, the characters are indecipherable. After GRAFTABL 437 is executed, however, the codes are displayable, as shown in Figure 11.10.

If you use this command, make sure that the path is set properly for finding it. Also make sure that you run the GRAFTABL command *before* invoking the programs that use the CGA graphics mode. Naturally, if you will be facing this problem on a regular basis, you should add the GRAFTABL command to your AUTOEXEC.BAT file (you will learn how later in this chapter).

PREPARING AN INTERNATIONAL DOS SYSTEM DISK

DOS provides a special command, SELECT, which can save you a good deal of trouble if your principal goal is to have a system disk that supports code-page switching. With the following methods and commands, the delimiter format and keyboard information for each country can be installed permanently on a disk.

INSTALLING COUNTRY AND KEYBOARD INFORMATION

The SELECT command expects to read all the necessary DOS information from your startup and operating disks, now located on a diskette on drive A or B. It will manage the formatting of the destination disk and the copying of all necessary DOS files onto this other disk. (The destination disk must not be the same as the source disk.) You must specify the desired three-digit country code and the two-letter keyboard code, both from the list in Table 11.2.

The required format of the SELECT command is

SELECT *Source Destination xxx yy*

Source is either A or B; it must contain the KEYBOARD.SYS, COUNTRY.SYS, FORMAT.COM, and XCOPY.EXE files. *Destination* is the drive and path to which the DOS command files will be copied. (The root directory is the default, but if you use the SELECT command to set up a hard disk, you would be advised to arrange a

Figure 11.10: Extended ASCII codes after GRAFTABL is used

specialized subdirectory to hold the appropriate files.) The *xxx* is the country code, and the *yy* is the keyboard code. Since the U.S. keyboard file is resident in the computer's memory, it does not need to be on the source disk.

When you first execute SELECT, the following message appears on the screen:

> **SELECT is used to install DOS the first time. SELECT erases**
> **everything on the specified target and then installs DOS.**
> **Do you want to continue (Y/N)?**

Entering Y will start the process, while N will abort it.

Here is an example of the SELECT command. Entering

SELECT B: C:\JUDD 001 US

will format and copy the DOS commands files to drive C, directory JUDD, executed from drive B, and install drive C with the U.S. rules for the date, time, and so on.

The SELECT command will also create two files on the destination disk. These are an initial AUTOEXEC.BAT file:

PATH \;\JUDD;
KEYB US 437 \JUDD\KEYBOARD.SYS

○ If you are using a high-density drive as the destination drive for the SELECT command, you *must* use high-capacity diskettes. Also, since the SELECT command uses the FORMAT command, anything on the destination disk will be destroyed during the preparation of the disk. If you prepare a hard-disk drive in this way, you must be careful.

```
ECHO OFF
CLS
DATE
TIME
VER
```

and the CONFIG.SYS file:

COUNTRY = 001,437,\JUDD\COUNTRY.SYS

The next section provides more details about these two files. SELECT will also copy all of the contents of the source disk, including COMMAND.COM, into the specified directory. The six files that must be accessible on your source drive for this command to work are COMMAND.COM, FORMAT.COM, SELECT.COM, XCOPY.EXE, KEYBOARD.SYS, and, finally, COUNTRY.SYS.

MODIFYING THE REQUIRED SYSTEM FILES YOURSELF

The CONFIG.SYS and AUTOEXEC.BAT files can contain statements that will automate some of this setup for you if you don't want to rely on SELECT alone. You've already read about using CONFIG.SYS, and you'll read about AUTOEXEC.BAT in more detail in Chapter 15. You can make these adjustments with your own word processor, with DOS's EDLIN editor, or by using the COPY command. COPY can be used to add a line (say, *FileName*) to any ASCII file in the following way. You can type the command

COPY *FileName* + CON

When you are done entering lines to be added, press Ctrl-Z and Return. You will now be back at the DOS prompt.

UPDATING THE CONFIG.SYS FILE FOR INTERNATIONAL SUPPORT

The DEVICE configuration command in CONFIG.SYS can be used to load the various drivers needed for code-page switching.

Assuming you have typed the above command or are in an editor and are creating or modifying a CONFIG.SYS file, adding the following lines will install the various required drivers. In these cases, you need a different DEVICE line in your CONFIG.SYS for each different printer and display device.

The sample entry

DEVICE = *D:*\DISPLAY.SYS CON: = (*Type,Hwcp,x*)

in your CONFIG.SYS file loads the specialized display device drivers. *D* is the location of the DISPLAY.SYS file. *Type* is either LCD or EGA, depending on the display being used. *Hwcp* is the code-page number(s) supported directly by the hardware device, and *x* is how many code pages will be added. The value for *x* should be 1 if 437 is the current code page, and 2 if it isn't.

This entry loads the specialized device drivers supporting the Proprinter and Quietwriter:

DEVICE = *D:*\PRINTER.SYS LPT1: = (*Type,Hwcp,x*)

The parameters are the same as those just described, except that *Type* can be 4201 or 5202.

The IBM Proprinter Model 4201 reserves a hardware memory area in its own read-only memory (ROM) specifically for code-page information. The IBM Quietwriter III Printer Model 5202 uses hardware font cartridges to perform the same support purpose.

You can also have the country automatically set at the time your system boots up. The line to add to your CONFIG.SYS file is

COUNTRY = *xxx*

where *xxx* is the appropriate country code.

UPDATING YOUR AUTOEXEC.BAT FILE

Commands can be added to the AUTOEXEC.BAT file in the same way as they are for the CONFIG.SYS file. Including the KEYB command in the AUTOEXEC.BAT file lets the keyboard translation table and country codes be loaded in automatically. For example, adding the following line to your AUTOEXEC.BAT file:

    KEYB FR 033

will automatically load the keyboard and country information for France.

You can also include versions of the NLSFUNC, MODE, and CHCP commands, which will work in conjunction with the CON-FIG.SYS statements. As an example, the following lines included in your AUTOEXEC.BAT file would initialize national language-support operations, prepare code pages 863, 437, and 850, load the keyboard information file for France, and then select 850 as the active code page for both output devices:

    NLSFUNC
    MODE CON: CP PREPARE = ((863,437,850) \DOS\EGA.CPI)
    MODE CON: CP PREPARE = ((863,437,850) \DOS\4201.CPI)
    KEYB FR 033
    CHCP 850

SUMMARY

Along with the PC family of computers, DOS has been a world-wide phenomenon. Recognizing this international influence, DOS provides certain features that allow you to customize your operating version. Although the specific commands and functions for national language support will be used primarily by only a small percentage of users, you may be one of that small group. This chapter is then critical to understanding the intertwined requirements of DOS setup.

- DOS supports many different languages and countries. DOS 3.3 supports five different groups of 256-character ASCII codes, called code pages.

- There are 11 different languages in 17 different countries, using 58 different keyboard layouts. DOS supports them all with a series of specialized commands.

- The code page is the fundamental table of information available to device drivers. Device drivers manage input from the keyboard (KEYBOARD.SYS) and output to printers and monitors (DISPLAY.SYS).

- Special identification codes exist in DOS 3.3 for each country (21 different codes for 17 different countries) and for each keyboard used in those countries.

- Keyboard device drivers convert scan codes, which represent the key that was pressed, to ASCII codes. The precise ASCII code depends on which of five code pages is active.

- Output drivers for the IBM Quietwriter III Printer Model 5202 and the IBM Proprinter Model 4201 support printing of any of the specialized code-page symbols. Also available to support international output are the output drivers for the Enhanced Graphics Adapter, the IBM PC Convertible LCD display, and the IBM Personal System/2 displays.

- The DOS 3.3 NLSFUNC command loads national language-support functions. It is an essential first command for the installation of international operations.

- DOS 3.3 expands the roles of the MODE command to include new parameters, which allow you to prepare an output device for code-page use, select a specific code page for a particular display or printer, present the current code-page status of a device, and to restore the code page in the hardware of certain output devices.

- Code pages can be activated or changed for all connected and prepared output devices by specifying a CHCP command along with the number of the desired code page.

- The KEYB command is needed to specify which country and keyboard combination is to be activated for keyboard input, once your national language-support operations have been fully installed.

- Certain keys on some foreign keyboards understand two-key sequences to implement accents. The first key selects the accent mark, but displays nothing; it is called a dead key. The second key selects the character to be accented and displayed.

- A single keystroke can switch between U.S. and foreign code-page selections.

- You may not have a fancy new monitor, but you may want to display the extended ASCII characters (codes 128–255) on your CGA monitor when it is in graphics mode. You can do that by loading in an alternate character set with the GRAF-TABL command.

- The SELECT command prepares a system disk that is properly configured for international operations. If you specify the desired code pages and the proper country code, DOS will create a system disk with all necessary files on it.

- SELECT also creates the useful CONFIG.SYS and AUTOEXEC.BAT files with the necessary initial lines for national language-support operations.

- You can adjust your own CONFIG.SYS file with the appropriate new DEVICE command for required keyboard and display output device drivers.

- You can update your own AUTOEXEC.BAT file to include the necessary NLSFUNC, MODE, KEYB, CHCP, and GRAFTABL commands for your system.

In the last four chapters, you've learned a good deal about customizing DOS. From controlling output and backups, to creating customized configurations and international layouts, you've done a good deal of work. The next chapter will present the last major subject in the "Revving It Up" section. It will focus on DOS's ability to redirect and filter all input and output information.

REDIRECTING THE
ACTION

A major benefit of DOS is its support commands, which affect whole files. Several additional features also enable you to manage your computer system more efficiently. These features offer you additional ways to control input and output in your system, as well as new ways to process your information. They are of great interest to programmers designing automated applications for DOS systems; they are also of practical value for anyone using DOS. In this chapter, you'll concentrate on three related features: redirection, filters, and pipes. These enable you to manage your computer information as it flows from one place to another in your system.

CONTROLLING THE FLOW OF INFORMATION BY REDIRECTION

Redirection refers to the ability of a program or a DOS command to choose an alternative device for input or output. As you know, most programs and commands have a default device. For example, when you enter the DIR command, the computer assumes that you want a directory to be displayed on the screen. This is because the default for DIR is the console (CON), which consists of the screen as the output device and the keyboard as the input device. Your normal "interface" with the microcomputer system is through the system console.

SENDING SCREEN OUTPUT TO THE PRINTER

You often need a hard-copy printout of the information that appears on your computer screen. As you learned in Chapter 7, the Ctrl-PrtSc key combination is limited to only one screenful of information at a time. However, it is often useful to send the complete output from a command such as DIR to another device, such as the printer. DOS has a simple way of redirecting the complete output, no matter how many screenfuls of data are involved.

Following a command with >PRN tells DOS to redirect the output to the printer. Think of the > sign as an arrow pointing to the destination. Entering the following command will redirect the standard DOS directory listing to the printer (PRN), instead of to the video screen:

DIR >PRN

The same principle of redirection applies to any DOS command that sends data to the screen. Entering

CHKDSK >PRN

will generate a status check of disk and memory and send it to the printer rather than to the video screen.

STORING SCREEN OUTPUT IN A DISK FILE

DOS can also direct the output to a text file. This means that the information displayed on the screen can be sent to a file on the disk. Screen displays are temporary; if a directory display is captured and stored in a file, however, its information can be used at a later time.

This redirection technique has many practical uses. If you're in a hurry and don't want to wait for printed output, you can quickly send the information to a disk file and then peruse it at your leisure. You can read it into your word-processing program and make modifications to it, or include it in reports. You can read it with a database management program and perform file management functions based on the information sent by DOS into the disk file.

An excellent use of redirection is to create a file that is a catalog of the contents of several diskettes. If you were working with a word processor or a database program, you could then get a master listing of all the files you have stored on all your working diskettes. If you were working with a hard disk, you could make a catalog of your backup disks.

The first step in creating your own diskette catalog is to decide where the master list will be placed. Let's assume you want to place the data in a file called CATALOG. The first cataloged directory will be that of the diskette in drive A. Entering

DIR A: > CATALOG

produces no visible result on the screen. You told DOS not to display the directory on the screen, but rather to store the information in a file called CATALOG. If you were watching, you would have seen the A drive light come on as the CATALOG file was being written.

To check the results of this command, you can ask DOS to type the contents of the CATALOG file:

TYPE CATALOG

The directory will be displayed just as if you had typed in the DIR command. However, this printout represents the directory when the original CATALOG file was created by DOS; it is like a snapshot of the original directory. It contains only the directory information that existed when the file was created.

Redirecting DOS output to a disk file can be misleading. Remember that the information contained in that file will not be current and will not be updated automatically to reflect any future changes to your system.

Try the following sequence now to reinforce your understanding of redirection. Redirect the output from the DIR and CHKDSK commands at the DOS prompt to a disk file. You can call this file CATALOG, or you can give it a name of your own. Then use the TYPE command to verify that the output was generated properly.

Later on, you can see that the contents of this file are unchanging. After doing some other work with the system, issue a DIR or CHKDSK command at the DOS prompt again. Then compare the results to the snapshot contained in your CATALOG file.

ADDING OUTPUT TO AN EXISTING FILE

Redirection also allows you to add the directory display of another drive to the CATALOG file. This requires a slightly different command. Look at the following two commands:

```
DIR A: > CATALOG
DIR A: >> CATALOG
```

They look quite similar. However, the first command has one > symbol and the second has two. What is the difference?

The first command simply replaces the old CATALOG file with a new one. The second command, on the other hand, causes the CATALOG file to contain the directory listings of *both* of the diskettes. The >> symbol indicates that the output from the DIR command should be *appended* to (added to) the existing CATALOG file. The directory listing of the new diskette placed in drive A will be appended to the directory listing of the diskette previously placed in drive A.

You can continue this process by placing other diskettes in drive A and repeating the >> command. CATALOG will grow as you store your diskette directories on it. If you are a hard-disk user, you can place your diskettes in A, and your CATALOG file will be updated on drive C.

To see the contents of this file, you can simply enter

```
TYPE CATALOG
```

The result will be a consolidated directory that spans the contents of a number of diskettes.

If you need a hard copy of the directories, you can redirect the data to your printer and use the TYPE command:

```
TYPE CATALOG > PRN
```

You can edit this command's output with your word processor, print the results on gummed labels, and attach them to your original diskettes. Some companies sell programs for $50 that do this simple task.

Try the redirection feature yourself right now. Create your own CATALOG file, listing all the file names on several diskettes. If you're interested only in the names themselves and not in the size or date and time information, use a DIR/W command to direct the output to your CATALOG file. Remember to use a single > sign to create the file and a double >> sign to append new directory output to it. Dual-diskette users should place the diskettes to be cataloged into drive B, creating the CATALOG file on drive A. Hard-disk users should place their diskettes into drive A, creating the CATALOG file on drive C.

RECEIVING INPUT FROM TEXT FILES

DOS can receive input from a text file. This means that instead of waiting at the console to enter data, make responses, or otherwise generate input for a DOS command or a program, you can type your responses in advance. DOS will then take each response from the input file as it is needed. Let's look at a simple example.

Input from a file is more unusual than output. In the normal course of computer use, most users will not take advantage of the feature described here. However, it can be useful.

You may have noticed that some DOS commands require the user to enter additional keystrokes after the program has begun. For example, the FORMAT command will always pause and ask you to press any key before actual formatting takes place. This safety precaution protects you from errors, giving you a moment to take a deep breath (and to check the disk in the drive) before actually committing yourself to the formatting process.

You could avoid that extra keystroke by creating an input file to be used with the FORMAT command. The input file would contain any keystrokes that you wanted typed in while the program was running. In this case, a simple press of the Return key will do. To create a file containing a Return character, you could use a word processor, or you could create the KEYS file from the DOS prompt using the COPY command you saw earlier. Enter

    COPY CON: KEYS

and press Return. Then press Return again. Enter

    N

and press Return. Then enter

    ^Z

and press Return. The KEYS file now contains the keystroke for the Return key. It also contains the No response (N) to the FORMAT command's request ''Do you want to format an additional diskette?''

To indicate that these responses are coming from a file and not from you at the keyboard, the < symbol is used:

FORMAT B:/S < KEYS

When you enter this command, the formatting does not pause—the Return keypress has been input from the KEYS file. When the single disk is completely formatted, the N tells FORMAT you're done, and the DOS prompt reappears. As you can see, this kind of feature can save you time and effort, and can be useful in many situations.

PROCESSING YOUR FILE INFORMATION WITH DOS FILTERS

Another powerful feature of DOS is its use of *filters* to process data directly. Just as a camera filter changes what you see through the lens, a DOS filter can process in unique ways any data that passes through it and can change what you see on the screen. There are three filters included in DOS: SORT, FIND, and MORE. They are stored on disk as the SORT.EXE, FIND.EXE, and MORE.COM files.

ARRANGING YOUR DATA WITH THE SORT FILTER

Let's look first at one of the most useful filters, the SORT filter. SORT rearranges lines of data. Take a look at the sample data files in Figures 12.1 and 12.2. These lists could have been prepared with a word processor, a database manager, a spreadsheet, or even with DOS itself. Lists like these usually grow in size, with the new entries added chronologically as your business acquires new clients or as you make new friends and acquaintances.

Every once in a while, you probably rewrite your own personal phone list. You usually want the list in last-name order, but you might want a special printout in nickname or first-name order. Even more often, businesses need to reprint their client list in some usable order. Perhaps the telephone receptionist needs an updated list in company-name order. The marketing department may need the

```
C>TYPE  BUSINESS.TXT
Cantonese Imports    134   Roberts   Joseph  212/656-2156
Brandenberg Gates    754   Bennett   Mary    415/612-5656
Sole Survivor,Inc.   237   Evans     Gail    415/222-3514
Presley Plastics     198   Presley   Robert  716/245-6119
Plymouth Granite Co  345   Williams  Peter   617/531-6145
Bucket Dance Wear    276   Lewis     Ann     415/635-2530
Intelli-Strategies   743   Griffiths Robert  415/362-9537
Benicia Balloons     983   Franklin  Marie   212/524-4157
Standard Shelters    690   Rucker    Sally   415/532-1107
Panama Rain Corp.    576   Cook      Freda   408/534-9739

C>_
```

Figure 12.1: A business contact list

```
C>TYPE PERSONAL.TXT
Klaar     Wim      213-968-2345   Ready
Torrance  Stan     415-567-4534   Stan
Quilling  Alan     415-526-4565   Al
Keepsake  Alice    415-249-3498   Jala
Bentley   Robert   415-654-4864   Speed
Hendley   Candice  415-212-3434   Candy

C>_
```

Figure 12.2: A personal phone list

same list printed in telephone-number order. Then again, the accounts payable department may want the list in customer ID order. All of these are very easy to obtain with the SORT filter.

Using the redirection concept presented in the previous section, you can take each of these representative lists and rearrange the data to suit your needs. The easiest form of filtering is to enter the following command at the DOS prompt:

SORT < BUSINESS.TXT

The resulting screen will display the original lines of the file in company-name order (see Figure 12.3).

A similar arrangement of your personal phone list could be obtained by entering

SORT < PERSONAL.TXT

In this case, the arrangement is by last name (see Figure 12.4).

In both examples just given, the .TXT files were directed to be *input* to the SORT command—the < arrowhead points to SORT. Since there was no redirection specified for output, the sorted results appeared on the video screen. Each of these commands could also specify an output redirection that would place the sorted results in a disk file. You could then work with the sorted file as you liked, perhaps delaying the printing until a convenient time.

The two sorted lists could be saved in the files CLIENTS.TXT and PHONES.TXT with the following commands:

SORT < BUSINESS.TXT > CLIENTS.TXT
SORT < PERSONAL.TXT > PHONES.TXT

> These lists are sorted by whatever data comes first on the line. Later in this chapter, you'll learn how to use SORT to arrange the data based on other information in each line.

```
C>SORT  <  BUSINESS.TXT
Benicia Balloons      983  Franklin   Marie  212/524-4157
Brandenberg Gates     754  Bennett    Mary   415/612-5656
Bucket Dance Wear     276  Lewis      Ann    415/635-2530
Cantonese Imports     134  Roberts    Joseph 212/656-2156
Intelli-Strategies    743  Griffiths  Robert 415/362-9537
Panama Rain Corp.     576  Cook       Freda  408/534-9739
Plymouth Granite Co   345  Williams   Peter  617/531-6145
Presley Plastics      198  Presley    Robert 716/245-6119
Sole Survivor,Inc.    237  Evans      Gail   415/222-3514
Standard Shelters     690  Rucker     Sally  415/532-1107

C>_
```

Figure 12.3: Sorting by company name

Figures 12.5 and 12.6 show the verification of these results with the TYPE command. Figure 12.7 shows how the SORT filter works.

PERFORMING TEXT SEARCHES
WITH THE FIND FILTER

Let's look at another DOS filter, the FIND command. It permits you to scan any text file for a series of text characters and to locate any

```
C>SORT  <  PERSONAL.TXT
Bentley   Robert   415-654-4864   Speed
Hendley   Candice  415-212-3434   Candy
Keepsake  Alice    415-249-3498   Jala
Klaar     Wim      213-968-2345   Ready
Quilling  Alan     415-526-4565   Al
Torrance  Stan     415-567-4534   Stan

C>_
```

Figure 12.4: Sorting by last name

```
C>SORT  <  BUSINESS.TXT  >  CLIENTS.TXT

C>TYPE CLIENTS.TXT
Benicia Balloons     983  Franklin  Marie   212/524-4157
Brandenberg Gates    754  Bennett   Mary    415/612-5656
Bucket Dance Wear    276  Lewis     Ann     415/635-2530
Cantonese Imports    134  Roberts   Joseph  212/656-2156
Intelli-Strategies   743  Griffiths Robert  415/362-9537
Panama Rain Corp.    576  Cook      Freda   408/534-9739
Plymouth Granite Co  345  Williams  Peter   617/531-6145
Presley Plastics     198  Presley   Robert  716/245-6119
Sole Survivor,Inc.   237  Evans     Gail    415/222-3514
Standard Shelters    690  Rucker    Sally   415/532-1107

C>_
```

Figure 12.5: Sorted client list in text file

lines in the file that contain the specified characters. For instance, let's take the business contact list from Figure 12.1 and try to find all clients located in the area code 415:

FIND "415" BUSINESS.TXT

```
C>SORT  <  PERSONAL.TXT  >  PHONES.TXT

C>TYPE PHONES.TXT
Bentley   Robert  415-654-4864   Speed
Hendley   Candice 415-212-3434   Candy
Keepsake  Alice   415-249-3498   Jala
Klaar     Wim     213-968-2345   Ready
Quilling  Alan    415-526-4565   Al
Torrance  Stan    415-567-4534   Stan

C>_
```

Figure 12.6: Sorted phone list in text file

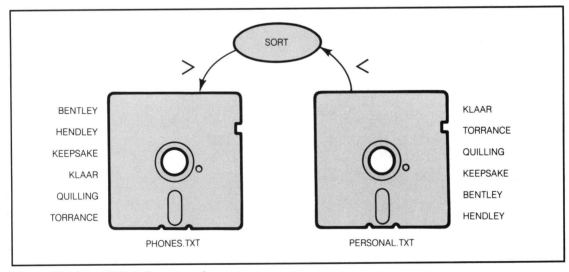

Figure 12.7: The SORT filter at work

The quotation marks around your character strings are delimiters. You must use them. They assist DOS in distinguishing a character string from the command line's other characters, which represent commands, file names, or parameters.

This command will locate all lines in the specified text file (the second argument) that contain the specified character string (the first argument). Figure 12.8 demonstrates the results. Note that the first line of the output identifies the input text file.

This is a typical database extraction request that has been handled by DOS *almost* satisfactorily. Notice that the Benicia Balloons company has been included in the results, even though its area code is not 415. You asked DOS to find every line in the file that included 415 anywhere in the line, and 415 is in the last four digits of that company's telephone number (524-4157). Therefore, the line was filtered into the resulting selection.

To solve this problem, you can specify ''415/'' as the character string. By including the slash you will be sure to extract only the telephone numbers that begin with the desired digits. Enter

FIND "415/" BUSINESS.TXT

Make sure your specified character string is unique enough to find only the data you're looking for. The fewer characters in your string, the greater the likelihood that DOS will find lines containing those characters.

Figure 12.9 shows the results. Your command has selected the correct lines from the file.

You can also name more than one file as input to the FIND filter. With the command shown in Figure 12.10, you could quickly see if any of your area code 212 business clients appeared on your personal phone list as well.

```
C>FIND  "415"  BUSINESS.TXT

---------- BUSINESS.TXT
Brandenberg Gates    754   Bennett   Mary    415/612-5656
Sole Survivor,Inc.   237   Evans     Gail    415/222-3514
Bucket Dance Wear    276   Lewis     Ann     415/635-2530
Intelli-Strategies   743   Griffiths Robert  415/362-9537
Benicia Balloons     983   Franklin  Marie   212/524-4157
Standard Shelters    690   Rucker    Sally   415/532-1107

C>_
```

Figure 12.8: Using the FIND filter to extract data

```
C>FIND  "415/"  BUSINESS.TXT

---------- BUSINESS.TXT
Brandenberg Gates   754   Bennett    Mary     415/612-5656
Sole Survivor,Inc.  237   Evans      Gail     415/222-3514
Bucket Dance Wear   276   Lewis      Ann      415/635-2530
Intelli-Strategies  743   Griffiths  Robert   415/362-9537
Standard Shelters   690   Rucker     Sally    415/532-1107

C>_
```

Figure 12.9: Making sure your character string is sufficient

```
C>FIND  "212"  BUSINESS.TXT  PERSONAL.TXT

---------- BUSINESS.TXT
Cantonese Imports   134   Roberts    Joseph   212/656-2156
Benicia Balloons    983   Franklin   Marie    212/524-4157

---------- PERSONAL.TXT
Hendley    Candice 415-212-3434    Candy

C>_
```

Figure 12.10: Filtering multiple files

In these sample situations, business and personal lives have been kept apart. The FIND command could just as easily have been used as in Figure 12.11, with two different business mailing lists, in order to identify duplicate entries that should be removed from data lists. This is an example of how DOS can help you weed out extra entries.

The example in Figure 12.11 requires you to specify a FIND character string like "415/". Therefore, only duplicates for the 415

```
C>FIND  "617/"  BUSINESS.TXT  PROSPECT.TXT

---------- BUSINESS.TXT
Plymouth Granite Co 345  Williams  Peter  617/531-6145

---------- PROSPECT.TXT
Williams  Peter  Plymouth Granite Co 617/531-6145
Kingland  Benson Ranger Treadmills   617/222-4543
Brandeis  Judd   Scholar Support,Inc 617/298-4455

C>FIND  "415/"  BUSINESS.TXT  PROSPECT.TXT

---------- BUSINESS.TXT
Brandenberg Gates   754  Bennett   Mary   415/612-5656
Sole Survivor,Inc.  237  Evans     Gail   415/222-3514
Bucket Dance Wear   276  Lewis     Ann    415/635-2530
Intelli-Strategies  743  Griffiths Robert 415/362-9537
Standard Shelters   690  Rucker    Sally  415/532-1107

---------- PROSPECT.TXT
Simpson    Robert Wellington Services 415/446-2345

C>_
```

Figure 12.11: Finding duplicate entries in multiple lists

calling area will appear; you would have to respecify more area codes to be complete. However, other tools that you've learned about can do the job even better. First use the COPY command to join the two business files into one temporary file, which you can delete later; then use SORT to filter the resultant file.

Using TYPE with the sorted file would now show you all possible duplicates. You could proceed to find any subset of records of interest (for example, the 415 calling area) with FIND. In each case, you would not have to look back and forth between two lists. Duplicates would appear one right after the other, like the two entries for Plymouth Granite Company in Figure 12.12.

Although Figure 12.12 shows the duplicates for the 415 calling area on the screen, remember that the TEMP2.TXT file still contains the sorted collection of *all* records from both the BUSINESS.TXT and the PROSPECT.TXT files. This file could be erased now, or you could use it in further processing.

When you are joining two files to create a third, or when you are creating any temporary file, make sure your disk has enough space on it for the operation.

CONNECTING DOS OPERATIONS WITH PIPES

You've seen how the SORT and FIND filters can work with data files as input. Now you'll explore how filters can work in connection with other programs or DOS commands. When these connections are made, they are called *pipes.* Earlier in this chapter, you saw how you could change DOS's default input and output devices using redirection. Pipes allow you to combine the power of redirection with that of filters. You can simultaneously change (filter) your data while it is being moved (redirected) from one location to another.

Even with the redirection techniques you have learned so far in this chapter, if you want to do several things in a row, you might still have quite a bit of work to do. You might need to run one program, send its results to a disk file, and then run another program to process the resulting data. Then you might have to take the next program's input from that disk file to continue the processing chain, perhaps creating several intermediate files before getting the final result. Piping allows you to take the output of one command or program and make it the input of another command or program. You can do this several times in a row. An entire series of programs that generate intermediate output for one another can be automated by using the sophisticated combination of filters and pipes.

COMBINING PIPING AND SORTING

As you know, the SORT filter can be used to create a sorted directory listing. By adding pipes, you can use any column that appears in a directory listing as the criterion for a sorting order. This is very

```
C>COPY  BUSINESS.TXT + PROSPECT.TXT  TEMP1.TXT
BUSINESS.TXT
PROSPECT.TXT
        1 File(s) copied

C>SORT  < TEMP1.TXT  >  TEMP2.TXT

C>FIND  "617/"  TEMP2.TXT

---------- TEMP2.TXT
Brandeis  Judd   Scholar Support,Inc 617/298-4455
Kingland  Benson Ranger Treadmills   617/222-4543
Plymouth Granite Co 345  Williams  Peter  617/531-6145
Williams  Peter  Plymouth Granite Co 617/531-6145

C>_
```

Figure 12.12: Merging files before looking for duplicates

helpful, because a normal directory display does not arrange the files in any particular order. Using the SORT filter, you can produce your directory listings in order of file name, file extension, file size, date of creation, or even time of creation. As you'll see, you can take any text file and arrange it in any way you like as well.

Pipes are created by using the vertical bar symbol (|). Entering the command

   DIR | SORT

sends the output of a DIR command to the SORT filter before it is sent to the screen. The filtered result is a sorted directory display. Figure 12.13 shows a standard directory listing before sorting. Figure 12.14 shows the SORT processing operation itself, and Figure 12.15 presents the sorted results.

This procedure required only a single piping sequence. Previously, you would have had to redirect the results of the DIR command into a disk file and then redirect the disk file so that it would be the input of the SORT filter. The pipe was created automatically by DOS to handle this job.

Note that the first three lines have also been sorted:

   17 File(s)   205824 bytes free
   Directory of A:\
   Volume in drive A has no label

```
A>DIR

  Volume in drive A has no label
  Directory of   A:\

ANSI      SYS      1678    3-17-87   12:00p
RESTORE   COM     34643    3-17-87   12:00p
SORT      EXE      1977    3-17-87   12:00p
SUBST     EXE      9909    3-17-87   12:00p
XCOPY     EXE     11247    3-17-87   12:00p
DISPLAY   SYS     11290    3-17-87   12:00p
KEYBOARD  SYS     19766    3-17-87   12:00p
PRINTER   SYS     13590    3-17-87   12:00p
VDISK     SYS      3455    3-17-87   12:00p
DRIVER    SYS      1196    3-17-87   12:00p
FIND      EXE      6434    3-17-87   12:00p
FORMAT    COM     11616    3-18-87   12:00p
JOIN      EXE      8969    3-17-87   12:00p
MORE      COM       313    3-17-87   12:00p
REPLACE   EXE     11775    3-17-87   12:00p
      15 File(s)     206848 bytes free

A>_
```

Figure 12.13: Unsorted directory listing

The "17 File(s)" line is indented seven spaces beyond the "Directory" and "Volume" lines, which themselves are indented one space. The file names that follow are not indented.

Two extra files, 0A3B0550 and 0A3B0727, appear in the sorted listing. These files are temporary work files created during the sort-

The default drive must not be write-protected—DOS needs to create temporary files while it is performing its filtering job. In addition, the default drive must have sufficient available space to create the temporary files. Otherwise, the automatic piping process will be unable to continue.

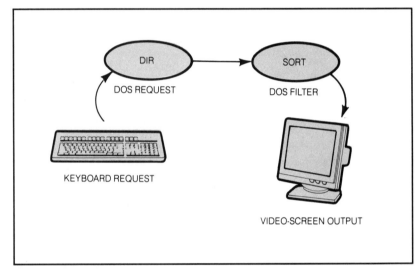

Figure 12.14: Information flow during filter operation

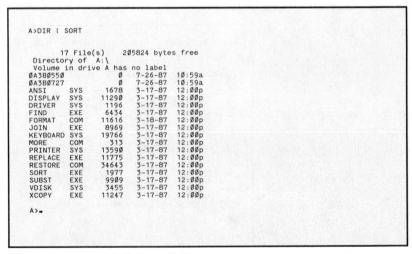

Figure 12.15: Sorted directory listing

ing operation by DOS on the default drive. They will be erased automatically after the piping operation is complete. Their obscure file names are based on the date and time of the actual SORT operation. They will always be different.

You can ignore these files completely if you wish. However, you may not want to have them appear in your sorted output—their inclusion may simply confuse others who read your output listing. To avoid this, you should set the default drive to a drive other than the one you want sorted. You can then use the PATH command to tell DOS where to find the SORT.EXE file. On a dual-diskette system, you might set the path to drive A; on a hard-disk system, you might set the path to the DOS directory on drive C.

Look at Figure 12.16 for further clarification. In this case, you first make drive C the default. The temporary files will be written on this new default drive. Then you ask for a directory listing of drive A. Finally, you ask DOS to direct the DIR command's output to the SORT command for filtering.

CUSTOMIZING YOUR DOS SORTS

Let's explore piping a little further, and in the process, look at some additional capabilities of DOS filters. The SORT filter allows

```
A>C:

C>DIR A: | SORT


        15 File(s)     206848 bytes free
   Directory of  A:\
   Volume in drive A has no label
ANSI      SYS       1678    3-17-87   12:00p
DISPLAY   SYS      11290    3-17-87   12:00p
DRIVER    SYS       1196    3-17-87   12:00p
FIND      EXE       6434    3-17-87   12:00p
FORMAT    COM      11616    3-18-87   12:00p
JOIN      EXE       8969    3-17-87   12:00p
KEYBOARD  SYS      19766    3-17-87   12:00p
MORE      COM        313    3-17-87   12:00p
PRINTER   SYS      13590    3-17-87   12:00p
REPLACE   EXE      11775    3-17-87   12:00p
RESTORE   COM      34643    3-17-87   12:00p
SORT      EXE       1977    3-17-87   12:00p
SUBST     EXE       9909    3-17-87   12:00p
VDISK     SYS       3455    3-17-87   12:00p
XCOPY     EXE      11247    3-17-87   12:00p

C>_
```

Figure 12.16: Creating automatic piping files on the default drive you several different ways to sort. For example, the /R switch tells the program to sort in reverse (descending) order. Entering

DIR A: | SORT /R

produces a directory listing in reverse alphabetical order (see Figure 12.17).

SORT also allows you to specify the column on which you want the sorting to take place. Normally, SORT begins with the first character in the line. However, you can tell SORT to sort from another position in the data line, which allows you to sort your directory in a variety of ways. The following command will sort by file extension rather than by file name (see Figure 12.18):

DIR A: | SORT / + 9

The +9 in this command tells DOS to sort based on the ninth character space. Since DOS uses eight-character file names, the ninth character space is always blank (to separate the base name from the extension). Beginning the sort here sorts on the following three characters, the extension. Extending this idea to the sixteenth character space in a directory listing, you could just as easily sort the direc-

```
C>DIR A: | SORT /R
XCOPY     EXE     11247    3-17-87    12:00p
VDISK     SYS      3455    3-17-87    12:00p
SUBST     EXE      9909    3-17-87    12:00p
SORT      EXE      1977    3-17-87    12:00p
RESTORE   COM     34643    3-17-87    12:00p
REPLACE   EXE     11775    3-17-87    12:00p
PRINTER   SYS     13590    3-17-87    12:00p
MORE      COM       313    3-17-87    12:00p
KEYBOARD  SYS     19766    3-17-87    12:00p
JOIN      EXE      8969    3-17-87    12:00p
FORMAT    COM     11616    3-18-87    12:00p
FIND      EXE      6434    3-17-87    12:00p
DRIVER    SYS      1196    3-17-87    12:00p
DISPLAY   SYS     11290    3-17-87    12:00p
ANSI      SYS      1678    3-17-87    12:00p
 Volume in drive A has no label
 Directory of  A:\
        15 File(s)    206848 bytes free


C>_
```

Figure 12.17: Directory sorted in reverse alphabetical order tory by file size (see Figure 12.19). Character space 16 gets you past the base name and extension, allowing sorting to begin with the file-size numbers.

DIR A:¦SORT / + 16

```
C>DIR A:  ! SORT /+9

MORE      COM       313    3-17-87   12:00p
FORMAT    COM     11616    3-18-87   12:00p
RESTORE   COM     34643    3-17-87   12:00p
SORT      EXE      1977    3-17-87   12:00p
FIND      EXE      6434    3-17-87   12:00p
JOIN      EXE      8969    3-17-87   12:00p
SUBST     EXE      9909    3-17-87   12:00p
XCOPY     EXE     11247    3-17-87   12:00p
REPLACE   EXE     11775    3-17-87   12:00p
DRIVER    SYS      1196    3-17-87   12:00p
ANSI      SYS      1678    3-17-87   12:00p
VDISK     SYS      3455    3-17-87   12:00p
DISPLAY   SYS     11290    3-17-87   12:00p
PRINTER   SYS     13590    3-17-87   12:00p
KEYBOARD  SYS     19766    3-17-87   12:00p
        15 File(s)    206848 bytes free
   Volume in drive A has no label
   Directory of  A:\

C>_
```

Figure 12.18: Sorting by file extension

```
C>DIR A:  ! SORT /+16

MORE      COM       313    3-17-87   12:00p
DRIVER    SYS      1196    3-17-87   12:00p
ANSI      SYS      1678    3-17-87   12:00p
SORT      EXE      1977    3-17-87   12:00p
VDISK     SYS      3455    3-17-87   12:00p
FIND      EXE      6434    3-17-87   12:00p
JOIN      EXE      8969    3-17-87   12:00p
SUBST     EXE      9909    3-17-87   12:00p
XCOPY     EXE     11247    3-17-87   12:00p
DISPLAY   SYS     11290    3-17-87   12:00p
FORMAT    COM     11616    3-18-87   12:00p
REPLACE   EXE     11775    3-17-87   12:00p
PRINTER   SYS     13590    3-17-87   12:00p
KEYBOARD  SYS     19766    3-17-87   12:00p
RESTORE   COM     34643    3-17-87   12:00p
   Directory of  A:\
   Volume in drive A has no label
        15 File(s)    206848 bytes free

C>_
```

Figure 12.19: Sorting by file size

COMBINING REDIRECTION WITH FILTERS AND PIPES

To make your job easier and quicker, a filter can also be combined with a redirection command. To print a sorted directory listing, you could enter

DIR A: ¦ SORT > PRN

As Figure 12.20 shows, the output of the DIR command is piped forward to become the input to the SORT command; the SORT command's output is then redirected from the screen to the printer.

As another example, you can create a text file containing a sorted directory listing by entering

DIR A: ¦ SORT > SORTDIR

Figure 12.20: Combining pipes, filters, and redirection

As Figure 12.21 shows, this is similar to the previous example, except that the final sorted directory listing is not sent to the printer but is instead redirected to the SORTDIR disk file. To see the contents of the SORTDIR file, you could enter

TYPE SORTDIR

With pipes and filters, you can also make reference to files located elsewhere within the DOS directory structure. As an example, Figure 12.22 shows a file called CAD.KEY that is contained in the CAD\VWF directory. CAD.KEY lists the internal macros (mini-programs) of a computer-aided design (CAD) program. It contains three columns of information: the numeric key code, an ASCII indication of which key on the keyboard invokes the macro, and the name of the file containing the macro instructions.

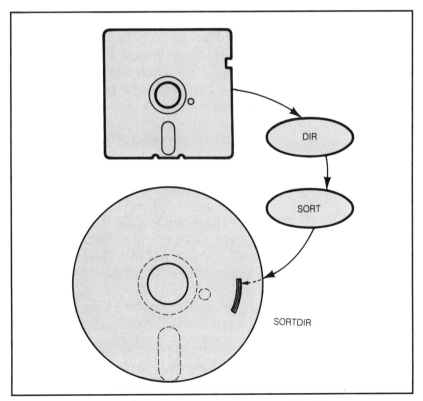

Figure 12.21: Creating a disk file with command combinations

```
C>TYPE \CAD\VWF\CAD.KEY
  316   F2  CLEARALL.MAC
   86    V  VERTSNAP.MAC
  318   F4  EXAMPLE2.MAC
   79    O  SNAPOFF.MAC
   71    G  SNAPGRID.MAC
   66    B  BACKUP.MAC
   76    L  LINE.MAC
   49    1  ALAN1.MAC
   65    A  ALAN2.MAC
   80    P  PLOTFIT.MAC
   51    3  ALAN3.MAC
   52    4  alan4.mac
  317   F3  EXAMPLE4.MAC

C>_
```

Figure 12.22: List of macro codes for a CAD program

The list of macro keys appears in the order in which the keys were created during previous use of the CAD program. Even with only a handful of possibilities, it is difficult to see which keys are taken and which are still available for macro assignment. A simple use of the SORT filter can rearrange the file lines within the same file, as shown in Figure 12.23. The command to use is

> SORT < \CAD\VWF\CAD.KEY > \CAD\VWF\CAD.KEY

Figure 12.24 shows the results of this simple sorting.

Test your understanding now of filters, pipes, and redirection. Select any subdirectory of interest on your hard disk, or put any diskette of interest into a disk drive. Construct and enter the proper command to ask DOS to produce a directory listing, sort it by file size, and then print the sorted results on your printer.

SOPHISTICATED TEXT SEARCHES USING REDIRECTION

From the output of a command or program, FIND can select lines that contain a certain character or group of characters. You can combine this feature with a piping operation for a sophisticated search. For example, the following command lists only those files that

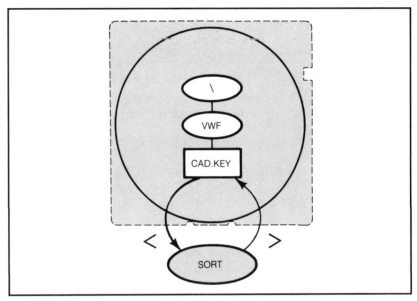

Figure 12.23: Sorting a file back into itself

```
C>SORT   <  \CAD\VWF\CAD.KEY  >  \CAD\VWF\CAD.KEY

C>TYPE   \CAD\VWF\CAD.KEY
   49    1  ALAN1.MAC
   51    3  ALAN3.MAC
   52    4  alan4.mac
   65    A  ALAN2.MAC
   66    B  BACKUP.MAC
   71    G  SNAPGRID.MAC
   76    L  LINE.MAC
   79    O  SNAPOFF.MAC
   8Ø    P  PLOTFIT.MAC
   86    V  VERTSNAP.MAC
  316   F2  CLEARALL.MAC
  317   F3  EXAMPLE4.MAC
  318   F4  EXAMPLE2.MAC

C>_
```

Figure 12.24: The sorted directory structure

When you are doing character searches in DOS or any other processing language, the case (upper or lower) of the characters is critical. You must always specify the character string *exactly* as you expect to find it in the file.

contain the letters OR:

DIR A: ¦ FIND "OR"

This command would produce such files as MORE.COM and FORMAT.COM (see Figure 12.25), since they contain the letters

OR somewhere in their file names. Because FIND includes a line if the search criteria are found anywhere in that line, SYS.COM and ANSI.SYS are also found.

The FIND filter can be used in reverse as well. For example, if you wanted to *exclude* all files that have an .EXE extension, you could use the /V switch, as shown in Figure 12.26. All files are found except those that have the letters EXE in their complete name.

```
C>DIR A: I FIND "OR"
MORE     COM     313    3-17-87  12:00p
FORMAT   COM   11616    3-18-87  12:00p
RESTORE  COM   34643    3-17-87  12:00p
SORT     EXE    1977    3-17-87  12:00p

C>DIR A: I FIND "SYS"
DRIVER   SYS    1196    3-17-87  12:00p
ANSI     SYS    1678    3-17-87  12:00p
COUNTRY  SYS   11285    3-17-87  12:00p
DISPLAY  SYS   11290    3-17-87  12:00p
PRINTER  SYS   13590    3-17-87  12:00p
KEYBOARD SYS   19766    3-17-87  12:00p
SYS      COM    4766    3-17-87  12:00p

C>_
```

Figure 12.25: Search capability with the FIND filter

```
C>DIR A: I FIND/V "EXE"

 Volume in drive A has no label
 Directory of  A:\

ANSI     SYS    1678    3-17-87  12:00p
RESTORE  COM   34643    3-17-87  12:00p
DISPLAY  SYS   11290    3-17-87  12:00p
KEYBOARD SYS   19766    3-17-87  12:00p
PRINTER  SYS   13590    3-17-87  12:00p
VDISK    SYS    3455    3-17-87  12:00p
DRIVER   SYS    1196    3-17-87  12:00p
FORMAT   COM   11616    3-18-87  12:00p
MORE     COM     313    3-17-87  12:00p
      15 File(s)    206848 bytes free

C>_
```

Figure 12.26: Excluding files with the /V switch

The FIND filter can also assign line numbers to the output. You can request this by adding the /N switch to the command:

DIR A: ¦ FIND/N "EXE"

Figure 12.27 shows the results of this command. Lines 1 through 6 of the directory in drive A did not contain EXE, so they were discarded. The first line with an EXE in it was the seventh line input to the FIND filter; therefore, the /N switch put [7] in front of it. The next lines containing EXE were lines 8, 9, 15, 17, and 19.

As always, switches can be combined in a FIND command to do double duty. Figure 12.28 shows a file sorted by both numbering and exclusion, which was produced by using the /N and /V switches.

FIND can also be used to count the number of line matches by invoking the /C parameter. For example, you might like to know how many .EXE files are on a disk or in a directory. Let's assume for a moment that you have added a file called AUTOEXEC.BAT to a disk in drive A. The command

DIR A:¦FIND/C "EXE"

would produce an answer of 7, shown in Figure 12.29. This seems inaccurate, since only six files have the extension .EXE. However,

```
C>DIR A: ¦ FIND/N "EXE"
[7]SORT        EXE      1977    3-17-87   12:00p
[8]SUBST       EXE      9909    3-17-87   12:00p
[9]XCOPY       EXE     11247    3-17-87   12:00p
[15]FIND       EXE      6434    3-17-87   12:00p
[17]JOIN       EXE      8969    3-17-87   12:00p
[19]REPLACE    EXE     11775    3-17-87   12:00p

C>_
```

Figure 12.27: Numbering feature of the FIND filter with /N

```
C>DIR A: ¦ FIND /N/V "EXE"
[1]
[2]  Volume in drive A has no label
[3]  Directory of  A:\
[4]
[5]ANSI      SYS      1678    3-17-87    12:ØØp
[6]RESTORE   COM     34643    3-17-87    12:ØØp
[1Ø]DISPLAY  SYS     1129Ø    3-17-87    12:ØØp
[11]KEYBOARD SYS     19766    3-17-87    12:ØØp
[12]PRINTER  SYS     1359Ø    3-17-87    12:ØØp
[13]VDISK    SYS      3455    3-17-87    12:ØØp
[14]DRIVER   SYS      1196    3-17-87    12:ØØp
[16]FORMAT   COM     11616    3-18-87    12:ØØp
[18]MORE     COM       313    3-17-87    12:ØØp
[2Ø]       15 File(s)   2Ø6848 bytes free

C>_
```

Figure 12.28: Combining FIND switches

```
C>DIR A: ¦ FIND/C "EXE"
7

C>DIR A: ¦ FIND "EXE"
AUTOEXEC BAT      152    7-Ø5-87   11:32a
SORT      EXE    1977    3-17-87   12:ØØp
SUBST     EXE    99Ø9    3-17-87   12:ØØp
XCOPY     EXE   11247    3-17-87   12:ØØp
FIND      EXE    6434    3-17-87   12:ØØp
JOIN      EXE    8969    3-17-87   12:ØØp
REPLACE   EXE   11775    3-17-87   12:ØØp

C>_
```

Figure 12.29: Counting occurrences with the /C switch

remember that FIND locates *all* occurrences of the specified string of
characters—and AUTOEXEC.BAT contains these characters
as well.

Once again, the solution is to specify a sufficiently unique character string. In this case, since the extension is always preceded by at
least one space in the directory listing, the string " EXE" would correctly identify the six .EXE files, as shown in Figure 12.30.

```
C>DIR A: | FIND/C " EXE"
6

C>DIR A: | FIND " EXE"
SORT      EXE     1977    3-17-87   12:00p
SUBST     EXE     9909    3-17-87   12:00p
XCOPY     EXE    11247    3-17-87   12:00p
FIND      EXE     6434    3-17-87   12:00p
JOIN      EXE     8969    3-17-87   12:00p
REPLACE   EXE    11775    3-17-87   12:00p

C>_
```

Figure 12.30: Specifying a sufficiently unique character string

SAVING TIME BY COMBINING FILTERS

Once you are comfortable with DOS filters, you can save yourself both typing time and waiting time. You don't need to wait for the SORT filter to finish its work before you ask the FIND filter to begin. Since you can use the SORT and FIND filters together, you can tell DOS to execute both filters, one after the other. Enter

DIR A: | SORT | FIND "EXE"

to receive a sorted listing of the .EXE files (see Figure 12.31). AUTOEXEC.BAT is again included in the listing.

You have probably seen advertisements for sorting programs that promise to sort your files by any field within them. You can do all of that kind of sorting with simple DOS commands now. You've learned how to use switches on the SORT command to arrange your directory lines by categories other than the first category. You've also learned how to send the sorted results from one filter to another through piping.

For another example of sophisticated DOS manipulation, you could now take the original business contact list shown in Figure 12.1, sort it by telephone number, pipe the results into the FIND filter to extract the 415 entries, and finally pipe the results back into the SORT command to be rearranged alphabetically:

SORT / + 43 < BUSINESS.TXT ¦ FIND "415/" ¦ SORT

Figure 12.32 demonstrates the results of this example. Notice that the first sort takes place using character space 43, the first space containing the phone number. If there were several contacts from the same

```
C>DIR A: ¦ SORT ¦ FIND "EXE"
AUTOEXEC BAT     152    7-05-87   11:32a
FIND     EXE    6434    3-17-87   12:00p
JOIN     EXE    8969    3-17-87   12:00p
REPLACE  EXE   11775    3-17-87   12:00p
SORT     EXE    1977    3-17-87   12:00p
SUBST    EXE    9909    3-17-87   12:00p
XCOPY    EXE   11247    3-17-87   12:00p

C>_
```

Figure 12.31: Combining SORT and FIND filters

```
C>SORT /+43  < BUSINESS.TXT ¦ FIND "415/" ¦ SORT
Brandenberg Gates   754  Bennett   Mary   415/612-5656
Bucket Dance Wear   276  Lewis     Ann    415/635-2530
Intelli-Strategies  743  Griffiths Robert 415/362-9537
Sole Survivor,Inc.  237  Evans     Gail   415/222-3514
Standard Shelters   690  Rucker    Sally  415/532-1107

C>_
```

Figure 12.32: Sorting, extracting, and sorting again

company, their entries would appear in phone number order for each alphabetized company.

This is another example of how a well-written DOS command can save you the purchase of a functionally simple piece of additional software. In the next chapter, you'll see an example of how you can set up a batch file to provide yourself with this kind of capability.

CONTROLLING SCREEN OUTPUT

The last filter available in DOS is named MORE. It causes the screen display to pause, just as the /P switch does with the DIR command. Why not just use the /P with the SORT filter? Try it, and see what happens. If you enter

    DIR A:/P ¦ SORT

you'll only get a blinking cursor if your directory required more than one screenful of information. This is because of the way the filter works. When data is filtered, it is stored in a temporary file; only then is the output filtered. Since the output is to be filtered, it's not sent to the screen. However, the now inappropriate pause required by the DIR A:/P command occurs anyway, so the computer is forced to pause when a screenful of information is sent *into* the pipe. This is not what you really want.

The proper way to handle pauses with filters is to use the MORE filter, like this:

    DIR A: ¦ SORT ¦ MORE

The MORE filter works because it pauses the output of the SORT filter, rather than pausing the input from the DIR command. This sequence will only display one screenful at a time from the sorted directory listing, signaling you with the "More" message that more output remains to be viewed. Pressing Return will display the next screenful of information. The command

    DIR ¦ MORE

will create a directory display like the one in Figure 12.33.

PIPES, FILTERS, AND REDIRECTION: AN EXAMPLE

Filters can help you overcome missing features in existing programs. One common problem is knowing how to sort a mailing list created by a word processor that does not contain a sorting feature. However, if you plan a bit, you can get the SORT filter to help you out.

Here is a typical mailing list, which uses commas to separate the name, address, and city fields (categories of information). WordStar uses a file arranged like this to produce MailMerge letters.

```
Smith,John, 12 Main St., Oakland
Goren,Nira, 10 Maple Dr., WC
Ornas,Diana, 1 Nut St., Pinole
```

Assume that this information is stored in a file called NAMES.TXT. The file could be created with the text mode of any word processor; in WordStar, you should use the nondocument mode to enter data for this special purpose. The data could also be entered using the COPY command, as you've seen earlier:

```
COPY CON: NAMES.TXT
Smith,John, 12 Main St., Oakland
```

```
Volume in drive C is ROBBINS
Directory of   C:\PROGRAMS\FW\SYBEX

.            <DIR>         3-16-87     4:34p
..           <DIR>         3-16-87     4:34p
FIG10-2   TXT      813     4-01-87     6:39p
DEMO      BAT       16     1-01-80    12:16a
FIG11-1B  BAT       60     3-23-87    10:21p
FIG12-2A  BAT       55     4-01-87     2:25a
FIG12-2B  BAT       40     3-25-87    11:05a
FIG12-2C  BAT       34     3-25-87    11:06a
FIG12-4   BAT       73     4-01-87     2:59a
HELP      BAT      412     3-24-87    11:41a
FIG11-1   CAP     4256     3-23-87     7:46p
FIG11-2   CAP     4256     3-23-87    11:39p
FIG11-3   CAP     4256     1-01-80    12:28a
FIG11-5   CAP     4256     3-24-87    11:42a
BOOKCRED  FW2    13888     4-02-87     4:42p
FIG10-50  CAP     4256     4-13-87     4:22p
FIG10-1   TXT      569     3-30-87    10:53a
FIG10-8   TXT      335     3-30-87    10:53a
FIG10-51  CAP     4256     4-13-87     4:27p
FIG7-5    CAP     4256     1-01-80    12:11a
-- More --
```

Figure 12.33: The MORE filter

Goren,Nira, 10 Maple Dr., WC
Ornas,Diana, 1 Nut St., Pinole
^Z

To sort this file by last names, you would enter

TYPE NAMES.TXT ¦ SORT > LIST.TXT

This would create a new file, called LIST.TXT, that would contain the sorted list of names. To see the contents of LIST.TXT, you could enter

TYPE LIST.TXT

The list would appear as shown in Figure 12.34. Since it is already sorted, it could now be used more readily by your word-processing program or any other application program.

The FIND filter can also be used to select entries based on some common text. For example, you could select all the people in your mailing list that live in a certain city. Look at the following command:

TYPE LIST.TXT ¦ FIND "Pinole" > P.TXT

This selects only those lines in LIST.TXT that contain the characters "Pinole". (Remember, the string of characters to be matched

```
B>TYPE NAMES.TXT
Smith,John, 12 Main St., Oakland
Gable,Nina, 1Ø Maple Dr., WC
Omney,Diane, 1 Nut St., Pinole

B>TYPE NAMES.TXT ¦ SORT > LIST.TXT

B>TYPE LIST.TXT
Gable,Nina, 1Ø Maple Dr., WC
Omney,Diane, 1 Nut St., Pinole
Smith,John, 12 Main St., Oakland

B>■
```

Figure 12.34: Mailing list sorted by filters and redirection must be entered in the same case in which the original text was entered.) The results of this selection are then redirected to P.TXT, the output disk file. P.TXT will contain only one of the mailing-list entries—the one containing ''Pinole'', as shown in Figure 12.35.

As in the earlier examples, this method is not a substitute for a real data management program. For example, if someone lived on Pinole street in Richmond, they too would appear on this DOS-generated ''Pinole'' list. However, features like FIND and SORT can be of great value, even to a new computer user. As you'll continue to learn in the next chapters on batch files, you can do many things with DOS alone that you otherwise would spend considerable money on.

SUMMARY

In this chapter, you've learned about powerful DOS features for specialized utility operations. You've seen that redirection allows you to specify alternative input and output devices for DOS commands. Pipes enable you to direct the flow of information with precision from one command to another. Filters permit you to process the data as it flows through your central processing unit under your direction. The

```
B>TYPE LIST.TXT | FIND "Pinole" > P.TXT

B>TYPE P.TXT
Omney,Diane, 1 Nut St., Pinole

B>_
```

Figure 12.35: File extraction with the FIND filter

chapter presented the following important points:

- Special symbols are used by DOS during redirection operations. The > sign indicates a new output device, and < indicates a new input source. If you use the >> sign, the output is appended to the specified file.

- Certain DOS commands can filter data. This data can be input at the keyboard, from an existing file, or even from another program or command.

- The FIND filter selects lines for output based on some selection characters. FIND offers three helpful switches: /N generates output lines that are numbered, /C counts the number of lines found, and /V excludes lines containing specified strings.

- The MORE filter performs the simple task of making the display pause when output fills the screen. This gives you the opportunity to read the complete display before continuing the processing.

- The SORT filter can easily arrange the lines of output from any command or data file. Optional switches add significant power to this command: /R produces a reverse-order listing, while / +*n* sorts the file by the *n*th character space instead of the first. This allows you to sort your data in meaningful orders.

- Pipes are preceded by the ┆ symbol. They transmit the output from one command to another, in effect making one command's output the next command's input.

- Pipes can be combined with both filters and redirection in sophisticated ways to produce powerful results.

The examples in this chapter should serve to spark your imagination—you can now create your own useful utility extensions. In Chapter 17, you'll learn about a number of utility programs that you can purchase to extend the power of DOS. With the tools from this chapter alone, however, you can develop your own programs for file sorting, text searching, and diskette cataloging.

PART 4

LIFE IN THE FAST LANE

Part 4 deals primarily with advanced commands and features. Chapters 13, 14, and 15 teach you how to use batch files to execute groups of DOS commands automatically. Chapter 13 describes the basic features and limitations of batch files and gives you practice in building simple batch files. Chapter 14 extends your knowledge by teaching you the DOS batch-file subcommands and parameters, enabling you to build more complex batch files. And Chapter 15 presents many batch files and techniques that you can use immediately on your computer.

In Chapter 16, you will learn a number of advanced DOS commands. These include special commands for advanced file and directory manipulation, for managing the DOS command processor, and for modifying the DOS environment. Lastly, Chapter 17 briefly describes a wide range of utility programs that you can purchase and use to enhance the power of DOS significantly.

THE POWER OF DOS
BATCH FILES

IN THIS CHAPTER, YOU WILL BEGIN TO LEARN ABOUT batch files. you've already learned several DOS features that give you added power. Batch files can multiply the power of DOS dramatically, not just add to it. This chapter will show you what batch files are, and how they can be created and used. You will learn why they are so important to you and to your effectiveness as a DOS user.

Up to this point, you've learned quite a bit about individual DOS commands. You know that when you want to execute a DOS command, you just type in the command at the prompt. When the command is complete, DOS displays the prompt again; then you can enter another command. You've seen that when you work with DOS, you must enter these commands one at a time.

Batch files allow you to enter a *group* of DOS commands automatically. A batch file is a series of ordinary DOS commands that the computer can execute automatically as a group (a *batch*) instead of one at a time.

You create batch files to automate DOS activities that require more than one DOS command. As you will see, this simple idea has some unexpected benefits. DOS's ability to understand simple batch files allows you to create sophisticated DOS programs, which are more complex batch files containing a series of commands and also special elements called variables, conditional statements, and subroutines.

BUILDING A BATCH FILE

Batch files can be as simple or complex as you want them to be. Let's take a simple task first. Assume you're working on a hard disk and would like to find out what .COM and .EXE files are available to you in the version of DOS installed on your disk. You would first need to change the active directory to the directory that contains the DOS files. Then you might clear the screen (with CLS) before you entered the appropriate DIR commands. You might successively enter each of the following DOS commands to obtain the desired output:

```
CD \DOS
CLS
DIR/W  *.COM
DIR/W  *.EXE
```

The result of this sequence would be the screen shown in Figure 13.1.

To complete the task, you had to issue four commands. If this were a task that you did often, you could automate the task with a batch file containing the commands. To do so, however, you'd need to know the rules for building batch files.

RULES FOR BATCH FILES

In order for DOS to properly recognize and process a file as a batch file, there are several rules you must follow. These rules apply to

- File type,
- Naming conventions,
- Limitations of the batch-file mechanism, and
- Running and stopping batch files.

BATCH FILES MUST BE STANDARD ASCII TEXT FILES

Standard text files contain normal ASCII characters, and each line ends with a carriage return (CR) and a line feed (LF). This definition

```
C>DIR/W *.COM

  Volume in drive C is ROBBINS
  Directory of  C:\DOS

ASSIGN   COM    BACKUP   COM    BASIC     COM    BASICA   COM    CHKDSK   COM
COMMAND  COM    COMP     COM    DISKCOMP  COM    DISKCOPY COM    EDLIN    COM
FDISK    COM    FORMAT   COM    GRAFTABL  COM    GRAPHICS COM    KEYBFR   COM
KEYBGR   COM    KEYBIT   COM    KEYBSP    COM    KEYBUK   COM    LABEL    COM
MODE     COM    MORE     COM    PRINT     COM    RECOVER  COM    RESTORE  COM
SELECT   COM    SYS      COM    TREE      COM    DEBUG    COM
        29 File(s)    2383872 bytes free

C>DIR/W *.EXE

  Volume in drive C is ROBBINS
  Directory of  C:\DOS

ATTRIB   EXE    FIND     EXE    JOIN      EXE    REPLACE  EXE    SHARE    EXE
SORT     EXE    SUBST    EXE    XCOPY     EXE    EXE2BIN  EXE    LINK     EXE
        10 File(s)    2383872 bytes free

C>_
```

Figure 13.1: DOS program-file listings

may not mean much to novice computer users; it is more important to know how to produce such files.

You can create a batch file using the DOS COPY CON command (see Chapter 12), the EDLIN line editor, or a word-processing program that can create an ASCII standard file or convert its files to ASCII standard. You can use the following word-processing programs to produce ASCII files directly:

- WordPerfect, using TEXT IN/OUT
- WordStar in nondocument mode
- WordStar 2000, using the UNFORM format
- Microsoft Word, saving the file as UNFORMATTED
- DisplayWrite III, using BLOCK ASCII SAVE
- Framework II, using DISK EXPORT ASCII

You can use the following programs to convert files to DOS standard text files after they have been saved as word-processing files:

- MultiMate, running the CONVERT program
- Samna, using the DO TRANSLATE ASCII command
- Symphony, using the PRINT FILE command

The best way to create and manipulate your batch files is to use one of these word processors, because a word processor offers the greatest range of commands for manipulating text. The next best way is with EDLIN; while it is less flexible than a word processor, EDLIN does have the advantage of being available with DOS. The ''least-best'' way is to use COPY CON, because it only allows text entry; it does not permit any manipulation of already entered text.

Because you may not have a word processor, this book assumes you are using EDLIN to create your batch files. If you need to refresh your memory on EDLIN, refer to Chapter 6.

BATCH FILES MUST FOLLOW CERTAIN NAMING CONVENTIONS   You've probably noticed by now that there are certain classes of files on your system: .COM and .EXE program files, .BAS BASIC language files, .WK1 spreadsheet files, .DBF database files, and probably many others. DOS must be able to distinguish a batch file from these other types of files on your system.

You can give a batch file almost any name you like, as long as you use the .BAT extension. Of course, the name must adhere to standard DOS file-naming rules, with no more than eight letters or numbers in the base name. SIMPLE.BAT and START.BAT are examples of acceptable batch-file names.

You should never create a batch file that has the same name as a DOS command (for example, DIR.BAT or FORMAT.BAT). If you do, DOS will become confused as to whether you wanted to execute the command with that name or the batch file with that name. DOS always assumes you want to execute a DOS command first; only if it can't find a DOS command (or any .EXE or .COM files) will it look to see if there is a batch file with the name that you typed in. DOS expects you to enter the command or batch-file name without typing the extension. Thus, you could create a file named DIR.BAT, but you could never use it—DOS would always assume when you entered DIR that you wanted the Directory command, not the DIR.BAT file.

Batch-file names should be unique. Never give a batch file the same name as either a DOS command or a program name (that is, the name of an .EXE or .COM file).

BATCH FILES HAVE CERTAIN LIMITATIONS   Only commands that work at the DOS prompt can be included in a batch file. You'll soon see that there are some additional controlling commands (called subcommands) that can be used in a batch file; you can also use variable input parameters, which will be covered in detail later in this chapter. However, the main commands that do something for you are always going to look just as they would if they were typed at the DOS prompt.

RUNNING AND STOPPING BATCH FILES   Executing all the instructions within a batch file is as simple as typing the name of the .BAT file containing those instructions. As with commands and programs, however, if you don't precede the batch-file name with a drive identifier and a directory name, the assumption will be the current drive and current directory.

You can stop batch-file execution at any time by pressing the Break key combination (Ctrl-ScrollLock). DOS will ask you if you want to terminate the batch job. Usually, you answer Y for Yes, since that's why you pressed the Break combination in the first place. However, if you have a change of heart and answer N, the current step in the batch file will be ignored and the rest of the commands will be executed.

Users of diskette systems should be aware that exchanging a diskette containing an executing batch file for another diskette will force DOS to stop after it completes the current instruction and prompt you to reinsert the original diskette. Only then can the next instruction in the batch file be executed properly.

CREATING YOUR FIRST BATCH FILE

Take a moment now to create your first batch file. Create your own version of SIMPLE.BAT, including all the statements seen in Figure 13.2. Use the EDLIN program unless you are familiar with an available word processor and plan to use it for all your batch-file work.

When you enter

EDLIN SIMPLE.BAT

```
CD \DOS
CLS
DIR/W *.COM
DIR/W *.EXE
```

Figure 13.2: The SIMPLE.BAT file

DOS will create a file called SIMPLE.BAT. Remember that when you use EDLIN, you are entering text into a file. This means that nothing appears to happen when you type in a command. Only after the SIMPLE.BAT file has been written can you tell DOS to read, process, and execute the instructions contained in it.

Write the file now using EDLIN's simple I (Insert) command. Leave insertion mode by pressing Ctrl-C, and then enter E (to end the edit). The DOS prompt returns, and you are ready to execute the batch file by typing in its name *without* the .BAT extension:

        SIMPLE

The results of typing in this one-word command are the same as those produced when all four commands were typed in separately. DOS executes each of the commands automatically, one after the other, without further assistance from you.

Like programs or disk-resident DOS commands, batch files can be located on any disk and in any directory, and they can be referenced by simply specifying the full path name to them. For example, if SIMPLE were located in a directory called UTILITY\MISC on drive C, you could execute it by entering

        C:\UTILITY\MISC\SIMPLE

Remember, if you wish to prevent the batch instructions from continuing to execute, you only need to press the Break key combination.

EDITING A BATCH FILE

You will notice that the batch file you just wrote displays the command lines contained within it as each one executes. This echoing of the commands to the screen is controlled by the ECHO command. The default status of ECHO is ON, which means that DOS commands executed from a batch file are displayed as they are executed. However, output results are sometimes more attractive or readable if the commands are *not* displayed. Let's add a line to the batch file that will set ECHO to OFF.

Bring up EDLIN again, specifying the full name of the file you want to edit, SIMPLE.BAT. Use the I command to enter

ECHO OFF

as the new line 1. To list the resulting file, enter the L command and press Return. EDLIN will display the five lines of your batch file:

```
*L
 1: ECHO OFF
 2: CD\DOS
 3: CLS
 4: DIR/W *.COM
 5:*DIR/W *.EXE
```

You can then save the file and return to DOS with the End command.

Now you can try the modified batch file. As before, just enter

SIMPLE

That's all it takes to execute all the individual DOS commands contained within the SIMPLE.BAT file. Note that since ECHO is OFF, only the results of the commands, not the commands themselves, will be displayed (see Figure 13.3).

Notice the extra DOS prompt on your screen after a batch file completes. This second prompt appears because EDLIN has inserted a carriage return before the end-of-file marker in SIMPLE.BAT. Don't be concerned; it won't cause any harm.

```
    Volume in drive C is ROBBINS
    Directory of  C:\DOS

ASSIGN    COM    BACKUP   COM    BASIC     COM    BASICA   COM    CHKDSK    COM
COMMAND   COM    COMP     COM    DISKCOMP  COM    DISKCOPY COM    EDLIN     COM
FDISK     COM    FORMAT   COM    GRAFTABL  COM    GRAPHICS COM    KEYBFR    COM
KEYBGR    COM    KEYBIT   COM    KEYBSP    COM    KEYBUK   COM    LABEL     COM
MODE      COM    MORE     COM    PRINT     COM    RECOVER  COM    RESTORE   COM
SELECT    COM    SYS      COM    TREE      COM    DEBUG    COM
        29 File(s)   2342912 bytes free

    Volume in drive C is ROBBINS
    Directory of  C:\DOS

ATTRIB    EXE    FIND     EXE    JOIN      EXE    REPLACE  EXE    SHARE     EXE
SORT      EXE    SUBST    EXE    XCOPY     EXE    EXE2BIN  EXE    LINK      EXE
        10 File(s)   2342912 bytes free

C>
C>_
```

Figure 13.3: Results of running SIMPLE.BAT

VARIABLES IN BATCH FILES

Until now, you've only seen batch files that have been designed for a specific use: for example, a batch file that quickly and easily lists all the .COM and .EXE files in the DOS directory. In such cases, the batch file works with constant values (*.COM or *.EXE). If batch files could accept variables, as more sophisticated programming languages do, they could be much more flexible.

You can create DOS batch files that will do just that. Variables in any language allow you to construct programs that differ in a well-defined way each time the program is run. In other words, the program stays the same, but the value used by the program to complete its tasks varies. You can consider the DOS batch-file feature to be a simple programming language.

Let's take a moment to look at the terminology involved. As you have seen throughout this book, many DOS commands accept a variety of parameters. These parameters are just additional pieces of information needed by DOS to clarify the task specified in the command. For example, the command COPY REPORT.DOC FEBRUARY.DOC contains the COPY command, and the REPORT and FEBRUARY documents are its respective source and destination parameters. Next month, however, you might want to run the COPY command again, with the REPORT.DOC file as the source and the MARCH.DOC file as the destination. Thus, the second parameter can be considered a variable parameter, since it needs to be changed each month.

Batch files can accept variables as easily as they can accept DOS commands. Variables always begin with a percentage sign (%) and are followed by a number from 0 to 9. Thus, DOS allows variables named %0, %1, %2, and so on.

To see how this system works, create a simple batch file called DEMO.BAT, consisting of the following two lines:

```
CLS
DIR *.%1
```

This batch file will clear the screen and then display a directory of all file names that have similar extensions (.COM, .BAT, .EXE, .WP, and so on).

Note that instead of entering .EXE or some other extension, you used the variable %1. This means that the batch file is not "locked in" to DIR *.EXE, DIR *.COM, or anything else. Instead, %1 can stand for anything you want.

Here's how the % symbol works. When you type in any DOS command, DOS assigns variable names to each section of that command. Look at the following command:

DEMO EXE

If this command were entered at the prompt, DOS would internally assign %0 to the first phrase (DEMO), %1 to the second phrase (EXE), and if there were other parameter entries on the line, % values up to %9. This allows you to refer to the phrases within your batch file. Since the DEMO batch file makes reference to %1, DEMO will actually use whatever phrase follows DEMO (in this case EXE) to complete the DIR command. Thus, the command

DIR *.%1

will be treated as if you had originally typed

DIR *.EXE

and the batch file will display all files with an .EXE extension, as shown in Figure 13.4.

Running the batch file again with a different value for the first parameter generates a different result.

DEMO COM

causes only the .COM files to be listed. You can refer to parameter %1 any number of times inside the batch file, even though DEMO-.BAT referred to it only once.

This technique is called *deferred execution,* since the decision as to what parameter will be used is deferred until the time of batch-file execution. In this example, a Directory command will be executed, but the decision as to what specific directory listing will be produced is deferred until the batch file has actually been called and the %1

```
A>DIR *.EXE

  Volume in drive A has no label
  Directory of  A:\

ATTRIB    EXE     8247  12-30-85   12:00p
IMSHOW    EXE    20090   6-20-85   10:09a
FIND      EXE     6416  12-30-85   12:00p
JOIN      EXE     8955  12-30-85   12:00p
REPLACE   EXE    11650  12-30-85   12:00p
SHARE     EXE     8580  12-30-85   12:00p
SORT      EXE     1911  12-30-85   12:00p
SUBST     EXE     9911  12-30-85   12:00p
XCOPY     EXE    11200  12-30-85   12:00p
          9 File(s)        6144 bytes free

A>
A>_
```

Figure 13.4: Running DEMO.BAT with one variable parameter (EXE)

parameter has been specified as the first parameter after the batch-file name.

Let's take another example of a batch file using variable parameters. This time, you'll use a second variable to create MOVE.BAT, a batch file whose purpose will be to move files from one drive or directory to another. As you know, you must do two things to move a file:

1. Copy the file to the new drive or directory.

2. Erase the file from the old drive or directory.

Your task is to create a batch file that will issue all the necessary commands, so that you only need to supply the file names to be moved and the identifier of the new drive.

The batch file MOVE.BAT requires two variables, %1 and %2. The first one will be a file name or a wild card to use for selecting a file or files. The second variable will be the letter specifying the destination drive. For example, you might want to move all the .EXE files from the current directory to drive B. To do that, you could enter the following four lines at the DOS prompt:

```
CLS
COPY *.EXE B:
ERASE *.EXE
DIR/W B:
```

Then again, you might want to move all the .PRG files from your DBASE\TEST subdirectory on drive C to the ACTIVE directory on drive C:

```
CLS
COPY C:\DBASE\TEST\*.PRG C:\ACTIVE
ERASE C:\DBASE\TEST\*.PRG
DIR/W C:\ACTIVE
```

There will probably be many occasions when you need to perform this operation between drives, between directories, or both, so this is a perfect opportunity to use variables. Write a batch file called MOVE.BAT, which contains these lines:

```
CLS
COPY %1 %2
ERASE %1
DIR/W %2
```

The MOVE.BAT batch file includes a dangerous command, ERASE. Since there is no automatic protection built into this batch program, a mistake can have serious consequences. If the COPY command in the MOVE batch file fails, the succeeding ERASE command will not allow you to effectively run the MOVE command again, since the original files will have been deleted. This can be a problem when your destination disk fills up or if you have a bad sector. Chapter 9 emphasized the importance of backup copies for your important files; writing and running a batch file such as MOVE.BAT reaffirms the need for such backup procedures.

This batch file issues the proper commands for you if you merely indicate the desired file source and destination. For example,

MOVE *.EXE B:

will move all the .EXE files from the current directory to drive B.

MOVE C:\DBASE\TEST*.PRG C:\ACTIVE

will move all the .PRG files from the DBASE\TEST subdirectory on drive C to the ACTIVE directory on drive C. The results are shown in Figure 13.5.

The same batch file can be used to move the files the other way. Simply reverse the parameters. Entering

MOVE B:*.EXE C:

will move all the .EXE files from drive B to drive C. (Substitute A for C in this command if you are using a dual-diskette system.)

Variable parameters are a mainstay of batch-file creation. You should stop here for a while and try out these new tools. Create a batch file called PARA.BAT that uses three variables: %1, %2, and %3. Have this program make a new directory (MD) using the first variable as the complete path name and directory name. Have it use

```
C>COPY \DBASE\TEST\*.PRG \ACTIVE
C:\DBASE\TEST\DB3BOOK.PRG
C:\DBASE\TEST\START.PRG
C:\DBASE\TEST\INVOICE.PRG
C:\DBASE\TEST\CERTIF.PRG
C:\DBASE\TEST\RECOMM1.PRG
C:\DBASE\TEST\RECOMM2.PRG
C:\DBASE\TEST\PAYROLL.PRG
C:\DBASE\TEST\PAYROLL2.PRG
C:\DBASE\TEST\EXPERT.PRG
C:\DBASE\TEST\EXPERT1.PRG
C:\DBASE\TEST\EXPERT2.PRG
C:\DBASE\TEST\EXPERT3.PRG
C:\DBASE\TEST\EXPERT4.PRG
C:\DBASE\TEST\MESSAGE.PRG
C:\DBASE\TEST\LEDGER.PRG
C:\DBASE\TEST\INVOICE2.PRG
C:\DBASE\TEST\BOOKS2.PRG
C:\DBASE\TEST\DISKPREP.PRG
      18 File(s) copied

C>ERASE \DBASE\TEST\*.PRG

C>DIR/W \ACTIVE
-- More --
```

```
   Volume in drive C is ROBBINS
   Directory of  C:\ACTIVE

.                   ..              DB3BOOK   PRG     START    PRG     INVOICE  PRG
CERTIF   PRG    RECOMM1  PRG    RECOMM2   PRG     PAYROLL  PRG     PAYROLL2 PRG
EXPERT   PRG    EXPERT1  PRG    EXPERT2   PRG     EXPERT3  PRG     EXPERT4  PRG
MESSAGE  PRG    LEDGER   PRG    INVOICE2  PRG     BOOKS2   PRG     DISKPREP PRG
      20 File(s)   1413120 bytes free

C>
```

Figure 13.5: Running the MOVE.BAT file

the second variable as a wild-card file name. Then have it copy all file names meeting the wild-card specification in the current directory to the directory specified in %1. The batch file should do a DIR/W on this new directory after the transfer, and should end with a CHKDSK on the disk drive specified in the third variable, %3. For example, if you wanted the following lines to be executed in your batch file:

```
MD \TRIAL
CD \TRIAL
```

```
COPY EX*.COM \TRIAL
DIR/W \TRIAL
CHKDSK B:
```

you should be able to invoke your batch file as follows:

```
PARA \TRIAL EX*.COM B:
```

SUMMARY

In this chapter, you took your first look at the DOS batch-file mechanism. It extends the power of your operating system by allowing you to build your own new set of commands. The new set of commands can be used just like any existing DOS command, except that it is your customized batch file that executes when requested, and not a prewritten command provided by DOS.

You learned the following key points about batch files:

- Batch files can be as simple as one line or as complex as many hundreds of lines.

- Batch files can contain a series of sequentially executed commands or programs, or even other batch files.

- Batch files can be invoked as easily as any DOS command— by simply typing the name of the batch file. This allows you to create your own set of specialized add-on DOS commands.

- You can terminate the execution of your batch program by pressing the Break key combination.

- Variable parameters make your batch files very flexible in terms of when and how you can use them. These variables are referred to as %0, %1, %2, %3, and so on through %9.

The next chapter will take your batch-file construction skills one giant step further. You'll learn about the set of specialized subcommands designed to work only within the batch-programming mechanism. These unique commands can be incorporated into any batch file, making DOS comparable to a high-level computer language.

SUBCOMMANDS IN BATCH FILES

BATCH FILES HAVE THEIR OWN SET OF SPECIALIZED support commands, known as *subcommands*. You don't need them to create simple batch files, but you greatly expand your possibilities when you learn them. You'll learn about all of these extra built-in tools in this chapter. Depending on what type of batch program you write, you may need to use one or several subcommands.

Some subcommands will be commonplace in your batch files; for example, you will frequently use ECHO or REM to insert messages both in the batch file itself and on the video screen. You'll use others only occasionally; for example, you'll use PAUSE only for batch files that must allow users sufficient time to read information on the screen. Still others will be used in specific situations only. In this category, you'll see the FOR subcommand, which allows the repetition of operations, the IF subcommand, which provides decision making, and the GOTO subcommand, which manages the flow of control.

In the preceding chapter, you looked at some simple examples of batch files, in which each command was executed successively. DOS also allows you to execute these commands nonsequentially, according to your own specified order. Changing the order of command execution is known as modifying the flow of control, or simply branching.

This chapter deals with elements that make the DOS batch-file feature into a simple but practical high-level programming language. A final section in the chapter discusses the distinction between creating a standard batch-file chain (which allows you to transfer control of execution from one file to another) and emulating true programming subroutines.

The SHIFT subcommand provides the virtually unnecessary capability of running a batch file that needs more than the allowable variable parameters (%0 to %9). Most DOS books make you struggle through the concept of shifting parameters, using trumped-up examples. However, no realistic batch file needs more than a few input parameters; this chapter won't waste your time on such an impractical subcommand.

INCORPORATING MESSAGES INTO BATCH FILES

In the last chapter, you briefly used the ECHO subcommand to suppress the display of the commands themselves while a batch file was processing. ECHO has some other uses. If ECHO is followed by text instead of by ON or OFF, it will print the text. Thus, ECHO can be used to display information on the screen during the execution of a batch file.

To see how this works, create a new batch file, called HELP1.-BAT, containing several ECHO subcommands, each of which contains helpful information for a user (see Figure 14.1). This batch file will explain how the previously created MOVE.BAT file can be used. (The figure contains a few sample lines of text to demonstrate the method of using the ECHO subcommand; the dots at the bottom indicate where you can add additional lines of text.) Running this batch file by typing in

    HELP1

at the DOS prompt results in Figure 14.2.

Notice that the first two commands set ECHO to OFF and clear the screen, so the remaining "echoed" messages appear without your seeing the actual ECHO subcommand for each line. Regardless of whether ECHO is on or off, the textual information on the ECHO line is always displayed. ECHO OFF only suppresses the display of any succeeding DOS commands in the batch file.

One of the command lines that is usually suppressed—and purposely so—is a REM statement. You will see many REM statements in batch-file listings. Here is an example:

    REM This is a simple internal commenting line.
    REM So is this... for the TYPICAL.BAT file

A REM (Remark) statement is used for internal documentation in a batch file. It usually contains notes to the programmer or to the future user of the batch program. Anything from the file name to information about algorithms and techniques will be welcomed by someone trying to understand the inner workings of a batch program. Nearly all of the remaining batch files in this book will have at

```
ECHO OFF
CLS
ECHO  The batch file MOVE.BAT is designed to
ECHO  transfer a file(s) from one drive or
ECHO  directory to any other drive/directory.
ECHO  =========================================
ECHO  MOVE first copies, then deletes the
ECHO  originals.  The general form is:
ECHO        MOVE  source  destination
  .
  .
  .
```

Figure 14.1: The HELP1.BAT file

```
    The batch file MOVE.BAT is designed to
    transfer a file(s) from one drive or
    directory to any other drive/directory.
    -----------------------------------------
    MOVE first copies, then deletes the
    originals.  The general form is:
         MOVE  source  destination

C>_
```

Figure 14.2: Results of executing the HELP1.BAT file

least one REM statement containing at least the name of the batch file itself.

If ECHO is set to OFF, then the REM statements will not be shown on the video screen during program execution. The more complex or obscure your batch-file logic, the more you need to have several REM lines built into it.

INTERRUPTING BATCH FILES DURING EXECUTION

There are two kinds of interruptions in life: permanent and temporary. DOS provides batch-file equivalents to these types of interruptions

In a batch file like HELP1.BAT, which displays text, it's a good idea to add PAUSE as a final command so that the screen information can be read. Information that is displayed to a user is usually only one part of a more complex batch file; pausing the execution allows the user to read the messages before continuing the program.

with the PAUSE subcommand and the Break key combination.

When a PAUSE subcommand is used in a batch file, the execution of the commands in the file stops temporarily, and DOS displays the message "Strike a key when ready...." When you press the Return key or the Spacebar (or virtually anything else), the next command in the batch file will execute.

The PAUSE subcommand is not necessary to the functioning of the program, but it has a practical function. Filling the screen with a lot of instruction is a sure way to lose a user's attention. Instead, you can display a little information, pause the display, clear the screen, and display a little more information. This will keep the user alert.

HELP2.BAT, an expanded version of the batch file that you saw in the last section, represents a two-screen help system (see Figure 14.3). This is implemented by inserting the two commands PAUSE and CLS into the middle of the batch file. PAUSE temporarily interrupts the execution of the batch file, prompting you to press any key when you are ready to go on. CLS simply erases the messages you've already read, so that you can concentrate on the new messages displayed. When you run the HELP2.BAT program, the results will be like those shown in Figure 14.4.

When a PAUSE subcommand is issued, almost any key will cause the batch-file processing to resume. One exception to this rule is

```
REM The HELP2.BAT File
ECHO  OFF
CLS
ECHO The batch file MOVE.BAT is designed to
ECHO transfer a file(s) from one drive or
ECHO directory to any other drive/directory.
ECHO .
ECHO MOVE first copies, then deletes the
ECHO originals.  The general form is:
ECHO      MOVE  source  destination
ECHO .
ECHO **********************************************************
ECHO Press Ctrl-BREAK key to terminate these messages, or
PAUSE
CLS
ECHO .
ECHO **********************************************************
ECHO Make sure you have a backup copy of all important files.
ECHO This batch file does an unconditional ERASE of
ECHO all the files requested to be moved.  It does this
ECHO even if the COPY command fails, and the files never
ECHO make it to the destination drive or directory (%%2)
```

Figure 14.3: The HELP2.BAT file

pressing Ctrl-ScrollLock, the Break key combination. If you press this, the batch file will be interrupted. DOS first displays a ^ C on the screen and then asks if you wish to terminate the batch job. Figures 14.5 and 14.6 demonstrate the screen results of your answer. In Figure 14.5, your Y answer causes the batch file to cease immediately and returns control to the DOS prompt. This is a permanent interruption.

Notice in Figure 14.6 that the ^ C occurred in the middle of the third ECHO statement's output. Because you answered N, the currently

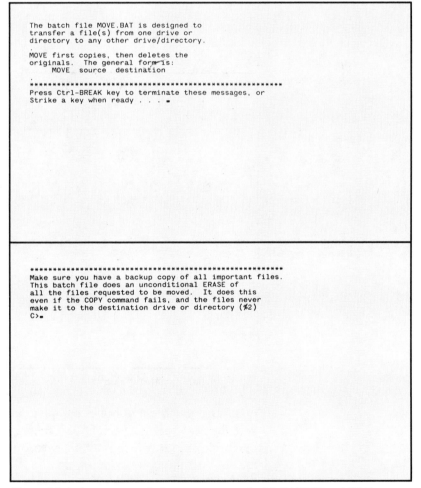

```
The batch file MOVE.BAT is designed to
transfer a file(s) from one drive or
directory to any other drive/directory.

MOVE first copies, then deletes the
originals.  The general form is:
     MOVE   source   destination

***********************************************************
Press Ctrl-BREAK key to terminate these messages, or
Strike a key when ready . . . ▪
```

```
***********************************************************
Make sure you have a backup copy of all important files.
This batch file does an unconditional ERASE of
all the files requested to be moved.  It does this
even if the COPY command fails, and the files never
make it to the destination drive or directory (%2)
C>▪
```

Figure 14.4: A two-screen help system created with PAUSE and CLS

```
The batch file MOVE.BAT is designed to
transfer a file(s) from one drive or
directory to any other drive/directory.
-------------------------------------------
^C

Terminate batch job (Y/N)? Y
C>■
```

Figure 14.5: Permanent batch-file interruption with the Break key combination

```
The batch file MOVE.BAT is designed to
transfer a file(s) from one drive or
d^C

Terminate batch job (Y/N)? N ----------------------------------------
MOVE first copies, then deletes the
originals.  The general form is:
     MOVE  source  destination

C>■
```

Figure 14.6: Continuing a batch file after interrupting its execution

executing statement does not complete, and the batch file continues with the next line. In short, DOS's message gets in the way of normal batch-file output, which is another reason to avoid asking a batch file to continue after you interrupt it.

The Break key combination will also work with DOS commands that have built-in pauses, such as FORMAT and DISKCOPY.

When these commands display such messages as "strike ENTER when ready," the Break combination will cancel the command. You may also want to use Break to stop the execution of a batch file that is not working as you desire.

DECISION MAKING IN BATCH FILES

DOS can test the value of certain variables and parameters during the execution of a batch file. Performing this test is known as *decision making,* or *logical testing.* A logical test allows branching within a program, which means that different actions will be performed based on the results of the test.

A branching statement (also called a *conditional* statement) might look like this:

IF Something = Something Else   Do This   Otherwise Do That

A more formal way of stating this is

IF A = B Then Perform Action C   Otherwise Perform Action D

A = B is called a *logical expression.* As in any language, it can stand for such things as Wage = 500 or Lastname = Robbins. If A = B is a true statement, then C will happen. On the other hand, if A = B is false, then action D will take place. This branching ability allows you to create batch files that evaluate circumstances and perform different actions according to the conditions found.

AN EXAMPLE BRANCHING PROGRAM

To get an idea of the usefulness of branching, let's create a batch file that takes advantage of it and also uses what you've learned already in this chapter. This program's purpose will be to help you to search a disk for a certain file and report if it is there or not.

After you've worked with your computer for a while, you probably will accumulate many diskettes with many files. Once in a while, you'll need to locate one file among those diskettes. Which diskette is usually the big question. You can easily miss the file name on a complete disk directory listing, even if you printed the listing out and kept it with the disk.

A new batch file, LOCATE.BAT, is just the ticket. Type in the LOCATE.BAT file as shown in Figure 14.7. (The line numbers are for your convenience only—don't enter them!) Once you've typed in this batch file, you can simply enter

LOCATE *FileName*

to learn if the file is on the diskette.

Figure 14.8 depicts the step-by-step flow of execution for the branching that occurs in the LOCATE.BAT file you've just entered. The first two commands, ECHO OFF and CLS, are familiar to you by now. The next subcommand is new: the IF subcommand. It is used to test a condition that the computer can evaluate as true or false.

The IF subcommand can be used in three ways:

1. IF EXIST or IF NOT EXIST. This form of IF is used to test if a file exists.

2. IF A == B or IF NOT A == B. This form tests the equality of A and B, where A and B represent character strings. Note that DOS uses == as the symbol for equality. The character strings can be literals or variables. A *literal* (also known as a constant) is any unchanging character string, such as JUDD or END. A variable is one of the changing parameters %0 through %9, which you learned about in Chapter 13. For example, the command

IF %1 == END

tests to see if the first variable parameter in the batch-file

> The batch program presented here for diskettes can also be used to locate a file in a hard-disk directory.

> DOS usually doesn't care whether information is entered in upper- or lowercase letters. However, when you are testing for the equality of groups of characters, as you do with the IF and the FIND subcommands, case does matter. If you enter the lowercase letters *end* as the first parameter in IF %1 == END, DOS will evaluate the IF as false. If you enter the uppercase letters *END*, the logical expression will be true.

```
1   ECHO OFF
2   CLS
3   IF NOT EXIST %1 GOTO NOFIND
4   ECHO The file %1 has been located!
5   GOTO END
6   :NOFIND
7   ECHO The file %1 cannot be found.  Look elsewhere.
8   :END
9   ECHO ON
```

Figure 14.7: The LOCATE.BAT file

command, %1 (a variable), is equal to the letters END (a literal). This is the most common use of the IF subcommand.

3. IF ERRORLEVEL #. This form tests to see if the preceding command has been executed correctly and failed. DOS or any individual application program can set a return code equal to a number from 0 to 255. Usually, a value of 0 means that the preceding command completed successfully; a number greater than 0 indicates a failure, the value indicating the different reasons for that failure. Only DOS commands like BACKUP, FORMAT, and RESTORE will affect this return-code value. (You can, of course, write your own programs to set the return code, but that requires a course in

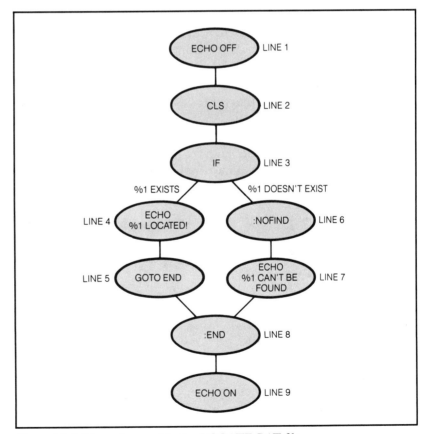

Figure 14.8: Flow of control in the LOCATE.BAT file

programming and goes beyond the scope of this book.) Note that ERRORLEVEL # means a return code of # *or greater*.

If any of these three DOS commands fail, the error level can be compared to a particular number, #, and different action can be taken depending on the severity of the error. The higher the return code, the more severe the error. The IF statement can control which succeeding section of the batch file receives control, depending on the value of this error level.

In this batch file you are using the IF NOT EXIST form of the IF subcommand to test whether a certain file exists. Line 3 is

IF NOT EXIST %1 GOTO NOFIND

What does GOTO NOFIND mean? The GOTO subcommand tells DOS to continue executing the batch file at a new place. NOFIND is a special placeholder, or label, that you enter into the batch file to indicate that desired location. Where is NOFIND? Look again at Figure 14.7. You will see :NOFIND on line 6. If the file name entered in the batch-file command line as %1 cannot be found on the disk (in other words, does not exist), then batch-file processing jumps from line 3 to line 6. The label line does nothing except facilitate this jumping, so the actual next line executed is on line 7. This branching technique is referred to in programming languages as the *flow of control*.

If, however, the file does exist, then the next command to execute will be the next available one in the batch file, the one on line 4. This is just an ECHO subcommand, which states that the sought-after file has been located:

ECHO The file %1 has been located!

The displayed message will contain the actual file name specified, typed in by you as %1, the first parameter on the command line.

The next line, line 5, is called an *unconditional transfer of control*. It is necessary in this batch-file language to enable the processing sequence to skip over the :NOFIND section of the program. The label :END is again just a placeholder to mark where processing can continue. If the desired file has been located (line 4), then the flow of execution should skip over the :NOFIND section, and the next line of code to be executed would be line 9.

Line 8 is called a *nonexecutable instruction,* because it does not represent any steps that the processor takes. It is simply a label for that place in the program. It can be compared to the address on your house, which is just a label that helps friends and the postal service find their way to you.

Let's go back now to the LOCATE command. To see how it works, try it with a file on a diskette or in a directory. Assuming your DOS operating disk is in drive A,

    LOCATE A:chkdsk.com

will produce the message ''The file A:chkdsk.com has been located!'' The command

    LOCATE A:topview.exe

will probably not find a file by that name. It will produce the message ''The file A:topview.exe cannot be found. Look elsewhere.'' If you wanted to search a large directory on your hard disk for the VTREE.COM file, you could enter

    LOCATE C:\utility\vtree.com

You might receive the message ''The file C:\utility\vtree.com has been located!''.

It's easy to see that the task performed by this batch file can be done in other—perhaps simpler—ways. However, you've used an IF subcommand, a GOTO subcommand, the label mechanism, and variable parameters. That's the main point of this batch file, not the actual job being performed. You can use these tools to make your own batch files, which will do meaningful work for you on your own system.

USING LOOPING AND REPETITION IN BATCH FILES

The FOR subcommand is similar to commands in other programming languages that facilitate repetition. Often, one or more commands in a program need to be repeated, sometimes a fixed number of times and sometimes a variable number of times. In either situation, the FOR subcommand enables you to meet this need.

The general form of the FOR subcommand is

FOR %%*Letter* **IN (***Possibilities***) DO** *Command*

Letter can be any single alphabetic letter. It is similar to the variable parameters you saw in Chapter 13 (%0, %1, %2, and so on). In this situation, however, double percent-sign variables are used. The %% tells DOS that you are referring to a batch-file variable in the looping FOR statement.

The *Command* in the FOR statement that will be executed repeatedly can change slightly during each repetition. This works similarly to the variable parameter method, which required you to write the batch file originally using %1 or %2 to refer to possible first or second input parameters. This method deferred execution so that when the batch file actually executed, it used the actual values typed in after the batch-file name, instead of using the placeholder % expressions.

In a FOR subcommand, execution is similarly deferred until the command executes. At that time, the *Possibilities* are evaluated, and the *Command* is executed for each possibility. When written into a batch file, this command can represent a more concise form of coding. For example, suppose you have a program called QRTLY.EXE that generates a quarterly business report. This program requires only that you specify the desired quarter for the current fiscal year. Entering the following at the DOS prompt would produce a report for quarter 3:

QRTLY 3

At the end of the fiscal year, you might want to generate current copies of the quarterly reports for each quarter. You would enter

QRTLY 1
QRTLY 2
QRTLY 3
QRTLY 4

and press Return after each line. All four of these successive requests

FOR is a batch-file subcommand. This means it can only be executed from within a batch file.

could be replaced in a batch file called REPORTS.BAT with one automatic FOR subcommand, as shown in Figure 14.9.

Using this looping mechanism would not require you to wait for each quarterly report to finish before you requested the next to begin:

FOR %%Y IN (1 2 3 4) DO QRTLY %%Y

Your first reaction might be that this is an awfully complicated-looking expression just to save typing in four simple QRTLY report requests. Again, it just demonstrates the technique. If you had a monthly report program called MONTHLY.EXE, you could just as easily request the printing of twelve monthly reports with

FOR %%Y IN (1 2 3 4 5 6 7 8 9 10 11 12) DO MONTHLY %%Y

The modified REPORTS file would look like REPORTS2.BAT, shown in Figure 14.10.

As you've seen in the general form of the FOR subcommand, there can be only one *Command* parameter executed after the DO portion of the command. It can be a program name, as you've just seen demonstrated, or it can be another DOS command, like DIR or CHKDSK. The following FOR subcommand exemplifies this:

FOR %%A IN (%1 %2 %3 %4) DO DIR %%A

This command would perform a DIR command for each variable

```
ECHO OFF
REM The REPORTS.BAT File
REM Produce the Four Quarterly Reports
FOR %%A IN (1 2 3 4) DO QRTLY %%A
ECHO ON
```

Figure 14.9: The REPORTS.BAT file

```
ECHO OFF
REM The REPORTS2.BAT File
REM Produce the Twelve Monthly Reports
FOR %%A IN (1 2 3 4 5 6 7 8 9 10 11 12) DO MONTHLY %%A
ECHO ON
```

Figure 14.10: The REPORTS2.BAT file

parameter (presumably, four different file names). If this FOR subcommand were in a batch file called HUNT.BAT, as shown in Figure 14.11, you might invoke HUNT in the following manner to determine if any of the four specified files were located in the current directory:

HUNT HEART.EXE, LUNGS.EXE, LIVER.COM, BRAIN.EXE

The result might look something like Figure 14.12. Even though you've suppressed the display of the DOS commands themselves with ECHO OFF, the remaining output still appears cluttered.

Using a batch subcommand as the object of DO can produce a more concise and attractive result. An IF subcommand can be used to replace the DIR command:

FOR %%A IN (%1 %2 %3 %4) DO IF EXIST %%A ECHO %%A FOUND

The results, shown in Figure 14.13, speak for themselves. The desired information about whether the files exist is not obscured by any additional DOS directory information. In this FOR subcommand, the actual command executed by DO is IF EXIST %%A ECHO %%A FOUND.

Note, however, that the ECHO OFF command itself is still displayed. This is because the echoing feature is on until ECHO OFF shuts it off. DOS 3.3 users can surmount this limitation by preceding the command with the @ symbol.

@ECHO OFF

will turn the echoing feature off for all succeeding commands, and the @ symbol will suppress the display of this command as well.

Try out all of the sample batch files in this section to affirm your understanding of the subcommands. In some cases, you will have to

```
ECHO OFF
REM The HUNT.BAT File
FOR %%A IN (%1 %2 %3 %4) DO DIR %%A
ECHO OFF
```

Figure 14.11: The HUNT.BAT file

```
C>HUNT HEART.EXE LUNGS.EXE LIVER.COM DRAIN.EXE

C>ECHO OFF

C>
C>_
```

```
    Volume in drive C is ROBBINS
    Directory of  C:\PROGRAMS\FW\CHAP11

HEART     EXE   186787   2-26-84   11:45a
          1 File(s)   1335296 bytes free

    Volume in drive C is ROBBINS
    Directory of  C:\PROGRAMS\FW\CHAP11

File not found

    Volume in drive C is ROBBINS
    Directory of  C:\PROGRAMS\FW\CHAP11

LIVER     COM   236398   1-13-86   9:55a
          1 File(s)   1335296 bytes free

    Volume in drive C is ROBBINS
    Directory of  C:\PROGRAMS\FW\CHAP11

File not found

C>
C>_
```

Figure 14.12: Executing HUNT.BAT to repeat a DOS command

change the directory references to references that will work on your system. Either in addition to or in place of the examples in this section, create a new batch file—for example, GYRO.BAT—that will provide extra information to a user about your chosen topics. The batch file could be invoked as follows:

GYRO HEART

This would determine if a text file called HEART.HLP existed. If it did, the screen would clear and the contents of the HEART.HLP file

```
C>TYPE HUNT2.BAT
ECHO OFF
REM The HUNT2.BAT File
FOR %%A IN (%1 %2 %3 %4) DO IF EXIST %%A ECHO %%A FOUND
ECHO OFF

C>HUNT2 HEART.EXE LUNGS.EXE LIVER.COM BRAIN.EXE

C>ECHO OFF
HEART.EXE FOUND
LIVER.COM FOUND

C>_
```

Figure 14.13: Subcommands within subcommands

would be displayed. If it did not, the message "No help is available on subject HEART" would be displayed. Create your own sample .HLP text files to test your batch file.

USING BATCH CHAINS AND BATCH SUBROUTINES

Since a batch file can execute any command that otherwise could be entered directly at the DOS prompt, a batch file can invoke another batch file. By simply entering the name of the second batch file, you can pass control from the first to the second file. Execution continues with the instructions in the second batch file and does not return to the first (calling) batch file. This is known as *chaining*. It is different from the calling procedure familiar to programmers.

Look at the listings of the three batch files in Figures 14.14, 14.15, and 14.16. These three files together demonstrate both the capabilities and the limitations of chaining. Carefully read the steps of each of the three batch files, while looking at the output results in Figure 14.17.

The first batch file executes three simulated instructions and then invokes the second batch file as its last instruction. These simulated instructions take the place of any other successive batch-file

```
ECHO OFF
REM The FIRST.BAT File
ECHO Simulated Instruction 1 in First.bat
ECHO Simulated Instruction 2 in First.bat
ECHO Simulated Instruction 3 in First.bat
SECOND
```

Figure 14.14: The FIRST.BAT file

```
ECHO OFF
REM The SECOND.BAT File
ECHO Simulated Instruction 1 in Second.bat
ECHO Simulated Instruction 2 in Second.bat
ECHO Simulated Instruction 3 in Second.bat
THIRD
ECHO Last Instruction in Second.bat
```

Figure 14.15: The SECOND.BAT file

```
ECHO OFF
REM The THIRD.BAT File
ECHO Simulated Instruction 1 in Third.bat
ECHO Simulated Instruction 2 in Third.bat
ECHO Simulated Instruction 3 in Third.bat
```

Figure 14.16: The THIRD.BAT file

```
C>FIRST

C>ECHO OFF
Simulated Instruction 1 in First.bat
Simulated Instruction 2 in First.bat
Simulated Instruction 3 in First.bat
Simulated Instruction 1 in Second.bat
Simulated Instruction 2 in Second.bat
Simulated Instruction 3 in Second.bat
Simulated Instruction 1 in Third.bat
Simulated Instruction 2 in Third.bat
Simulated Instruction 3 in Third.bat

C>_
```

Figure 14.17: Batch-file chaining

commands that you might write. (You should focus on chaining here, rather than on other command lines; the simulated instructions are displayed merely to give you a representative context for the chaining technique.)

After FIRST is done, it passes control to SECOND by invoking as its last instruction the name of the file (SECOND) to which control will be passed. Then batch file SECOND executes another three simulated instructions before passing control to batch file THIRD. THIRD executes its own three simulated instructions before the chain process is complete. However, the line "Last instruction in Second.bat" is never executed, because the third batch file was invoked *in the middle* of the second batch file!

True subroutines provide you with the ability to write modular batch files that perform well-defined task sequences, and to temporarily leave one batch file to execute a sequence *without losing your place* in the first batch file. If you need to run a batch file while in the middle of another batch file, you can do this in two ways. If you are using DOS 3.3, you can use the CALL subcommand. If you are using an earlier version of DOS, you must invoke the COMMAND.COM program itself. The forms required are

Proper chaining of batch files requires the new batch-file name to be the last instruction of the preceding batch file in the chain.

CALL *BatchFileName*

for DOS 3.3 users, and

COMMAND/C *BatchFileName*

for all earlier versions. Since under most circumstances DOS batch files can only chain, the COMMAND/C version brings into memory a completely separate copy of DOS for the express purpose of running the named batch file.

With either the CALL or COMMAND/C method, when the batch file has executed all its commands, control will be returned to the very next line in the running batch file—the one *following* the CALL or COMMAND/C instruction—and execution will continue from there.

Look again at the THIRD.BAT file shown in Figure 14.16, and then look at FOURTH.BAT, shown in Figure 14.18. You can use these two files and the secondary command processor technique to invoke and run the instructions within the THIRD.BAT file, as shown in Figure 14.19. The results are different from the results of chaining.

Running FOURTH by this method will result in the same first three simulated instructions as with chaining. When those three have executed, control will be transferred to the THIRD batch file, at which point its three simulated instructions will execute. However, unlike the previous chaining example, control returns to FOURTH, which can execute its last instruction. If there were another instruction in FOURTH, or another hundred instructions, they would then all execute. In this way, sophisticated, structured application environments and systems can be built up by using only DOS commands and the batch-file mechanism.

```
@ECHO OFF
REM The FOURTH.BAT File
ECHO Simulated Instruction 1 in Fourth.bat
ECHO Simulated Instruction 2 in Fourth.bat
ECHO Simulated Instruction 3 in Fourth.bat
CALL THIRD
ECHO Last Instruction in Fourth.bat
```

Figure 14.18: The FOURTH.BAT file

```
C>FOURTH
Simulated Instruction 1 in Fourth.bat
Simulated Instruction 2 in Fourth.bat
Simulated Instruction 3 in Fourth.bat
Simulated Instruction 1 in Third.bat
Simulated Instruction 2 in Third.bat
Simulated Instruction 3 in Third.bat
Last Instruction in Fourth.bat
C>_
```

Figure 14.19: DOS supports true subroutines

SUMMARY

In this chapter, you extended your understanding of batch files. You learned about a variety of specialized commands that only work from within batch files. These subcommands provide DOS with the kind of features normally reserved for a high-level computer language:

- Messages can be included for internal documentation with the REM subcommand. You can also include messages to be displayed during the execution of the batch program with the ECHO subcommand.

- All batch-file command lines are displayed on the console as they execute. You can suppress any particular one by preceding it with the @ character in column 1 of the command line (DOS 3.3 only), or you can suppress all succeeding command lines with the ECHO OFF command.

- Batch files can contain the standard logic seen in most programming languages. Branching is managed by the GOTO subcommand in conjunction with simple labels.

- Decision making is provided with the IF subcommand. DOS allows decisions on whether a file exists or not (EXIST), decisions on whether character strings equal each other or not (==), and decisions about the severity of command errors (ERRORLEVEL #).

- The FOR subcommand controls the sophisticated features of looping and command repetition.

- You can interrupt your own batch program temporarily with the PAUSE subcommand or permanently with the Break key combination.

- You can implement true programming subroutines by using the CALL subcommand (DOS 3.3 only) or by invoking a secondary command processor with COMMAND/C (for earlier versions of DOS).

Now that you possess these fundamental batch-file construction skills, the next chapter will make a more advanced user out of you. You will learn many tricks and techniques that will lead you to develop fancy implementations and systems of your own.

SOPHISTICATED BATCH-FILE EXAMPLES

YOU'VE SEEN IN CHAPTER 13 THAT THE PRIMARY ROLE of batch files is to allow you to conveniently group together a collection of DOS commands, other programs, and other batch files. You've also seen how this entire collection of commands can be run by entering the batch-file name with any special parameters at the DOS prompt.

As you've learned in the last two chapters, there are two situations in which you should write batch files:

1. When you have a time-consuming sequence of unattended operations to be performed.

2. When you need to run a complex sequence of commands frequently, and you would like to ensure that they are performed consistently.

If a batch file you write works, *it's right*. It may not be the fastest, most efficient, or most elegant file, but it's still right.

In this chapter, you will see a wide range of batch files. These examples provide you with usable programs: you can type them in yourself, or you can send for the diskette with the files already on it (see the coupon at the end of this book). These examples will also give you ideas for creating similar programs for your own computer system.

AUTOMATING SYSTEM JOBS

When you turn on your computer and load DOS, DOS scans the root directory of the disk for a batch file called AUTOEXEC.BAT. If it finds that file, it executes the commands within it automatically.

AUTOEXEC.BAT is a valuable tool. In both diskette and hard-disk systems, it can be used to execute any number of DOS commands or other programs. For example, you can set the time and date if you have a battery-powered clock in your computer, or you can configure your PROMPT and MODE commands for specific serial-port and video-screen requirements. There is no limit to the variations you can make in your AUTOEXEC.BAT file.

Let's take a look at some of these AUTOEXEC.BAT variations. You'll look first at how to load and run a specific program automatically when you power up your computer. Then you'll see how to set up a customized PROMPT command. Finally, you'll explore some possibilities for more complex system setup.

> DOS does not supply a default AUTOEXEC.BAT file. However, many application programs do supply one on their system disks. When loading a new application program, be sure that the program's AUTOEXEC.BAT file does not overwrite an existing AUTOEXEC-.BAT file that you carefully created.

AUTOMATING THE SYSTEM STARTUP

It's easy to add an automatic startup feature to your system disk. As soon as DOS is loaded, the computer will run a particular program. Let's assume you want to run the BASICA program each time you start your system. Since BASICA is totally self-contained, all you need to do is use the COPY command to place a copy of BASICA-.COM on your new system disk.

Assuming your new system disk is on drive B for dual-diskette systems and on drive C for hard-disk systems, you would use the command

> The AUTOEXEC-.BAT file must be stored in the root directory of the disk. It will be ignored if it is stored in any other directory.

    COPY BASICA.COM B:

for a dual-diskette system, or the command

    COPY BASICA.COM C:

for a hard-disk system.

A simple task your AUTOEXEC.BAT file can do is to enter the name of a particular application program you want to execute. The principle shown here will apply to any program that you want to start up automatically when your system boots. For this example, you'd like to invoke BASICA.COM automatically on startup. Use whatever text-editing method you like to create an AUTOEXEC.BAT file containing the one line that invokes the BASICA program:

BASICA

If you'd like to try out this method with another program such as a word processor—say, WP.COM—make sure you copy WP.COM to the new system disk. In this case, your AUTOEXEC.BAT file will contain one line:

WP

Since many application programs include overlay files, you must be sure to copy those files to your new system disk. For instance, suppose your word processor requires a file called WP.OVL. You would need to have that file on the system disk containing your new AUTOEXEC.BAT file.

To see if your new setup will work as planned, restart the computer from your system disk. You can do this in two ways. First, you can turn off the computer, wait a few seconds, and then turn the computer on again. When the disk spins, DOS should be loaded and the program should run automatically.

As an alternative, you can use the keyboard rebooting procedure produced by the Ctrl-Alt-Del key combination. This will also restart the computer. However, it will not perform the same internal hardware and memory checks that occur with an actual startup.

Don't get casual about the Ctrl-Alt-Del rebooting method. If you are in the middle of running a program like a word processor, a database manager, or a spreadsheet, rebooting may destroy your current working file.

Using the Ctrl-Alt-Del key combination is also simple. If you have a hard-disk system, remember to remove any disk that is currently in drive A, since the computer defaults to that drive automatically. Hold down the Ctrl and the Alt keys, and press the Del key at the same time. Then release all of the keys. The system will load, and your AUTOEXEC.BAT will be executed. This is called a *warm boot,* since the computer has already been turned on. A *cold boot* occurs when you first turn on the computer's power; the same sequence takes place then, with the addition of several internal hardware tests.

Either of these rebooting procedures can be followed with most programs, and any main program can be run automatically at system startup. However, keep in mind that some copy-protected programs have their own instructions for automatic startup.

CHANGING THE DEFAULT SYSTEM PROMPT

Changing your default system prompt is often so useful that you might want to have it set automatically when you turn on the computer. You can use the AUTOEXEC.BAT file to accomplish this. Not only individual software programs, but also DOS commands themselves can be executed automatically during startup.

Create an AUTOEXEC.BAT file in the root directory that contains the single line

PROMPT pg

Even though this AUTOEXEC.BAT file contains only one command, there is no limit to the number of automatic commands you can have in this file. To see how this particular command is activated, reboot your system.

OTHER POSSIBILITIES WITH AUTOEXEC.BAT

There is no limit to the number of command lines you can have in any batch file. However, you should not write batch files with too many commands in them. They become harder to read, understand, modify, and debug as they get larger.

The possibilities are limitless when it comes to adding useful instructions to your AUTOEXEC.BAT file. Just about everything else you'll read about in this chapter could be included in it. For that matter, just about anything you've already learned, from setting the prompt uniquely to initializing function keys, could be included in your startup AUTOEXEC.BAT file.

For example, suppose that you want to simply press the function key F9 or F10 to generate a wide directory listing or a clean screen. As you learned in Chapter 10, the following two commands will provide that setup:

PROMPT $e[0;67;"DIR/W";13p
PROMPT $e[0;68;"CLS";13p

Include these in your AUTOEXEC.BAT file, and voila—your wish has become DOS's command. Use the more sophisticated versions of the PROMPT command presented in Chapter 10 if you'd like an even more useful prompt than this.

Use your own judgement and creativity in including commands in your AUTOEXEC.BAT file. The rest of this chapter contains a host of tips, tricks, and techniques that can be used with batch files. You'll want to include some of these in your AUTOEXEC.BAT file. The next section provides a good example of using batch files in AUTOEXEC.BAT.

CREATING YOUR OWN MENU SYSTEM

It's always helpful to set up a mechanism that makes it easy for you and others to run programs. Hard-disk menu systems are designed to provide that very capability. Of course, you can always buy one; you'll read more about that in Chapter 17. However, an inexpensive way to set up a menu system is to use DOS's batch-file feature. A series of batch files stored on your hard disk can enable anyone to access the programs you have installed. You'll now see one possible design for such a series of batch files.

The first step in creating your own menu system is to create a file that will contain a listing of the programs available on your system. Let's put this display menu into a text file called MENU.SCR, as shown in Figure 15.1.

This file of text can be displayed each time your system boots up. All you must do is write an AUTOEXEC.BAT file containing these two simple commands:

```
CLS
TYPE MENU.SCR
```

Remember that nearly everyone designs and programs differently, and that all of the batch files you see here are demonstrations. Feel free to add embellishments or to design the instruction sequences differently.

```
              MENU OF AVAILABLE HARD DISK PROGRAMS
    TO SELECT ONE, TYPE ITS NUMBER AND PRESS <RETURN>

    1  -   INVENTORY MANAGEMENT SYSTEM

    2  -   BUDGET ANALYSIS SYSTEM

    3  -   WORD PROCESSING

    4  - .SYSTEM UTILITIES


    ENTER YOUR CHOICE NOW, PLEASE:
```

Figure 15.1: Menu management file

To make this menu work, you must create other DOS batch files for each option listed on the menu. For example, to run your inventory management system, you need to create a batch file called 1.BAT. Because the file's base name is the number 1, and all batch files have the extension .BAT, typing 1 and pressing Return will execute the commands in that file.

A typical batch file for a menu system would contain a set of actions like the following:

1. Changing the directory to the correct one (for example, C:\DBMS\INVNTORY).

2. Running the program. For example, to run a dBASE III PLUS customized inventory program called INVENT.PRG, the batch file would execute the command DBASE INVENT.

3. Returning to the root directory after the program has completed.

4. Displaying the menu again, so that the user can make another choice.

Of course, many other things could be done in a file like 1.BAT; for example, it could set a specialized path and then reset it at the end of the program. The rest of this chapter will focus on the many different things you can do in any batch file.

Figure 15.2 shows the contents of example .BAT files that perform three minimum steps. The three sets of commands shown in this figure perform the actions required for choices 1, 2, and 3 on the menu in Figure 15.1. The 1.BAT file brings up a database management program, the 2.BAT file brings up a spreadsheet program, and the 3.BAT file brings up a word-processing program. The contents of each of these batch files are almost exactly the same, except that the directory and program have been changed in each.

The fourth choice on your sample menu, SYSTEM UTILITIES, is interesting because it suggests the possiblity of a flexible multilevel menu system. You could create a batch file called 4.BAT that would contain a new screen display, listing several utility choices. The utility operations could be safely nestled inside other batch files, and another entire set of menu choices could be automated.

```
CD \DBMS\INVNTORY
DBASE   INVENT
CD \
TYPE MENU.SCR

------------------

CD \LOTUS
LOTUS
CD \
TYPE MENU.SCR

------------------

CD \WP
WP
CD \
TYPE MENU.SCR
```

Figure 15.2: The 1.BAT, 2.BAT, and 3.BAT files

At this point, you should write your own 4.BAT batch file and any necessary subordinate batch files to complete the menu example. Although you can use your imagination, start off with the following simple tasks:

1. Clear the screen, and display a file of new choices with TYPE. Call this file UTIL.SCR, and give the user these options:

   A. Display the current date and time
   B. Format a new diskette in drive A

   Remember that 1.BAT, 2.BAT, and so on are already used for your main menu, so your utility files will have to be named differently. For example, you might want the two options just presented to be contained in batch files named A.BAT and B.BAT. Or you could display the menu choices as 1 and 2, and then name the files U1.BAT and U2.BAT. (The latter method is preferable, since it presents a consistent appearance to any user; all choices are numbered 1, 2, 3, and so on.) In fact, you could even create new batch files called 1.BAT, 2.BAT, and so on, but you would have to place them in a separate directory and run them from there.

2. When done, display the main menu again (MENU.SCR).

Remember to add REM statements for documentation to all batch files that aren't transparently simple. Use them for your successor, for another programmer who uses your batch file, and for yourself—after all, *you* could be the one who, two months later, tries to figure out why a certain statement was included.

3. The final step is to create a new AUTOEXEC.BAT file that will start up your menu system automatically when the computer is turned on. Although you may come back throughout this chapter to change the file, start off with an AUTOEXEC.- BAT file that looks like the one in Figure 15.3. This file contains commands that change the prompt, open a path, clear the screen, and display the menu.

You are now ready to test the menu system you've created. Before you do, let's review the several files that make up your menu system:

- MENU.SCR. This file contains the menu display. It has no DOS function. Its only purpose is to tell the user what options are available on the hard disk.

- AUTOEXEC.BAT. This file executes when the computer is turned on or booted. It opens the path needed for hard-disk operation and displays the menu for the user to read.

- 1.BAT, 2.BAT, 3.BAT, 4.BAT. These files execute the choices listed on the menu. You should create one batch file for each choice.

- If you completed the exercise, you also wrote UTIL.SCR and several other batch files.

To test the entire menu system, reboot your computer. When the computer starts up, it should display your menu. You should test each option on the main menu, as well as each option you programmed into the submenu. Be careful to use a new disk or scratch disk when testing the FORMAT choice on your Utility menu.

IMPROVING PERFORMANCE WITH BATCH FILES

There are many ways to improve performance with batch files. Some of these are ridiculously easy—what's hard is thinking of them at all. In this section, you'll learn a host of simple possibilities for batch files. Since the lines of code are few, you can implement these approaches quickly if you choose.

```
ECHO OFF
PROMPT $P$G
PATH \;\DBMS;\WP;\LOTUS;\DOS
CLS
TYPE MENU.SCR
```

Figure 15.3: AUTOEXEC.BAT file for hard-disk menu management

SIMPLIFYING CONSISTENT SEQUENCES

Most of us are not great typists. Even for those who can speed along, there is great value to be gained in reducing the number of keys to be pressed. In the music world, there is much debate on the value of pressing one button and getting the sound of an entire rhythm section. No such debate rages in the PC world; anything that gets the same result with fewer keypresses receives a broad welcome.

ABBREVIATIONS Any DOS command can be abbreviated to the ultimate in simplicity with a one-line batch file. For example, the CHKDSK command can be shortened to the letter C simply by creating a batch file called C.BAT, and including in it the one instruction

CHKDSK

When you type C at the DOS prompt, the batch file C.BAT will be given control, and its one instruction will be executed as if you had typed it at the DOS prompt.

This technique can also be used for commands that normally take parameters, such as the RENAME or the XCOPY command. You could just as easily create a batch file called R.BAT that only contains the one executable instruction

RENAME %1 %2

When you wanted to use this command, you could type R instead of typing RENAME along with the variables. For instance, if you wanted to rename OLD.TXT to NEW.TXT, you could now type

R OLD.TXT NEW.TXT

DOS would quickly discover that R is a batch file, and the job would be handled through the batch-file invocation of the RENAME command, using the parameters represented as %1 and %2.

This simplification technique can be extended to commands with multiple lines. If you frequently do a CHKDSK on your A and C drives, your version of C.BAT could contain the following lines:

```
CHKDSK A:
CHKDSK C:
```

In this case, you won't even have to type C twice and press Return twice. On the other hand, the C.BAT file will be less flexible for other purposes, since it will always issue the CHKDSK command for two disk drives, A and C.

SHORTHAND NOTATION FOR COMMANDS   Certain commands that perform fixed chores can also be simplified with batch files. For instance, you learned in Chapter 8 how to use the MODE command to manage various aspects of different devices. If your system has both a color and a monochrome monitor, you could use a batch file to invoke the proper version of the MODE command. To switch output to the monochrome monitor, you could enter

```
MODE MONO
```

in a file called MONO.BAT. To switch output to the color monitor using 80 columns with color enabled, you could enter

```
MODE CO80
```

in a file called COLOR.BAT. Then, whenever you needed to switch, you would only have to enter the simple batch name, MONO or COLOR, to obtain the desired result. With this method a user doesn't have to remember (or even know) the actual DOS command or command/parameter sequence that produces a particular result.

Another good use of this technique is turning on the compressed printing mode for your Epson- or IBM-compatible printer, which you learned about in Chapter 7 as well. You could create a batch file called COMPRESS.BAT that contains one line:

```
MODE LPT1: 132
```

You could create another batch file called NORMAL.BAT that would also contain only one line:

MODE LPT1: 80

Anyone could now type COMPRESS at the DOS prompt to send a wide spreadsheet or database information to the printer. When they were done, they could enter the command NORMAL to return the printer to its normal configuration.

Another benefit of this method appears when you acquire new printers at a later date. Only the inside portion of the batch file has to be changed once, and only by one knowledgeable person. Everyone else using the system still only has to remember to type COMPRESS or NORMAL.

REPEATED AUTOMATIC INVOCATION

Any time you need to execute the same command repeatedly, the following technique can come in handy. Perhaps you need to find a text string in a series of files located in different directories; or perhaps you just need to obtain a directory listing of several diskettes successively. This method relies on the fact that %0, as a batch-file variable, represents the actual name of the batch file itself.

Take a look at the CONTENTS.BAT file shown in Figure 15.4. In this batch file, the PAUSE command prompts you to enter a new diskette into drive A and then waits for you to do so (see Figure 15.5).

If you press the Return key at this point, you will receive a directory listing of the diskette you placed in drive A, as shown in the top portion of the figure. However, this is also the point in the batch program at which you can terminate the otherwise unending sequence by pressing Ctrl-C. If you do not, the batch file will retype its own

Remember that the line numbers in this batch file and in the other files listed in this chapter are there for reference only. If you type in these batch programs for yourself, leave out the line numbers.

```
1   REM   CONTENTS.BAT
2
3   PAUSE Load diskette into drive A:
4   DIR  A: /P
5   %0
```

Figure 15.4: The CONTENTS.BAT file

```
COLORBAR BAS     1427  12-30-85  12:00p
COMM     BAS     4254  12-30-85  12:00p
DEBUG    COM    15799  12-30-85  12:00p
DONKEY   BAS     3572  12-30-85  12:00p
EXE2BIN  EXE     3063  12-30-85  12:00p
LINK     EXE    39076  12-30-85  12:00p
MORTGAGE BAS     6178  12-30-85  12:00p
MUSIC    BAS     8575  12-30-85  12:00p
MUSICA   BAS    13431  12-30-85  12:00p
PIECHART BAS     2180  12-30-85  12:00p
SAMPLES  BAS     2363  12-30-85  12:00p
SPACE    BAS     1851  12-30-85  12:00p
VDISK    LST   136315  12-30-85  12:00p
        18 File(s)     107520 bytes free

C>contents

C>REM  CONTENTS.BAT

C>
C>PAUSE Load diskette into drive A:
Strike a key when ready . . . ^C

Terminate batch job (Y/N)? y
C>_
```

Figure 15.5: Running the CONTENTS.BAT file

name and the word ''contents,'' and the batch file will begin to execute again; you will be prompted to enter another diskette.

The key to this repetitive behavior is in line 5 of the listing. The %0 is only a variable parameter that substitutes for the original batch-file name typed at the DOS prompt.

PROGRAM SETUP AND RESTORATION

This section offers different approaches for initiating your own programs. You've already seen a typical small application method in Figure 15.2. In that example, a main program was run (perhaps with initial parameters) after the proper directory was entered. Now let's look at two other times you'll want to consider using batch files.

INVOKING THE SAME SEQUENCE OF PROGRAMS You sometimes perform a recurring series of steps in the computing world. For instance, you may run your word processor (WP.EXE) to create a new document and then, as a matter of course, run your grammar and style checker (STYLE.COM). You may also run a specialized spelling checker (SPELL.EXE) before you rerun your word processor to implement any suggested changes. The sequence, then, is as follows:

1. Word processor runs.

2. Style checker runs.

3. Spelling checker runs.

4. Word processor runs again.

If these programs do not allow parameter passing, you could write a batch file called WRITE.BAT, which would consist of the following lines:

```
WP
STYLE
SPELL
WP
```

On the other hand, many programs now allow you to specify a parameter to indicate the name of a file to be selected. If a program allows such a specification, then a batch file can be even more useful. Suppose you are working on a proposal called PROPOSAL.DOC. Your WRITE.BAT file could do more work if it contained these lines:

```
WP PROPOSAL.DOC
STYLE PROPOSAL.DOC
SPELL PROPOSAL.DOC
WP PROPOSAL.DOC
```

Simply typing WRITE at the DOS prompt would bring you successively through all four program invocations, each one bringing in the specified PROPOSAL file.

Here's another example. You may be working on the Great American Novel, and each chapter you write undergoes the same painstaking care and attention as the rest of your word-processed documents. You can take the simplifying process one step further by using the variable parameter technique. Look at the following batch file:

```
WP CHAPTER%1
STYLE CHAPTER%1
SPELL CHAPTER%1
WP CHAPTER%1
```

If you've named your files CHAPTER1, CHAPTER2, and so on, you can then invoke your four-program sequence by typing at the DOS prompt the chapter number as the parameter:

WRITE 5

Keep in mind that if your novel has more than nine chapters, you'll have to name them differently so that you don't exceed DOS's maximum limit of eight characters in a file name.

SETUP AND RESTORATION FOR TWO-DRIVE OPERA-TIONS   Some programs assume that the data they use is available on the default disk drive and directory. Since DOS allows you to run a program that isn't in the current drive and directory, you can first switch to the drive or directory containing your data and then run the program. After the program is done, you can change back to your original drive or directory. This is usually the root for hard-disk systems, and drive A for dual-diskette systems. The technique for returning to the root was shown in Figure 14.2. On a dual-diskette system, you can perform a similar sequence of steps.

Figure 15.6 shows a typical configuration, in which programs reside on drive A and data files on drive B. Suppose you want to run a main program called ESTATE.EXE, which is on your program

Figure 15.6: Typical configuration for a two-drive operation

disk and which uses several real estate data files on the data disk in drive B. The following batch file (SWITCH.BAT) will change the default drive to B for the duration of the execution of ESTATE.EXE, and then reset the default drive back to A. DOS will look on B for any files referenced by the ESTATE program.

```
REM SWITCH.BAT
B:
A:ESTATE
A:
```

CHAINING FOR DISKETTE-SWITCHING APPLICATIONS

As you know, any batch file can contain references to other batch files. Now you'll learn how those referenced batch files can also be on different drives. You can use this technique to develop sophisticated multidiskette applications. For example, you could have a batch file called FIRST.BAT on drive A, which has a number of instructions in it, ending with an invocation of a SECOND.BAT file, located on drive B. A segment of the FIRST.BAT file might look like Figure 15.7.

The SECOND.BAT file, which could control the backing up of your files onto a clean diskette, could be located on your data disk. SECOND.BAT might look like Figure 15.8. When control transfers to SECOND.BAT, its first instruction pauses the computer, prompting you to remove the main program diskette from A and replace it with a backup diskette. After performing the XCOPY backup sequence, the batch file pauses again so you can reinsert your original system diskette in drive A.

The last statement in SECOND.BAT is your opportunity to continue the execution chain. This ''last line'' can be the name of

```
Instruction 1
Instruction 2
   .
   .
   .
Last instruction
B:
SECOND
```

Figure 15.7: Segment from FIRST.BAT file

```
PAUSE Place your data backup diskette into drive A:
XCOPY  *.*  A:
PAUSE Replace your original system diskette in drive A:
**** last line ****
```

Figure 15.8: Sample SECOND.BAT file

another batch file to execute, on either A or B. You can even include a variable such as %1 in this last line, transferring it from the original FIRST.BAT file to a THIRD.BAT program. The %1 could also be a command that would be executed as the last instruction of the SECOND.BAT file. In short, the last line in the SECOND.BAT file could contain A:FIRST, which would rerun the original starting program; %1, which would run a command passed from FIRST-.BAT to SECOND.BAT; or the name and location of any other batch file to continue the chain. If your last line uses %1, then of course the FIRST.BAT file should be modified to include a parameter in the final line.

INITIALIZING YOUR RAM DISK

A batch file is an obvious place for the series of commands necessary to set up your RAM disk. If you use the VDISK or RAM-DRIVE options of your CONFIG.SYS file, your RAM disk will already be created. However, some memory boards (like AST boards) come with a program that can initialize a RAM disk whenever you choose. If this is the case on your system, you should invoke the program with a batch file.

Say you have created a RAM disk called D. The following RAMINIT.BAT file could copy programs and files to it—for instance, commonly used batch files like HELP.BAT and frequently used DOS programs like CHKDSK.COM, SORT.EXE, and the command processor COMMAND.COM.

```
COPY HELP.BAT D:
COPY CHKDSK.COM D:
COPY SORT.EXE D:
COPY COMMAND.COM D:
```

You could also set the COMSPEC environment here to tell DOS

where to find the command processor. (COMSPEC is a special DOS variable, designed to specify where a copy of COMMAND.COM can be found. You will learn more about this variable in Chapter 16.)

Finally, you could reset the path to check the RAM disk for referenced files that are not in the default directory:

```
SET COMSPEC = D:\COMMAND.COM
PATH D:\;C:\LOTUS;C:\WP;C:\UTILITY;C:\DOS
```

> If you use this RAM disk method for improving your system's performance, remember to put the RAM disk on your path *before* any other references to directories that may contain the original copies of the files. Then the fast-access RAM copy of the referenced file is located first, before the slower disk-resident version of the same file.

In Chapter 10, you learned about a wide range of uses for a RAM disk. Placing all of those things in this RAMINIT.BAT file is a good technique, even if you eventually include a reference to RAMINIT-.BAT in your AUTOEXEC.BAT file for automatic initialization of your RAM drive.

INITIALIZING YOUR COLOR MONITOR

You learned in Chapter 10 how to use the PROMPT command to set up the foreground and background colors on a color monitor. Having to look up or remember the codes can be tedious. This is a perfect opportunity for a batch file. RGB.BAT will expect two parameters, each specifying what colors the monitor should use for the foreground and background. The calling sequence will be

RGB *Foreground Background*

Entering the following sequence at the DOS prompt will cause all future output to appear in blue letters on a white background:

RGB BLUE WHITE

The batch file itself can be seen in Figure 15.9.

Several interesting points are demonstrated in this file:

- There are two major sections in the logical flow. The first section (lines 3–28) controls the setting of the foreground colors, according to the first color parameter specified after the batch-file name RGB. The second section (lines 30–58) controls the background color settings, based on the value of the second parameter on the batch file line.

```
 1   REM   RGB.BAT
 2
 3   ECHO OFF
 4   IF ARG==ARG%1 GOTO BKGROUND
 5   GOTO %1
 6   :BLACK
 7   PROMPT $e[30m
 8   GOTO BKGROUND
 9   :WHITE
10   PROMPT $e[37m
11   GOTO BKGROUND
12   :RED
13   PROMPT $e[31m
14   GOTO BKGROUND
15   :GREEN
16   PROMPT $e[32m
17   GOTO BKGROUND
18   :BLUE
19   PROMPT $e[34m
20   GOTO BKGROUND
21   :MAGENTA
22   PROMPT $e[35m
23   GOTO BKGROUND
24   :CYAN
25   PROMPT $e[36m
26   GOTO BKGROUND
27   :BROWN
28   PROMPT $e[33m
29
30   :BKGROUND
31   ECHO ON
32   ECHO OFF
33   CLS
34   IF ARG==ARG%2 GOTO DONE
35   GOTO BK%2
36   :BKBLACK
37   PROMPT $p$g$e[40m
38   GOTO DONE
39   :BKWHITE
40   PROMPT $p$g$e[47m
41   GOTO DONE
42   :BKRED
43   PROMPT $p$g$e[41m
44   GOTO DONE
45   :BKGREEN
46   PROMPT $p$g$e[42m
47   GOTO DONE
48   :BKBLUE
49   PROMPT $p$g$e[44m
50   GOTO DONE
51   :BKMAGENTA
52   PROMPT $p$g$e[45m
53   GOTO DONE
54   :BKCYAN
55   PROMPT $p$g$e[46m
56   GOTO DONE
57   :BKBROWN
58   PROMPT $p$g$e[43m
59   :DONE
60   ECHO ON
61   CLS
```

Figure 15.9: RGB.BAT sets foreground and background colors

- This batch file is not case-sensitive, as other batch programs that relied on the IF subcommand would be. In other words, each of the following commands would produce the same result:

```
RGB      BLUE
WHITE    rgb
blue     white
```

- If no color is specified for the foreground or background, you can use the IF ARG = = ARG %1 technique to test for the absence of a variable parameter. This IF test will only be true if the variable (either %1 or %2) is missing.

- ECHO ON and OFF, followed by a screen clearing, is necessary between the setting of the foreground and background colors. The foreground prompt must take effect while ECHO is off and before the background color is set.

- As written, this RGB.BAT file requires that a user enter both parameter values (foreground and background colors). If you enter only one color, the foreground will be set to that color, and the background will not be set at all. However, losing the background color will also lose the pg portion of the prompt. This program, like all programs, could be improved by separating the setting of the background color from the pg. You could include PROMPT pg at the end of the batch file so it would always be executed (after line 59). Try it now as an exercise. Remember to include an ECHO ON, ECHO OFF sequence.

The overall flow of this program can be seen in Figure 15.10.

SOPHISTICATED BATCH FILES

This section deals with some specific batch files used by experienced DOS users. People's perceptions of advanced subjects differ dramatically; what one person views as sophisticated, another views as old hat. The batch-file techniques presented here are beneficial. If they're new to you, that's all the better. If they're old hat, perhaps

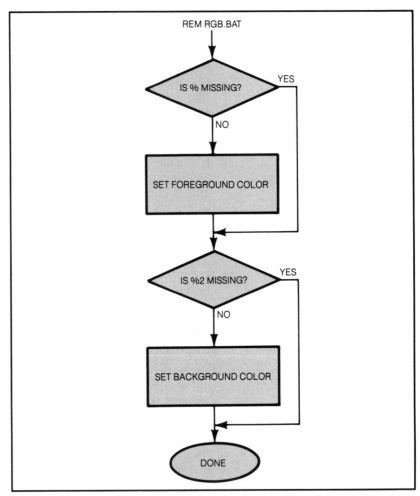

Figure 15.10: Logical flow in the RGB.BAT file

you'll learn some new approaches by the manner in which these batch programs are implemented.

CUSTOMIZED SYSTEM HELP SCREENS

Some systems are used by many people at different times. A desirable feature for such a system is customizable help screens. You can use the batch-file mechanism in DOS to easily set up this capability. All it takes is the INFO.BAT file, shown in Figure 15.11.

```
1   REM   INFO.BAT
2
3   ECHO OFF
4   IF EXIST %1.HLP  GOTO OK
5   ECHO Sorry.   No help available for %1
6   GOTO END
7
8   :OK
9   TYPE %1.HLP
10  PAUSE
11
12  :END
```

Figure 15.11: Customizable help screens with INFO.BAT

Once you've installed this batch file in your path, you can use it from any directory. All you need to do is write a text file with an .HLP extension. This file should contain the text information you'd like displayed for anyone requesting help. The user, in turn, will only need to run the INFO.BAT file, specifying the first parameter as the topic for which help is desired.

For example, if there is a subject named GOBBLEDY for which you wish to provide users with helpful on-line information, you should place the information in a text file called GOBBLEDY.HLP. Then the user need only enter

INFO GOBBLEDY

to display the predefined textual information (see Figure 15.12). If help is not available on your system (that is, an .HLP file does not exist for the subject), then a simple message to that effect is given (see Figure 15.13).

The program in Figure 15.11 can be understood quickly by looking at the logic-flow diagram in Figure 15.14. The heart of the batch program begins at line 4, after the initial REM and ECHO OFF statements. If an .HLP file exists for the subject (entered as %1), then the batch file continues executing at line 8. This is really only the label :OK, which is needed by the GOTO statement in line 4. The help information is presented to the user by the TYPE statement in line 9. The PAUSE statement ensures that the user will have time to read the information before anything else appears on the screen or before the screen is cleared.

If no help file exists, the IF statement in line 4 causes line 5 to be executed next. The ECHO statement displays a "Sorry ..." message

In this example of a help file, no CLS instruction is executed. It was omitted so that Figures 15.12 and 15.13 could show the entire resulting sequences. If you were to write a similar INFO system for yourself, you might want to consider inserting CLS instructions before lines 5 and 9, the output lines in the INFO.BAT batch file.

```
C>INFO GOBBLEDY

C>REM  INFO.BAT

C>
C>ECHO OFF
GOBBLEDYGOOK is a specially coined phrase which means wordy and
generally unintelligible jargon.  It is symptomatic of many
computer textbooks.  No one believes that the phrase could
possibly apply to their writings or utterances.

Strike a key when ready . . . . ▪
```

Figure 15.12: INFO.BAT makes on-line help available

```
C>INFO ARRAYS

C>REM  INFO.BAT

C>
C>ECHO OFF
Sorry.  No help available for ARRAYS

C>▪
```

Figure 15.13: Screen display when help is not available

to the user, and the batch program ends immediately. This is handled by the GOTO statement in line 6, which ensures that none of the instructions between lines 7 and 11 execute.

APPOINTMENT REMINDER SYSTEM

Some computer systems offer the luxury of automatic appointment reminders. In addition, some utility packages like Sidekick per-

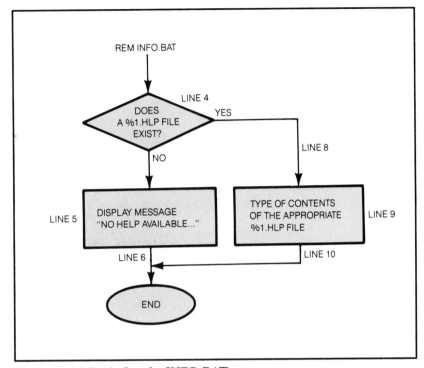

Figure 15.14: Logic flow for INFO.BAT

mit the entry and retrieval of date-oriented information (however, this is not automatic). The following example can take away the problem of forgetting to check your message or appointment log.

Unless you're very self-disciplined, the easiest way to implement this method begins by including a couple of reminders in your AUTOEXEC.BAT file. For instance, these three lines should jog your memory:

```
ECHO Remember to enter the following command to
ECHO get your messages for today (or any day).
ECHO TODAY mm-dd-yy
```

When you want to see the message or appointment file for, say, January 1, 1988, you only need to enter

```
TODAY 01-01-88
```

The results of this sequence can be seen in Figure 15.15.

The actual batch file that manages this simple operation is shown in Figure 15.16. As you can see, it is only a variation on the help method of the preceding section. The date files are text files, differing only in name and content from the .HLP files.

The way in which these text files are used (via the TYPE command) also reflects a similar batch-file approach. With the INFO method, all the files were similarly named with an .HLP extension, and their base names reflected the actual topic for which help was desired. In this appointment reminder system, the actual file name is understood (via %1) to be the date itself, a simple enough naming convention. The batch file types out the text file by that precise name. Here, you cannot assume that the batch-file code has the intel-

○ The naming convention for date files must be adhered to precisely. If you use dashes, slashes, or even leading zeros to create the text files, then you must also use them when you call up the TODAY.BAT file.

```
C>TODAY 01-01-88

C>REM  TODAY.BAT

C>
C>ECHO OFF
Happy new year!
You probably shouldn't be at work today at all.
However, since you are, don't forget to start writing 1988
        on all your checks, memos, etc.
Also, don't forget the paperwork for the new tech writer
        beginning work tomorrow.

C>TODAY 1/1/88

C>REM  TODAY.BAT

C>
C>ECHO OFF
No messages for 1/1/88

C>_
```

Figure 15.15: Running the TODAY.BAT file

```
 1   REM   TODAY.BAT
 2
 3   ECHO OFF
 4   IF NOT EXIST %1 GOTO ERROR
 5
 6   TYPE %1
 7   GOTO END
 8
 9   :ERROR
10   ECHO No messages for %1
11
12   :END
```

Figure 15.16: The TODAY.BAT file

ligence of the DOS DATE command; in other words, 01-01-88 could not be replaced by 1/1/88 or any other variation.

The logic flow for this batch file can be found in Figure 15.17. You can see that it is only slightly different from the logic flow in the INFO.BAT file.

One of many additions to this batch file could be the simple addition of the line

DATE %1

just before line 6 (the TYPE instruction). In systems that do not have a battery-backed clock/calendar, you usually have to run the DATE command when you bring up the system. Since you must enter the date once for your appointment-making system, you can let the batch-parameter mechanism do the work of setting the date as well. Programmers are always looking for ways to reduce user intervention time, system program time, or both. Minor improvements like this will add up dramatically over time.

Remember to erase your older date files when you no longer need them. Date files tend to proliferate quickly if they are not erased after use.

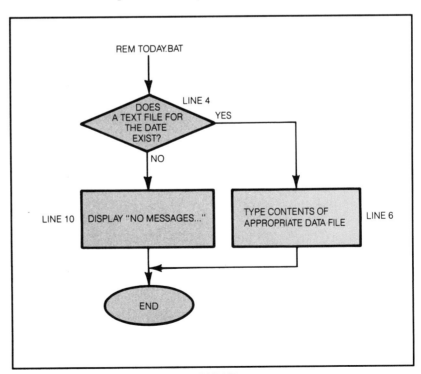

Figure 15.17: Logic flow for TODAY.BAT

BROADCASTING SYSTEM MESSAGES

Yet another variation on the theme of this section can be seen in the ANNOUNCE.BAT file of Figure 15.18. This batch program uses an area in memory called the *DOS environment,* which contains a set of variables and the values assigned to them. The DOS environment always includes the COMSPEC variable and the values you assign to PATH and PROMPT variables, as well as other arbitrarily named variables used by some programs or by the batch files described here.

A little-known technique of referencing DOS environment variables from within batch files allows you to broadcast messages to your system's users. This technique is useful for systems that have a number of different users, with perhaps one primary user. The goal is to have a simple command like

ANNOUNCE

display any and all current system messages for a user (see Figure 15.19).

In this figure, the first line is the key to the technique. You initialize a DOS environment variable (MESSAGE) equal to the name of this week's message file. In this case, the primary system operator only has to make the assignment of WEEK34.TXT to MESSAGE once, usually at the beginning of the day. For the rest of the time that the system is up, simply typing ANNOUNCE at the DOS prompt will display the current message file. Only the system operator needs to know the name of the actual message file, and from week to week, everyone's procedure for displaying system messages remains the same. Even the naming conventions can change, and the system operator is the only one who needs to know it.

This batch program can be modified slightly to allow for recurring messages that don't change from week to week. For instance, you could insert another line before line 5, like

TYPE ALWAYS.TXT

Then the ALWAYS.TXT file could contain any constant that you wished to display always, regardless of the week. This could contain such things as the operator's name and phone number, the service bureau's phone number, the security guard's extension, and so forth.

```
1   REM ANNOUNCE.BAT
2
3   ECHO OFF
4   ECHO Current System Messages:
5   TYPE %message%
```

Figure 15.18: The ANNOUNCE.BAT file

```
C>SET MESSAGE=WEEK34.TXT

C>TYPE WEEK34.TXT
Messages for Week 34 of FY88:
        Ted Bishop is on vacation.  Susanne Powers will be filling in.
        Next Saturday is the company picnic.  Mary has the tickets.
        Don't forget.  Backup, backup, backup.
        Time cards due on Thursday this week!

C>ANNOUNCE

C>REM ANNOUNCE.BAT

C>
C>ECHO OFF
Current System Messages:
Messages for Week 34 of FY88:
        Ted Bishop is on vacation.  Susanne Powers will be filling in.
        Next Saturday is the company picnic.  Mary has the tickets.
        Don't forget.  Backup, backup, backup.
        Time cards due on Thursday this week!

C>_
```

Figure 15.19: ANNOUNCE.BAT displays all current system messages

USING BATCH-FILE SUBROUTINES FOR STATUS TRACKING

Programmers use a variety of techniques for debugging their code. One of those techniques places additional printing statements at critical points in the source code. These are like snapshots. When the execution flow reaches these points, various parameters and variable values are printed out. The current program status can then be assessed and the problem discovered.

Programmers using this technique quickly learned the value of sending these debugging snapshots to a disk file instead. In this way, their program is not slowed down, and normal screen output is not compromised by debugging output.

You can borrow a page from the programmer's book for your own batch-file programming. Your batch files may at times become complicated, especially if you use the multifile technique of chaining. In writing any batch file, consider writing your own SNAPSHOT.BAT file. In a simple implementation, it could consist solely of the following two commands:

```
DIR > > AUDIT.TXT
CHKDSK > > AUDIT.TXT
```

Whenever SNAPSHOP.BAT was invoked, the current directory and disk status would be noted, and the > > redirection symbol would ensure that the AUDIT.TXT file would receive this information. You could later peruse the contents of this "tracking file" at your leisure.

The CALL subcommand in DOS 3.3 (or the COMMAND/C feature of earlier DOS versions) is also critical to effective use of the snapshot method. You may want to note the current disk directory and memory status at various points during the execution of one of your batch files.

The ANYOLD1.BAT file shown in Figure 15.20 is representative of any batch file you might write; the vertical dots just stand for your own instructions. Some example DOS commands, like COPY, DIR, and ERASE, have been included. The snapshot is taken by inserting a line that runs the SNAPSHOT.BAT file immediately.

In the figure, lines 8 and 18 use the CALL subcommand. If you're using a version of DOS earlier than 3.3, you could just replace the CALL subcommand with the following:

```
COMMAND/C SNAPSHOT
```

This invokes a secondary copy of the command processor, which then runs the SNAPSHOT batch file before continuing with other statements in the batch program you are testing.

When you are creating your batch file, you can insert as many of these secondary command processor lines as you need to assess the actual actions of your batch program. All of the snapshot results will be placed in the AUDIT.TXT file. You can erase this file any time you'd like to clear it out, since the > > redirection parameter will recreate the AUDIT.TXT file if it does not exist. After your batch file is complete and working just the way you want it to, you can remove all of the snapshot lines.

Note the use of the PAUSE command in ANYOLD1.BAT. Since the next command is ERASE, you're giving the user of your batch program a last chance to cancel out the continuation of the batch file. This is made especially useful by the preceding display of the A and C directories in the ANYOLD1 program.

Several creative variations on this method are available to you. Look at the modified SNAPSHOT.BAT file in Figure 15.21. In this version, two additional lines have been added before the DIR and CHKDSK lines. In fact, the DIR and CHKDSK commands are now being executed for both of the disks affected by commands in ANYOLD1.BAT. Line 4 is an add-on utility program that displays the system date and time. It is one of the Norton Utilities (see Chapter 17), and it presents this information in an attractive and readable format.

You could, of course, use DOS's DATE and TIME commands instead of an additional utility, redirecting their output to the AUDIT.TXT file. However, doing this would require you to press the Return key twice. This is because DOS will place its normal request for any date and time changes in the AUDIT.TXT file

```
REM ANYOLD1.BAT

             .
             .
             .

COPY A:*.DBF   C:\DATABASE
CALL SNAPSHOT

             .
             .
             .

DIR C:\DATABASE
DIR A:
PAUSE Everything look OK? BREAK, if not.
ERASE A:\*.WK1
CALL SNAPSHOT
```

Figure 15.20: The ANYOLD1.BAT file

```
1   REM   SNAPSHOT.BAT
2
3   ECHO Snapshot at point %1  >> AUDIT.TXT
4   TM          >> AUDIT.TXT
5   DIR/W  A:   >> AUDIT.TXT
6   CHKDSK A:   >> AUDIT.TXT
7   DIR/W  C:   >> AUDIT.TXT
8   CHKDSK C:   >> AUDIT.TXT
```

Figure 15.21: The SNAPSHOT.BAT file

Naturally, you can modify the snapshot examples presented here to include any other utility program lines or DOS commands that will provide you with useful information.

instead of on your video monitor. You won't see the requests, but DOS will wait for your response anyway.

Line 3 represents another useful variation. The AUDIT.TXT file will expand to include many entries, depending on the complexity of your batch file and how often you invoke the COMMAND/C instruction. Each entry can be tagged so that it indicates where the snapshot was taken.

Figure 15.22 shows the beginning of the AUDIT.TXT file. The first AUDIT entry sequence is labeled anyold1-A. When the secondary processor begins each time, it runs the SNAPSHOT program, passing the first parameter (%1) along. Line 3 accounts for the value of this parameter (anyold1-A) appearing in the output file AUDIT.TXT. You need only type a different string of characters each time you make a COMMAND/C entry in a batch file you want to trace through.

TIPS, TRICKS, AND TECHNIQUES

Earlier in this chapter, you used several batch files that will be useful in your system either directly or with slight modification. They represent stand-alone batch files that can provide you and others with useful additional tools, like the customized help screens or the color monitor initialization. This section will present a number of techniques that you can apply to your batch files. The methods can either be used as you see them, or they can be incorporated into the more sophisticated batch programs you may write.

USING RAM DISKS EFFECTIVELY

You learned in Chapter 10 how to initialize a RAM disk. You only needed to include one of the following two lines in your CONFIG.SYS file:

    DEVICE = VDISK.SYS 256

for PC-DOS, or

    DEVICE = RAMDRIVE.SYS 256

for MS-DOS. You've then created a 256K RAM disk (of course, the

```
Snapshot at point anyold1-A
                                              5:56 pm, Wednesday, June 17, 1987

   Volume in drive A is INVENTORY
   Directory of  A:\

   INVENT   EXE    INVENT2 EXE    STORES   DBF    STORES   NDX    PRICES   DBF
   ANALYSIS WK1
          5 File(s)     43008 bytes free
   Volume INVENTORY created Nov 23, 1987 3:37p

      362496 bytes total disk space
           0 bytes in 1 hidden files
      319488 bytes in 5 user files
       43008 bytes available on disk

      524288 bytes total memory
      132304 bytes free

   Volume in drive C is ROBBINS
   Directory of  C:\PROGRAMS\FW\CHAP13

   .                 ..                 1        BAT    2        BAT    3        BAT
   QUANCHAH FW2      CHAP12A  FW2      CHAP12B  FW2    FIG12-4  TXT    FIG12-5  TXT
   -- More --■
```

```
   FIG12-6   TXT    FIG12-1   TXT    FIG12-2A TXT    FIG12-2B TXT    FIG12-2C TXT
   FIG12-3   TXT    FIG12-10  TXT    FIRST    BAT    GOBBLEDY HLP    C        BAT
   R         BAT    MONO      BAT    RGB      BAT    COMPRESS BAT    NORMAL   DBF
   COLOR     BAT    01-01-88         CONTENTS BAT    FIG12-8  CAP    ANYOLD1  BAK
   FIG12-7   TXT    FIG12-14  CAP    TODAY    BAT    HELP     BAT    FIG12-13 CAP
   FIG12-12  TXT    FIG12-17  TXT    FIG12-16 CAP    ANNOUNCE BAT    WEEK34   TXT
   ANYOLD1   BAT    FIG12-19  TXT    FIG12-20 CAP    AUDIT    TXT    FIG12-21 TXT
   ANYOLD1   TXT    SNAPSHOT  BAT    FIG12-22 TXT    FIG12-21 BAK    SNAPSHOT BAK
   FIG12-22  BAK
          51 File(s)    1292288 bytes free
   Volume ROBBINS        created Mar 22, 1987 4:43p

     21204992 bytes total disk space
       108544 bytes in 4 hidden files
       149504 bytes in 62 directories
     19654656 bytes in 1442 user files
      1292288 bytes available on disk

       524288 bytes total memory
       132304 bytes free


   C>■
```

Figure 15.22: Contents of AUDIT.TXT after running ANYOLD1.BAT

These examples
assume that you
have previously trans-
ferred the correct main
programs, help files,
overlays, and so on, to
your RAM disk.

disk's size can vary according to what you intend to use it for), and you can proceed to transfer the proper files to it.

If you want your RAM disk to run a word processor, you could use the lines

REM RAMWP.BAT

CD\PROGRAMS\WORDPROC
D:
WP

```
C:
CD\
```

to create a file called RAMWP.BAT.

Storing the RAMWP.BAT file in your root directory, and assuming your root is on your path, you could switch to rapid RAM-based word processing easily and quickly by simply typing

```
RAMWP
```

> If you use this RAM drive technique for running more than one major program (for example, both a word processor and a DBMS), you must have enough space reserved for both. If you do not, you may need to write a separate batch program to copy the required programs onto the RAM drive. Of course, you can use the IF and EXIST subcommands to check the RAM drive itself. They will do the work for you, determining what files are needed and whether any existing files need to be erased to make room for the new ones.

You can use the same technique for your database management program, or for any other program that is slow because of normal disk-access speed. A variation of the RAMWP.BAT file for a database management system might contain these lines:

```
REM RAMDBMS.BAT

CD\PROGRAMS\DATABASE
D:
DBMS
C:
CD\
```

This batch file also makes the C hard-disk directory the obvious one for containing your document or data files. D, the RAM disk, is made the current drive so that the WP or DBMS program that executes is the one found on the RAM disk. Any references to C alone, with no directory path, will access the files in the current default directory on the C drive (in this case, either PROGRAMS\WORDPROC or PROGRAMS\DATABASE).

CONTROLLING USER ACCESS

Entire books have been written on the subject of password protection. Even more advanced tomes discuss the subject of *resource allocation,* which involves usage as well as access. Resource allocation means controlling access to both the contents of data files and the running of program files. Let's look at a simple but subtle form of password protection that you can implement with DOS alone.

The DOS environment affords you a special password feature. You can initialize a PASSWORD variable at the DOS prompt or in another batch file. For instance, you can enter

SET PASSWORD = EELS

Then the code segment shown in Figure 15.23 must be contained in a batch file to restrict access to only those people who know the password. If PASSWORD was set correctly to EELS before a batch file containing this code was run, then PROGRAM will run. Otherwise, the invalid password message will be echoed, and the batch file will terminate. In short, only those users who know that the password is EELS and set it correctly will be able to run the particular program. The program could be contained in any .EXE or .COM file, and of course, the batch file could properly reset the directory if necessary in the :RUN section.

The password feature can easily be extended by using several DOS environment variables, each containing different passwords. Your batch programs can check for the proper values. For instance, you can have three passwords controlling access to the inventory, personnel, and accounting programs. Doing this might require several blocks of code like the code just seen, and three passwords, PASS1, PASS2, and PASS3, controlling access to INVENTRY.EXE, PRSONNEL.EXE, and ACCOUNTS.EXE.

You might have a menu system that passes control to three batch files (see Figure 15.24) instead of directly to the three main programs. Only users who properly knew and set the appropriate DOS environment variable would be allowed access to the program they chose

> This password code uses IF statements to check for entry of the password in uppercase and in lowercase. You never know what case a user's keyboard might be in when he or she tries to run your batch file or menu system.

```
IF %PASSWORD%==EELS GOTO RUN
IF %PASSWORD%==eels GOTO RUN

ECHO Sorry. That's an invalid password.
GOTO END

:RUN
PROGRAM
:END
```

Figure 15.23: Code segment for password protection

```
          IF %PASS1%==STORE GOTO RUN
          IF %PASS1%==store GOTO RUN

          ECHO Sorry.  That's an invalid password.
          GOTO END

          :RUN
          INVENTRY

          :END

------------------------------------------------

          IF %PASS1%==JOSHUA GOTO RUN
          IF %PASS1%==joshua GOTO RUN

          ECHO Sorry.  That's an invalid password.
          GOTO END

          :RUN
          PRSONNEL

          :END

------------------------------------------------

          IF %PASS1%==1812 GOTO RUN

          ECHO Sorry.  That's an invalid password.
          GOTO END

          :RUN
          ACCOUNTS

          :END
```

Figure 15.24: Three batch files for a multiple password system

from the menu. Notice in the figure that the third password contains digits only, so IF tests for upper- and lowercase do not have to be performed.

SUMMARY

You've come a long way in this book. Not only have you learned a wide variety of commands and DOS features, but you've learned how to knit those features into seamless and sophisticated automatic batch files. This chapter presented the following examples:

- The AUTOEXEC.BAT file offers you a host of useful applications. Besides automating the system startup, you can change the default system prompt and automate anything you wish at power-up time. This ranges from automatically running any DOS command to automatically running add-on utility software packages.

- Batch files can be used to create simple but functional menu systems to drive the most sophisticated application setup.

- Batch files can simplify consistent instruction sequences. Through the use of abbreviations and shorthand notation, you can reduce your typing burden while simultaneously speeding up your system processing.

- The variable parameters allowed in batch files can provide a valuable tool for repeating critical application tasks automatically.

- A batch file quickly and automatically invokes any application program that is nested in its own subdirectory structure. The current directory and DOS path can be set up before program execution and restored afterwards.

- Operations involving multiple disks and diskettes, as well as sophisticated modular batch systems, can easily be developed with batch-file chaining.

- You can make batch files that will prepare and initialize your RAM disk automatically. This increases system efficiency and improves response time.

- Color monitors can be controlled easily through judicious batch-file development. You saw how a single batch file can make short work of setting the foreground and background colors on color screens.

- With batch files, you can create customized system help features, as well as an appointment reminder system. You can also broadcast messages to system users. These features can be very useful on systems that involve many people sharing the computer at different times.

- The CALL subcommand (DOS 3.3 only) or a secondary command processor can be woven into sophisticated applications. You saw how to do this for capturing system status snapshots, which can help you debug and analyze your system.

- You also learned a couple of new tricks for dealing with RAM disks. Batch programs can load main word-processing, spreadsheet, or database programs onto a RAM disk, and then execute the RAM-resident version of the main program using data files from your hard disk.

- The DOS environment can be used with batch files to manage a password control system.

Congratulations! There is nothing more you need to know in terms of DOS itself to consider yourself an advanced DOS user. However, keep reading. Chapter 16 offers you a chance to learn about advanced DOS commands. Chapter 17 discusses add-on and add-in utility programs, which enhance the power of DOS. They fill in DOS's functional gaps and add new features.

ADVANCED DOS
COMMANDS

YOU HAVE NOW LEARNED ALL THE COMMANDS NEC-
essary for using your DOS system effectively. In this chapter, you'll
extend your knowledge to include a special advanced set of commands. None of the standard uses of DOS require these commands,
but they can help you immeasurably in dealing with special situations. With their help, you can tailor your system to your specific
needs and increase the overall efficiency of your applications.

The commands presented in this chapter will allow you to expand
the range of ways in which you manage and manipulate files. Others
will enable you to use and traverse your directory and disk structures
more easily and more quickly. A final group of commands will help
you get more mileage from the main DOS controlling program,
COMMAND.COM.

ADVANCED FILE MANIPULATION

A file attribute is something that describes that file. Height is an
attribute of a person; disk storage space is an attribute of a file.
Another attribute of a file, indicated by the archive bit, is whether it
has been changed since the last time it was backed up with the
BACKUP command. Yet another attribute, indicated by the read/
write bit, is whether you are allowed to make or delete permanent
changes. Several advanced DOS commands have been designed to
work specifically with files and attributes such as these.

CHANGING A FILE'S ATTRIBUTES

Most files can be read from and written to; they are said to be *read/write* and to have an attribute of −R. Some files are restricted, only permitting data to be read from them. These files are called *read-only* and have an attribute of +R.

ATTRIB, a DOS disk-resident command, is used to change the read/write and archive file attributes. This command can be very useful; since you can change a file's read/write attribute bit to read-only, you can block the deletion of the file, which could prevent accidental erasure or changes to a file or group of files.

Influencing the archive bit allows you to control which files will be backed up. If you are using many temporary files, for example, you can reset their archive bits to 0 (off). Those files will then be ignored by the BACKUP /M and XCOPY /M commands. No backup or copy will take place; as a result, the backup and copy operations for the rest of your files will be faster, and less disk space will be required.

One version of the ATTRIB command affects the attributes of one or more files. A second, simpler version displays the current attributes of one or more files. The format of the command is

ATTRIB *Switches FileNames*

The *Switches* parameter controls the on/off status of the two file attributes. If *Switches* is not specified, the current attribute values of the specified files are displayed. *FileNames* is any standard file name. Wild cards are allowed, as well as drive and path-name prefixes.

Figure 16.1 shows the ATTRIB command applied to the root directory on drive C of a sample system. It indicates that three files have the A bit (archive attribute) set (files COMMAND.COM, AUTOEXEC.BAT, AND QD2.LOG), while only one file has the R bit (read/write attribute) set to read-only (COMMAND.COM). The CONFIG.SYS file has no attributes set, which means that it does not need to be backed up, and it can be read from and written to with no restrictions.

If switches are included, both the archive and read/write attributes can be modified simultaneously with one ATTRIB command. The first switch, which affects the read-write bit, is specified either as +R for read-only or −R for read/write. If the read-only status is set (+R), then the file may not be deleted or modified in any way.

The second switch affects the archive bit. It is specified either as +A, which sets the archive bit, or −A, which resets the archive bit. The archive bit is normally set whenever a file is rewritten to disk (after it has been changed). When a BACKUP command is issued, it

If read-only status is
set, it may not
always be obvious why
later operations become
difficult. Trying to use
EDLIN on a read-only
file, for example, pro-
duces the understandable
message "File is READ-
ONLY," but trying to
erase such a file produces
"Access denied," a less
than obvious message.
Worse still, you may be
in another application
program like dBASE III
PLUS, which only pro-
duces the cryptic message
"File cannot be
accessed!"

checks the archive bit. If the archive bit is set, BACKUP will back up the file; otherwise, it won't. After BACKUP has scanned a file and either backed it up or not, the archive bit will be reset to 0. Using the −A switch forces the archive bit to be reset, so that a file will be skipped over during a backup. This allows you some measure of control over whether your files will be backed up.

Table 16.1 shows the different states of a file's attributes when different combinations of these two switches are used. Remember that 1 in a binary system indicates that the attribute bit is on, and 0 indicates that it is off.

```
C>DIR

  Volume in drive C is ROBBINS
  Directory of  C:\

COMMAND  COM    25307   3-17-87   12:00p
CONFIG   SYS      160   8-10-87    6:03p
WP            <DIR>     8-10-87    9:44p
FW            <DIR>     8-10-87    9:45p
AUTOEXEC BAT      276   8-10-87    6:08p
QD2      LOG     3206   8-11-87    4:46p
DBASE         <DIR>     1-01-80   12:06a
DOS           <DIR>     1-01-80   12:10a
UTILITY       <DIR>     1-01-80   12:14a
        9 File(s)   3715072 bytes free

C>ATTRIB *.*
    A    R   C:\COMMAND.COM
             C:\CONFIG.SYS
    A        C:\AUTOEXEC.BAT
    A        C:\QD2.LOG

C>_
```

Figure 16.1: Attribute status of sample root files

COMMAND	READ/ WRITE BIT	ARCHIVE BIT
ATTRIB +R +A SAMPLE.TXT	1	1
ATTRIB +R −A SAMPLE.TXT	1	0
ATTRIB −R +A SAMPLE.TXT	0	1
ATTRIB −R −A SAMPLE.TXT	0	0

Table 16.1: Attribute combinations with the ATTRIB command

As Figure 16.1 showed, you can determine the current status of a file by using the ATTRIB command without switches. Using the switches, however, lets you control those attribute values yourself. If the command

ATTRIB +R –A SAMPLE.TXT

were used to set the read/write attribute to read-only (on), and the archive attribute off, then the command

ATTRIB SAMPLE.TXT

would produce the following result:

R   A:\SAMPLE.TXT

This shows that the read/write bit for the SAMPLE.TXT file is set to read-only, and that the archive bit is not set—no A indicator appeared.

UPDATING SETS OF FILES

If you work with a specific application program (for example, a word processor or a spreadsheet), you might want a backup disk to contain only copies of the most recently modified files. REPLACE allows you to make selective backups of files without using the BACKUP command. It can replace (update) the files on the backup disk that were recently changed or newly created on your working disk. It can also ignore any of your older and unchanged files.

The format of this command is

REPLACE *Source Destination Switches*

As always, the command may be prefixed by an optional drive and path name indicating where the REPLACE command file is located. *Source* represents the changed or newly created files that are to be written to the destination disk. *Destination* is optional; it specifies the destination drive and path to receive the copies of the specified files. If no destination path is given, the default is the current directory.

The *Switches* parameter represents one or more switches: /A, /P, /R, /S, or /W. Because the REPLACE command is defined primar-

The REPLACE command is simply an advanced, selective version of the COPY command. It is most commonly used when you change versions of DOS and need to update various system files. REPLACE can also be used to update an entire DOS directory on your hard disk when you upgrade your version of DOS. It also comes in handy when regularly backing up a small set of files at the end of a workday, either adding new files or updating modified files on your designated backup diskette.

ily by these switches, some of them cannot be used together. Let's use the two directories in Figure 16.2, SOURCE and DEST, to demonstrate the behavior of the REPLACE command with its switches.

The /A switch allows you to add files to the destination directory. DOS will only copy source files that are not in the destination directory. The /P (Prompt) switch instructs DOS to pause and ask you if it is all right to copy each file that meets the criteria of *any other* switch that is used.

Let's use the /A and /P switches together. If you issue the command

C> REPLACE \SOURCE*.* \DEST /A /P

for the files shown in Figure 16.2, the results on your screen will be

Add C:\DEST\FILE2.TXT? (Y/N) Y
Adding C:\DEST\FILE2.TXT

1 file(s) added

The one file in the source directory (FILE2.TXT) that did not already exist by name in the destination directory was selected for replacement. As Figure 16.3 shows, FILE2.TXT was added to the DEST directory; FILE1.TXT and FILE3.TXT were left as they were.

```
C>DIR

   Volume in drive C is ROBBINS
   Directory of  C:\SOURCE

   .              <DIR>      3-05-88    3:00p
   ..             <DIR>      3-05-88    3:00p
   FILE3          12176     11-16-88   10:30a
   FILE1           1056      8-18-88    4:23p
   FILE2           3616      9-26-88    6:42a
          5 File(s)    2535424 bytes free

C>DIR \DEST

   Volume in drive C is ROBBINS
   Directory of  C:\DEST

   .              <DIR>      3-05-88    3:00p
   ..             <DIR>      3-05-88    3:00p
   FILE3          12784      8-15-88    7:06a
   FILE1           1040      1-08-88    4:57p
          4 File(s)    2535424 bytes free

C>_
```

Figure 16.2: Example directories

```
C>DIR \DEST

    Volume in drive C is ROBBINS
    Directory of  C:\DEST
    .            <DIR>      3-05-88   3:00p
    ..           <DIR>      3-05-88   3:00p
    FILE3        12784      8-15-88   7:06a
    FILE1         1040      1-08-88   4:57p
    FILE2         3616      9-26-08   6:42a
         5 File(s)   2525184 bytes free

C>_
```

Figure 16.3: Adding files with the REPLACE command

The /R switch overrides the read/write attributes of read-only files on the destination directory. It allows you to replace those read-only files without generating an error message, so you will not be denied the implicit file update performed by REPLACE. This switch should be used with caution, since you or someone else may have set the read/write attribute bit to read-only for a good reason.

The /S switch will only replace or update old files, not add new ones. Therefore, it cannot be used with the /A switch. Be careful when you use the /S switch with a wild-card character—it will replace *all* files matching the source specification, including those in any sub-directories of the destination directory.

Figure 16.4 shows how the /S switch works. This example uses the original DEST directory from Figure 16.2, which only contained FILE1.TXT and FILE3.TXT. The command shown in the figure tells the computer to use files in the SOURCE directory to replace any files they match in the DEST directory. Since only FILE1.TXT and FILE3.TXT are common to both directories, only they are replaced in the DEST directory.

The /W switch allows you time to insert a new source diskette before the replacement process begins. DOS pauses to give you time to place a new source diskette into a drive. For example, you can execute a REPLACE command from a DOS diskette in drive A, replace that disk

⊙ Be careful to enter the source and destination directories in the correct order in your command. Performing a REPLACE backwards could copy your old data over your new versions.

```
C>REPLACE  \SOURCE\*.*  \DEST  /S
Replacing C:\DEST\FILE3 file.
Replacing C:\DEST\FILE1 file.
2 files were replaced.

C>DIR \DEST

 Volume in drive C is ROBBINS
 Directory of  C:\DEST

 .            <DIR>       3-05-88   3:00p
 ..           <DIR>       3-05-88   3:00p
 FILE3          12176    11-16-88  10:30a
 FILE1           1056     8-18-88   4:23p
         4 File(s)    2525184 bytes free

C>_
```

Figure 16.4: Updating matching files with REPLACE

with the correct source disk, and then proceed to replace files on B with files from the newly inserted source diskette in A.

RESCUING LOST FILES

RECOVER is DOS's "Humpty Dumpty" command—it puts a file or a complete disk back together again. There may be times in your future when something will happen to a file or to a part of the disk containing your file. A file may become unreadable, and access to that file may be denied. (This usually stems from the deterioration of the magnetic disk surface, rather than from the simple attribute modification discussed in the last section.)

The RECOVER command can read a file part by part (actually, disk cluster by disk cluster), skipping over the parts that have gone bad. This command rewrites the file without the bad data and allows you to access what's left. The format to recover specific files is

RECOVER *FileNames*

and the format to recover an entire disk is

RECOVER *DriveName*

File loss may also be due to corruption of the file allocation table (FAT). Even RECOVER is not likely to help you much in this instance.

RECOVER is not designed to work properly on a network disk. Disengage a disk completely from any network before you try to recover files with this command.

Only try to recover an entire drive when your disk's directory has been damaged completely. RECOVER does not distinguish between normally accessible and inaccessible files, so all files in the directory will be renamed in this format.

Like all DOS commands, RECOVER can be prefixed with a drive and path name to indicate where the disk-resident DOS command file may be found. In the first format, the file names to be recovered can also be prefixed by their directory locations.

Recovering all files on a disk is necessary when the directory or file allocation table of the disk has been damaged. After you use the second version of this command, the directory will be made up of files of the form FILE*nnnn*.REC, where *nnnn* is a number. All of the recovered files will be numbered sequentially in the order in which they were recovered. This is not necessarily the order in which they appeared in the directory before the damage was done.

When you try to recover all files on a disk, you are limited to the maximum number of files that can fit into the root directory of the disk. If your disk has a subdirectory structure that contains more than this maximum, you'll have to invoke RECOVER several times, clearing out the recovered files from the root in between invocations. When you have finished recovering your text files, you will probably need to go through each one and edit the end of the recovered files, since the recovery process is likely to capture meaningless data at the end of the last disk cluster occupied by your original file.

IMPROVING DISK AND DIRECTORY REFERENCING

The following commands influence the way that DOS looks at its disk drives and disk directory structures. These commands can be very useful when you are running older programs that make fixed assumptions about drives, when your programs do not contain a changeable path specification, or when a path name simply gets too long. These commands will also make your DOS application references easier and faster.

TREATING DISKS AS DIRECTORIES

JOIN is used to make DOS treat a whole disk drive as if it were a subdirectory on another drive. This extraordinary command allows individual DOS commands to treat files on multiple disk drives as if they were part of one sophisticated directory on a single drive.

The JOIN command can be very helpful when it is used with a directory management program like XTREE. Each time XTREE switches disks, it totals all of the files to determine the amount of space already used and the amount of space still available. This takes quite some time and can be a burden to power users. Switching a new disk with JOIN allows you to switch the current directory rather than current drive, and is a significantly faster operation.

There are three versions of the JOIN command. As usual, all of them allow you to precede the command itself with a drive and path name specifying where DOS can find the JOIN.EXE file. Entering JOIN with no parameters at the command prompt will display all the current directory and disk names that have been joined. Entering JOIN with two parameters specifies what directory and drive are to be joined. Entering JOIN with only one parameter (a drive identifier) and the /D switch *disjoins* the drive from a directory to which it had been joined.

Executing the following JOIN command will connect the two drives internally:

    JOIN D: C:\ACCOUNT

This can be read as "Join the entire drive *D* to the C:\ACCOUNT directory." Any disk drive identifier may be substituted for D, and any empty directory of files may be substituted for C:\ACCOUNT. To see how this works, look at Figure 16.5, which shows two disk directory structures. Figure 16.6 shows the new directory structure after this JOIN command was executed. Drive D appears to be a subdirectory on drive C.

When you invoke JOIN with no parameters, DOS will display the results of any joining. The computer will show the joined drives and the directories they have been attached to. For example, entering

    JOIN

The JOIN command applies only to root directories and the first level of subdirectories beyond root directories. You'll receive an "invalid parameter" message if you try to join to a directory any further into your hierarchical structure.

Figure 16.5: Sample disk directory structures

produces

D: = > C:\ACCOUNT

This tells you that the root directory of drive D can only be accessed now through the ACCOUNT directory on drive C. In effect, C:\ACCOUNT is the new root directory of drive D, and all of drive D's subdirectories are now subdirectories of C:\ACCOUNT.

When you use the primary form of the JOIN command, in which you specify a drive and a directory to be joined, DOS will simply respond with a new prompt if everything went well. You won't receive any notice that the join was made—and in this case, no news is good news. For example, if ACCOUNT is an empty directory, the command

JOIN D: C:\ACCOUNT

will produce no obvious result.

You must use a completely empty directory when you join another disk drive to it.

If the proposed root directory (C:\ACCOUNT) had not been empty of files, you would have received the error message "Directory not empty," and the JOIN command would have failed. Although a proposed root directory *may* have subdirectories and the JOIN command can still be made, any subdirectories in existence will be sup-

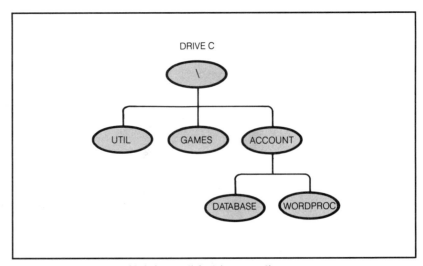

Figure 16.6: Results of joining a disk drive to a directory

pressed temporarily until the drive and directory are disjoined. You won't be able to access any information in that part of your directory structure.

Continuing with this example, if a DIR command is executed on drive C after the join has been made, the remaining amount of disk storage shown will be that of drive C, not of drive D. If anything is saved in the ACCOUNT subdirectory (actually, drive D), then disk storage will be used on drive D, not on C. Thus, it is possible to save in ACCOUNT (drive D) a file that is larger than the apparent amount of disk storage space left. In addition, access to drive D will be denied, so any command using drive D explicitly (such as DIR D:) will generate the error message "Invalid drive specification."

The last version of the JOIN command cancels the effects of a previous JOIN command. You must specify the JOIN command you wish to disengage (there may have been many). The following command would disengage the join just executed in our example:

    JOIN D: /D

If the destination drive (that is, the proposed root directory of the JOIN command in question) is omitted, with the intention of undoing all joinings, the error message "Incorrect number of parameters" will appear. Similarly, disjoining a drive that has not been joined will generate the error message "Invalid parameter."

Now let's work through an actual session with the JOIN command. The following sequence will show what happens if you are using drives A and B on a dual-diskette system. The drives contain the directories shown in Figure 16.7. The first JOIN command in Figure 16.8 appends the root directory of B to the directory A:\ACCOUNT, as a DIR command shows. A:\ACCOUNT has become drive B's root directory.

The two commands in Figure 16.9 change the active directory and then create a file in that directory; this file is actually being created in drive B. To see that the file is actually on drive B, you need to disjoin the directories and take a look at the files on drive B (see Figure 16.10).

TREATING DIRECTORIES AS DISKS

The SUBST (Substitute) command is the opposite of the JOIN command: it will create a new disk drive out of any existing directory.

```
A:\> DIR A:

  Volume in drive A has no label
  Directory of  A:\

UTIL         <DIR>      6-04-87    2:12p
GAMES        <DIR>      6-04-87    2:12p
ACCOUNT      <DIR>      6-04-87    2:12p
JOIN     EXE   8955   12-30-85   12:00p
SUBST    EXE   9911   12-30-85   12:00p
       5 File(s)    339968 bytes free

A:\> DIR B:

  Volume in drive B has no label
  Directory of  B:\

WORDPROC     <DIR>      6-04-87    2:12p
DATABASE     <DIR>      6-04-87    2:12p
       2 File(s)    359424 bytes free

A:\> ■
```

Figure 16.7: Directory listings of drives A and B

```
A:\> JOIN B: A:\ACCOUNT
A:\> DIR A:\ACCOUNT

  Volume in drive A has no label
  Directory of  A:\ACCOUNT

WORDPROC     <DIR>      6-04-87    2:12p
DATABASE     <DIR>      6-04-87    2:12p
       2 File(s)    339968 bytes free
A:\> ■
```

Figure 16.8: Joining drive B to the ACCOUNT directory on A

To visualize this, look at Figure 16.6 first and Figure 16.5 next. Starting with one directory structure, you can take a directory (ACCOUNT) and all of its subdirectories and make that directory the root directory of a new drive.

A frequent use for this command is running older software packages that cannot reference files in a hierarchical directory structure. By fooling these packages into thinking they are only addressing files

```
A:\> CD \ACCOUNT
A:\ACCOUNT> COPY CON: TEST.TXT
This is a test file.  This will be saved in the
\ACCOUNT directory which is actually the root directory
of drive B.  Therefore, the available storage space
shown with the DIR command will be that remaining on
drive A.  When this file is saved, it will actually use
space on drive B, so the available storage space shown
on the screen (for A:) will not change.  However, it
will be decreasing the available disk space on drive B.
^Z
        1 File(s) copied

A:\ACCOUNT> DIR

 Volume in drive A has no label
 Directory of  A:\ACCOUNT

WORDPROC    <DIR>        6-04-87    2:12p
DATABASE    <DIR>        6-04-87    2:12p
TEST     TXT      380    6-04-87    2:58p
        3 File(s)     339968 bytes free

A:\ACCOUNT>
■
```

Figure 16.9: Directory files as files on another drive

```
A:\ACCOUNT> CD \
A:\> JOIN B:  /D
A:\> DIR B:

 Volume in drive B has no label
 Directory of   B:\

WORDPROC    <DIR>        6-04-87    2:12p
DATABASE    <DIR>        6-04-87    2:12p
TEST     TXT      380    6-04-87    2:58p
        3 File(s)     358400 bytes free

A:\> ■
```

Figure 16.10: Disjoining a drive and directory

The SUBST command also reduces your typing burden. You can redefine any directory, no matter how deep in your hierarchical structure, as a single-letter drive identifier. All future command references will be shorter, faster, and less liable to contain typing errors.

on a disk drive, you can still make use of the DOS directory structure for file storage.

The SUBST command comes in handy in another common situation. If you have a hard disk with a directory structure containing many levels of subdirectories, this command allows you to avoid typing long path names. For the same reason, it is useful when you have a program that requests a file name and path but only allows a certain amount of characters to be entered. WordPerfect is an example of this type of program.

Like the JOIN command, SUBST has three versions. The first actually performs a substitution, the second displays all current substitutions, and the third cancels a previous substitution.

Let's look at an example. Specify a directory structure, as shown in Figure 16.11. Then suppose you need to run an older general ledger program that needs the files in ACCOUNT\GL, but the older program does not support paths. You would issue the following command:

> Since a substituted drive is really only a portion of another drive, don't mistake it for a RAM drive. SUBST offers convenience, not increased performance.

SUBST F: C:\ACCOUNT\GL

This command makes DOS assume there is a disk drive F, and that the contents of this drive are the contents of the ACCOUNT\GL subdirectory on drive C. Drive F now includes all of the directory's subdirectories (in this example, however, there are no subdirectories).

You can refer to the directory just as you would a normal disk drive. If you typed

DIR F:

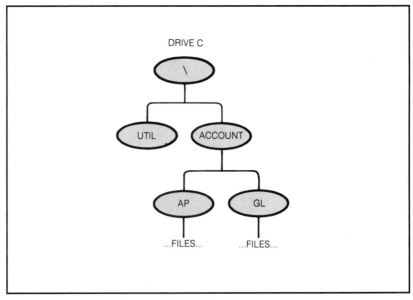

Figure 16.11: Sample directory structure

DOS would return the same result as if you had typed

DIR C:\ACCOUNT\GL

Unlike the JOIN command, the SUBST command allows you to access the specified subdirectory directly after the SUBST command has been issued. If you save a file on F (or in the subdirectory), it will also be saved in the subdirectory (or on F), because both access the same part of the disk (see Figure 16.12). In effect, this command opens up another "window" into a directory, and you can access that directory's contents through the window simply by using a drive specifier.

The second version of SUBST causes all currently active substitutions to be displayed. DOS will show you the created drive identifier and the drive and directory to which it is linked. For example,

C:\ > SUBST
F: = > C:\ACCOUNT\GL

shows you that drive F is being used as a substitute for

> By default, DOS only supports drives lettered A through E. In order to create and access drives lettered beyond E, you must include in your CONFIG.SYS file the command LASTDRIVE = *n*, where *n* is the last letter allowed for a drive. For example, LASTDRIVE = E is the default condition, whereas LASTDRIVE = Z allows drives labeled A through Z.

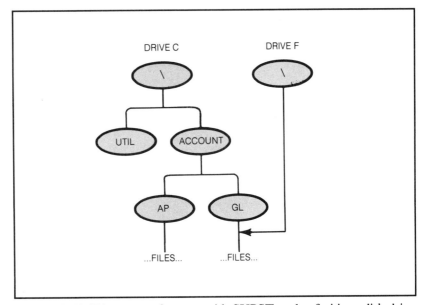

Figure 16.12: Directory references with SUBST and a fictitious disk-drive identifier

ACCOUNT\GL on drive C. As a result, the ACCOUNT\GL directory can be accessed normally (on drive C) or through its substitute (on the fictitious drive F).

The final version of SUBST is used to undo a substitution. To undo the SUBST command shown in the previous example, you would type

SUBST F: /D

The /D switch disjoins, or disassociates, the directory from the fictitious drive F.

Let's take a look at an example of using all three versions of this command. The first step is to examine the root directory on drive A to verify that no drive F exists (see Figure 16.13). Next, issue the SUBST command to create drive F, as shown in Figure 16.14. Then activate the "windowing" feature of this command by creating a file on drive F and verifying that it actually resides in the linked subdirectory (see Figure 16.15).

Finally, you can undo the SUBST command to restore the system to its original state by issuing this command:

A:\> SUBST F: /D

```
A>DIR

 Volume in drive A is DEMO
 Directory of  A:\

UTIL         <DIR>      3-05-88   2:40p
ACCOUNT      <DIR>      3-05-88   2:40p
        2 File(s)    358400 bytes free

A>DIR ACCOUNT

 Volume in drive A is DEMO
 Directory of  A:\ACCOUNT

.            <DIR>      3-05-88   2:40p
..           <DIR>      3-05-88   2:40p
GL           <DIR>      3-05-88   3:35p
AP           <DIR>      3-05-88   3:35p
        4 File(s)    358400 bytes free

A>_
```

Figure 16.13: Root directory of drive A

Trying to use the DIR command on drive F will now result in the following:

A:\\> DIR F:
Invalid drive specification

```
A>SUBST F: \ACCOUNT\GL

A>DIR F:

 Volume in drive F is DEMO
 Directory of  F:\

 .            <DIR>       3-05-88    3:35p
 ..           <DIR>       3-05-88    3:35p
        2 File(s)    353280 bytes free

A>_
```

Figure 16.14: A directory treated as a disk drive

```
A>COPY CON: F:TEST.TXT
This file should appear in both F: and \ACCOUNT\GL^Z
        1 File(s) copied

A>DIR F:

 Volume in drive F is DEMO
 Directory of  F:\

 .            <DIR>       3-05-88    3:35p
 ..           <DIR>       3-05-88    3:35p
 TEST     TXT      50    3-05-88    4:31p
        3 File(s)    347136 bytes free

A>DIR \ACCOUNT\GL

 Volume in drive A is DEMO
 Directory of  A:\ACCOUNT\GL

 .            <DIR>       3-05-88    3:35p
 ..           <DIR>       3-05-88    3:35p
 TEST     TXT      50    3-05-88    4:31p
        3 File(s)    347136 bytes free

A>_
```

Figure 16.15: Substituted and original drive

REROUTING DISK INPUT AND OUTPUT

Some older programs have hard-coded drive references, which means they are internally frozen, with no way for you to make use of a hard disk. The ASSIGN command can help you solve this problem. It causes any requests for one drive to be carried out on another drive. ASSIGN is very useful with older software packages designed to work only with drives A and B. You can have your files in a directory on your hard disk, and the older program will be tricked into believing it is accessing the files on a single drive without any hierarchical structures.

This command has two versions. The first will make or break assignations, while the second cancels all assignations currently in effect. The first version is the most frequently used:

ASSIGN *DriveX* = *BigDrive*

In this version, DOS will cause all future references to files and directories on *DriveX* to be treated as if they had been made to *BigDrive*. As always with DOS transient commands, you can prefix the command name with a drive identifier and a path name.

A simple example of this command is assigning to drive C any references to the files on drive A.

ASSIGN A = C

can be read as "Let the current working directory on drive C handle everything requested of drive A." When the command DIR A: is executed, a directory of drive C will appear. To undo ASSIGN commands, use ASSIGN by itself without any drive assignments:

ASSIGN

You should not use ASSIGN with BACKUP, RESTORE, LABEL, JOIN, SUBST, or PRINT. These commands act on the contents of drives and directories; serious problems can result if your intended destination drive has previously been reassigned to another drive. As a matter of protection, DOS ignores reassignments when you invoke the even more dangerous FORMAT, DISKCOPY, and DISKCOMP commands.

SPEEDING UP DISK ACCESS

When you have a directory structure that contains many levels of subdirectories, DOS can take a very long time to search for a file or directory. To combat this problem, Microsoft developed the new DOS 3.3 FASTOPEN command, which maintains a list of the most recently accessed directory and file locations. This means that if you repeatedly reference a directory or file, DOS will be able to locate it more quickly on the disk. The FASTOPEN memory buffer will contain the disk location of that directory or file; DOS can then access it without having to check the disk directory structure itself.

The general format of this command is

FASTOPEN *Drive:* = *Size*

Drive is the drive you want FASTOPEN to work for. You must repeat the *Drive:* and = *Size* parts of the command for each drive you want FASTOPEN to affect. *Size,* an optional parameter, represents the number of directory or file entries that FASTOPEN will remember.

Make sure that the FASTOPEN command file is available on the current directory or path. As with all DOS 3.3 commands, you can precede the command name with the full path name leading to it.

The most common use of the FASTOPEN command is simply to specify the disk drive whose performance you want to improve. For example, entering

FASTOPEN C:

will enable DOS to remember the last 34 directories and files accessed (the default), and thus be able to go right to them on the disk.

FASTOPEN can only be used once per boot session and reserves 35 bytes per entry. A buffer size of 100 (FASTOPEN C: = 100) would therefore consume about 3500 bytes of memory. It is recommended that *Size* be at least as great as the highest number of levels in the directory structure, so that any file in the directory can be quickly found. In fact, unless you are only working with one file, *Size* should be larger. The default is reasonable, unless you have special usage requirements and perform some actual timing tests.

FASTOPEN may not be used on a drive defined by the JOIN, SUBST, or ASSIGN command. In addition, it should not be used on network drives.

INFLUENCING THE COMMAND PROCESSOR AND ITS ENVIRONMENT

The command processor on your system disk, COMMAND-.COM, is the program that interprets all of the commands you type in from the keyboard. It has been primarily responsible for interpreting all the commands you've learned so far. It takes your command

and first scans its own internal command list to see if it can handle your request without going to the disk. If the command is a resident command, then the way in which that command will work is defined somewhere in COMMAND.COM. If it is a transient command, COMMAND.COM will check the directory to see if the command file is present. If it is not, and your command is not in a batch file, you will get an error message. However, if it does find the command file, control will be transferred to that file.

Let's look at some examples. TYPE is a resident command used to display the contents of ASCII files. When COMMAND.COM is ready to accept a command, it displays the DOS prompt. Say you type in the command TYPE OUTLINE.TXT. COMMAND-.COM first determines that TYPE is a resident command. It then looks internally for the instructions that tell it what to do when the TYPE command is used. Following these instructions, it gets the file name you typed in and displays the file.

Transient commands are not really commands at all—each transient command request actually runs a program contained in a separate file. These files are called .COM or .EXE files. For example, a file named ASSIGN.COM contains the program that performs an ASSIGN command. Say you issue the command ASSIGN A = B. COMMAND.COM first checks that it is not a resident command. After first checking the current working directory, it will then find the file called ASSIGN.COM somewhere along the specified path and transfer control of the system to that file. When ASSIGN is done assigning, control passes back to COMMAND.COM. Of course, this assumes you've set the path properly (PATH \DOS).

When COMMAND.COM is doing all of this, it must not only access those parts of itself that contain definitions and instructions, but it also must access the DOS environment. This contains user-defined definitions, such as the current path and the last available drive (LASTDRIVE in CONFIG.SYS). The SET command gives you direct control over the contents of the DOS environment.

RENAMING COMMANDS

The SET command is used to change character strings and definitions within the DOS environment. Both you and DOS can set aside named areas of this environment for character strings. You can use them for anything you like—for example, individual path names for future commands, file names for later DOS operations, or variable values used by several batch files.

The SET command with no parameters

SET

can display the current DOS environment settings. A modified format can erase any existing entry:

SET *Name =*

will erase the DOS environment variable $\overset{\bullet}{Name}$. To create a completely new DOS environment string or to change one that already exists, use the format

SET *Name = String*

where *Name* is either a variable name defined by you, or one of the system's predefined names like PROMPT, PATH, LASTDRIVE, or COMSPEC.

Let's take a look at a sample sequence that demonstrates this command. First, you can display the existing DOS environment, which includes all externally defined system defaults and user definitions. For example, issuing the SET command at the DOS prompt:

A:\ > SET

will display the following:

```
COMSPEC = A:\COMMAND.COM
PATH = \
PROMPT = $p$g
LASTDRIVE = Z
FILES = \wordproc\wordperf\files
```

The first four of these environment names are predefined and have special meaning to the system. You've seen all of these except for COMSPEC, which is only modified infrequently, when you've relocated your command processor to some drive or directory other than the root of the boot disk. COMSPEC is usually used when you place

You are limited by default to 127 bytes of total available DOS environment space, although this default may be increased by using the /E switch of the SHELL command (see Chapter 18).

COMMAND.COM on a RAM disk to speed up applications that invoke the command processor frequently.

The next version of the SET command will remove an entire string definition from the DOS environment. With the DOS environment defined as just shown, executing the command

    SET PATH =

will clear the value of the PATH variable. If you then execute the SET command, you will see that the PATH variable has been removed:

```
A:\> SET
COMSPEC = A:\COMMAND.COM
PROMPT = $p$g
LASTDRIVE = Z
FILES = \wordproc\wordperf\files
```

The entire path definition has been removed. Asking for the current path at the DOS prompt now will result in a ''No Path'' message.

The last version of SET will define or modify a DOS environment string. Say you want to replace the path. You can do it in one of two ways: by using the PATH command (see Chapter 5), or by using the SET command. Using the command

    SET path = \utility

would change or create the path definition, as shown here:

```
A:\> set
COMSPEC = A:\COMMAND.COM
PATH = \utility
PROMPT = $p$g
LASTDRIVE = Z
FILES = \wordproc\wordperf\files
```

Notice that the variable name ''path'' was changed to ''PATH,'' but ''utility'' stayed in the same case. This is because the case of the DOS environment's character string may have meaning to you and affect how you intend to use it.

Definitions contained in the DOS environment can only be used (that is, actually referred to) by programs or batch files. For example, typing CD FILES at the DOS prompt will not work. You can, however, create a batch file that accesses the DOS environment string FILES:

A:\ > COPY CON: TEST.BAT

dir %FILES%
 ^Z

As you learned in Chapter 15, a leading percent sign indicates a batch variable, while leading and trailing percent signs together indicate a DOS environment string.

The command dir %FILES% would cause the command processor to look up FILES in the DOS environment and, when found, substitute its definition (in this case, \wordperf\wordproc\files) for %FILES%. Remember, this is *not* available directly from the DOS prompt.

As you can see, the DOS environment can be used by programs and batch files and is a convenient way to pass information to these programs. For example, suppose a program needs a certain file name or path, but for some reason the program does not ask the user directly for this information. (Security reasons often account for this situation.) The path information can be put into the DOS environment, which then can be made inaccessible to the user but readily obtainable from the program.

CREATING A SECOND COMMAND PROCESSOR

There will be times when it may be useful to create or invoke a second command processor. COMMAND.COM, the first command processor, is invoked when the computer is turned on. It is the part of DOS that takes in, translates, and executes your standard commands. However, invoking a second command processor with COMMAND can give you the ability to execute DOS commands from inside a program (written in BASIC, Pascal, and so on) and then return to that program. This command also allows you to load and customize a command processor that has special functions and abilities or altered command definitions. The COMMAND command has several switches: one to specify the memory residency status of the new command processor, one to name a file to be run upon invocation, and one to change the size of the DOS environment.

The general format of this command is

COMMAND *Location Switches*

Location is the optional drive and path where the command processor to be invoked is located. This parameter gives you the ability to prepare and then use a nonstandard or restricted version of a command processor. The *Switches* parameter represents any or all of the optional switches /P, /C *String*, and /E:*xxxxx*.

The new command processor must be named COMMAND.COM as well. Once the new processor is invoked, however, the directory containing the new processor will not become the new root directory. Everything will run as it did before you reassigned the processor, but the processing rules of the new processor will be in effect.

The optional switches define the new processor's environment. The /P (Permanent) switch causes the new command processor to become the primary processor. DOS will assume as initial values all the existing DOS environment variables defined by the prior command processor. You may change any of them, but you will not be able to exit to the previous DOS environment. Without /P, the new DOS environment exists only temporarily, and you can exit from it only by using DOS's EXIT command. This comes in handy if you are using a modified command processor for security reasons.

The /C *String* parameter tells the new processor to execute the command in *String* when it is invoked. If this is left out, the new command processor will be invoked and prompt you for commands. For example, the normal processor that is run every time you start the computer, COMMAND.COM, has a built-in *String* value of AUTOEXEC.BAT, which causes the AUTOEXEC.BAT file to be run when the system starts.

The /E:*xxxx* parameter can define a new DOS environment size, so that extensive use of the SET command will be permitted. This is only necessary when you begin doing fancy things with your batch files (as you saw in the previous chapter) or your application programs.

For example, suppose you have a command processor in the UTILITY directory, in which the ERASE command has not been defined. You would like 500 bytes of DOS environment, and you would like this processor to supplant the COMMAND.COM processor permanently. The following command will do all of this:

```
COMMAND \UTILITY /P /E:500
```

COMMAND is the command name, and UTILITY is the directory containing the new command processor. The /P switch makes the newly active command processor (the secondary command processor) the permanent primary processor, and /E:500 tells the computer to allow half a kilobyte of DOS environmental memory.

Invoking a secondary processor without the /P parameter will cause the DOS environment to appear as in Figure 16.16. You may terminate the secondary processor invoked without /P by using the DOS EXIT command. This will deactivate the secondary DOS environment and reactivate the main processor. On exiting from the secondary processor, the computer will reenter the DOS environment of the first processor. Therefore, any changes made to any of the DOS environment variables of the secondary command processor will be lost when you exit to the primary DOS environment.

While any changes you make to the DOS environment while you are running the secondary processor will be lost when you exit to the primary processor, anything else you have done—such as changing drives and deleting files—will be permanent.

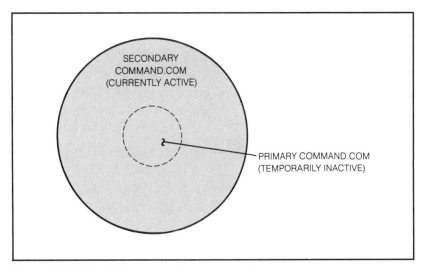

Figure 16.16: Invoking a secondary command processor

This can come in handy in a number of instances. If necessary, you could even use this command to increase the available DOS environment. Simply reinvoking the original command processor with

    COMMAND \ /P /E:5000

would activate the same processor, but expand the DOS environment to 5000 bytes and make the new processor the primary processor.

You should not invoke a secondary command processor lightly, since each new invocation of COMMAND.COM requires a finite additional amount of physical memory to be allocated. Permanent attachment of a secondary processor is better used as a technique for customization or security, rather than for simply expanding the DOS environment.

SUMMARY

You have now mastered some of the most advanced features of DOS. The sophisticated capabilities you've seen in this chapter often lie buried under unreadable documentation. In this chapter, however, you've seen how these advanced features can be used to your advantage.

- The ATTRIB command gives you complete control over the file attributes that govern whether and when the file can be erased, modified, or backed up.

- Files, and even entire disks, that have become physically damaged stand an improved chance of being recovered with the RECOVER command.

- You can upgrade backups and software easily and quickly by using the REPLACE command.

- Entire disk drives can be seen as only a single directory branch of another disk structure by using the JOIN command.

- The SUBST command allows you to treat an entire directory branch as a separate and unique (but fictitious) disk drive. This is useful with older programs that don't allow directory path references. The ASSIGN command is also useful for hard-coded programs; it lets you reroute disk references.

* Speedier disk access can be obtained by DOS 3.3 users with the FASTOPEN command, which enables DOS to remember the disk locations of recently used files and directories.

* You can create sophisticated application environments with the SET command, which controls the creation and modification of DOS environment string variables.

* You can exercise control over the command processor itself by invoking a secondary processor with the COMMAND command. This allows unique security and customization possibilities.

You now have a complete picture of DOS, and you can see that it is a very useful operating system. However, software developers have created a vast body of new software designed to extend and enhance the power of DOS. The next chapter presents the best examples of add-on and add-in software that you should consider acquiring to make even more effective use of your DOS software.

EXTENDING THE POWER
OF DOS

CHAPTER *17* _____

MICROSOFT SUPPLIES MANY USEFUL PROGRAMS WITH
your DOS; as with all things, however, there is still room for
improvement. For instance, when you back up hard disks, DOS does
not tell you how many diskettes you will need. In this chapter, you
will learn about a program that provides this feature, and about other
programs that "fill the gaps" in DOS's operations.

You will also learn about a number of programs that provide functionality well beyond the current scope of DOS. For example,
different computers often have different disk formats, and different
word processors often have different internal file-storage formats.
Offices with several computers and different types of word processors
can benefit from the special-purpose *conversion utilities* that work
with DOS.

Because they provide you with added utility features, these programs are usually known as *utility programs*. Some utility programs are
similar to the transient (disk-resident) commands of DOS, like
CHKDSK or FORMAT. You can execute them whenever you
choose, as long as they are accessible in the current directory or on
the path. They require a certain amount of memory to run, but they
release it back to DOS when they are done. Some people refer to
these disk-resident enhancement programs as *add-on* utilities.

Other utility programs are similar to the resident commands of DOS, like DIR or ERASE. This second type of utility is called a *memory-resident* or *terminate and stay resident* (*TSR*) program. A memory-resident program is loaded from disk only once as part of its required setup phase. It is read into a certain area of memory that will not be used later by any other program. It then terminates, but stays resident for rapid activation at some later time. Some people refer to these memory-resident programs as *add-in* utilities.

Most memory-resident software will do nothing—not even offer a command prompt—until you type a unique key combination, called a *hot key,* to call it into action. For instance, Sidekick leaps into action when you press the Ctrl-Alt key combination. Keyworks presents its own menu of options when you summon it with the gray Plus key (usually on the right side of most keyboards). The appealing aspect of these memory-resident programs is that their complete capabilities are instantaneously available when you need them, even during the execution of another program.

In some cases, you can make more than one memory-resident program available simultaneously. If you do load one or more memory-resident programs, however, you should use the CHKDSK command afterwards to see if enough memory is still free to run your main application program.

Some memory-resident programs and main application programs will not work together, because each will try to use the same area of memory. This can result in many problems, from the memory-resident program or main program simply not working correctly, to having to reboot a frozen system, to having your entire hard disk erased. Check the documentation before you begin to be sure there are no incompatibilities with your current software.

Thousands of utility programs are available on the market today; advertisements for such products appear in the backs of all major PC-oriented magazines. In this chapter you will see how some programs improve the performance of hard disks, while others speed up your keyboard and screen. You'll see utilities designed to enhance your printed output, to organize your desktop functions, and to make hard-disk file management easier. This chapter will only select a few examples in the most useful categories of utility programs; keep in mind that there are many excellent alternatives to the programs presented here.

Memory-resident utility programs are fast; however, the cost for this responsiveness is that part of the physical memory on your machine must be allocated to them. That reduces the amount remaining for your main programs, and even for other memory-resident software.

Back up your data files before running any new memory-resident utility in conjunction with existing software. You should protect yourself in the event of an unexpected memory conflict or a system crash.

IMPROVING YOUR
HARD-DISK MANAGEMENT

Managing many directories on a hard disk can require great effort and care. However, a class of utility programs can relieve your burdens. In this section, you'll look at Q-DOS II, a hard-disk file manager; PreCursor, a hard-disk menu system; the Norton Utilities, a wide-ranging file and directory support tool; and Back-It, a powerful substitute for DOS's BACKUP and RESTORE commands.

MANAGING YOUR FILES
AND DIRECTORIES WITH Q-DOS II

Q-DOS II makes standard DOS features much easier to use. Many of DOS's functions, such as formatting disks, displaying directories, and listing and copying files, are implemented in Q-DOS II. Those commands that are not directly available in DOS can be executed easily from within Q-DOS II. Figure 17.1 shows the main menu of Q-DOS II.

As you can see from the main menu line at the top of Figure 17.1, Q-DOS II offers you much more convenience in implementing many standard DOS commands. For example, instead of having to

```
Directory Tag View Copy Move Find Erase Rename Space Attribute Print
Change current directory, make or remove directory, see directory tree

PATH  >> C:\TYPESET

Count        Total Size          File Name      Size      Date      Time

 99  Files      323,228          &BOOK-P1.CAP      156    7-29-86   5:44p
                                 &BOOK-P1.CHP    1,862    7-29-86   5:44p
  0  Directories                 &BOOK-P1.STY    3,868    1- 1-80   1:22a
                                 &BOOK-P2.CAP      156    7-29-86   5:44p
  0  Tagged           0          &BOOK-P2.CHP    1,848    7-29-86   5:44p
                                 &BOOK-P2.STY    4,068    7-29-86   2:44p
                                 &BRO-L2 .CHP      844    7-29-86   5:44p
F1- Help       F2- Status        &BRO-L2 .STY    2,868    7-29-86   5:44p
F3- Chg Drive  F4- Prev Dir      &BRO-L3 .CHP    1,178    7-29-86   5:44p
F5- Chg Dir    F6- DOS Cmd       &BRO-L3 .STY    2,868    9- 1-86   3:22p
F7- Srch Spec  F8- Sort          &BRO-P3 .CHP    1,178    7-29-86   5:44p
F9- Edit       F10- Quit         &BRO-P3 .STY    2,668    9- 1-86   3:22p
   SPACE BAR- Tag file           &EXAMPLE.PUB      732    9-19-86  11:44a
   ESC- Abort Command            &INV-P1 .CHP      824    9-19-86  11:33a
                                 &INV-P1 .STY    2,468    9- 1-86   3:22p
Q-DOS II -- Version 2.00         &LSTG-P2.CHP    1,097    7-29-86   5:55p
   Copyright (c) 1986            &LSTG-P2.STY    1,868    9- 1-86   3:33p
GAZELLE SYSTEMS - Provo, Utah
```

Figure 17.1: Q-DOS II's main menu

type a complete COPY command, specifying file names and path names, you use a more visual technique. You *tag*, or graphically select, which directories and files you want copied and where they should be copied to. You can easily see directories by moving along the directory tree (see Figure 17.2) and pressing Return, which will bring up a sorted list of files that reside in the selected directory.

You can sort directory entries by anything on the entry's line, such as the date or extension. Although you see the files sorted in the Q-DOS II directory window, they will not be physically rearranged on the disk. Although the screens may appear crowded at first glance, they are quite comfortable in actual use.

Q-DOS II is available from

> Gazelle Systems
> 42 North University Avenue, Suite 10
> Provo, Utah 84601
> (800) 233-0383
> (801) 377-1288

SETTING UP MENU SYSTEMS WITH PRECURSOR

A menu program enables you to predefine paths and program names, and to present to a user a simple and familiar list of choices.

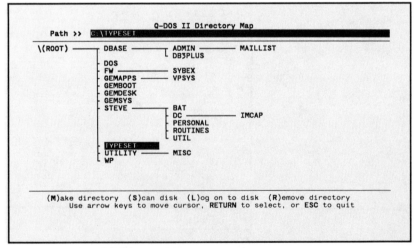

Figure 17.2: Q-DOS II's graphic representation

No commands need be entered at the DOS prompt, since all required DOS commands will have been incorporated into the menu system setup.

Some users prefer to enter commands at the DOS prompt because they only run one simple application, and they are more comfortable entering individual commands. Others feel that a menu system is too slow or restrictive, or that they simply cannot give up the memory required for the menu program itself. For most users, however, understanding and using DOS at the command level is unnecessary. This is especially true if the operations performed are repetitive and require little variation.

If the set of programs you run on your machine is fairly constant, a menu program can be a definite convenience. It can save you the trouble of changing directories or remembering where a particular program is located on your hard disk. This is particularly convenient in a large office environment, where it may not be feasible to teach all users enough about DOS to enable them to get on with their jobs. A menu system can be set up once by a knowledgeable user, leaving only a simple, one-key selection for individual users.

PreCursor is an excellent menu program. Beyond offering a menu system, it provides most of the key DOS functions on its own special DOS menu. You can do most things from PreCursor that you can do from DOS, without having to remember or know as much about formats and restrictions. The main menu of PreCursor is very cleanly laid out, and shows you exactly what you can do and where to go (see Figure 17.3).

The program is organized into menus and submenus. You can categorize your programs, placing them on different menus by function. By choosing an option, you can execute a DOS program, a batch file, or a DOS command, or you can go to another menu of predetermined choices. The DOS function keys are used to obtain special PreCursor services, such as creating and editing menu screens, initializing program parameters, and setting up passwords (see Figure 17.4).

Menu systems can be set up for a large number of users, and access can be restricted by a powerful password mechanism. Separate passwords can be created for each individual menu choice, as well as for entire menus.

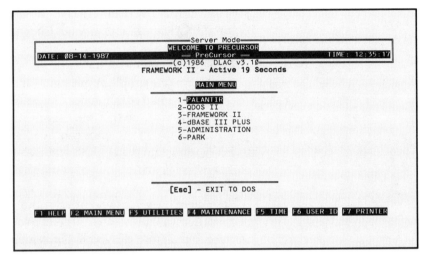

Figure 17.3: PreCursor's main menu

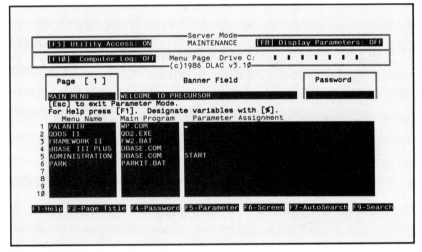

Figure 17.4: PreCursor's maintenance menu

PreCursor is available from

> The Aldridge Company
> 2500 City West Boulevard, Suite 575
> Houston, Texas 77042
> (713) 953-1940

INVESTIGATING DISK CONTENTS WITH THE NORTON UTILITIES

The Norton Utilities is a group of programs designed to increase your control over the data that is actually stored on your disk. For example, you can look at specific parts of the disk and modify the data you find there. You can also recover files that have been accidentally erased, and even recover complete hard disks that have been formatted. Utilities of this kind come in very handy when you've made a major blunder. Even if things are going smoothly, the Norton Utilities can provide you with a greater understanding of how your system is set up, as well as an insider's glimpse into previously inaccessible disk files.

The latest version of the Norton Utilities features a menu-driven system. The system shows you various screens of information. For example, you can see a screen of all the files on the disk, including hidden files, system files, and those that have been deleted but not yet overwritten since their deletion. You can change the attributes of any file, controlling even more attributes than you can with the ATTRIB command in DOS. You are even able to change any individual byte in any file anywhere on the disk. All of this can be displayed when you request file information. For the technical user, detailed data about specific files and the hard disk as a whole is also available on another screen choice.

Included in the Norton Utilities are many individual utility programs that are both easy in form and powerful in function (see Table 17.1). For example, the DS (Directory Sort) program will first display your current directory on the screen. You can then specify how you want to sort the directory's files, using several levels of sorting. The sorted directory is then displayed, and you have your choice of resorting it differently or writing it to the disk.

The main hub of the utilities is the NI (Norton Integrator) program. This program brings information about all of the other Norton programs onto one screen, where you can choose which program to execute. Each program, when highlighted, has a format and functional description displayed on the right side of the screen. At the bottom of the screen is a command line that changes whenever you highlight a different program. It allows you to enter parameters for a

UTILITY NAME	PROGRAM DESCRIPTION
ASK	Creates interactive batch files
BEEP	Controls the computer's speaker
DS	Sorts a directory's file names
DT	Tests disks for physical errors
FA	Sets, resets, and scans file attributes
FF	Finds disk files by name
FI	Assigns and retrieves file comments
FR	Recovers an accidentally formatted hard disk
FS	Lists and totals file sizes
LD	Creates a graphic view of directory structure
LP	Prints files with line numbers and headers
NCD	Allows fast directory navigation
NI	Integrates all utilities for easy selection
NU	Allows detailed disk and file exploration
QU	Allows quick unerase capability
SA	Sets screen colors and attributes
SD	Reorganizes disks to remove fragmentation
SI	Reports system information
TM	Displays time and offers stopwatch capability
TS	Searches text in files and disks
UD	Recovers removed directories
VL	Views, adds, removes, or changes disk labels
WIPEDISK	Completely blanks out file contents
WIPEFILE	Completely blanks out disk contents

Table 17.1: The Norton Utilities, Advanced Edition (4.0)

specific command. The right half of the screen explains the high-lighted command and its possible switches (see Figure 17.5).

The Norton Utilities are available from

Peter Norton Computing, Inc.
2210 Wilshire Boulevard
Santa Monica, California 90403
(213) 453-2361

MAKING BACKUPS WITH BACK-IT

Backups can sometimes get very complicated, especially if you don't want or need to back up an entire disk. They can also take a long time and can be subject to simple mistakes, such as inserting the wrong diskette or forgetting a group of files. Back-It provides a way to back up and restore files easily on your hard disk. You can use it in place of DOS's BACKUP and RESTORE commands.

Back-It's main menu (see Figure 17.6) shows you a well-grouped approach to its chores. The top line provides all desired options. When you are ready to back up, Back-It lets you choose exactly which directories to back up by showing you the directory tree and letting you move around in it, tagging the directories you want or don't want backed up.

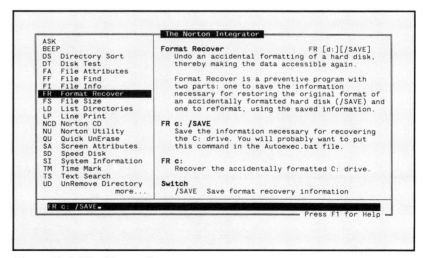

Figure 17.5: The Norton Integrator menu

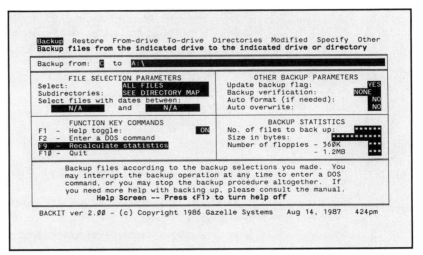

Figure 17.6: Back-It's main menu

The program is very easy to use. It will even tell you how many disk-ettes you will need for the backup. You move around the menu screen by using the arrow keys. You can select different functions of the program from the menu bar at the top of the screen, and then modify the parameters that accompany a certain function on the main screen. Back-It is fast and truly user-friendly, offering you many additional options such as different standard backup sets, variable levels of data verification, and automatic formatting of target diskettes.

Back-It is available from

>Gazelle Systems
>42 North University Avenue, Suite 10
>Provo, Utah 84601
>(800) 233-0383
>(801) 377-1288

SPEEDING UP YOUR HARD DISK

If you have a hard-disk system, the efficient operation of the hard disk is crucial to the efficient use of your entire computer system. As the number of files on your hard disk gets larger, the time involved to access a file increases, slowing down your system. There are several reasons for this slowdown.

As you know, when DOS writes a file on the disk, it writes it in groups of sectors called clusters. The number of 512-byte sectors in each cluster does vary by the version of DOS you are using, but the principle of cluster writing creates the speed problem. As an example, let's say that you write a first file to disk, and it uses up a full cluster. Then you write another file to the disk, and it uses up the next (contiguous) cluster. Your disk looks like this:

Cluster	Contents
1	File 1 (first cluster of file 1)
2	File 2 (first cluster of file 2)

Then you go back and double the size of the first file, perhaps by expanding a database or adding a new page of text with your word processor; you then save it again.

Instead of pushing the second file up to make room for the two clusters of the first file, DOS saves the additional information for the first file in cluster 3, leaving cluster 2, which contains the second file, untouched. If you were to expand the second file next, and then add a third file, the disk would look like this:

Cluster	Contents
1	File 1 (first cluster of file 1)
2	File 2 (first cluster of file 2)
3	File 1 (second cluster of file 1)
4	File 2 (second cluster of file 2)
5	File 2 (third cluster of file 2)
6	File 3 (first cluster of file 3)
.	.
.	.
.	.

As you can see, files get broken up as you work on them. The time it takes to move the disk's read/write head can increase dramatically as the number of your files increases and as your files become more and more fragmented. *Fragmentation* occurs when pieces of the same file are stored in nonadjacent clusters on a disk. As this condition evolves, the first half of a file could be on an outside track, whereas the second half could be on an inside track. Head movement across the disk would take a lot more time than it would with sequential clusters.

Reducing or eliminating fragmentation speeds up the disk. The way to do this is to go through the whole disk and rearrange the clusters so that all clusters for every file are contiguous. With a great deal of effort, you can actually do this yourself. All you need to do is to copy all files in all directories onto backup disks, reformat the entire disk, and then rewrite the files back onto the disk. An easier way is to buy one of the utilities described in this section, such as VOPT or H.D. Tuneup.

A less-obvious solution to speeding up the disk, which relieves the symptoms but does not really solve the problem, is to cut down on disk access. The memory-resident program Lightning will actually remember disk sector data every time it is used, so that continued access to the same sector will, instead of accessing the disk drive, access a memory area (called a *cache*) that already has the data in it. This is much faster than accessing the disk, but does cost you a certain amount of memory for both the Lightning program and the memory cache.

Another problem with disks of all sizes is that they can run out of space. This is especially true if you use large databases or manage hundreds or thousands of files. A creative solution to the problem of space availability is to shrink your existing files down to a much smaller size. This is sometimes called *data compression*. When you need to use the files, you can expand them back to their normal size and then compress them again when you're through. This provides extra disk space, and your files are available for use when necessary. The utility program Squish provides this capability for your system.

File sizes and numbers always seem to expand to fill whatever size hard disk you are using. Be sure you take the time to delete older files or early versions of files regularly.

OPTIMIZING THE DISK HIERARCHY WITH H.D. TUNEUP

H.D. Tuneup is a *disk optimizer*. It takes fragmented files and makes them contiguous, which eliminates excessive head travel and thus speeds up disk operations.

The main program of H.D. Tuneup, TUNEUP.EXE, performs the optimization. It moves all directories and subdirectories as close as possible to the root directory and then places remaining files after these directories. Any time you run the DIR command after running

H.D. Tuneup, all of your subdirectories will be at the top of the list, with the remaining data and program files following.

A companion program, FILECHK.EXE, can be run more frequently. It uses the same logic as H.D. Tuneup to decide on the degree of disk fragmentation. However, it doesn't perform the reorganization, so it is much faster. Using it allows you to assess the amount of fragmentation and to decide whether to actually go through the time-consuming process of reorganizing files. If there are any problems, it lets you know. Otherwise, you simply receive information and statistics about the status of your hard disk and its files.

Using an optimizer is a good idea, and the developers of H.D. Tuneup recommend running it once a month. This function is also duplicated by one of the many utilities contained in the more extensive Norton Utilities.

H.D. Tuneup is available from

SofCap, Inc.
364 Parsippany Road, Unit 9
Parsippany, New Jersey 07054
(201) 386-5876

RAPID FILE REORGANIZATION WITH VOPT

VOPT is an interesting package of utilities from Golden Bow Systems. It features a hard-disk optimizer that can optimize a badly fragmented disk in only a few minutes. It is so fast that it can be used in your AUTOEXEC.BAT file to optimize the disk every time you boot up; this takes only a few seconds.

The VOPT program itself is very easy to use: just issue the VOPT command at the prompt, and you have started. First the program uses its own version of CHKDSK to make sure there are no lost clusters or disk errors. Should there be, VOPT will end and you will be instructed to use the DOS command CHKDSK/F to correct the problem. Once this is done, or if no errors are found, optimization is started. Figure 17.7 shows a map of the disk space before optimizing, created by another utility program (VMAP) included on the VOPT diskette.

VOPT itself displays a version of this disk map, which changes during the optimization process. When the process is complete, you

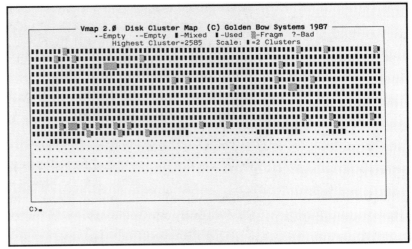

Figure 17.7: VMAP disk-space display before optimizing

The probability of a utility package containing extra utility programs is directly proportional to the pizzazz and usefulness of its first utility.

are shown statistics about the overall effort, as shown in Figure 17.8. The cluster display is more colorful than necessary, but flair and drama are always attractive in a good program.

VOPT is available from

> Golden Bow Systems
> 2870 Fifth Avenue, Suite 201
> San Diego, California 92103
> (619) 298-9349

INSTALLING A MEMORY CACHE WITH LIGHTNING

The Lightning program remembers the information stored in disk sectors. For example, you may need to access file information contained in disk sectors 1 and 2. The actual data stored in the sectors is placed in a memory buffer, or cache. If you need to access the data again, Lightning locates it in memory, eliminating the need for DOS to access the disk again.

Lightning must be executed only once at the command prompt (or from a batch file), along with all parameters. It then becomes memory-resident, the memory cache is set up, and no further intervention on your part is required. It uses a default memory cache of

```
Vopt Version 2.10  serial no. 701162        ·-Empty ▌-Used ▒-Fragm ?-Bad
Copyright (C) Golden Bow Systems 1987       Lo Cluster=1599  Scale: ▌=1 Clus.

Volume ROBBINS
20672 sectors total disk space
  112 sectors in 3 hidden files
   88 sectors in 11 directories
14552 sectors in 428 user files
 5920 sectors available on disk

    3 empty files
   48 erased files
  176 clusters in 18 fragmented files
 1894 is the highest used cluster
 1806 is the lowest empty cluster
   49 empty clusters in the used space

   86 files (541 clusters) were moved
   36 directory sectors were updated
  101 seconds to compact disk


C>_
```

Figure 17.8: VOPT display after optimizing

60K, but you can expand that (even to extended memory, if it exists in your system). Lightning can also display statistics on speed improvement, by disk, in your system.

Lightning is available from

> The Personal Computer Support Group
> 11035 Harry Hines Boulevard, Suite 206
> Dallas, Texas 75229
> (214) 351-0564

COMPRESSING DATA WITH SQUISH

Squish is one of those programs that may, with its first use, save you hundreds of dollars in the cost of purchasing a new disk, not to mention reducing the time it takes to create backup diskettes. Files stored by DOS on a disk are usually stored with a lot of unused space. For example, all the blank characters and lines in your word-processing files, and all those empty fields in your database files, take up a lot of unnecessary disk space. In other words, many files are stored inefficiently, taking up more room than is needed on both your hard disk and on your backup diskettes.

To get around this, Squish "runs interference" between your disk drive and DOS. When you save a file, Squish intercepts the request, compressing the file into the least amount of space possible, and then writes the "squished" file to disk. For example, a single Pascal program that originally takes up over 36K can be squished to less than 27K, an improvement of 25 percent.

Squish runs invisibly—that is, you do not know that it is running, but it is there. It has a memory-resident portion (about 40K), which is activated not by a hot key, but by any request to DOS for a task requiring disk access. Squish converts files automatically when you access them; if you save a file, it will be squished automatically. You will never see anything to indicate that it has been compressed except that it will take up less space than it normally would.

> Programs that improve system performance typically trade speed for space; that is, if the utility improves speed, you usually have to give up memory space for this improvement. On the other hand, if the utility improves space usage, you usually have to give up operational speed to obtain that benefit.

To "unsquish" a file, just load it in as usual. Squish will intercept the load command, get the file, decompress it, and send it on to your application. It does all of this in memory, so you don't need to budget extra disk space for decompressed files. Again, there will be no indication that the file is being unsquished, except that it may take slightly longer to load than usual.

You can also run Squish for existing files stored on your disk. You may want to do this for a few large files only. When memory-resident, however, Squish can tell the difference between a squished and an unsquished file.

Squish is available from

> SunDog Software Corporation
> 264 Court Street
> Brooklyn, New York 11231
> (718) 855-9141

ENHANCING YOUR CONSOLE'S POWER

Your console is the most important part of your computer system in that it is the means by which you control the system and by which the system responds to you. Should the keyboard not "feel" right to you, or should you be uncomfortable with its setup or behavior (mushy keys, poor key layout, and so on), it will influence the way you use your system and the amount of time you spend on it. Therefore, it is important that you feel comfortable with the keyboard and the display.

There are many ways to customize the keyboard, making it much more powerful. This means that you can redefine the keys so that more can be done from the keyboard. For example, by using the Keyworks program, you can redefine any key on your keyboard to actually type a different character, word, command, sentence, or paragraph. When you redefine a key into some sort of an instruction set, such as redefining the F3 key to type DIR A: and press Return, you have created your own keyboard macro. (Remember, a macro is a set of instructions that are executed at once, whether the instructions are stored in memory or in a file on the disk.)

Another utility acts on your display. Scroll & Recall gives you the ability to take a second look at any data that has been displayed for you in a line-by-line manner, but has since scrolled off the screen. How many times have you wanted to go backwards to see something that scrolled too quickly off the screen? Or how often have you run a long program that produced results that you didn't write down, and that you'd like to see again?

EXTENDING KEYBOARD POWER WITH KEYWORKS

In many application programs, long sequences of keystrokes are often needed to accomplish something. For instance, many commercial database services require you to connect your computer to theirs through a dial-up telephone connection. You may have to sign on to their computer, enter a password, and then pass through five different levels of menus just to read some news. The keystrokes might be LOGON JUDD 123456 3 2 1 4 5 READ #1. Typing this out every time is a real chore.

To alleviate this, programs like Keyworks have been written to enhance the keyboard by giving key combinations like Alt-F, which normally doesn't do anything, the ability to substitute for a string of keystrokes. By using one of these programs, you can even represent a whole paragraph with one key, and then whenever you hit that key, the paragraph will appear. If you use WordStar or any other program that requires a series of keystrokes to implement certain features, this type of program is for you.

Keyworks is a keyboard macro program with extraordinary versatility. It actually includes a complete programming language. One of the many features of this memory-resident program allows you to directly edit the macros that you have defined. When you select this option, Keyworks goes into full-screen mode, similar to many word processors, allowing you to edit the macros directly. Cut and paste capabilities allow you to create new, complex macros from old ones.

Several other useful capabilities come with Keyworks, such as a way to encrypt confidential disk files for security purposes. Most essential DOS features are implemented as well, enabling you to reproduce DOS commands in a *pop-up* display while other programs are running. (In a pop-up display, all of the screen's contents appear instantaneously, instead of appearing line-by-line as they are written to the screen.) All of Keyworks's features are available from a pop-up system of menus.

Keyworks's menu system is very accessible. You can also use Keyworks to set up your own system of menus and help screens. Although it does take a bit more work than using the PreCursor utility described earlier, Keyworks has more potential power because of its macro language, which is as powerful as many high-level programming languages and allows decision making, looping, and flow-of-control commands.

Keyworks is available from

> The Alpha Software Corporation
> 30 B Street
> Burlington, Massachusetts 01803
> (617) 229-2924

RECALLING FORMER SCREEN OUTPUT WITH SCROLL & RECALL

Scroll & Recall recalls past commands issued at the DOS prompt or other program prompts. It also remembers a variable number of lines that have been shown on the screen but that have been scrolled off the screen. This comes in handy when you are issuing a lot of DOS commands and need to see the exact format of an earlier command. Also, if you need to look back at a computer session or see part of a listing or directory that has scrolled off the screen, this program is for you.

Scroll & Recall is available from

Opt-Tech Data Processing
P.O. Box 2167
Humble, Texas 77347
(713) 454-7428

REISSUING PREVIOUS DOS COMMANDS WITH RECOMM

Many commands you issue in DOS are repetitions of commands you issued earlier in the same session. Sometimes you issue the same command several times; other times, you issue a similar command with only minor variations. ReComm is a utility that can instantaneously call back to the DOS prompt any command issued previously. It even saves and recalls command and text sequences from within many application programs.

ReComm has a built-in line editor, so you can use the cursor keys to make any desired edits to the recalled command prior to reissuing it. This means that you can easily correct errors in the last issued DOS command as well. (You merely press Return to reissue the command.)

All of ReComm's activities occur at the bottom of the screen when you call the screen up with a redefinable hot key. Help is also available at the touch of the usual F1 key (see Figure 17.9). Active screens

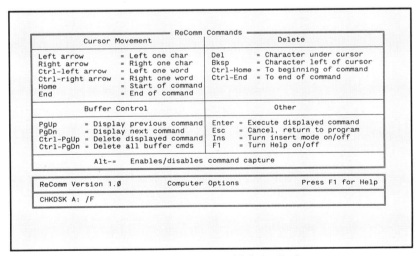

Figure 17.9: ReComm's Activity screen with help display

are saved and restored after ReComm has completed its operations. ReComm is available from

Computer Options
198 Amherst Avenue
Berkeley, California 94708
(415) 525-5033

DRESSING UP YOUR PRINTED OUTPUT

So far in this chapter you have seen how you can enhance the console and and disk drives by means of utility programs. You can also enhance your printer. Since it generates the physical output of the work you do, it is very useful to have additional control over it.

For example, if you have a large spreadsheet that stretches over 200 columns and you have only a 9-inch wide printer, you have a problem. The two programs listed here, however, will print your spreadsheet sideways, so it can be as wide as you wish. The Printworks program also allows you to change character sets, styles, fonts, and sizes, which is important if you need to make signs or overhead transparencies, or if you just want to vary the appearance of your typed text.

PRINTING WIDE OUTPUT WITH SIDEWAYS

You may deal with databases containing many fields or with spreadsheets containing many columns. The usual solution to printing all the information is to carefully extract for printing specific portions of the database or spreadsheet, and then tape the printed pieces together.

Sideways is perhaps the best-known program for solving the wide-output problem. This utility prints the extremely wide output sideways on the printed page. In other words, it rotates the output by 90 degrees, giving a whole new sequence of control commands to your printer. This solution usually is reserved for use on dot-matrix printers with continuous-feed paper.

Sideways is available from

Funk Software
P.O. Box 1290
Cambridge, Massachusetts 02238
(617) 497-6339

MODIFYING TYPE SIZES AND STYLES WITH PRINTWORKS

Printworks is another program that allows sideways printing. It also allows you to control a wide range of other printing features. Many printers have built-in hardware that can produce condensed, boldface, and wide characters. Some can also print pica, elite, and even proportionally spaced output characters.

Printworks gives you a full-screen display that presents all the possibilities for customizing your printer. After a required installation phase, you merely select the options you want for your printed output. With Printworks you can also generate your own special fonts and characters, including graphics, foreign, or special characters not available on your keyboard.

Printworks is available from

SoftStyle
7192 Kalanianaole Highway, Suite 205
Honolulu, Hawaii 96825
(808) 396-6368

CONVERTING FILE AND DISK FORMATS

There are many programs available that perform the same task—for example, there are many word-processing programs. However, a file from one word processor cannot be moved directly into another word processor, because most word processors make extensive use of special control codes to perform their text formatting. The file must first be converted to a format that the new word processor can understand. Many conversion programs perform this function, although their ability is limited to converting to or from only a very few programs.

Like word processors, some computer systems are not compatible. To load a disk from one operating system into another (from CP/M to DOS, for example, or from DOS to UNIX), you must convert the entire contents of the disk to a format acceptable to the other system. Each operating system writes its files in a certain way at certain places on a disk; in addition, different operating systems use different storage and formatting schemes.

For example, you may be using 5¼" diskettes, but their different layouts inhibit compatibility. In other cases, you may even be using the same operating system (such as DOS) but have switched to a different machine (from an IBM PC-AT to a Personal System/2, for example). One machine might use 3½" diskettes, while the other machine might use 5¼" diskettes. Both can use identical application programs and the same version of DOS, but the data must be converted from one diskette format to another. The following programs offer just this kind of service.

CHANGING DISK SIZES WITH BROOKLYN BRIDGE

Ambitious utility software vendors will always create innovative software solutions to hardware problems and software oversights. However, you may not learn of such a product unless the vendor also possesses sufficient marketing skills.

The Brooklyn Bridge utility package offers two separate programs. One program runs on a computer with 3½" diskettes, while the other program runs on a computer with 5¼" diskettes. This utility package is similar to a communications program, but its purpose is more focused: it allows you to specify file names to be transferred between two different disk drives.

Brooklyn Bridge transfers the specified files between machines by means of cables connecting the required serial ports on each machine. This is an inexpensive and creative solution to the problem of hardware incompatibility.

Brooklyn Bridge is available from

White Crane Systems
6889 Peachtree Ind. Boulevard
Norcross, Georgia 30092
(404) 454-7911

READING DIFFERENT
MACHINE FORMATS WITH XENOCOPY-PC

XenoCopy-PC converts the diskette formats of files from various operating system formats. It is no longer as necessary for DOS users as it once was, since fewer and fewer offices have multiple machines with incompatible operating systems. However, if your office still has an old TeleVideo running a CP/M word processor, and various newer IBMs and compatibles running the same word processor, XenoCopy-PC is the right package to own.

XenoCopy-PC pays for itself every time a file written on a TeleVideo must be used by someone using a differently formatted IBM diskette on his or her machine. It is very easy to use, offering a simple menu-selection procedure to specify each of the two incompatible diskette formats.

XenoCopy-PC is available from

XenoSoft
1454 Sixth Street
Berkeley, California 94710
(415) 525-3113

REWRITING WORD-PROCESSING
FORMATS WITH R-DOC/X

R-Doc/X is a very handy program to have around when one or more people are using two or more word processors. It converts word-processing files to different formats for use by other word processors. If your office has several people using different word processors, you don't necessarily have to force them to select one for consistency. You also don't have to sacrifice the required time and effort to learn a new word-processing system if you are already comfortable with your current one. Instead, you can just convert it to someone else's word-processing format; they will be able to work on the file as well.

R-Doc/X does a pretty good job of converting files, but there are a few things it cannot understand and hence will not convert properly. Some of these are headers and footers, multicolumn documents, and specific types of tab stops. Therefore, if one of your word processors uses these, you should make sure the conversion will be sufficient before you actually select this program.

R-Doc/X is available from

Advanced Computer Innovations
1227 Goler House
Rochester, New York 14620
(716) 454-3188

ORGANIZING YOUR WORK

The best thing to have when you work is organization. If you spend a lot of time on the computer, you know how much of a chore keeping manual records (such as a date book or a phone directory) can become. Having to swing around and look at a clock is also a chore, as is rifling through your drawers or under papers for a calculator. The worst visible signs of wasted effort are those little notes to yourself, scrawled half-legibly on scraps of paper, that multiply over the course of a day.

Computers are good at keeping things straight, so why not give them a few extra tasks? The Sidekick program does just that. It should make your life quite a bit easier.

ORGANIZING YOUR DESKTOP WITH SIDEKICK

Sidekick is a desktop organizer. Its name derives from the sidekicks of the old West, who were always trusty companions. You can call up Sidekick at any time by pressing its hot key, since it is a memory-resident program.

Sidekick incorporates many features. Its main menu, shown in Figure 17.10, outlines everything Sidekick can do. For example, you can move the menu bar or type in a letter. If you type in the letter N or press F2, you will find yourself in the NotePad section of Sidekick, which allows you to type and save notes for yourself or for later inclusion into a file. It is actually a mini-version of a word processor, using a set of control codes similar to that found in WordStar. This feature is useful as a rapid editor for small database programs, as well as for small batch files in DOS.

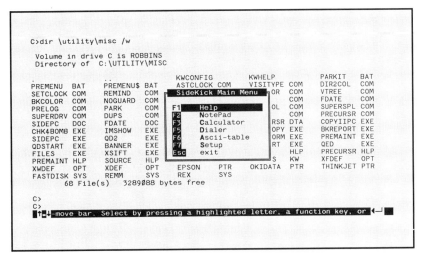

```
C>dir \utility\misc /w

Volume in drive C is ROBBINS
Directory of  C:\UTILITY\MISC
                              KWCONFIG        KWHELP          PARKIT   BAT
     .           ..           ASTCLOCK COM     VISITYPE COM   DIR2COL  COM
PREMENU  BAT   PREMENU$ BAT  ┌─SideKick Main Menu──────┐OR COM    VTREE    COM
SETCLOCK COM   REMIND   COM  │                         │  COM    FDATE    COM
BKCOLOR  COM   NOGUARD  COM  │ F1  Help                │OL COM    SUPERSPL COM
PRELOG   COM   PARK     COM  │ F2  NotePad             │  COM    PRECURSR COM
SUPERDRV COM   DUPS     COM  │ F3  Calculator          │RSR DTA   COPYIIPC EXE
SIDEPC   DOC   FDATE    DOC  │ F5  Dialer              │OPY EXE   BKREPORT EXE
CHK4BOMB EXE   IMSHOW   EXE  │ F6  Ascii-table         │ORM EXE   PREMAINT EXE
SIDEPC   EXE   QD2      EXE  │ F7  Setup               │RT EXE    QED      EXE
QDSTART  EXE   BANNER   EXE  │ Esc exit                │  HLP    PRECURSR HLP
FILES    EXE   XSIFT    EXE  └─────────────────────────┘S KW     XFDEF    OPT
PREMAINT HLP   SOURCE   HLP                                      THINKJET PTR
XWDEF    OPT   XDEF     OPT   EPSON    PTR    OKIDATA PTR
FASTDISK SYS   REMM     SYS   REX      SYS
        68 File(s)   3289088 bytes free

C>
C>
↑↓-move bar. Select by pressing a highlighted letter, a function key, or ←┘
```

Figure 17.10: Sidekick's main menu

You can also access an on-screen calculator, a calendar, and an automatic phone dialer, should you have a modem hooked up. Sidekick also includes a phone directory that works with the autodialer, and a datebook that can keep track of your appointments.

Sidekick is available from

> Borland International
> 4585 Scotts Valley Drive
> Scotts Valley, California 95066
> (800) 255-8008
> (800) 742-1133 (CA)

SUMMARY

DOS is clearly not the end-all for your computing needs. There are thousands of additional utilities, from hundreds of utility vendors, that can extend the power and capabilities of your disk operating system dramatically. In this chapter you have seen only a few of the many excellent products available to you.

- Hard disks require considerable management. Q-DOS II is a powerful file and directory manager that simplifies hard-disk maintenance.

- If simple but professional menu systems are your goal, you should purchase PreCursor, a program whose primary (but not only) strength is the easy setup of program menus.

- The Norton Utilities is one of the oldest and most respected of the utility packages you can buy for your PC. It's a must-have for all PC owners.

- Back-It extends the range of backup and recovery features offered by DOS's BACKUP and RESTORE commands. A more flexible and powerful alternative, it is a worthy choice for reducing your maintenance effort.

- Speeding up your hard disk can be accomplished in several ways. A disk optimizer like H.D. Tuneup or VOPT will reduce head movement during file accesses. A memory cache like Lightning will reduce the number of disk accesses. A file compressor like Squish will shrink the files themselves, so that fewer disk accesses are needed to obtain the same data.

- Several programs enhance the power of your console. Keyworks is an extraordinarily powerful keyboard enhancer. Scroll & Recall is useful for looking back at data already lost from the screen. ReComm saves typing effort during sessions in which you issue the same or similar DOS commands many times.

- Printed output can be dressed up with several programs like Sideways, which prints out extremely wide data files, and Printworks, which prints output in a variety of type styles and sizes.

- Conversions are important because of the multiplicity of computers, disk formats, and software products. Examples of conversion programs are Brooklyn Bridge, which converts different diskette sizes, R-Doc/X, which converts different word-processing formats, and XenoCopy-PC, which converts different diskette formats.

- Sidekick is a popular product containing an attractive collection of desktop tools, including a small word processor, a phone dialer, a calendar, and a calculator.

This book has taken you from the basic concepts of DOS, disk files, and formats to advanced commands, batch-file programming, and now to add-on and add-in utility programs. You can now perform any computing task with assurance, and do it easily and quickly. You know what commands exist, what the options for batch files are, and what extra utility software exists.

Use this book now as a reference. Chapter 18 contains capsule summaries of all DOS commands with their switches and parameters. The appendices contain additional information about vocabulary, character sets, numbering systems, and configuring your fixed disk. The index to this book should point you to anything you'll want to reread.

PART 5

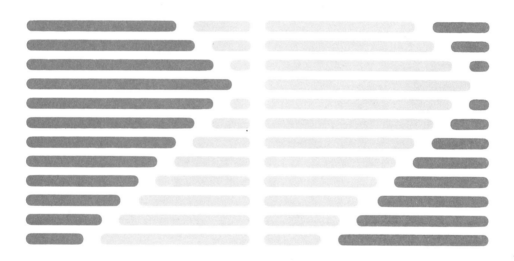

GOING BEYOND

Part 5 is designed for those who want to go beyond the standard limits of DOS. Chapter 18 presents Windows from Microsoft, a program that enables you to run many DOS programs simultaneously. This is called multitasking and is accompanied in Windows by a completely new visual interface consisting of screen windows and mouse support for program and command selection.

Chapter 19 covers the latest software technology for stretching the memory limits of DOS. The 640K limit of DOS programs can be overcome by several techniques. This chapter explores the most common methods of expanded and extended memory and gives a historical perspective including the most recent LIM 4.0 specification.

Chapter 20 completes this DOS extendability section by introducing you to the ultimate step forward—the new operating system from Microsoft and IBM, OS/2. This new system not only eradicates the 640K limit but uses the enhanced memory addressability to support a sophisticated form of multitasking. You will learn the specific steps necessary to run your current DOS programs within this new OS/2 environment.

WINDOWS AND DOS

MICROSOFT WINDOWS OFFERS A GRAPHICS- OR object-oriented interface to a multitasking DOS operating environment on IBM and compatible personal computers. The Windows operating environment provides an additional layer of control between DOS and applications software to allow you to use your computer's capacity more fully.

Although Windows may appear to be primarily a graphics-interface extension of DOS, it is in fact an enhanced operating environment that permits multitasking and data transfer operations that are difficult to perform under DOS alone.

INTRODUCTION TO WINDOWS

Only those programs designed to operate under Windows can take complete advantage of the special benefits of this windowing environment.

This chapter discusses Windows Version 2 and does not attempt to cover all the differences between Versions 1 and 2. If you have the option of buying one version or the other, you will probably find the later one easier to use.

This chapter describes the operation of Windows and some of its utility programs. These programs are all designed specifically to operate under and interface with the Windows environment; they cannot run without Windows. As the number of personal computer systems running Windows grows, more commercial software packages are being introduced, redesigned, or upgraded to operate under or interface with this environment.

Two principal characteristics distinguish the Windows operating environment from the more recognizable command-line orientation of DOS. First, it is a completely new visual interface for users. Your connection to the computer and its operations no longer requires carefully constructed command requests. Instead, the interface consists of full screen displays controlled by a pointing device, typically a mouse. The mouse controls the location of the screen cursor, and therefore the selection of various operations, applications, and DOS commands. All programs and commands are selectable by the mouse, so you are no longer forced to learn and remember the commands. When a selection requires more information, such as additional parameters on a DOS command, Windows prompts you for the additional information in what is called a dialog box (a small screen window).

The second distinguishing feature of the Windows environment is *multitasking*. In DOS, you can only run one program at a time. In Windows, multiple programs can run simultaneously. Windows can manage the sharing of the CPU time cycles in a manner similar to the way DOS can enable print spooling to proceed concurrently with a main foreground program. All programs installed under Windows are able to proceed, sharing the CPU under the supervision of the main Windows software.

In fact, Windows itself is simply a program that runs under DOS. Its role, then, is to present a user interface that is easier both to use and to understand, as well as to manage the concurrent running of several programs designed to run under the Windows environment. Unlike a true multitasking environment such as OS/2, which provides its multiprocessing features to all programs running on your computer, Windows provides multitasking ability only to those programs installed within it.

Furthermore, Windows is limited by the standard DOS restrictions (like 640K of memory), and so must multitask its programs within that restrictive memory span. A true multitasking operating system like OS/2 can directly use and allocate much more memory (up to 16Mb) to the various programs sharing both the CPU and the available memory.

WINDOWS AND DOS

Most software packages currently available are designed to run under DOS as stand-alone applications. Most such applications can run under the Windows operating environment, but they generally can make no use of the graphics interface or multitasking capacities of Windows. The primary benefit to be derived from running standard

DOS applications under Windows is that you can load and run several of these applications at the same time. Once multiple applications are loaded, you can switch from one to another without first exiting the current application. In addition to reducing the amount of time required to load individual software packages, Windows lets you transfer data between various applications.

RUNNING DOS PROGRAMS UNDER WINDOWS

A particular advantage of programs designed to run under Windows is that they continue to execute, even after you've activated another DOS program.

Although you can load and run several programs simultaneously under the Windows environment, you can directly access only one of these programs, the *active* program or window, at any one time. The program executing in the active window operates in much the same way as any program running under standard DOS. Programs designed to run under Windows continue to run even when they are not in the active window. Standard DOS programs, on the other hand, run only when they are in the active window. When another window is active, these programs suspend execution.

There are two principal ways to switch between different windows, using the keyboard or the mouse. You may press the Alt-Esc key combination one or more times; pressing Alt-Esc switches windows successively. Depending upon how many windows you have, you will activate one after the other, stopping when you have reached the desired one. Alternatively, if your system has a mouse, you can simply move the cursor to any point within the desired window, then click the mouse.

If the desired window is currently represented as a symbol at the bottom of your screen (an *icon*—see below), you may select it with the mouse, then select either the Restore or Maximize options from the pop-up dialog box that will appear. Windows will then either restore the window to its original size or enlarge it to fill the screen.

MULTITASKING UNDER WINDOWS

Windows affords increased hardware independence to software, and provides users an intuitive graphic interface to DOS. Windows also lets both users and programs more fully utilize the processing capacity of personal computers. The original concept of personal computers "One user, one machine, one program" gradually evolved to "One user, one machine, several RAM-resident utilities, one main program." Windows extends this concept the next logical step: to "One user, one machine, many programs."

As noted above, multitasking works by sharing the CPU among various programs. It is a form of time sharing. Since the CPU performs its tasks much faster than most peripheral devices (like printers) and certainly much faster than most users can type, there is always time to spare from the processing chip's point of view.

These spare time cycles can be used by other programs, rather than have everything grind to a halt while one program waits for a user to press Return, or a printer to complete a slow I/O operation. This rapid switching from one program to another creates the *appearance* of multiple programs actually running simultaneously. This is not the real case, since there is only one CPU, and it can at any given moment service only one program. But the rapid context switching creates what is commonly called a multitasking or multiprocessing environment.

> Very rapid switching between programs is what provides PC's with the *appearance* of true simultaneous processing.

HARDWARE REQUIREMENTS OF WINDOWS

Version 1.0 of Windows runs on any IBM PC, XT, AT, 386, PS/2, or compatible computer equipped with at least 320K of RAM, two 360K disk drives, and a CGA graphics display. Version 2.0 requires at least one 1.2Mb disk drive. Running Windows on just these minimal configurations, however, is only minimally productive as the environment requires considerable disk activity and CPU processing. In part because of this overhead, a realistic minimum configuration is a PC-AT or compatible computer with 640K of RAM, a 20Mb hard disk, an EGA graphics display, and a mouse pointing device. Windows can also use extended memory (see Chapter 19) to increase operating speed.

INSTALLING WINDOWS

The Windows operating environment and its associated utilities and programs require a significant amount of disk storage space.

Version 2.0 is delivered on nine 360K disks. Before you can run Windows on your personal computer, you must install it for your specific hardware configuration.

 Do not have an APPEND list active when installing Windows.

Installing Windows on your computer is extremely easy. However, be sure *not* to use the DOS command APPEND prior to running the Windows setup procedure; you should temporarily remove this command from use before taking the steps described here.

Regardless of whether you are installing Windows on a dual-diskette or a hard-disk system, the simple instructions begin the same way. Place the Setup diskette into drive A and enter

A:
SETUP

If you place the wrong Windows disk in drive A at any time, Setup merely prompts you again for the correct one.

Microsoft's initialization program takes over, as Figure 18.1 shows, and prompts you for information regarding your particular hardware configuration. This first screen illustrates the type of information you must have to continue with the Windows installation. You must, for example, know enough about your system to tell Setup what kind of mouse, monitor, and printer you are using, and the port to which your printer is connected.

During the actual installation, you are prompted for specific information regarding your individual hardware configuration. You must answer the questions displayed during your actual installation of

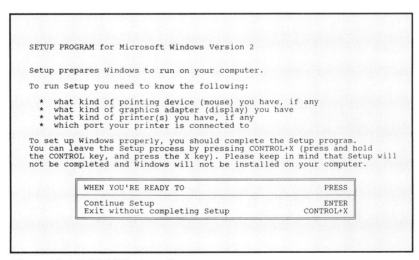

Figure 18.1: Initial Windows Setup screen

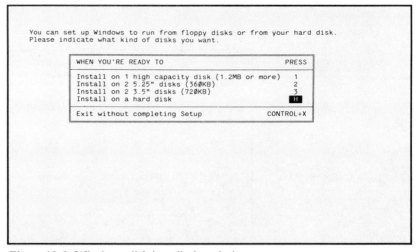

During the specification of your disk drives, you can install and run the Windows environment from any of the three diskette combinations listed or from a hard disk. The hard-disk option, H, is highlighted as the default choice.

If you select your computer's class and then press Return and find that your computer is not one of the listed IBM, AT&T, or Tandy computers, the compatibility of your system will now be tested.

Windows. Press Ctrl-X to exit from the setup process to determine the answers before continuing, or press Return to continue setting up your system.

You can run Windows from floppy diskettes, although the program works exceedingly slowly under such a setup. The following example of an installation sequence assumes that you are using a hard disk, choice H in Figure 18.2. Choice H is the default selection.

A typical Windows installation creates a directory for the Windows files. As Figure 18.3 shows, the default directory is called WINDOWS, although you can change this name before Windows actually creates and uses that directory on your system.

Windows creates a directory during setup to store all of its support files. Although most systems accept the default name, WINDOWS, you can change that name here before Windows actually makes the directory and copies the files from your Windows diskettes into it.

Although the Windows SETUP program supports primarily IBM, AT&T, and Tandy computers (see Figure 18.4), in fact, it supports literally hundreds of compatibles as well. You need only select which class of computer you are using.

Once you have identified the general class of your computer, you must specify which of many different display adapters your system

```
You can set up Windows to run from floppy disks or from your hard disk.
Please indicate what kind of disks you want.

 WHEN YOU'RE READY TO                                          PRESS

 Install on 1 high capacity disk (1.2MB or more)          1
 Install on 2 5.25" disks (360KB)                         2
 Install on 2 3.5" disks (720KB)                          3
 Install on a hard disk                                  [H]

 Exit without completing Setup                         CONTROL+X
```

Figure 18.2: Windows disk installation choices

uses. Windows supports all of the standard CGA, EGA, and VGA adapters, as well as a host of other popular alternatives, as shown in Figure 18.5.

DOS recognizes many different international keyboards. Chapter 11 discussed the steps required to prepare your DOS for using a different

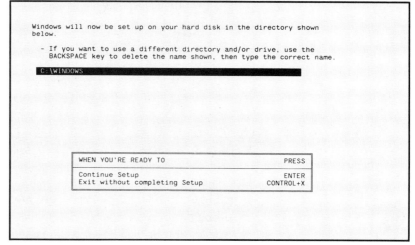

Figure 18.3: Setup of Windows default directory

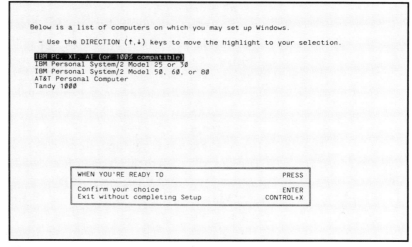

Figure 18.4: Computers supported by Windows

When selecting the display adapter for your system, you use the cursor keys to highlight the display adapter installed on your computer and then press Return. As is true during the entire setup operation, you can abort the process by typing Ctrl-X.

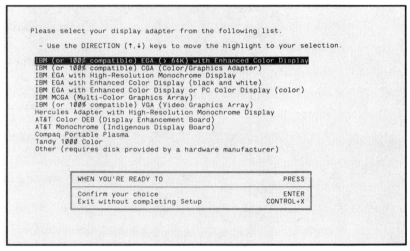

Please select your display adapter from the following list.

- Use the DIRECTION (↑,↓) keys to move the highlight to your selection.

```
IBM (or 100% compatible) EGA (> 64K) with Enhanced Color Display
IBM (or 100% compatible) CGA (Color/Graphics Adapter)
IBM EGA with High-Resolution Monochrome Display
IBM EGA with Enhanced Color Display (black and white)
IBM EGA with Enhanced Color Display or PC Color Display (color)
IBM MCGA (Multi-Color Graphics Array)
IBM (or 100% compatible) VGA (Video Graphics Array)
Hercules Adapter with High-Resolution Monochrome Display
AT&T Color DEB (Display Enhancement Board)
AT&T Monochrome (Indigenous Display Board)
Compaq Portable Plasma
Tandy 1000 Color
Other (requires disk provided by a hardware manufacturer)
```

WHEN YOU'RE READY TO	PRESS
Confirm your choice	ENTER
Exit without completing Setup	CONTROL+X

Figure 18.5: Windows display adapter options

keyboard. You must tell Windows which keyboard layout your system uses. Figure 18.6 lists the choices currently available from Windows.

Although you can operate Windows without a pointing device, you really shouldn't. The program is designed for use with a mouse, or at least with some form of pointing device such as a trackball or joystick. Figure 18.7 shows the choices available to you during Windows installation.

The default U.S. keyboard is highlighted, but you can use the cursor keys to select one of the other layouts.

The choices seen in Figure 18.7 are the most popular pointing devices for Windows use. Using one of these devices facilitates your use of Windows, since software support for them is included in the Windows package.

After you have responded to the various setup screens (Figures 18.1 to 18.7), Setup displays a summary of the key information it gathered from you (see Figure 18.8) and prompts you for confirmation. Press Return if the information is accurate or select any of the answers for correction; Windows will return to the appropriate screen to let you modify your earlier answer.

When you have confirmed your answers, Setup loads several programs (KERNEL.EXE, USER.EXE, MSDOS.EXE, and MSDOS-D.EXE). Setup also copies from the Setup diskette to your hard disk a number of necessary files and then prompts you to insert your other Windows diskettes in succession. Figure 18.9 shows the first of several prompt screens.

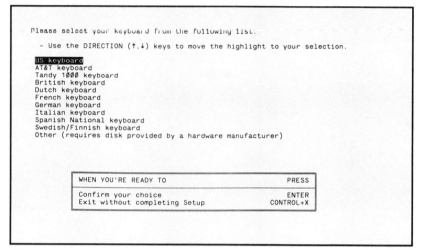

Figure 18.6: Keyboard layouts known to Windows

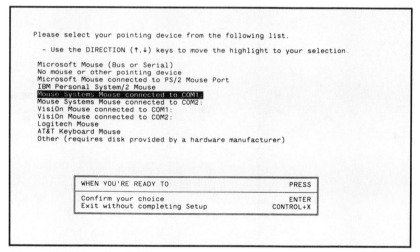

Figure 18.7: Pointing device selection screen

The first step in the primary setup process loads the main Windows file and overlay instructions. Among other, smaller files, the Windows drivers for your earlier choices are loaded at this time (for the mouse, the keyboard, and so on).

Next, you'll need to install one or more printers or plotters in your Windows configuration. The screen shown in Figure 18.10 prompts you for this step, allowing you to select choice I repeatedly until you

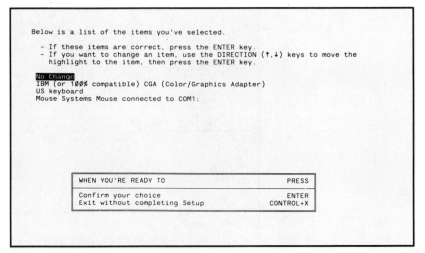

Figure 18.8: Setup confirmation screen

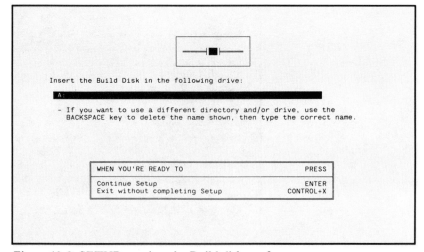

Figure 18.9: SETUP requires the Build diskette first

have installed all printer and plotter devices. You can then continue with the rest of the installation.

You can continue with the installation, or you can specify one or more output devices at this point. Choosing I on this screen displays the screen shown in Figure 18.11, which presents a series of output device choices.

Figure 18.10: Output device configuration

Figure 18.11: Output device screen

Selecting I produces a multiscreen list of output device choices, part of which is shown in Figure 18.11. Use the up and down cursor keys to scroll through the many printer and plotter choices.

The setup program lists several screens displaying output devices compatible with Windows. Use the cursor-control keys to select the desired device; then press Return. You will then be asked to indicate the port being used for the specified device.

Windows must know the port to which each device used for output is connected. Even though DOS can support more than two serial communications ports, Windows offers only COM1 and COM2 serial support. Figure 18.12 lists the output port selections available.

You must select one of these ports for each printer or plotter you specify during the Windows setup. After this is done, the screen shown in Figure 18.10 will be redisplayed. If you have more than one printer or plotter installed, you can specify it now by selecting I once again and then specifying the port to which the device is connected. When you have finished specifying devices, you can continue with the rest of the Windows setup.

Continuing the Windows setup displays the screen shown in Figure 18.13, which allows you to specify the country for your Windows operation. Just as for DOS (see Chapter 11), this specification determines the currency symbol, separator symbols for the date and time, and other country-specific features used by Windows.

Windows 2.03 supports 27 country settings. Selecting one of these countries automatically specifies such country-specific features as currency symbols and date and time separators.

Once this initial configuration is complete, you must load several required Windows utilities into your system. Just as you were prompted to insert the Build diskette into drive A, you now are prompted to insert the Utilities 1 disk (see Figure 18.14). Depending on the hardware you

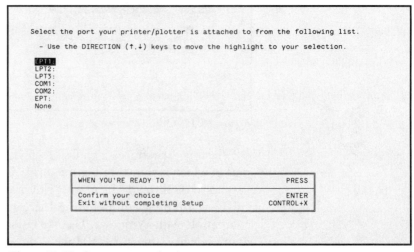

Figure 18.12: Output port selections

specified as part of your system configuration, you may also be prompted to insert the Utilities 2 and Displays disks, which contain many of the alternative choices for Windows support software.

After reading from the Utilities 1 disk, Setup asks for the Fonts (1 and 2) disks. After reading the necessary files from the Fonts disks and copying those files to the \WINDOWS directory, Windows prompts you to insert your Desktop Applications disk.

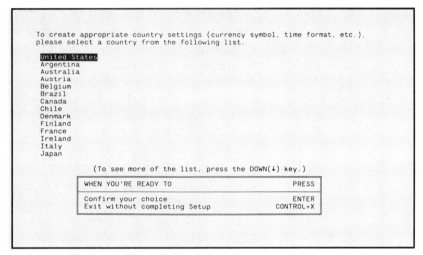

Figure 18.13: Country settings for Windows

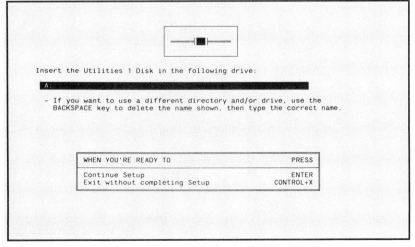

Figure 18.14: Utilities are loaded after the Build

Pressing Return after placing the Desktop Applications disk into drive A copies the primary desktop application modules (CALC.EXE, CALENDAR.EXE, CARDFILE.EXE, CLOCK.EXE, PAINT.EXE, NOTEPAD.EXE,and so on) to your \WINDOWS directory.

You are next prompted to insert your Windows Write disk in drive A. In fact, this prompt is misleading; the correct disk to load at this point is labeled Program disk. This disk contains the primary software for the Windows word processing program, called Write.

You are nearly done with the Windows setup. The screen shown in Figure 18.15 now appears. This screen displays information about the software that was changed after the manuals and documentation were complete. The special files containing this last-minute information are disk resident. Setup tries to make sure that you read this information by including this screen in the installation process.

When you are done viewing the text information, your current directory will be \WINDOWS, and you can begin operating the WINDOWS program by typing WIN. You can later modify the path (perhaps set from AUTOEXEC.BAT) to include \WINDOWS; this will allow you to initiate Windows at any time, regardless of current drive or directory.

Do not skip the final steps of reading the README files during the setup process. The advice and information contained in those text

```
Now you can view the README files. The README files contain updated
information about Windows that is not available in your manual.
Topics include new features, information on running applications
efficiently, and answers to common questions.

   WHEN YOU'RE READY TO                          PRESS

   View README files                               V
   Finish Setup                                    F

   Exit without completing Setup              CONTROL+X
```

Figure 18.15: README text is part of the setup process

Skipping the README information may cause you to be unaware of important Windows information not included in the standard documentation.

files may be relevant and even critical to your system. For instance, information about many popular laser printers, and the use of soft fonts on those printers, is contained only in the README files. Additional information about Windows performance and advice regarding system modification for performance and convenience also appears on these important text screens.

The Windows operating environment that results from the initial installation procedure is more than sufficient for a beginning user. From this environment, you can use utility programs and follow printed instructions to modify Windows to accept changes in system hardware and in the use of current hardware.

You can also have Windows automatically load one or more software applications whenever you load Windows into the computer. Although this may significantly increase the amount of time required to start Windows, you will have all the applications opened in this manner available at the beginning of the Windows session instead of having to load them one by one later.

When installing programs under Windows, load those programs requiring the most amount of memory first.

Because of the way Windows manages memory during multitasking operations, it is more efficient to load programs into the Windows environment by order of decreasing memory requirements (that is, starting with the program with the largest memory requirement first). Although this sequential loading of programs can be performed manually, allowing Windows to do it for you is obviously easier.

USING WINDOWS

You usually load Windows by entering WIN at the DOS prompt. You can write a simple batch file to set the default drive and directory and to enter the request to DOS to run WIN. When installed on a hard disk, Windows is usually stored in the \WINDOWS subdirectory, so you must either change to that directory (using the DOS CD command) or ensure that \WINDOWS is on the path.

Once you have entered the WIN command, by whatever means, Windows displays the Microsoft logo and begins operation. The time required for Windows to become functional depends on the speed of your computer and disk drives and on the number of applications that Windows has been configured to start automatically. When the

Windows operating environment is completely set up, a full-screen window similar to the one in Figure 18.16 appears.

Files in the current directory (\Windows) of the current drive (C) are displayed. The default drive is represented by a highlighted icon; the first entry in the directory also is highlighted. Available options include the three main menu choices: File, View, and Special.

The window in Figure 18.16 is for the Windows MS-DOS Executive application program in Version 2. MS-DOS Executive is always available during a Windows session and is used to initiate other applications and perform some DOS disk operations. The use of the MS-DOS Executive will be discussed shortly, but first take a brief look at the areas of the window and the icons on it.

THE COMPONENTS OF A WINDOWS SCREEN

The standard window in a Windows application has three primary and two secondary (optional) components. The first primary area consists of the top two lines of the window: the title bar and the Command menu. The title bar contains the name of the application and (in Versions 2.X) three icons, one on the left and two on the right. The Command menu displays the names of the commands associated with a particular application (File, View, and Special, in Figure 18.16). The second primary area is the work area, or working

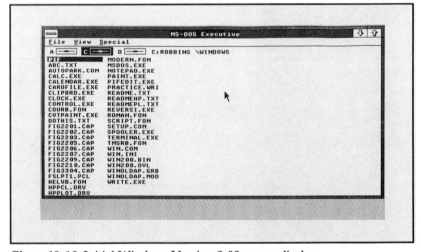

Figure 18.16: Initial Windows Version 2.03 screen display

window. The third primary area, which appears as a dark or inverse stripe across the bottom of the screen, is the icon display area. Applications that are loaded but not shown in the work area as full or partial windows are displayed here as icons.

Depending on the application, two other components, vertical and horizontal scroll bars, may appear in the window. If present, the vertical scroll bar (see Figure 18.20) appears at the right side of the work area, and the horizontal scroll bar (see Figure 18.72) appears immediately above the icon display area. When displayed, the scroll bars can be used to scroll the work area to display any information that exceeds the number of lines, or the number of characters in a line, of the work area. The scroll bars are used as they are in programs that display only a portion of a document or spreadsheet at a time. The use of scroll bars is described later in this chapter.

The title bar in Figure 18.16 displays three icons. The two icons that appear on the right side of the title bar, a down arrow and an up arrow, control the display of the associated window. The down arrow, or minimize box, changes the window into an icon. The up arrow, or maximize box, expands the window to a full-screen display. When a window has been maximized to a full-screen display, the up arrow changes to a double up arrow, or window restore box. This box restores the window to its previous display size.

The third icon, on the left side of the title bar, is the Control menu box. This box provides access to the Control menu, which is common to all Windows applications. Choices on this menu control the size, location, display status, and termination of an application and its associated window. They are outlined in the section "Using the Control Menu."

The components of the title bar just described are included in Version 2 only; the title bar in Version 1 simply displays the name of the application program. Similar features are available in Version 1, but they are generally less convenient to use.

RUNNING WINDOWS

Windows provides a graphics-oriented interface that allows a user to perform various operations by selecting the appropriate commands from pull-down menus. Displaying a pull-down menu and selecting commands can be accomplished by using a pointing device, such as a mouse, or by entering a series of multikey keyboard commands (which are entered as Alt plus the selected key). The keyboard commands are inconvenient at best and confusing at worst; using a mouse is strongly recommended for users of Windows. The examples in the remainder of this chapter assume the use of a mouse pointing device.

If your cursor is not positioned on one of the Windows icons or on a text choice, it will appear as a small arrow on your screen. This arrow is the mouse pointer. To select an icon on a window, you position the pointer by moving the mouse so that the pointer tip is on the icon. After you have correctly positioned the pointer, you can activate the icon by pressing the mouse button. On mouse devices that have two or more buttons, this is usually the left button. When you press the button, either the icon will change color, indicating that it can be moved to another location on the screen, or a pull-down menu will appear.

In Figure 18.17, the Control menu box has been selected, and its menu is displayed because the mouse button has been pushed. If the mouse button is released while the pointer is inside the icon, the menu will remain on screen. If the mouse button is clicked with the pointer on some empty area of the screen, the menu will disappear. However, if you move the pointer to the Command menu with the mouse button

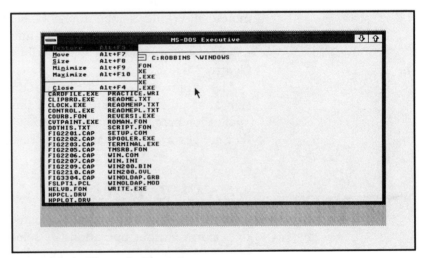

Figure 18.17: The main Control menu

still pressed, the menu command that is touched by the pointer will change its display characteristics (usually to white letters on a colored background) to indicate it has been selected. If you move the pointer off the command, the command will revert to its original display and will not be selected. To execute a command on a menu, select it with the pointer and release the mouse button. If you don't want to execute any of the commands on a menu, move the pointer back to the menu icon or to an empty area of the screen before releasing the mouse button.

This menu appears after you select the horizontal box icon in the upper-left corner of any window. The six controls displayed are available to you for managing any window. From the menu, you can move a window around the screen and adjust its size any way you like. You can replace the entire window with an icon only, expand the window to fill the screen, restore the window to its original size, or close the window.

Frequently, one or more of the commands in a pull-down menu will be disabled because they are invalid or meaningless at the time. When a command has been disabled, it is displayed in a different color, shade, or font than valid commands. For example, the Print choice in Figure 18.47, later in this chapter, appears dimmer than the other options. This indicates that it is not a valid choice for the currently selected file. When the pointer touches a disabled command, the display characteristics do not change. If you release the mouse button while it is touching a disabled command, the menu will disappear.

Windows displays commands in a different color, shade, or font if they are invalid or temporarily disabled.

USING THE CONTROL MENU

The Control menu, shown in Figure 18.17, is available in every application designed to operate in the Windows environment. It controls the display of an application window and closes (terminates) an application program. The commands on this menu are as follows:

Restore: Restores window appearance and size to original values. Also accessible as Alt-F5 key combination.

Move: Moves the window to another location on a multiple window display. Also accessible as Alt-F7 key combination.

Size: Adjusts the size of the window in a multiple-window display. Also accessible as Alt-F8 key combination.

Minimize: Closes the active window, reduces it to an icon, and places the icon in display area at the bottom of the screen. Also accessible as Alt-F9 key combination.

Maximize: Expands a window or an icon to the largest possible screen size. Also accessible as Alt-F10 key combination.

Close: Closes a window, terminating the current application program and removing it from the Windows environment. Also accessible as Alt-F4 key combination.

As you can see, each of these commands also can be activated by an Alt-keystroke combination. You can use keystroke commands regardless of whether a pointing device (a mouse) is installed, but pointing is usually easier.

USING MS-DOS EXECUTIVE

MS-DOS Executive is the primary control application in the Windows environment. It is initiated automatically when Windows is loaded into the computer system, and it must remain active as long as Windows is running. MS-DOS Executive performs the following three primary functions:

1. It loads and runs other application programs in Windows.

2. It displays the current disk directory listing.

3. It provides access to DOS disk-control operations such as file COPY, DELETE, and RENAME; disk FORMAT; and subdirectory creation and alteration.

When Windows is first loaded, MS-DOS Executive is the only application window open. If additional applications have been open, they appear as icons in the display area at the bottom of the screen.

Figure 18.16, presented earlier, shows a sample MS-DOS Executive window. The actual directory list and disk drive icons vary between different computer systems. At the top of the work area, a disk drive icon is displayed for each disk drive on the computer system. The icon for the current default disk drive is displayed in inverse video. To the right of the disk icons, the default drive letter, volume label, and current subdirectory path are displayed. Below the disk icons is a directory listing of the files in the current subdirectory. Generally, the first file in the directory listing is displayed in inverse video to mark it as the default selection.

CHANGING THE DEFAULT DISK DRIVE

You can change the default disk drive by positioning the pointer inside the icon for the disk drive that is to become the new default drive and then clicking the mouse button once. The icon for the original default disk drive will revert to normal video display, and the new default drive icon will change to inverse-video display. The new default drive letter, volume label, and subdirectory path of the new default drive will then be displayed, as will a directory listing of the files in that subdirectory.

SELECTING A FILE FROM THE DIRECTORY LIST

To change the selected file in the directory list, move the pointer onto the file name and click the mouse button once. The previously selected file name will be restored to normal display, and the new file name will display in inverse video.

USING THE MS-DOS EXECUTIVE COMMAND MENU

MS-DOS Executive provides three pull-down menu commands (File, View, and Special) in the Command menu at the top of the window. The functions of the commands available under these three menus are described in the following sections. Position the pointer on a Command menu command and hold down the mouse button; the pull-down menu for that command will be displayed.

With the mouse button still pressed, move the pointer down through the pull-down menu. As the pointer passes over a command, the command is selected and displayed in inverse video. If you release the mouse button, the selected command will be performed on the selected file or files in the work area. If additional information or verification is required to complete a command, one or more pop-up windows will appear.

CONTROLLING DOS FILES   Figure 18.18 shows the File command pull-down menu. The command functions available here are performed on the currently selected file shown in the work area. The command functions are as follows:

RUN: Brings an application .COM, .EXE, or .BAT file into the Windows environment and executes it. If a Windows application is to be run, a window will be open for it on the screen. If a standard DOS application is being run, the display screen will revert to normal DOS mode. The application will then run as it normally does under DOS, using the entire screen for display.

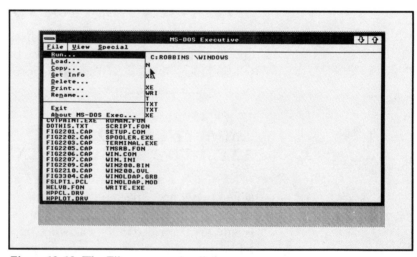

Figure 18.18: The File command pull-down menu

LOAD: Loads and executes Windows and standard DOS applications in the Windows environment, but with the applications displayed as icons in the icon display area. No window will be open for the application.

COPY: Copies one or more selected files to another disk or directory. You can copy more than one file at a time by selecting multiple files from the work area directory list. To select more than one file, press and hold the Shift key on the keyboard while pointing to and selecting the files with the mouse.

GET INFO: Displays full directory information for the selected file.

DELETE: Deletes the selected files.

PRINT: Sends one or more ASCII text files to the Windows print spooler.

RENAME: Renames the selected file.

This menu lets you perform DOS operations on the files in the displayed directory. You can run a program or batch file, load a program or batch file for later execution, or obtain the equivalents of the DOS commands COPY, ERASE, RENAME, and DIR. If the highlighted file is printable, the PRINT command option is also available.

VIEWING DOS DIRECTORY CONTENTS   Figure 18.19 shows the View command pull-down menu. The command functions available here determine how the file list appears in the work area. Normally, the file name and extension of all files in the current subdirectory are displayed in alphabetical order by file name. By selecting different options, you can organize the file list by date, time, size, or extension. Only program files or files matching a specified naming convention are displayed. The \WINDOWS directory files listed behind the pull-down View window appear in the default short format.

As you can see, check marks indicate the default choice in each of the three categories of this menu. By default, all files appear in name order using the short format, which displays showing only the base name and extension of each file.

Moving the mouse down the menu to select the long format results in a display similar to Figure 18.20. Notice that a vertical scroll bar appears on the right side of your screen since there are more files in

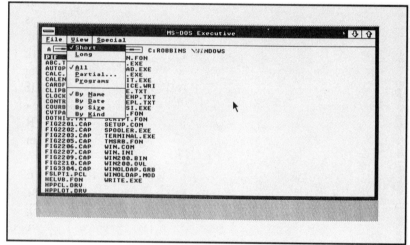

Figure 18.19: The standard View pull-down menu

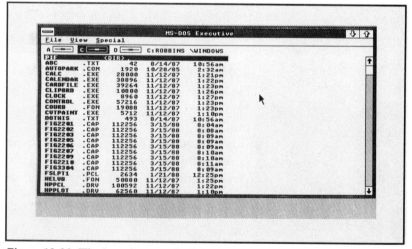

Figure 18.20: The long format of a Windows directory

this directory than can be displayed on one screen. You can move the mouse to the scroll bar and select a different portion of the directory list for display, by clicking the mouse button on different portions of the scroll bar. The long file-name format (which includes date, time, and size) will remain in effect until you again select the short format.

USING SPECIALIZED DOS COMMANDS   Figure 18.21 shows the Special command pull-down menu. The command functions available from this menu provide access to common DOS operations associated with hard disk use (formatting new disks, changing or assigning a disk volume label, creating new disk subdirectories, or changing the current subdirectory on a disk drive).

Miscellaneous but important DOS command capabilities are available from this Special menu. The choices here are equivalent to the DOS MD, CD, FORMAT, FORMAT/S, and LABEL commands. The Windows command for ending the Windows session is also available from this menu.

The Special menu also includes the command to terminate a Windows session (End Session). If you select End Session, a window appears requesting verification (see Figure 18.22). If you select the OK icon, Windows closes any open windows. If an open window or loaded application contains new or modified data that has not been saved, a pop-up window allows you to save or discard that data.

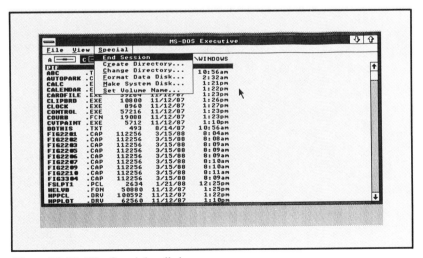

Figure 18.21: The Special pull-down menu

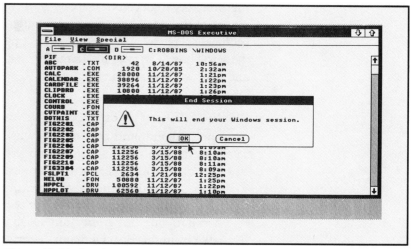

Figure 18.22: Confirmation screen at Windows termination

Selecting End Session on the Special pull-down menu of MS-DOS Executive results in this simple pop-up confirmation panel. You use the mouse or cursor-control keys to select whether to terminate your entire Windows session or to cancel the request and return to the Windows session.

SAVING TIME AND ENERGY WITH WINDOWS APPLICATIONS

> ✍ This display of available .EXEs appears when you select the Programs choice on the View pull-down menu. Running any one of these programs requires only that you highlight its name (either by selecting it with the mouse or the cursor-control keys) and then press Return.

The Windows directory contains several built-in .EXE files. Most of these (shown in Figure 18.23) are unique application programs included with your Windows software. In this section, you'll explore these useful tools. You can then decide which ones best serve your own needs.

PERFORMING ON-SCREEN CALCULATIONS

The Calculator application, shown in Figure 18.24, functions as a standard 10-key calculator. When this application is active, you can use it to perform calculator operations by positioning the pointer over the appropriate key and clicking the mouse button or by typing the appropriate keys on the keyboard. This application also can transfer and receive information from other applications.

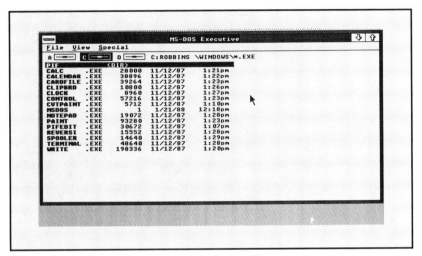

Figure 18.23: .EXE programs included with Windows

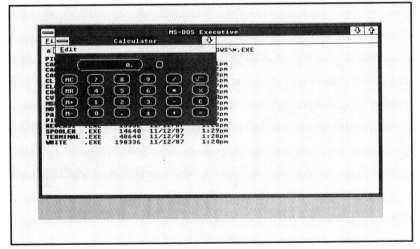

Figure 18.24: On-screen calculator function

The on-screen calculator resembles a pocket calculator. It includes the standard number keys, arithmetic functions, and single-value memory location. The only additional feature of the Windows calculator is a square-root button located above the percent key.

The screen cursor (normally an arrow elsewhere on the screen) appears as a small octagonal symbol. You can move this symbol directly over any of the calculator keys with your mouse. Pressing the mouse button is then equivalent to pressing that key on the keyboard. Calculations proceed as they would on any portable calculator, with intermediate and final numeric results shown in the calculator display window. In Figure 18.24, this window shows a value of 0. The push-button cursor is located just to the right of the calculation window.

MAINTAINING YOUR APPOINTMENT CALENDAR

Various desktop software packages offer a date and time appointment calendar. Windows offers CALENDAR.EXE, which runs in a window on the desktop. Figure 18.25 shows the initial view of this software facility. Optional settings dictate the size, shape, and contents of each window application when it first appears on the desktop. In this case, the appointment calendar is set to November 15, 1988 (today's date), beginning with 8:00 A.M. and showing one-hour intervals.

Current time and date is displayed, as are the entries for this date, beginning at 8:00 A.M. No appointments have yet been entered on this system for this date. Notice the small icon at the bottom of the screen. It represents the active and available Calculator program, whose desktop window has been minimized by a Control menu choice.

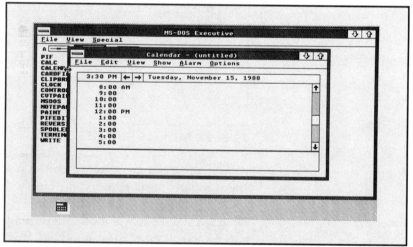

Figure 18.25: Initial window display of the Calendar feature

As you can see in Figure 18.25, the previously active Calculator function is still available. Its window has simply been shrunk (minimized) to a small icon. Windows places this icon at the bottom of the screen to remind you of the program's availability. MS-DOS Executive is still available and can be partially seen on the screen. It is said to be in the *background*, since the primary window is running the Calendar program.

In Figure 18.26, two steps have been taken. First, MS-DOS Executive has been minimized to reduce the visual clutter. This leaves only the window containing the Calendar on the screen, plus the two icons now visible in the display area at the bottom of the screen.

Only the Calendar window is being displayed at full size. Other active programs are MS-DOS Executive and the Calculator. Both of these programs appear as small icons at the bottom of the screen. The disk represents MS-DOS Executive; the miniature calculator represents the Calculator program.

You can make entries for different times on the visible schedule. In Figure 18.26, appointments have been made for 8:00, 9:00, 10:00, 12:00, 2:00, and 4:00. The cursor for the next entry is on the 3:00 line. This calendar is completely new and has not yet been named; thus, the file name *untitled* appears on the top title bar.

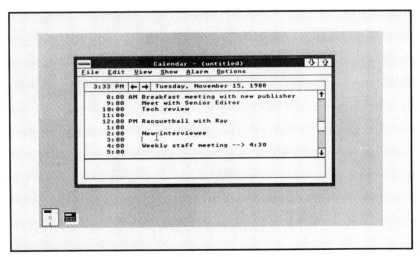

Figure 18.26: A completed appointment calendar

The Calendar program has six pull-down menus: File, Edit, View, Show, Alarm, and Options. Figure 18.27 displays the pull-down contents of the File menu. This File choice is common across the desktop applications, as are most of the features listed here.

As you can see, you can create new entries or files (New), open existing entries or files (Open), save your current work to a new or already existing file (Save), back up your current work to a uniquely specified file (Save As), print your schedule (Print), or delete files (Remove). You can also always close an application window (Exit) or display information about the application (About ...).

Save is highlighted, indicating that the file will be saved under its current name, SCHEDULE.CAL (shown in the title line at the top of the window).

To save a copy of your appointments schedule under a different name, you select the Save As choice, which displays the screen shown in Figure 18.28. The dialog box shows the current name as the default name and permits you to type over that name with another.

After entering a new file name in the dialogue box, you need only select OK with your mouse to initiate the file save process. Selecting Cancel withdraws your request to save the file at all.

The Edit menu provides a number of standard editing features, including the deletion (cutting) and reinstatement (pasting) capabilities common to most desktop applications. You'll explore these

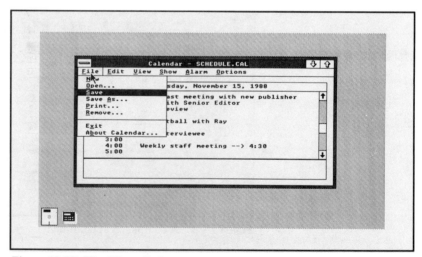

Figure 18.27: The File pull-down menu

editing capabilities in the context of the next desktop application discussed, the Cardfile.

The View menu lets you display the Calendar by day (as shown in Figure 18.26), or by month (as shown in Figure 18.29).

The entire current month is displayed, with the currently selected day shown in reverse video. The symbols > and < indicate that the

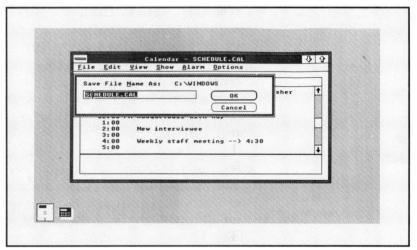

Figure 18.28: Saving a Calendar file under a different name

Figure 18.29: Calendar display by month

selected date is also today's date. Move the cursor with the mouse and then press the button once to select another day.

Notice in Figures 18.28 and 18.29 that the vertical scroll bar is visible. You can use the mouse to move the time or date forward or backward by moving the cursor to the scroll bar and pressing the mouse button. Moving downward in the scroll bar is equivalent to moving forward in time.

You can also move forward or backward using control-key and function-key combinations, as shown in Figure 18.30.

No matter what date you are currently working with, you can quickly return to today's date (that is, the system date). You can also move forward (Next) or backward (Previous) by one day, or you can specify a particular date. Each of these choices is available from this mouse-selected pull-down menu or by using the keystrokes Ctrl-PgUp, Ctrl-PgDn, or F4.

Mouse-based software such as Windows usually encourages the use of the intuitive mouse interface, using pull-down menus and mouse button selections. However, for reasons sometimes of speed and personal style and preference, the software also offers keystroke combinations that provide the same functionality. As Figure 18.30 shows, Windows often displays these keystroke alternatives on the pull-down menu to remind you of them.

Keystroke possibilities are not available once you've pulled down a menu; they are alternatives to the menus.

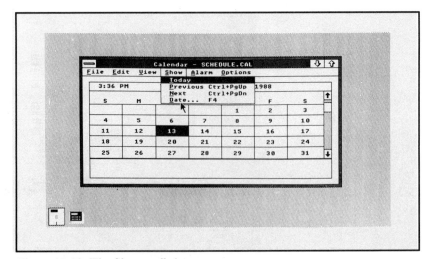

Figure 18.30: The Show pull-down menu

As you'll learn shortly, you can set an alarm to go off on your computer when a particular appointment time arrives. As Figure 18.31 demonstrates, you can also set the alarm to go off up to 10 minutes in advance of an appointment time. At the specified time, a dialog box will appear or an icon will flash. Figure 18.31 shows the screen when you select the Alarm pull-down menu. In this dialog box, you set the time precedence value and indicate whether you want your alarm to be audible as well as visible.

You can specify how many minutes (up to 10 minutes) in advance of an appointment the alarm is to go off. You can also specify whether the alarm is to be audible (by clicking the sound box and displaying an X) or visible only.

Up to this point, the screen displays have all shown 1-hour intervals using a 12-hour clock and beginning at 8:00 A.M. These settings all are adjustable from the Day Settings choice of the Options pull down menu. Figure 18.32 shows the day settings available to you.

You can set the appointment interval to 15, 30, or 60 minutes by selecting the number with your mouse. Similarly, you can switch between a standard 12-hour clock or a 24-hour format. You can directly enter the starting time for your display in the starting time box.

If you prefer your appointment calendar based on 15-minute intervals rather than 60-minute intervals, you choose this option to

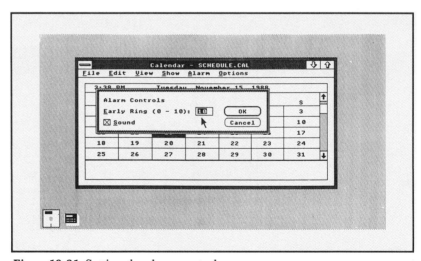

Figure 18.31: Setting the alarm controls

change the specification. Naturally, if you use 15-minute intervals, any single screen will display less total time.

When an alarm has been set for a particular appointment, the visual indicator appears as a small bell icon to the left of the appointment time, as seen next to the 3:00 slot in Figure 18.33.

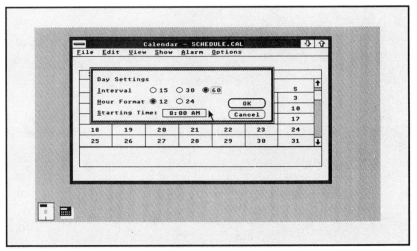

Figure 18.32: Day Settings dialog box, available on the Options pull-down menu

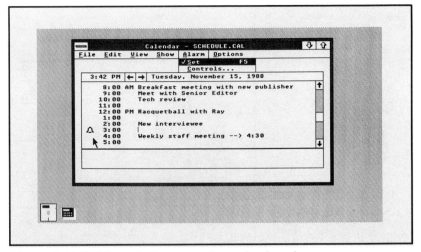

Figure 18.33: Bell icons indicate any alarms that have been set

An alarm has been set for 3:00 on Tuesday, November 15, so the bell icon appears next to that line on the display. You set alarms by using the Set choice on the Alarm pull-down menu. The Controls choice produces the dialog box shown in Figure 18.31.

Scrolling on a particular date is easily accomplished using the cursor keys (up and down arrows) or the vertical scroll bar and the mouse. Figure 18.34 shows the result of scrolling down the day from the range 8:00 A.M. to 5:00 P.M. to the range 2:00 P.M. to 11:00 P.M.

You scroll down the time intervals of a day using either the scroll bar at the right of the screen or the up and down arrow keys. Position the mouse at the desired time, then press the button once to enter new information for that time.

BUILDING YOUR OWN SIMPLE DATABASE

Complex database management systems provide powerful capabilities for managing large amounts of data. The commands and tools available in these DBMS program are often much more than is necessary for many simple files of information. The concept behind the Windows card file program is that much information is easily stored on the equivalent of a 3 × 5-inch card. Thus, with the Cardfile, you create visual cards on your computer screen. When you run the Cardfile program from MS-DOS Executive, the screen shown in Figure 18.35 appears.

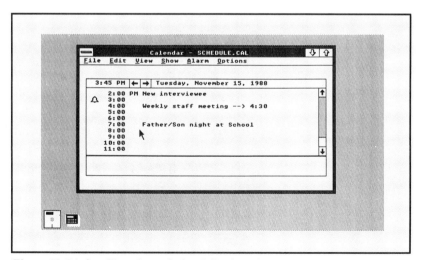

Figure 18.34: Scrolling through the daily time slots

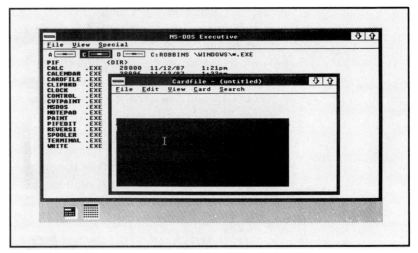

Figure 18.35: First appearance of the Cardfile window

As with the Calendar, you can give each card file a unique file name. Card files are untitled until you enter a name. The first blank is displayed for your information entry.

As the figure shows, the Cardfile offers five pull-down menus. The first three menus perform functions similar to those they perform in the Calendar program. The Card and Search menus are unique to the Cardfile program. Notice in the figure that the MS-DOS Executive window has been maximized and no longer appears as an icon. However, the Calendar program has been minimized and now appears only as an icon at the bottom of the screen.

When setting up a card file, the first step to take is to give your card a title, or index line. Select Index on the Edit menu, shown in Figure 18.36, to obtain the proper dialog box.

Selecting the Index choice on the Edit menu allows you to give each card a unique title, or index line. The name refers to the method Windows uses internally to store and retrieve individual file cards (via an index into the file).

The resulting dialog box, shown in Figure 18.37, allows you to enter a brief title for the card. This *index line* appears at the top of each card on the computer screen. The Cardfile also uses the characters in these index lines to arrange the cards for display. The default arrangement of the cards on your monitor is standard alphabetic order.

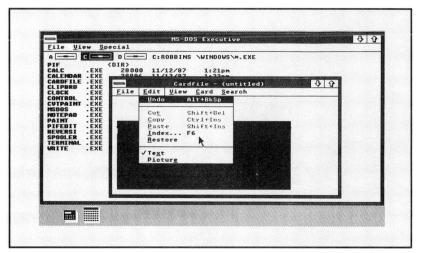

Figure 18.36: The Index choice on the Edit menu

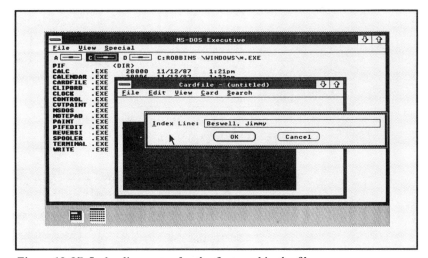

Figure 18.37: Index line entry for the first card in the file

The last name is entered first, so that later automatic alphabetizing by the Cardfile program will sort the cards into a logical order. After you enter the index line, the dialog box disappears, and the card is redisplayed with the index line entry appearing as the first line on the card. You can then begin typing any information you would like to appear and be stored on this card. Figure 18.38 shows a completed card entry for Jimmy Beswell, a racquetball opponent of the person keeping this example card file.

The individual's name is used as the index line, for easy alphabetizing. Notes about each individual's game skills are kept for later reference.

To add additional cards to this simple card file select the Card pull-down menu. As Figure 18.39 shows, you then choose Add (or alternatively press F7) to create a new blank card on your screen.

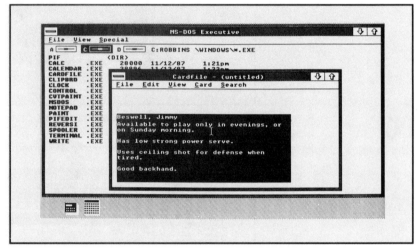

Figure 18.38: First card entry in file of racquetball opponents

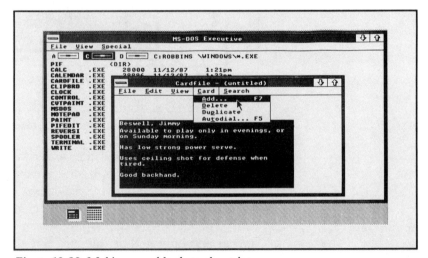

Figure 18.39: Making new blank card entries

You can add new blank cards to your card file with the Add choice on the Card pull down menu. You will be asked to give the card a title (index line) before you enter new information on that card. Adding a new card to your file causes the Cardfile program to ask you for the title of the card. Figure 18.40 shows the dialog box that appears.

A new card added after your first one (Beswell, Jimmy) must first be given a title line. This second card is given the index line Kayple, Robert. This card, like all cards, will later be quickly accessible via the Search menu simply by entering the first letters of the index line (in this case, the person's name).

The resulting display shows a new card that is blank except for the index line at the top of the card (see Figure 18.41). The former card is obscured except for the index line (Beswell, Jimmy). The new current card is now ready for information entry.

This facilitates the expected entry of information onto the card. Once this display appears, you can begin typing, and the text will appear on the card.

Figure 18.42 shows the completed second card. All notes about Robert Kayple have been entered onto his card and are visible.

A second card is entered in the card file under the index line Kayple, Robert. The card file program displays the top index line for several cards at a time, so that you can easily select cards with your

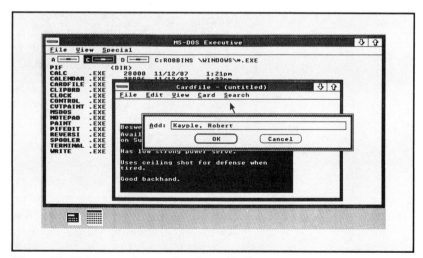

Figure 18.40: New cards must be given title lines

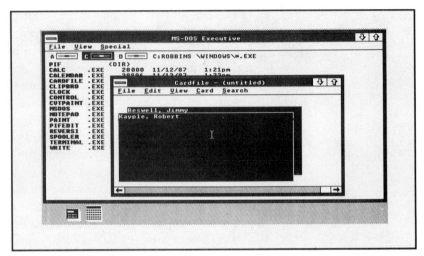

Figure 18.41: Newly added cards at the top of the deck, or file

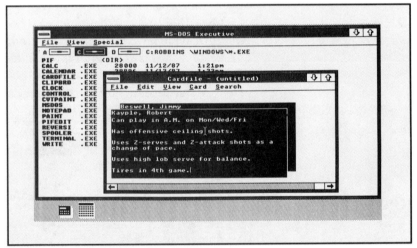

Figure 18.42: Multiple cards have their index lines visible

mouse. Selecting an index line moves its card to the top of the deck, where you can read the card's contents.

You can add other cards by selecting Card/Add. Figure 18.43 shows a deck containing a third racquetball opponent's card. Since all three cards fit on one screen, Windows does not yet need to display a scroll bar.

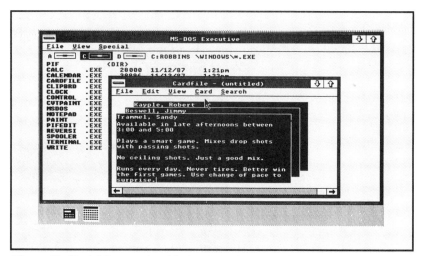

Figure 18.43: Adding cards with the Add choice on the Card menu

You can easily add more cards with the Add choice from the Card menu. If more cards were created than fit on one screen, a horizontal scroll bar would appear, allowing you to scroll through the deck from front to back (left to right on the scroll bar).

A useful tool when your card deck becomes much larger is the Search pull-down menu. As you can see in Figure 18.44, you only need to enter the first several characters of the index line to enable the Cardfile program to quickly find a particular card.

The GoTo choice on the Search menu lets you enter several characters from the card's title, or index line. The program quickly finds the specified card and makes it the topmost card on the deck, as the next figure shows.

At any time you can change the appearance of your card file from its default view of complete cards, as shown so far, to an alternative view displaying only the index lines for the card entries. These two choices appear on the pull-down View menu, shown on Figure 18.45.

You can view your card file in two ways: either as a deck of titled cards (the Cards option), or as a list of card titles (the List option). Selecting List displays the screen in Figure 18.46.

Figure 18.46 displays the card file as a list of index lines, or titles, for easy reference. Naturally, more card titles can appear on one screen display in this format than in the alternative format displaying complete cards.

2

Your card file has a list of titles, or index lines. In this format, you can see more entries on a single screen and thus can easily and quickly select the next card you want to see or modify.

When you're done working on your card file, you will most likely want to save it to a disk file. In fact, you should probably save it earlier than that to ensure that a power failure doesn't cost you a great deal of work. Once you've saved your work, your data will be protected.

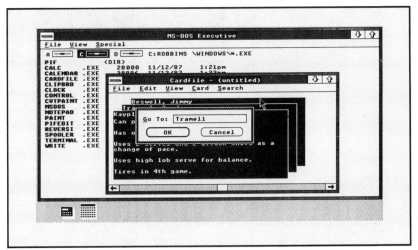

Figure 18.44: Finding a particular card quickly with Go To

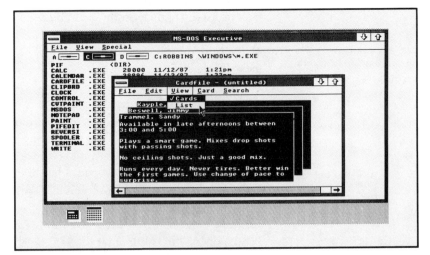

Figure 18.45: Alternative viewing possibilities

Figure 18.47 displays the File menu, including the standard options for creating, opening, and saving files. It also contains useful choices for printing individual cards (one to a page) and for printing your entire card file (multiple cards per printed page).

In particular, the printing choices provide you with the ability to print individual cards, one to a page, and to print several cards on a

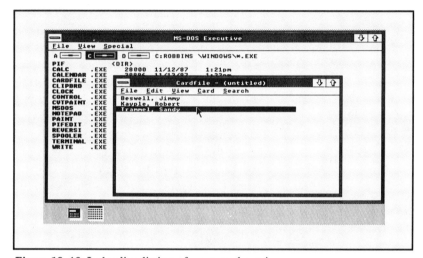

Figure 18.46: Index line listing of your card entries

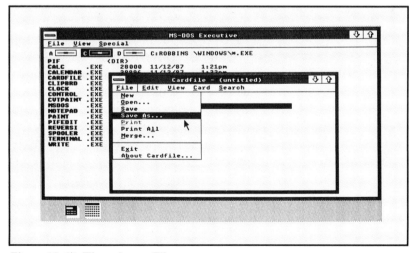

Figure 18.47: The primary File menu

single page. All cards are printed with a solid border for easy visual separation. Figure 18.48 shows a printout of the three cards created in this card file session.

All three cards appear on one page; each card is printed with a solid border for easy identification and perhaps cutting.

One last feature of the Cardfile program is its ability to dial a telephone number. This feature is included in case your cards represent a person or business that you want to call. Selecting the Autodial choice from the Card menu displays the screen in Figure 18.49.

You can enter a phone number in the Dial text box (for example, 212-234-5476), or you can allow the program to automatically find the phone number on the topmost card in your file. The first phone number, if any, on the topmost card is placed in the Dial text box. That number is then dialed through your connected modem as soon as you select OK.

In the Phone Settings dialog box, you can set the baud rate to 300 or 1200, the port to COM1 or COM2, and the dialing to pulse or tone (touch tone). The card file program will automatically enter the first phone number it finds on the topmost card displayed on your screen, or you can enter another number. Once you are ready, selecting OK causes the card file program to send the appropriate signals to your modem to dial the phone.

Suppose at this time that you have correctly saved your card file as RACQUET. As you can see in Figure 18.49, the formerly untitled card file is now called RACQUET.CRD. The default .CRD extension was added when the file was saved as RACQUET from the File menu.

You can now maximize the MS-DOS Executive window to select the Special menu and end the Windows session. Windows will check to verify that other sessions have had their data updates properly saved. In Figure 18.50, Windows discovered that your calendar entries have not been updated in the file named SCHEDULE.CAL.

Windows will not allow you to end a session with outstanding data changes that have not been saved to a disk. In this example, you tried to end the session after saving your card file work. Windows discovers that the SCHEDULE.CAL file had not been updated and so provides you the opportunity to correct this possible oversight before you lose your work.

```
Beswell, Jimmy
Available to play only in evenings, or
on Sunday morning.

Has low strong power serve.

Uses ceiling shot for defense when
tired.

Good backhand.


Kayple, Robert
Can play in A.M. on Mon/Wed/Fri

Has offensive ceiling shots.

Uses Z-serves and Z-attack shots as a
change of pace.

Uses high lob serve for balance.

Tires in 4th game.


Trammel, Sandy
Available in late afternoons between
3:00 and 5:00

Plays a smart game. Mixes drop shots
with passing shots.

No ceiling shots. Just a good mix.

Runs every day. Never tires. Better win
the first games. Use change of pace to
surprise.
```

Figure 18.48: Results of selecting Print All from the File menu

Sophisticated spooling needs can be better met through the features of Windows or OS/2 (see *Essential OS/2*, SYBEX, 1988) than by standard DOS alone.

SPOOLING YOUR OUTPUT INFORMATION

Spooling (see Chapter 7) is even more powerful under Windows than under DOS alone. You can configure Windows to understand several pieces of output hardware (during the Setup procedure) at

Figure 18.49: Autodial option on the Card menu

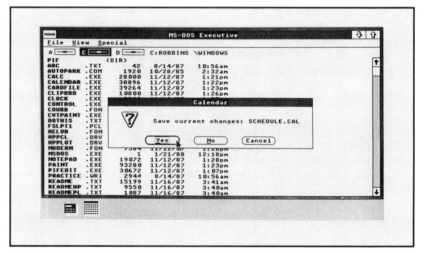

Figure 18.50: Automatic protection against inadvertent data loss

one time, and because of the multitasking capabilities of Windows, you can just as easily have different output spools, or streams, actively working at the same time. Each separate output device in your system can print files from a different queue of file names. Different programs in your system can be responsible for sending output to each of the output ports and the different devices connected to those ports. Using MS-DOS Executive to run SPOOLER.EXE, you can view and manipulate all of this simultaneous output. The example system in Figure 18.51 has been configured to expect output to LPT1 to actually be connected to an HP LaserJet printer. Also, output to LPT2 will be directed to an HP plotter.

The initial window displays all configured output devices, the ports associated with them, and two pull-down menus: Priority and Queue. This display also indicates whether each queue is actively open for accepting and processing output data (Active), or is paused and temporarily closed to output processing. Notice that MS-DOS Executive is being displayed in a background window, and that the recently used Cardfile program has been minimized and is visible as a new icon at the bottom of the screen.

Since you can have multiple output streams executing simultaneously, Windows provides the Priority pull-down menu (see Figure 18.52) to let you influence which queue(s) achieves better response. No matter how many queues exist, you can specify whether each queue is to receive low or high priority service. Since Windows intercepts CPU timer interrupts and then allocates time to each of the programs running under it (including the spools), a high-priority spool will achieve better output processing performance than will a low-priority spool.

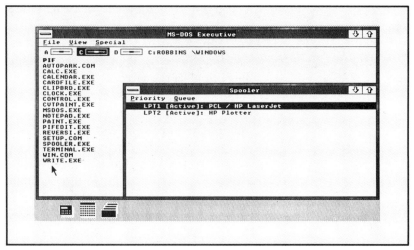

Figure 18.51: Results of executing the SPOOLER.EXE program

You can set the processing priority of each spool to one of two relative values: high or low. This lets you specify which of multiple output streams should achieve faster performance results.

When the Spooler program begins, after Windows itself begins, all configured output devices have separate spools that are open and actively queueing output information. Each of the possible file names queued for printing on a particular device is listed in the main SPOOLER window, just below the port and device line shown earlier in Figure 18.51. You can control whether any of these individually queued up file names are to be temporarily paused or canceled completely.

Figure 18.53 shows the Queue pull-down menu. Notice that the Terminate option is dimmed, since there is currently no file name in the highlighted queue (HP LaserJet) available for cancellation.

Each queued file can be paused, or halted from printing. When you are ready to continue printing, you must return to this menu and select Resume. Although the Terminate option is not currently available, you can normally use this choice to completely remove (cancel) a print job from a queue.

MAKING NOTES AND PERFORMING OTHER SIMPLE FILE EDITING

Windows lets you manipulate text in several ways. The easiest and simplest mechanism for text manipulation is the Notepad program, shown in Figure 18.54. Notice that before Notepad was run, the Spooler window was minimized; it now appears as a new icon at the bottom of the screen.

Only three pull-down menus are provided: File, Edit, and Search. Use File to manipulate all the data on the notepad at once, Edit to manipulate individual characters and strings in the file, and Search to locate specific text strings on the Notepad.

When the Notepad program begins, the cursor appears as a blinking vertical bar, as it did in the Cardfile program. You can simply begin typing text onto the Notepad; in fact, you are entering information into the memory-resident portion of what will later become a disk file. Figure 18.55 shows a typical entry sequence.

Typically used for jotting down short and simple notes, the Notepad can be used as a handy programming editor or as a simple, word-wrapping text processor. Note that word wrap is an option, not a default feature.

Although it's not apparent until you enter some text, the default status of the Notepad is line mode. All text stays on a single line until you press the Return key. If you enter more text than can be seen on the screen, the Notepad scrolls the viewing window to the right so you can see your most recently entered characters.

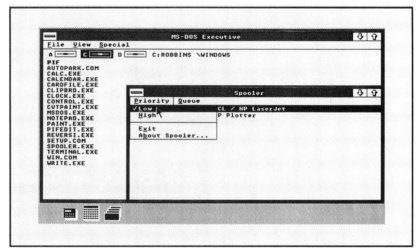

Figure 18.52: The Priority pull-down menu of the SPOOLER.EXE

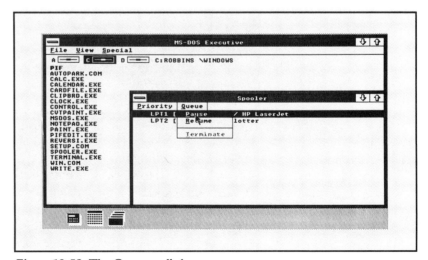

Figure 18.53: The Queue pull-down menu

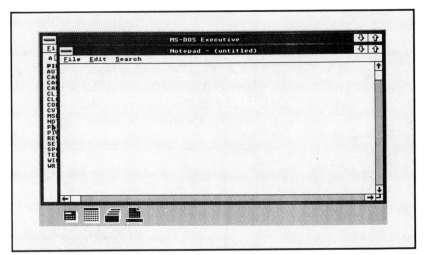

Figure 18.54: The initial Notepad program window

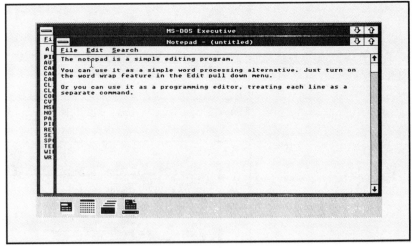

Figure 18.55: First data entry in the Notepad

Programmers can take advantage of the Notepad's simplicity by using it as a convenient programming editor. Computer languages typically work on a line-by-line command basis.

This wide scrolling mode is not the typical way in which the Notepad was designed to work. It is more likely that your text entries will be short notes, and the Notepad will perform the function anticipated by its name of simply storing brief remarks or notes.

The File menu visible in Figure 18.56 works like other file menus discussed so far. Note the vertical scroll bar on the right side of the screen. Windows expects note files to exceed the size of the on-screen

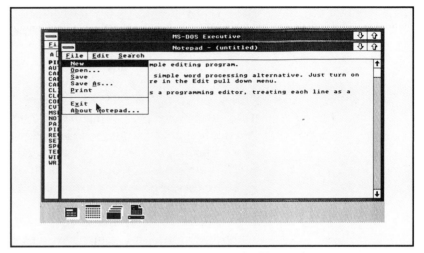

Figure 18.56: The File pull-down menu on the Notepad

window; you can use the vertical scroll bar to move up and down through the file's contents.

You can create a new file to store the Notepad's contents, open an old file and display its contents on the Notepad, save the current Notepad contents to disk, save the contents of the current Notepad in a specifically named alternate file, and send the Notepad's contents to a queue for printing.

Selecting the Edit menu displays the screen in Figure 18.57. Word wrap has been turned on in this figure to allow the Notepad to be used as a simple letter writer; paragraphs flow more easily when word wrap is used. However, note that you cannot yet use the text-manipulation commands since you have not selected any text for them to operate on.

Word wrap has been turned on as a feature of text entry. None of the text-manipulation commands (Cut, Paste, Undo, and so on) are available, because no text has been highlighted or just recently deleted.

Built into the Windows environment is both a concept and a program called the Clipboard (CLIPBRD.EXE). Whenever character data is deleted, copied, or moved around in the Windows environment, a copy of that data is stored in a memory buffer. This buffer is analogous to a clipboard and paper. Unless the paper on the clipboard is actually thrown away, you can retrieve it and restore the data placed on it to its former location, and you can just as easily insert a copy of that data at any other location as well.

In Windows, data that has been highlighted (selected) by cursor and mouse manipulation can be operated on by the Edit menu commands. The data usually is moved temporarily onto the internal Clipboard until you decide what its final disposition will be. In Figure 18.58, the second paragraph on the Notepad has been selected by the mouse. It appears in reverse video behind the Edit pull-down menu. Since a text string has been selected and can be acted upon, the formerly italicized Cut, Copy, and Clear options are now available.

These three options are available because a text string has been selected on the Notepad for manipulation in some way. Cut removes the string from its current location, saving a copy of the string on the Clipboard for later use. Copy leaves the string as it is and where it is, but deposits a copy of it on the Clipboard for later access. Clear erases the text completely; you will be unable to transfer it to another application, although you can use the Undo command to restore the deleted text in this application.

Suppose, for instance, that you had selected Cut in Figure 18.58. The entire second paragraph would have been removed (cut) from its existing location. Since there is now information on the Clipboard, the next time you call up the Edit menu, the Undo and Paste choices will be displayed in normal letters, indicating that they are available as choices.

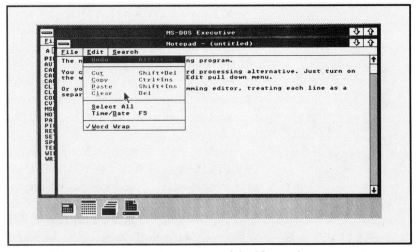

Figure 18.57: The Edit pull-down menu of the Notepad

Use the *Undo* choice immediately to correct an error. Waiting until after other operations may nullify Undo's ability to perform its job successfully.

Figure 18.59 shows the screen after the second paragraph was first cut, the cursor was moved to the end of the notes, and Paste was selected. The paragraph was reinserted (pasted) into the Notepad at the location of the cursor. The net effect in this case was to move the second paragraph from the middle of the document to the end. You could now select Undo to reverse the editing steps. You can use

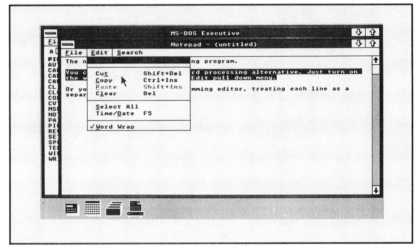

Figure 18.58: The Edit menu shows Cut, Copy, and Clear available

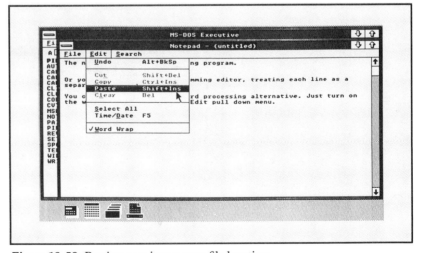

Figure 18.59: Pasting text into a new file location

Undo to undo any editing step, whether a cut-and-paste or a simple deletion (clear).

In this moving operation, the middle paragraph was first cut, then the cursor was moved to the end of the Notepad text, and finally the paragraph was pasted back into the Notepad at the new location.

When your notes become more voluminous, you may need the help offered on the Search pull-down menu. As shown in Figure 18.60, you can find any specified character string. When you select Find, a dialog box appears where you can enter the string for which you want the Notepad program to search.

Find was selected to locate occurrences of the string *you* in the document. The first occurrence is displayed in reverse video. You can select Find Next on the Search menu to locate the next occurrence of the string in the text. Case is ignored in the search, so the *You* at the beginning of the next paragraph would be highlighted next.

When searching through an entire file for text, first position the cursor to the top of the file. Searching proceeds from current cursor location to the end of the file.

After each occurrence of the specified string is found, you can press F3 or select Find Next from the Search menu to ask the Notepad program to find the next occurrence of the same string. It's important to realize that the searching begins at the point where the cursor is located and proceeds until the end of the notes is reached. Therefore, you should move the cursor to the top of the file before you issue a search request. When the program can find no more occurrences of the string a dialog box appears (see Figure 18.61).

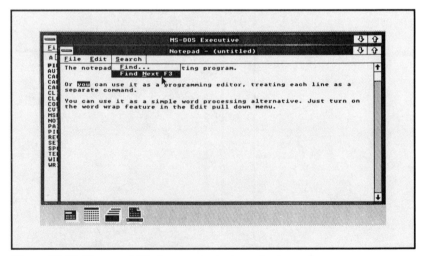

Figure 18.60: Repeated Find requests during a text search

After finding all occurrences of the specified string in the Notepad, the program displays a pop-up window, indicating that no more occurrences can be found. In this case, the string was found twice before this dialog box appeared. The same type of box would appear immediately if no occurrences at all could be found.

CONTROLLING
YOUR WINDOWS CONFIGURATION

When your Windows environment is initially configured, the Setup program asks you to enter a number of important items of information. You can change some of these values at any time by invoking the CONTROL.EXE program (see Figure 18.62).

Three pull-down menus (Installation, Setup, and Preferences) are provided, and the initial display contains the system date and time and a sliding-scale control of the cursor blink rate and the mouse double-click time separation. All of these values can be changed from this window.

You can directly change the system date and time from this window, known as the Control Panel, achieving the same results as when you use the DATE and TIME commands at the DOS prompt. The other features unique to the Control Panel are the cursor blink rate

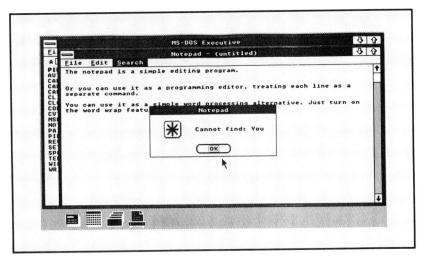

Figure 18.61: When no more matches can be found

and the time interval between double clicks from your mouse. Notice the word TEST underneath the double-click box.

Some applications require that you double-click the mouse button. To distinguish between a double-click and two successive yet separate clicks, Windows tests the amount of time that elapses between the clicks. The scroll bar in the Double Click box allows you to adjust this interval. You can then move the cursor into the TEST box and try to double-click the mouse. If Windows recognizes the two clicks as a double click, based on your interval setting, then the word TEST will invert (white on black to black on white, or vice versa).

The Control Panel also lets you install or remove printer and font information. Figure 18.63 shows the options available under the Installation pull-down menu.

This Installation pull-down menu lets you add or delete printer and font information. Selecting Add brings up a dialog box that lists the various supported devices you can install. Associated driver files are displayed when you select a device for installation.

The printer driver files used during this control function are obtained from the Utilities disk files on your original disks or from the \WINDOWS directory on your installed hard disk. You can also add or remove output fonts to your Windows installation with this menu. Although the minimum required fonts are automatically

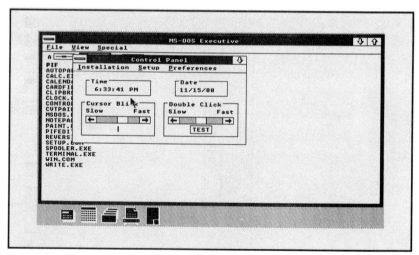

Figure 18.62: The Control Panel as it first appears

loaded during setup, you can override the initial settings and add or delete specific font files available to you.

You can review the current output device and port connections by selecting the Printer choice on the Setup pull-down menu, shown in Figure 18.64.

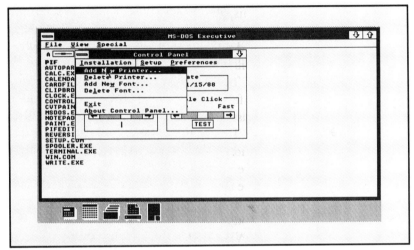

Figure 18.63: The Installation pull-down menu

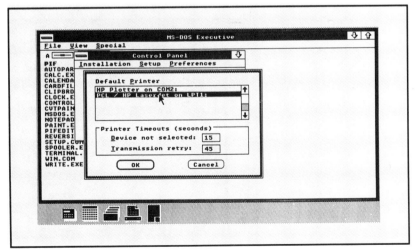

Figure 18.64: The Printer selection on the Setup pull-down menu

Currently configured printers and plotters are displayed. You can specify the system default printer and adjust its timeout values (in seconds) on this screen. This example shows a maximum 15 seconds wait before Windows will notify you of an offline condition. Also, Windows will wait for 45 seconds for an online printer to print successfully before notifying you of an error.

The Printer choice lets you specify which printer is to be used as the default printer for output from applications designed and configured for Windows operation. Simply move the cursor to the name of the desired printer and click OK. After selecting the default printer, you can enter the printer timeout information in the new dialog box that appears (already visible in Figure 18.64).

A second option on the Setup pull-down menu is Connections. Selecting this option results in the display in Figure 18.65, which lists currently configured printers and plotters and the port to which each is connected.

As you select any one of these choices, with the mouse or cursor keys, the port to which that device is connected is highlighted on the right. You can change the port connection by selecting a different port name in the Connection box.

Miscellaneous Windows system values can be set from the Preferences menu, shown in Figure 18.66.

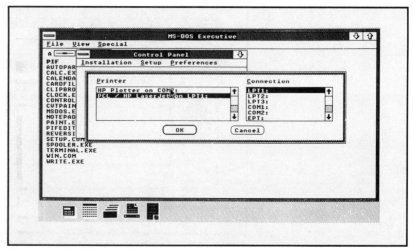

Figure 18.65: The Connections choice on the Setup menu

Miscellaneous Windows settings are accessible on this Preferences menu: country settings, mouse speed and click settings, system beep status, window borders thickness, and color intensity and hues for color monitors.

A dialog box is displayed when you select any of the choices on the Preferences menu, further information clarifying your requirements is solicited by Windows. For example, Figure 18.67 shows the result of selecting Screen Colors from the Preferences pull-down menu.

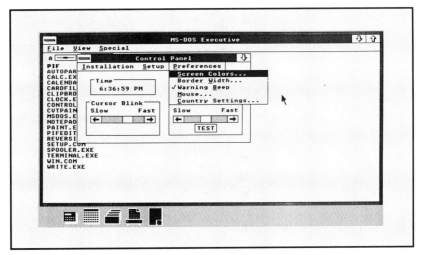

Figure 18.66: The Preferences pull-down menu

Figure 18.67: The Screen Colors submenu of the Preferences pull-down menu

Moving the bright-
ness and color bars
to extreme rightmost and
leftmost values produces
the sharpest contrast
between background and
foreground. This also
reduces the intensity of
color on color monitors,
however.

You can now determine, on a sliding scale, values to be used for
the hue, brightness, and color saturation of all items displayed by
Windows. First, you must select which item is to be influenced (such
as the menu bar or the screen background). Then you use your
mouse to point to different places on the graduated bars for hue,
brightness, and color. The Sample window on the right changes
appearance to reflect your choices.

All aspects of a Windows display, including the backgrounds of the
different portions and the contents of those portions of the screen, can
be controlled from this Preferences menu.

PLAYING REVERSI: HAVING SOME FUN

Microsoft includes a game called Reversi in the Windows desktop
applications package. As Figure 18.68 shows, this game looks similar
to the more sophisticated game, go; Reversi follows similar rules for
moves to capture territory owned by your opponent's pieces (circles).

The object of Reversi is to trap the opponent's circles between
your own, thereby turning an opponent's white circles to black,
enlarging the territory on the board owned by circles of your color.

At the end of the game, the player owning the most territory wins.
The game goes quickly (very quickly, if you play against the computer), and it's both intellectually challenging and fun. It can be

Figure 18.68: The game of Reversi

more fun if you pull down the Game menu before each of your moves to select the Hint choice. The computer then places the cursor in the best location for your next move. Naturally, do this only for the first game or two to quickly learn how to play the game successfully.

PRODUCING ANALOG CLOCK DISPLAYS

Computers typically display time in digital format. Windows has a program called CLOCK.EXE, however, that displays the time of day in analog format (see Figure 18.69).

This analog display of time shows standard hour and minute hands and a moving second hand. Notice that the control panel and the Reversi game have both been minimized to icons at the bottom of the screen.

This analog clock keeps and displays accurate time, regardless of where you move it on your screen. You can use the control box menu (in the upper-left corner of the clock display) to move the clock or to change the size of the clock. In fact, as Figure 18.70 (presented later) shows, even if you minimize the clock to an icon, it continues to keep and display the correct time. Of course, this is because Windows is a multitasking environment, and the Clock program continues to run, even though its visual output appears only in the minimized icon.

Figure 18.69: A colorful way to tell time when in Windows

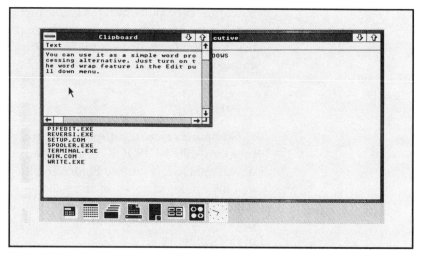

Figure 18.70: Initial display of the Clipboard (CLIPBRD.EXE)

ACCESSING THE CLIPBOARD DIRECTLY

When you learned about the Notepad earlier in this chapter, you learned that any text that is deleted or cut is actually temporarily stored in a memory-resident buffer called the Clipboard. During normal use of the other application programs, you never actually see or manipulate the temporary data stored in this Clipboard.

You can run the program CLIPBRD.EXE under Windows to display the current contents of the Clipboard. As Figure 18.70 shows, the Clipboard contains the character string last cut from the Notepad, in Figure 18.58. This cutting could have been undone in the Notepad by selecting Undo from the Edit menu, or this data acquired from the Notepad and now available on the Clipboard could be placed in another application. For example, if you activate the Cardfile application and select the Paste function, the current contents of the Clipboard (the two sentences in Figure 18.70) will be inserted on the top card in the Cardfile.

In this example session, the contents of the Clipboard were deposited by the Cut command last used from the Notepad application and shown in Figure 18.58.

Suppose, for example, that you minimized the Clipboard and MS-DOS Executive and then restored the Cardfile. Figure 18.71

Figure 18.71: Restoring the Cardfile window

displays the new screen display. The Clipboard icon appears at the bottom of the screen, and MS-DOS Executive returns to the leftmost position at the bottom of the screen. The Cardfile icon is removed in favor of the real Cardfile display.

Text on one card is first selected. This is followed by the Copy function on the Edit menu. This text is immediately available for pasting into another application because all of it is now on the Clipboard.

If you select all the text information on Jimmy Beswell's card and then pull down the Edit menu, you can then copy that data. This choice leaves the card untouched, but deposits a copy of all the text on the Clipboard, wherever the icon or window representing it happens to be located. However, whatever used to be on the Clipboard is now gone forever.

Figure 18.72 shows the information most recently acquired from the Cardfile now available on the Clipboard (whose window size has been adjusted using the Size choice on the Control menu).

Data on the Clipboard is usually placed there by the Delete, Cut, or Copy commands. The Clipboard immediately reflects the copy operation most recently performed in the Cardfile program (see Figure 18.71). When this occurs, the former contents, shown in Figure 18.70, are discarded.

Once again, remember that you should save your work at regular intervals. In a complex Windows environment containing many simultaneous applications, such as the example you've worked with here, it is easy to forget what data has been saved and what has not. Windows will not allow you to end a session (by selecting End Session on the MS-DOS Executive Special menu) without prompting you to save any new data. Figure 18.73 displays one of the prompt boxes displayed by Windows if you forget to save recent updates.

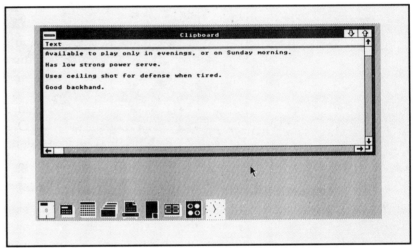

Figure 18.72: The Clipboard contains only the most recent information deposited in it

Figure 18.73: Windows reminds you to save your work

In this case, the Notepad data had previously been saved to a file called TEST1.TXT, but further adjustments during the session have not been saved. Selecting Yes now correctly updates the disk file to reflect these changes. A similar box appears for each application with changes or updates that have not been saved.

SUMMARY

In this chapter, you have learned about the Windows multitasking operating environment. It offers a dramatic step beyond the single program, command line interface, environment of standard DOS.

- You have seen how to run multiple DOS programs simultaneously and how to relate DOS commands to Windows' more intuitive, graphic, mouse-based user interface.

- You have learned the steps necessary to install and configure Windows for your computer system.

- The MS-DOS Executive offers a range of file management, command selection, and window controlling choices.

- Built-in application programs offer a variety of utility capabilities, such as on-screen calculation, appointment calendar maintenance, output spooling, note and text manipulation, and even cutting and pasting operations between utilities.

Now that you've seen how Windows offers you the opportunity for multitasking in DOS, turn to Chapter 19 for a peek behind the scenes. In the next chapter, you'll learn how Windows as well as other advanced DOS programs make use of large amounts of additional memory to break through the DOS 640K memory barrier.

BREAKING THROUGH THE
640K MEMORY LIMIT

CHAPTER *19*

TWENTY YEARS AGO, SOPHISTICATED PROGRAMS could be (and were) written using computers with as little as 4K of memory. In the early 1980s, users and developers alike marveled at the DOS facility for addressable program space of up to 640K. Times change.

And they continue to change. Within a few years, applications were being written that consumed all of that 640K and begged for more. Spreadsheets frequently displayed a "memory full" message as the range of cells and formulas quickly exceeded available space. Integrated packages discovered scarce file space left in memory after all the requisite code to support the multiple applications was loaded.

Users discovered that DOS and their individual application programs didn't always do everything they wanted. Consequently, memory-resident software surged in popularity in the mid-eighties. These packages consumed portions of the 640K memory limit.

Users also wanted easier access to multiple programs. This situation led to various programming solutions, from common data-file formats to conversion programs to simultaneous program execution. Programs such as Desqview and Windows approach this requirement for simultaneity in different ways (see the discussion that follows), but the performance of both still suffers when available memory is limited.

EARLY SOLUTIONS TO MEMORY RESTRICTIONS

Limitations on memory affect programs in two primary ways. In the first case, the program must reference data files that are larger than can fit into what little memory remains after the program itself is loaded. This limitation affects word processors such as WordPerfect and WordStar. In the second case, the program itself requires more memory for its own code routines and logic than is available. This limitation affects more recent and sophisticated DOS programs such as dBASE IV and Framework II. Some programs struggle with both limitations and meet those constraints with the two solutions presented in this section.

REFERENCING LARGE DATA FILES

Databases are often quite large, easily exceeding 640K. In fact, the most common database applications on microcomputers are inventory files and customer or client mailing lists. These files often exceed one megabyte in size. Database programs and word processors don't even fight the constraint; these packages simply spill excess memory requirements right over into disk space.

In essence, then, a large file is maintained on disk; the application program brings into memory only a piece of the file at a time. The application uses this piece and then updates the disk file. Then the program brings another piece of the data file into the memory buffer area to be used by the application program. Most word processors and database managers use this technique (see Figure 19.1).

A program can reserve a small data area within its own address space and designate it as an input/output buffer. Depending on what portion of the disk-based data file you reference, the program fills the buffer with the portion of the file containing the desired data.

The solution seen here is implemented when a program must access a data file whose size exceeds available physical memory. A portion of memory (a buffer) within the application program's addressable space is designated to hold the desired portion of the data file. Whichever portion of the data file is being referenced determines at each moment the contents of the memory-resident buffer.

LOADING LARGE, SOPHISTICATED PROGRAMS

Most popular application software packages contain more instructions and coding sequences than can fit at once into conventional

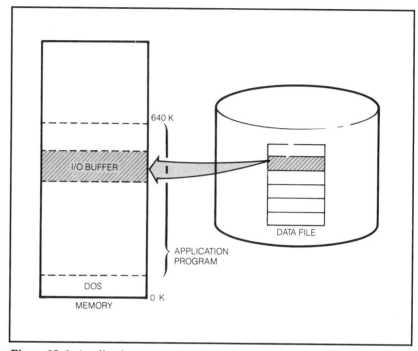

Figure 19.1: Applications can manage their own memory buffers.

DOS memory. Remember that this conventional memory is constrained to 640K, as shown in Figure 19.2.

Conventional memory is limited to 640K and spans both the memory requirements of your DOS version and the needs of your individual application program. Upper memory is accessible to the Intel chips that run DOS, but is used only for special purposes: 128K is reserved for video memory, and the remaining 256K is reserved for read-only memory tasks, primarily the built-in BIOS.

The actual limit of 1Mb is a constraint of the 8086 and 8088 chips from Intel, which construct their memory addresses using 20 bits ($2^{20} = 1$Mb). IBM PC and PC-XT computers and compatibles are absolutely restricted by the hardware in this way. This is also true for machines using the newer 80286 chip in real mode; the IBM PC-AT and compatibles fall into this category.

Many users do not avail themselves of all the capabilities of programs that offer advanced features. Recognizing this reality is fundamental to this next solution to memory limitation. Figure 19.3

Figure 19.2: Standard DOS memory usage (map)

illustrates how *overlays*, or submodules, provide a solution to the memory-limitation problem.

Memory overlays solve the problem of limited space by splitting program code into a main module and one or more submodules. If the main code, loaded at program startup, does not contain the needed instruction sequence, then the appropriate overlay module containing the required code is loaded into memory. This code overwrites a clearly designated portion of memory called the overlay area.

When designing an application, the program designer can specify certain routines as always resident. These should be the most common routines, the ones the user will probably want to use frequently.

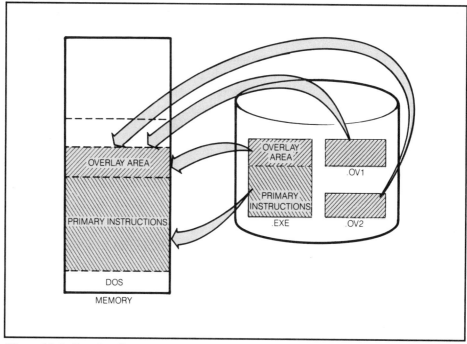

Figure 19.3: Overlay files use the same memory but at different times.

The designer can place less frequently needed routines in an auxiliary load module, known as an *overlay file*. Some extremely feature-rich software packages, such as CAD (computer-aided design) programs, often have two or three overlay files.

When the program runs, it determines which feature the user is calling, either via a command prompt or through a menu mechanism. If that particular feature is not supported by the instructions in the portion of the package currently in memory, then the overlay file containing the proper instructional routines is loaded into memory. Typically, a designated portion of memory, called the *overlay area*, is used as the temporary home for these overlay routines.

In this way, an application can contain an unlimited number of features. If loaded at the same time, these features could easily consume hundreds of kilobytes more than can fit into conventional memory. The overlay mechanism ensures that conventional memory is never exceeded, and that when a particular feature is activated, the code to support the feature is loaded.

The primary disadvantage of this technique is the extra processing overhead required to load a disk-based module to obtain access to specific code when requested.

Overlays are a form of demand loading that works quite successfully for many programs. However, besides the CPU drain, an additional problem of the overlay technique is the designer effort and knowledge necessary to split the support routines into separate modules and properly prepare the overlay files.

Overlays were a good first solution to the memory limitation problem. Faster and easier methods have since been developed, although they are not all available to all programs and to all processing chips.

USING EXTENDED MEMORY TO BREAK THE MEMORY BARRIER

The most obvious solution to memory constraints is to increase the amount of memory available in the system. If memory were easily added without limit, then such techniques as those discussed in the previous section would be unnecessary. Entire data files and program files supporting an enormous range of features could, regardless of their size, be easily loaded into memory.

Even though memory is becoming increasingly inexpensive, simply adding memory chips or boards is not the answer. Physical availability of memory on a system is not enough. The processing chip must be able to address that memory, and the operating system must also be able to gain access to the program code and data stored in that memory; the application programs themselves may need to modify their addressing techniques to make effective use of the new addresses located outside of conventional memory.

USING PROTECTED MODE TO EXTEND MEMORY ADDRESSABILITY

The 80286 chip from Intel offers a feature called *protected mode*. Whereas the 8088/8086 chips used 20 bits to construct an address (gaining access to 1 megabyte of memory), this chip uses 24 bits for addressing. Those extra 4 bits allow the protected mode of the chip to directly access 16Mb of memory ($2^4 = 16$), many times that allowed by earlier chips. Figure 19.4 depicts this enhanced feature of the 80286 chip.

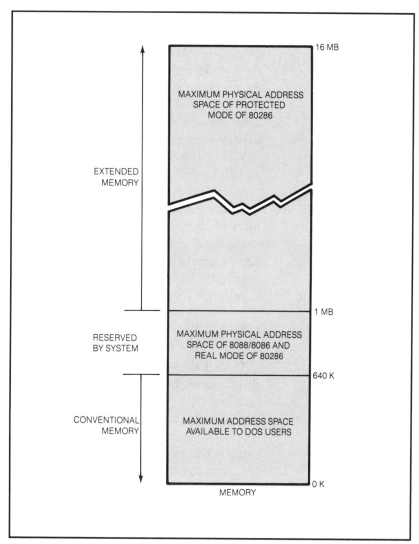

Figure 19.4: 80286 chips can address 16 megabytes of memory.

The 80286 chip has a split personality. With only a few assembly language instructions, the operating mode of the chip can be changed from real mode to protected mode. In protected mode, the extra address lines on the PC-AT and PS/2 computers allow access to 16 megabytes. This extra memory beyond one megabyte is called *extended memory*.

Unfortunately, most software (including DOS itself) has not been adapted to actually use any of the address space beyond one megabyte. However, DOS 3.X has been able to use this extra memory in the form of a RAM disk (called VDISK in IBM PC-DOS systems). Remember that RAM disks use memory addresses to store files in a special format that emulates the organization and accessibility of a disk drive. This allows disk operations such as on-line overlay transfers to work at memory speeds rather than at the much slower disk speeds.

With a RAM disk, only RAM disk software knows that the data and file access is actually from memory, not from a real disk drive. In fact, earlier RAM disk drivers often created virtual disks from unused memory locations in the conventional memory space below the 640K limit. In either case, however, you must first copy data files or overlay files from their real disk locations to the RAM disk before any programs can access them. After using the data files, you must remember to copy any changes back to their permanent file locations, typically on your hard disk.

LIMITATIONS OF EXTENDED MEMORY

Extended memory is just a tool. The 80286 chip provides access to that memory, but DOS is limited in its ability to use it. Instruction support in the ROM BIOS is extremely limited, being restricted to determining how much memory is installed and transferring data to and from conventional memory. DOS and the BIOS do not manage this extended memory in any sophisticated way, so it is difficult for multiple programs to use portions of extended memory simultaneously.

DOS still does not directly address the extended memory locations. The newest IBM operating system, OS/2, from Microsoft and IBM, does introduce a sophisticated memory manager that uses this extended memory directly. See my *Essential OS/2* (SYBEX, 1988) for more information about how this mechanism is implemented.

Certainly, extended memory can be used as more than just an area for large RAM disk operations. That's just what industry leaders proclaimed in 1985 when they announced new standards for memory utilization. These standards, known as the LIM specification, form the basis for the discussion in the next section.

USING EXPANDED MEMORY FOR MORE POWERFUL OPERATIONS

The next creative solution to memory constraints was developed in 1985 by Lotus Development Corporation and Intel. In an attempt to further stretch the capabilities of the millions of existing microcomputers, these companies announced a new specification for what they called *expanded memory*. After viewing early presentations of their specifications, Microsoft Corporation joined Lotus and Intel to release the LIM EMS (Lotus-Intel-Microsoft expanded memory specification 3.2.) This common standard became an overnight hit.

USING BANK SWITCHING TO EXPAND YOUR MEMORY

Like the size of conventional memory, the size of your desk surface is finite. You can assign a central portion of your desk to papers and folders, selected from a potentially unlimited number of files in your file cabinet. You can have a series of relevant papers on your desk, reserving one area for reference folders you get from and return to your file cabinet (see Figure 19.5).

Even though your desktop is physically limited in size, you can use unlimited reference materials by switching among file folders, reserving one portion of your desk as a "switching area." Although your desk may contain a variety of other materials that does not change, you can access 2, 5, or 50 file folders during your own personal information processing, though only one of these folders is open and accessible at any given moment.

Similarly, a computer can reserve a portion of conventional memory as a central "switching area." If this area is analogous to the file folder area in the center of your desk, then any number of similarly sized (or smaller) portions of extended memory can be logically brought into this area. This technique is called *bank switching* (a *bank* of storage addresses in memory is a physically and logically addressable unit). Figure 19.6 depicts this approach to memory expansion.

In the original LIM 3.2 specification, up to 8Mb of expanded memory could be accessed through one 64K reserved lower memory area. This area was typically carved out of an unused area of contiguous memory located in the sparsely used ROM area at the upper end of addressable memory (below 1Mb).

Figure 19.5: Desktop analogy for memory bank switching

The LIM EMS specification contained many details of expanded-memory management and of the interface between that memory and programs wanting to gain access to it. Many of these details are embodied in a program called the Expanded Memory Manager (EMM.SYS) which expanded memory systems must include as a device driver in the CONFIG.SYS file.

During system booting, when all device drivers are installed, EMM.SYS looks for a contiguous, available area of 64K in the uppermost 256K of memory reserved for ROM programs. When it finds such an area, EMM.SYS takes control of these addresses and uses them as a window into the separate expanded memory locations. IBM PCs and PC-XTs, as well as PC-ATs and PS/2S in real mode, can address only up to one megabyte; however, these 64K address locations are directly addressable by the processing chip.

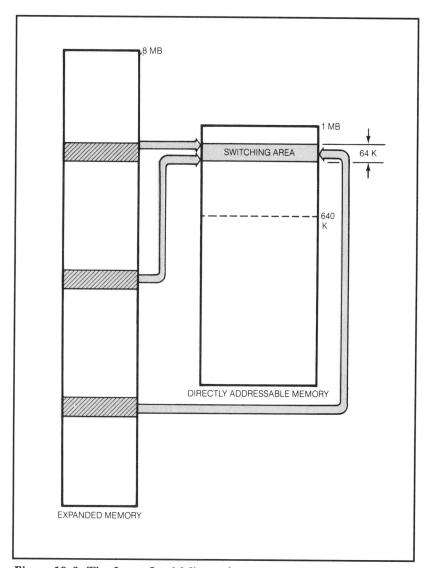

Figure 19.6: The Lotus-Intel-Microsoft expanded memory specification (LIM EMS 3.2)

When a program wants access to the additional memory locations in the expanded memory area, it must make a precisely defined interrupt call to EMM.SYS that provides the uniform interface to any of those locations. EMM.SYS enables this access by providing a unique programming handle to each program using expanded memory.

Figure 19.7: 8Mb of expanded memory is managed 16K at a time.

These programs can be single-tasking or multitasking programs, other device drivers, or even written memory-resident programs.

Even though the area reserved by the expanded memory manager is 64K in size, EMS 3.2 actually called for the banks to be only 16K in size. Hence, as can be seen in Figure 19.7, the EMM must manage the necessary access to up to 8Mb of physical expanded memory through the regimen of switching base addresses in units of 16K.

the necessary access to up to 8Mb of physical expanded memory through the regimen of switching base addresses in units of 16K.

Conventional memory programs can use this technique to access up to 8Mb of additional expanded memory, according to the original expanded-memory specification 3.2. They do so through software-interrupt calls to the EMM.SYS device driver. EMM.SYS switches banks of 16K memory addresses. The window into these expanded memory pages is provided and maintained by EMM.SYS in a contiguous block of 64K, carved out of the 256K ROM area at the top of the typical 1Mb address space.

All expanded memory is treated as a collection of memory banks, divided into 16K pages. Simple instructions are part of the memory specification, allowing programs to switch new 16K pages into the 64K addressable window or to switch existing pages and their data out of the window and back to expanded-memory locations.

In total, EMM.SYS provides a variety of services to a requesting program, well beyond the standard initialization and output functions of a standard device driver. EMM.SYS also provides information, through software-interrupt 67H, regarding hardware and software module statuses and the current allocation of expanded-memory pages. Diagnostic routines are available, as are routines to manage the actual mapping of logical pages into and out of expanded memory into physical pages in the 64K window.

The LIM EMS specification was the possible groundwork for the next generation of multitasking operating systems. But progress continued in the DOS world with the introduction of new products from industry competitors.

ENHANCING THE EXPANDED MEMORY SPECIFICATION

AST Research and Quadram are two of the industry leaders in the production of add-on memory boards, and Ashton-Tate is a major producer of personal computer software. Together, these three companies released their own new specifications for expanded memory use. Their enhanced version of EMS was called EEMS (enhanced expanded memory specification).

EEMS was more complex than EMS 3.2 and differed in key ways. Whereas EMS located the switching area above the DOS 640K program area, EEMS mapped expanded memory into addressable

EEMS enabled program code, not just data, to be switched into addressable memory locations below 640K.

space anywhere under the 1Mb address limit. This feature allowed easy switching of memory pages that contain addressable code because they could be switched into the lower memory addresses accessible by DOS programs.

EEMS also offered an expanded mapping window. Whereas EMS allowed the mapping of only four 16K logical expanded memory pages into physical memory, EEMS allowed the mapping of 64 logical pages (64 × 16K = 1Mb). EEMS also supported a minimum window size of 16K. In fact, as it turns out, the upper limit on window size was somewhat unrealistic, since much of that 1Mb is needed by DOS, application program code, video buffers, and system ROMs. The new EEMS specification did, however, realistically make available all free space: often as much as 20 logical pages.

EEMS also allowed software specification of mapping areas at runtime. Under EMS 3.2, you had to take great care setting the proper switches and jumpers on the memory boards to specify the mapping area. Additionally, EMS 3.2 required one contiguous 64K memory area. EEMS allowed the use of several areas that are not necessarily physically contiguous.

For a while, it was unclear which of these two heavyweight standards would emerge the winner. Microsoft's Windows used EMS to implement its multitasking strategy, and Quarterdeck's Desqview used EEMS in its more powerful multitasking operating environment. The differing concepts and implementation strategies of these memory specifications made writing programs that run easily under both specifications difficult. In fact, memory boards conforming to one specification do not necessarily work under the other.

EVERYONE WINS WITH THE LIM EMS 4.0 SPECIFICATION

Users of DOS and designers of programs in the DOS environment were gratified in 1987 by the announcement of the latest evolution of the expanded memory specifications. This latest announcement, variously referred to as LIM 4.0 or EMS 4.0, specifies a new set of developer functions that support much larger DOS application programs, as well as multitasking. These new specifications permit the use of these improved features on all DOS machines, even the seemingly more limited 8088/8086 PC and PC-XT models.

EMS 4.0 incorporates all of the best aspects of the earlier EMS 3.2, as well as the improvements made in EEMS, thus reducing confusion among program developers and setting EMS 4.0 apart as a viable standard for future program growth in the DOS world. The AST/Quadram/Ashton-Tate group has accepted the new standard.

The new standard defines more than twice the number of functions and subfunctions (30 versus 15) contained in EMS 3.2. In addition, accessible expanded memory has been increased from a maximum size of 8Mb to 32Mb. Incorporating some of the EEMS techniques ensures that EMS 4.0 supports the execution of both standard program code as well as TSR (terminate and stay resident, or memory-resident) programs in expanded memory.

EMS 4.0 directly supports multitasking. An occasional requirement of programs when they run concurrently with other programs is that they be able to share data. This new standard also defines how, specifically, common data access and sharing can take place.

The developers of EMS 4.0 clearly state that it is not itself a multitasking operating system. It does, however, provide a formidable array of features that allow applications to perform multitasking in expanded memory. A variety of programs, RAM disks, and print spoolers all can run simultaneously in expanded memory.

The new OS/2 system for IBM computers, on the other hand, is a full-blown multitasking operating system, with significantly enhanced features over both DOS and EMS 4.0. However, if your computer does not run OS/2 or you do not upgrade your system to OS/2, EMS 4.0 can breathe new life into your system. New software will undoubtedly be designed, and certainly much old software will be upgraded, to work in this enhanced DOS environment.

SAVING MONEY WITH EXPANDED MEMORY EMULATORS

If you have no available slots in your IBM PC or PC-XT for a specially designated expanded memory board, or if you choose to avoid the expense of a new expanded memory board, several vendors now offer help. This help may be especially relevant if you've already spent money on an AT-type extended memory board.

Since the expanded memory specification is device independent, the source of the expanded memory is unimportant to applications using it. Therefore, just as surely as a piece of software can cause memory to be perceived as a RAM disk, so a piece of software can cause a disk to be perceived as memory.

In fact, the same concept can be taken one step further. Expanded memory-emulation software can adhere to the EMS requirements, providing memory pages not from an expanded memory board, but from any one of the sources shown in Figure 19.8.

The emulation software conforms to the expanded memory specifications, so the source of the data is irrelevant to an application program making the proper EMS calls. The source could be a standard expanded memory hardware board, as shown at the top of figure 19.8, or it could be one of the two sources for emulated expanded memory, as shown at the bottom of the figure.

If your system already includes extended memory, you can configure the emulation software to use that memory as if it were expanded memory. Naturally, the drawback of this method is the extra software overhead (which can be considerable) required for the emulated access.

Even if your system has no additional memory installed, you still can run software requiring expanded memory. The emulation routines can create a disk file equal in size to the simulated expanded memory that you need but don't have. The emulator handles the reading and writing of the disk file to obtain the 16K pages needed by the expanded memory manager. This solution permits you to run software in an expanded memory environment, albeit at significantly reduced speeds because of the relatively enormous disk input/output overhead.

Although emulation may seem attractive, it has some obvious drawbacks. As pointed out, using it is markedly slower than using expanded memory directly. The overhead for the software emulation is considerable, and, if you are using a disk file to emulate expanded memory, the disk I/O overhead further reduces overall system performance. In addition, emulation software is not always completely compatible with programs designed to run using actual hardware boards. So even if you're willing to endure reduced performance, you still may not be able to run your favorite expanded memory program.

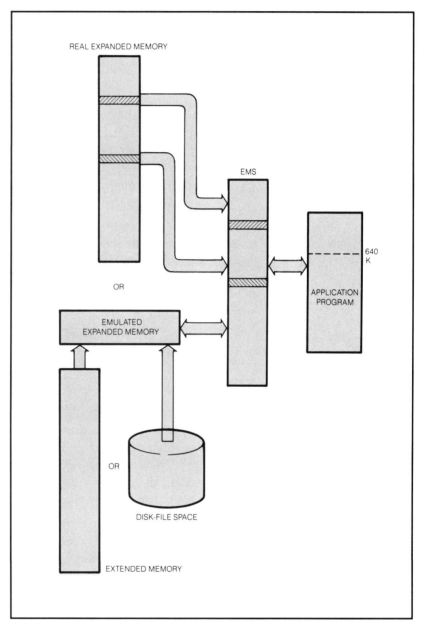

Figure 19.8: Expanded memory can be emulated in either AT-style extended memory or in disk files created just for this purpose.

SUMMARY

You've learned a variety of creative approaches in this chapter, all aimed at surmounting the 640K limit imposed by DOS on application programs.

- Early solutions concentrated on reusing memory within the application's .EXE space. Large amounts of data was managed within internal buffers maintained by the program. Larger amounts of executable code were managed by grouping the instructions into separate *overlay* files which would later use the same area of memory, but at different times.

- 80286 chip technology enabled direct addressing of up to 16Mb of extended memory. However, very few programs written for DOS took advantage of this possibility, since it required the special *protected* mode of the hardware. DOS itself used extended memory only for its RAM disk configuration feature.

- Major industry leaders (Lotus, Intel, and Microsoft) defined a set of specifications (LIM 3.2) for addressing up to 8Mb of *expanded* memory through small 16K blocks of memory reserved from locations in lower memory (under 1Mb). This is called "bank switching".

- The Enhanced Expanded Memory Specification (EEMS) was created by Ashton-Tate and Quadram to improve upon the LIM definitions. Both groups of specifications have been collectively grouped and improved in the 1987 announcement of the LIM 4.0 Expanded Memory Specification.

- As an alternative to those unwilling or unable to buy or add expanded memory boards to your computers, you can emulate expanded memory with either extended memory or even disk files. Both of these techniques save money, but have a severe performance impact on your system.

RUNNING DOS PROGRAMS
IN OS/2

OS/2 PROVIDES MANY DRAMATIC IMPROVEMENTS
over DOS. The range and nature of these new capabilities are presented in detail in my 1988 book, *Essential OS/2*, from SYBEX. Each
of the preceding two chapters in this book presented techniques and
programs designed for the DOS arena which provide some of OS/2's
standard capabilities. Chapter 18 concentrated on the multitasking
capabilities of Windows, and Chapter 19 focused on methods for
addressing memory in excess of 640K.

OS/2 features multitasking for all new programs written for its
special protected mode environment. This protected mode is an
inherent, but previously little-used capability of the 80286 and 80386
processing chips. OS/2 also features memory management logic
which enables programs to address physical memory up to 16 Mb,
and even enables programs to write code for addressing memory
beyond what physically exists; this then is called *virtual memory*.

In this chapter, you'll learn an important OS/2 benefit: you are
not required to buy or write completely new programs, because
almost all of your DOS programs can run under OS/2. OS/2 can
give you the benefits of a dramatically improved operating system,
including the enhanced new features, without losing the functionality
of your current DOS programs.

The compatibility between DOS and OS/2 is provided through the
OS/2 *real mode*, which emulates DOS 3.3. Real mode provides an operating environment that allows you to run most of your DOS 3.X programs with no changes. In fact, many programs that predate DOS 3.X
will also run in OS/2's real mode. This real mode is the portion of OS/2
that only uses the portion of the 80286/80386 chips, also called real

mode, that merely acts like a very fast DOS 8088/8086 processing chip. You may sometimes hear this real mode referred to as the DOS Compatability Box.

This chapter also explains the steps necessary to make a smooth transition from DOS to the OS/2 environment including setting up, starting up, and configuring your OS/2 environment to permit DOS programs to run. Additionally, you will learn a number of important distinctions between the two operating environments, and potential obstacles to running DOS programs in OS/2. The chapter examines a broad range of issues, from proper configuration to initial batch file contents to some of the more complex programming issues of OS/2 function calls.

WORKING IN REAL MODE

In order to run DOS programs, you must switch the processing chip from OS/2's protected, multitasking mode to its DOS compatible real mode. When OS/2's protected mode (the normal default mode) starts up, you are presented with one of several possibilities. First, you may see the primary Session Manager screen which lists all running programs, as well as program and mode possibilities. Second, you may see some main program (perhaps a menu screen) running. Or, you may simply see the normal protected mode command interpreter prompt, [C:\]. If your version of OS/2 does not automatically display the Session Manager, perhaps because someone has configured it in a special way, you can easily display this important management screen. Pressing the Ctrl-Esc key combination displays Figure 20.1, the Session Manager screen. At this point under OS/2, you can use your cursor keys and the Return key to start new programs or switch to a running program from the Session Manager.

If you want to run a DOS application, the simplest method is to bring up the Session Manager screen and use the right arrow key to highlight the MS-DOS Command Prompt choice. Then press the Return key. This moves you and the processor into real mode and the DOS command line prompt. If you had selected CMD.EXE, you would have been switched to the OS/2 (protected mode) command prompt. The OS/2 CMD.EXE command file interpreter handles all protected mode OS/2 command requests, while the COMMAND.COM command

If you follow the instructions in this section and get a message saying Insufficient Memory, don't worry that the 3Mb of RAM you bought aren't enough to run your old program. They are. The next section on configuration explains how to configure your new OS/2 system to understand the different memory requirements of the DOS programs you'll be running in OS/2's real mode.

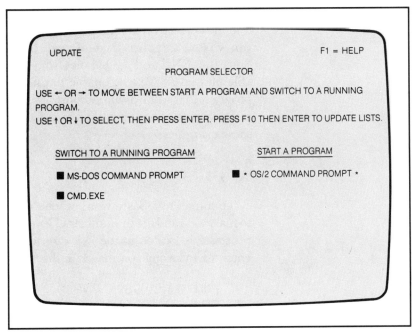

Figure 20.1: OS/2 Session Manager program selector menu at startup

line interpreter handles all real mode command line requests. Once you have brought up COMMAND.COM, you can continue as if your machine were running DOS alone. If you've loaded your disk with your applications, set your PATH and your working directory as required to run the DOS program.

If you try to run one of your DOS programs (.EXE or .COM) from the protected mode command prompt, you will receive one of the following two error messages:

> **DOS0191E: The system has detected an unacceptable signature in the file, *Filename*.**

or

> **DOS0193E: The system has detected an unacceptable executable format in file, *Filename*.**

OS/2 displays one of these two messages when you try to run a file that is either formatted incorrectly for OS/2, or represents an incorrect version of the program. Under most conditions, you would try to find the correct version of the program. In this case, you are trying to run what you know is the real mode or DOS version of the program. Since the .EXE and .COM files from DOS are unreadable as executable files in OS/2, it is unable to understand the instructions. Any program that was originally compiled, assembled, or prepared to run in DOS mode can be run only in OS/2's real mode. Let's look at some examples.

RUNNING YOUR WORD PROCESSOR

To run a DOS-based word processor on OS/2, you must first switch to real mode and get the familiar C> prompt. In this example, the word processor is located in the WP directory of the C drive. To access it, enter the following commands at the C> prompt:

```
PATH C:\;C:\OS2;C:\WP
CD \WP
WP
```

The first line augments the system search path in order to look for files in the root first, then to search the OS2 directory for any necessary supporting routines (such as the external commands CHKDSK or XCOPY), and lastly to look in the WP directory (where the word processor in this example can be found). The second line performs the standard change directory (CD) request to make the word processing directory the current default. The final step in real mode asks the COMMAND.COM interpreter to pass control to your version of WP.COM or WP.EXE, depending on which word processor you are using.

RUNNING YOUR DATABASE MANAGEMENT PROGRAM

Now suppose that you have a database program whose main and support files are located in a directory called DBMS. You want to run your inventory program located in a subdirectory of the DBMS directory called INVNTRY. You want to switch to the INVNTRY subdirectory that contains the inventory database information, but you must still ensure that the principal DBMS files are accessible through the PATH. Use the following sequence of statements in real mode:

```
PATH C:\;C:\OS2;C:\DBMS
APPEND \DBMS
CD \DBMS\INVNTRY
DBASE
```

In this example, your working directory is now the INVNTRY directory. This is where the dBASE.COM program will look for the appropriate database files or create new ones. The PATH command meanwhile ensures that OS/2 knows how to find its appropriate system files in either the root or the OS2 directory. Because of the PATH command, OS/2 can also find the main dBASE program in the DBMS directory. The APPEND command, on the other hand, enables the system to locate any required overlay files used by the main executable dBASE programs.

RUNNING YOUR SPREADSHEET PROGRAM

Finally, you may wish to run a favorite spreadsheet, like Lotus 1-2-3. All of Lotus's main system files may be located in the LOTUS subdirectory, while all of your budget worksheets are located in a subdirectory called BUDGET, and your accounting worksheets are located in a different subdirectory called ACCOUNTS. Like database managers, sophisticated spreadsheets usually work on an overlay basis. You therefore need the following sequence of steps to run this kind of application in OS/2's real mode:

```
PATH C:\;C:\OS2;C:\LOTUS
APPEND \LOTUS
CD \LOTUS\ACCOUNTS
123
```

As you can see in Figure 20.2, the CD command makes the ACCOUNTS directory the current working directory (pointed to by the arrow in Figure 20.2). To OS/2 this means that your worksheet

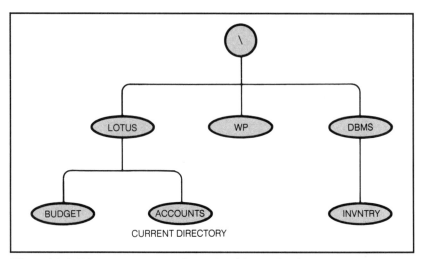

Figure 20.2: Directory structure for real mode applications

files will be accessible in that directory. If you want to switch to the BUDGET directory, do so either from within Lotus, or modify the CD command before running the 123.EXE program. The PATH and APPEND lines again direct the OS/2 system to find the main 123.EXE program (via PATH), and any subordinate overlay files (via APPEND), in the LOTUS directory.

Most DOS programs will run if you follow the instructions above. As mentioned at the beginning of this section, however, some programs may not run directly because they require more memory than the default number of kilobytes allotted by OS/2 to real mode. If this is the only problem, you'll get an Insufficient Memory message, and you should follow the guidelines for configuring your system in the next section.

If your program doesn't run in real mode for some other reason, read about potential obstacles in the "Distinctions and Obstacles" section of this chapter. Your program may use certain system interrupts or DOS function calls for manipulating hardware that are not allowed in any program in the OS/2 environment, even in real mode. In these cases, you must either find a replacement program or get the errant program rewritten for the OS/2 environment.

CONFIGURING YOUR OS/2 SYSTEM FOR DOS PROGRAMS

Some versions of OS/2 offer a dual boot feature which enables a single hard disk to maintain complete and separate OS/2 and DOS systems. During the bootstrap process, you are asked to choose which of the two systems you want to establish as the actual controlling operating system.

In both DOS and OS/2, the system assumes certain default values if you do not specify new ones with a CONFIG.SYS file. In OS/2 as in DOS, there is only one controlling configuration file. However, in some versions of OS/2 from Microsoft, you have the option of installing both DOS and OS/2 on a single hard disk. In this case, a CONFIG.SYS file controls the booting of DOS, while a separate CONFIG.OS2 file oversees the booting of OS/2. If both systems are not installed on the same disk, then CONFIG.SYS becomes the controlling file containing all configuration information.

OS/2 allows you to override any or all of a host of initial values for internal systems parameters. The control you have via this initial file is so much enhanced over DOS that an entire chapter of *Essential OS/2* is entirely devoted to the initial setup conditions now under your control. This chapter, however, addresses only the minimum required to enable DOS programs to run in real mode. Figure 20.3 shows an example CONFIG.SYS file.

When you first install OS/2, the installation program (INSTAID.EXE) prepares a CONFIG.SYS (or CONFIG.OS2) file such as this one for you. As you can see in line 12, the SHELL command specifies that the DOS COMMAND.COM program will be a permanently resident command interpreter for real mode instructions (indicated by the /p switch). All of the lines in this prototype CONFIG.SYS file are as they appear during initial installation of OS/2, except lines 13, 18, and 19. Line 13 is essential to DOS programs. During OS/2 initialization, the default is to install a real mode memory size of 256K (RMSIZE = 256).

If you configure OS/2 to run DOS applications, use the maximum RMSIZE value of 640 to help protect running OS/2 programs from errant DOS programs running at the same time.

At first glance, the RMSIZE parameter enables you to simply tell OS/2 how much of its low memory to reserve for DOS program execution. If you do not use all 640K for the real mode area, OS/2 uses the remainder of these low memory addresses for running OS/2 (protected mode) programs. Unfortunately, since errant DOS programs have access to all memory addresses below 1Mb, a failed DOS program can adversely affect protected mode programs and data which happen to be occupying low memory addresses. For this reason, you should always configure your OS/2 system (with the RMSIZE parameter) to consume all 640K.

```
 1   REM
 2   REM    Prototype Config.sys file for OS/2 when booting off a hard disk
 3   REM
 4   REM
 5   REM    If your system has less than 2MB of RAM, shrink the size of the
 6   REM    diskcache and the real mode box.  If you are not going to use the
 7   REM    compatibility mode then remove the REM statement from the line that
 8   REM    reads PROTECTONLY=yes
 9   REM
10
11   BUFFERS=50
12   SHELL=Command.com /p /e:512 c:\
13   RMSIZE=640
14   PROTSHELL=Shell.exe Cmd.exe
15   IOPL=yes
16   LIBPATH=C:\
17   MEMMAN=Noswap,move
18   DEVICE=Ansi.sys
19   DEVICE=Hardrive.sys
20
21   REM    The rest of the file contains commented out lines.  Delete the word
22   REM    REM from the begining of the command lines if that feature is needed
23   REM    or wanted.
24
25   REM PROTECTONLY=yes
26   REM DISKCACHE=512
27   REM SWAPPATH=C:
28   REM DEVICE=C:\Com01.sys
29   REM DEVICE=C:\Vdisk.sys 256 512 16
30   REM DEVICE=C:\Pointdd.sys
31
32   REM    Select one of the following drivers:
33   REM     02 - serial, 03 - Bus, 04 - Import
34   REM DEVICE=C:\Mousea02.sys mode=b
35   REM DEVICE=C:\Mousea03.sys mode=b
36   REM DEVICE=C:\Mousea04.sys mode=b
37
38   REM    The following lines enable the Code Page support drivers.
39
40   REM DEVINFO=scr,ega,C:\Viotbl.dcp
41   REM DEVINFO=kbd,us, C:\Keyboard.dcp
42   REM DEVINFO=lpt1,4201,C:\4201.dcp,rom=(437,0)
43   REM CODEPAGE=437,850
```

Figure 20.3: Sample CONFIG.SYS file

In any event, if your automatically generated configuration file does not allocate enough real mode memory, you can use your line editor or word processor to change the value in line 13. It is not unusual to use all 640K in real mode for large, demanding programs like computer-aided design programs, or for certain memory resident utility programs that are run in conjunction with standard software. In this case, the DOS real mode will almost surely need to occupy 640K and you must make sure that your CONFIG.SYS file contains the line

RMSIZE = 640

In fact, since OS/2 itself occupies approximately 100K of low memory, you really only have about 540K left for DOS applications running

OS/2 uses up 100K of the low 640K memory locations. DOS programs which formerly required all 640K will not be able to run in OS/2's real mode.

in the real mode. Naturally, then, some DOS applications with extensive DOS memory requirements will not even be able to run in this OS/2 emulation environment (real mode).

Depending on need, applications, and installed hardware, you may also have to add extra lines such as lines 18 and 19. Some application programs, like the PreCursor menu management application program, require that the ANSI.SYS device driver be added to your CONFIG.SYS file (line 18). It is available at all times in protected mode for OS/2 programming and applications. However, you must load the ANSI.SYS device driver yourself (by including the line DEVICE = ANSI.SYS in your CONFIG.SYS file) if you intend to use special ANSI escape sequences in real mode such as cursor movement, graphics characters, and colors on color monitors. (Read the section on the PROMPT command in Chapter 10 for a full explanation of ANSI escape sequences.)

The last example insertion in this CONFIG.SYS file is seen on line 19: DEVICE = HARDRIVE.SYS. This line is for a system with a nonstandard hard disk installed, and a hard-disk device driver called HARDRIVE.SYS. Your system may have this or other unique installed devices, each of which requires the insertion of a line of this kind:

DEVICE = *drivername*

As you can see in Figure 20.3, there are a number of other sample features that are included as remarks (REM statements). These are suggested additions and you can invoke any of the special configuration parameter situations by removing the REM from the beginning of the desired line (as lines 21 through 23 explain). Read Chapter 9 of *Essential OS/2* for further information on any of these additional commands. If you're only interested in the minimum requirements for running DOS programs at this time, continue to the next section on startup programs and procedures.

CONTROLLING AUTOMATIC STARTUP IN OS/2 REAL MODE

When you first boot up your OS/2 system, the internal setup of OS/2 is completely initialized according to the command requests placed in the CONFIG.SYS file. These commands influence OS/2 and its internal settings one time only. They are acted upon at system bootup, and are not interpreted or acted upon again until the next time you boot up OS/2.

In contrast to this, Figure 20.4 represents the system flow that can be influenced by you at system start. In DOS, the system would automatically run a special startup batch file called AUTOEXEC-.BAT immediately after configuration and before giving you control at the command prompt. OS/2 has a similar mechanism.

In real mode, the same AUTOEXEC.BAT runs with the same results. If you have a file called AUTOEXEC.BAT in the root directory of your boot drive, all of the individual command line entries contained within it will be executed one after the other the first time OS/2 switches

Your AUTO-EXEC.BAT and STARTUP.CMD batch files must reside in the root directory of your boot disk.

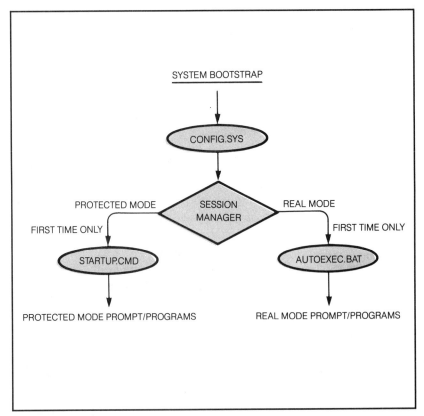

Figure 20.4: Automatic system startup flow

to real mode. Just as in DOS 3.X systems, all real mode batch files are named with a .BAT extension; the AUTOEXEC.BAT allows for this automatic execution of a "batch" of commands. Paralleling this automatic invocation of the AUTOEXEC.BAT file is another batch file called STARTUP.CMD that is automatically invoked the first time OS/2 switches to protected mode. However, unlike the CONFIG.SYS file, which can only be invoked at system startup, both these batch files can be run at any time. As OS/2 is implemented, the processor comes up in protected mode, so the STARTUP.CMD file (if it exists) is run automatically. This is directly comparable to the automatic running of AUTOEXEC.BAT in a DOS system.

The AUTOEXEC.BAT file can be a sequence of commands like those you are familiar with from DOS as shown below:

```
SET COMSPEC = C:\COMMAND.COM
SET PATH = C:\;C:\OS2
PROMPT $n$g
```

The system PATH is set for system files and external command files. The COMSPEC parameter is also set (for clarification only, because C:\COMMAND.COM is the usual default file and directory), which tells OS/2 where it will be able to find the real mode interpreter (COMMAND.COM). The PROMPT command in the third line initializes the default system prompt to $n (the working drive) followed by $g (a chevron symbol). As you read in Chapter 15, there is no end to the many additions and modifications you can make to this AUTOEXEC.BAT file, allowing a more flexible and utilitarian startup sequence for your system.

You can use this AUTOEXEC.BAT file to tell OS/2 how to access your old DOS files automatically. To do so, look at a copy of your own DOS system AUTOEXEC.BAT file, and then add your own appropriate adjustments or new lines to OS/2's default AUTOEXEC.BAT file. In the simplest case, you can leave the COMSPEC and the PROMPT lines alone. You might adjust the PATH command in your AUTOEXEC.BAT to include reference to the DBMS and LOTUS directories, by changing it as follows:

```
SET PATH = C:\;C:\OS2;C:\DBMS;C:\LOTUS
```

An APPEND line of the following sort tells the system where the overlay files can be found for your application programs:

APPEND C:\DBMS;C:\LOTUS

At the end of your Autoexec.BAT file, you can pass control to a hard-disk menu-management utility you've already set up by adding the following line:

PREMENU

This passes control to the main menu program of a hard-disk management package, giving you and other users of your system potential access to all executable DOS programs on your hard disk.

DISTINCTIONS AND OBSTACLES

If you follow the simple guidelines in the previous sections, you should have your old DOS programs up and running in no time. In most cases, it's as simple as adding a couple of lines to the CONFIG.SYS file and a couple of lines in an AUTOEXEC.BAT file. But life is not always so simple, and certain DOS programs will never run under OS/2. For example, a sophisticated backup system such as Back-It Version 3.0 uses direct memory access (DMA) to achieve very high performance. Data are written to floppy disks at the same time as data are read from the hard disk. This particular program does not work successfully under OS/2, because OS/2 does not allow some of the interrupt-based techniques that are used. However, it can (and probably will) be rewritten using the simultaneous threads technique so that it will run in OS/2.

Some programs can be made to run with slight adjustments to the code, but this requires that you are either able to get into the code to adjust it, or that the programmer can provide you with an upgraded version of the code. In this section, you will learn some of the distinctions that should be considered in attempting to make or rewrite these programs.

Let's take a look first at some of the overlapping issues in the DOS and OS/2 operating environments. Figure 20.5 shows a number of

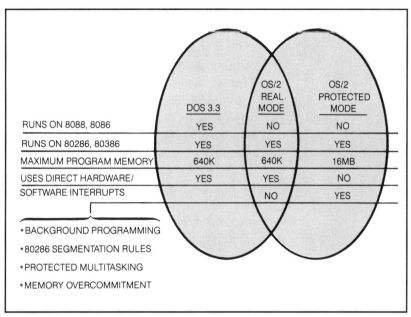

Figure 20.5: Overlap of OS/2 and DOS 3.3 features

the key distinctions between OS/2 and DOS 3.3. It also shows the overlap that allows DOS 3.3 applications to run in OS/2's real mode.

OS/2 uses the hardware features of the 80286 and 80386 chip for protected mode operations, and will not run on machines based on 8088 or 8086 chips. DOS, although it will run on the more advanced chips, uses only the real mode portion of the chip. Because they do not take advantage of any of the advanced hardware operations of the new chips, DOS programs, whether run under DOS directly or in OS/2's real mode, are limited to 640K of addressable memory.

Although they can make direct use of hardware interrupts, DOS programs running under OS/2 cannot participate in protected multitasking. This means that during protected mode operations, your real mode DOS program is frozen. It receives no interrupts and does not continue executing, because it receives no CPU service while you are executing in protected mode. In addition, the advanced programming features of *segmentation* and *memory overcommitment* can't be used completely by DOS programs.

Segmentation refers to the partitioning of memory by logical addresses rather than physical addresses, enabling you to run

If your program is timer or clock dependent, it will not work properly.

programs that can reference more memory than actually exists. Virtual memory, through OS/2's sophisticated memory manager, provides the ability to offer more apparent (virtual) memory to a running process than there is physical (actual) memory available. This is called memory overcommitment.

Some DOS programs are version specific and will only run on versions 2.X or 3.X. These may not work under OS/2, because the numbering of versions is different. As well, the set of system calls and returned error values differs from version to version.

Those of you accustomed to programming with interrupts may have written your programs to use interrupt 21H services under DOS. Most of the working but undocumented services through this interrupt are no longer supported by OS/2 real mode. Certain service interrupts that access ROM video services by address won't work either, because the management of interrupt 10 has been dramatically changed in OS/2.

There are many internal distinctions in the methods programmers must use to handle interrupts, manage devices, and code their applications. As a result, Microsoft has defined a special subset of its total system calls that are designed to work in both real mode and protected mode environments. This subset is called the Family Application Program Interface (FAPI) of the complete OS/2 Application Programming Interface (API), and is the suggested subset for programs run in both real mode and protected mode. Programs written in this way can also be run on machines using DOS 2.X or 3.X, depending on which actual subset of instructions are chosen by the application programmer.

If you are writing commercial code that you want to run in either environment, you would certainly do well to write it with the FAPI set of functions. It ensures that users will have much greater ease running your code in either operating system environment, eliminates the drain on physical memory, and enhances the performance and usefulness of the entire OS/2 system.

Since interrupt handling has changed drastically under OS/2, older special purpose DOS device drivers will surely not work in the OS/2 environment.

SUMMARY

One of the first ways you will probably use your OS/2 system is to run your DOS programs. Even if you are using OS/2 primarily for new programs, there will probably be times you will want to run DOS programs. This chapter detailed the steps to take to exploit this attractive functionality of OS/2.

- Real mode runs DOS programs in OS/2. OS/2 allows you to reserve (through CONFIG.SYS) a portion of physical memory (up to 640K) for emulating a DOS 3.X environment.

- When you switch to real mode, you can run most existing application programs and all standard DOS commands, like CD or PROMPT.

- A CONFIG.SYS file initializes both real mode and protected mode operations. Some configuration commands control initial conditions in real mode, and others control these startup system values in protected mode. To run real mode programs, the most important command is the RMSIZE parameter, which must be set equal to the number of kilobytes your DOS program requires.

- The first time real mode is entered from the Session Manager, a batch file called AUTOEXEC.BAT executes. All commands within it are assumed to be standard batch file commands, adhering to standard batch file processing rules.

- When OS/2 first boots, a special batch file called START-UP.CMD executes in protected mode, enabling you to initialize your working environment for protected mode operations.

- If no STARTUP.CMD file exists in the root directory of the boot drive, OS/2 starts up with the Session Manager screen. A special keystroke, Ctrl-Esc, can bring this special screen into view, regardless of what happens to be running on your OS/2 system.

- The number of overlapping features between OS/2 and DOS 3.3 explains the compatibility that allows many DOS programs to run in OS/2 real mode. But because DOS and OS/2 are not completely compatible, some DOS programs cannot run at all, while others require rewriting.

Now that you understand how to run your favorite DOS programs in your new operating environment, OS/2, you can take a closer look at OS/2 itself. In this way, you'll gain a better appreciation for the significant improvement in capability and flexibility offered by this new operating system. *Essential OS/2* covers the fundamentals of OS/2, while *Mastering OS/2* (forthcoming from SYBEX) was designed to concentrate on the broader graphics-based Presentation Manager version of OS/2.

PART 6

DOS COMMAND REFERENCE

Chapter 21 contains a detailed, alphabetized reference to all the DOS commands, parameters, and switches. These include commands that were too specialized to describe in the main body of the book, and infrequently used parameters and switches for the more common commands. Refer to Chapter 18 as you read this book to obtain a complete understanding of each command. After you finish reading the book, you can use Chapter 21 any time you want a quick reference to a command's format and options.

Three appendices are also included to make your use of DOS a little easier. Appendix A is a complete glossary of important computer terms used in this book. As you are reading, you should refer to the glossary every time you run across an unfamiliar term. Appendix B is an extended table of ASCII codes, with an explanation of character sets and numbering systems. Appendix C contains complete instructions for configuring or reconfiguring your hard disk.

DOS PROMPT, BATCH-FILE AND CONFIGURATION COMMANDS

CHAPTER *21*

THIS CHAPTER PROVIDES CAPSULE SUMMARIES OF all DOS 3.3 commands. The majority of these commands are described in more detail in previous chapters of this book (see the index for specific pages); however, the summaries presented here can be used for quick reference to each of the individual commands.

Some commands not covered previously in this book are only needed occasionally, but are presented here for completeness. All batch-file subcommands and all configuration (CONFIG.SYS) commands are reviewed in this chapter as well.

Each capsule summary begins with a general description of the command, followed by its format or formats and the definitions of its switches and parameters. Brackets indicate optional switches and parameters. Vertical bars indicate "either/or" choices. The command's type, and any restrictions on the command's use, close each command capsule.

APPEND

The APPEND command causes the computer to search through a predetermined set of directories. It will not, however, search for files ending in .COM, .BAT, or .EXE, but for files with extensions other than these. The APPEND command allows DOS to open files that will be read from or written to. The PATH command must therefore still be used to find executable files.

Format
[D:Path]APPEND[D1:Path1][;D2:Path2...][/X][/E][;]

D:Path is the drive and path where the command file is located if it is not in the current directory.

D1:Path1 is the first drive and directory searched after the default drive and directory.

D2:Path2... is the second drive and directory searched after the default drive and directory, and so on.

/X causes APPEND to process the searching methods SEARCH FIRST, FIND FIRST, and EXEC (for programmers only).

/E stores the paths in the DOS environment (which means they can be changed through SET, but that they will be lost when a secondary processor exits).

The ; symbol alone nullifies the APPEND command by erasing the path list.

Type
Transient upon first execution, resident after first execution.

Unless specified, files will be saved by APPEND in the default directory instead of in the directory they were called from, if that directory was not the default directory.

Restrictions
There are 128 bytes of space in which to specify the paths. Do not use this command in conjunction with the different APPEND command used in the IBM PC Network program 1.00 or in the IBM PC LAN program 1.10.

ASSIGN

The ASSIGN command causes any requests for one drive to be carried out on another drive. With parameters, assignments are made. Without parameters, ASSIGN cancels all current assignments.

Format
[*D:Path*]ASSIGN [*SourceD = DestD*] [...]

D:Path is the drive and path where the command file is located if it is not in the current directory.

SourceD is the drive to be rerouted.

DestD is the drive that will handle *SourceD*'s requests.

... are additional assignments.

Type
Transient.

Restrictions

Do not use ASSIGN with BACKUP, RESTORE, LABEL, JOIN, SUBST, or PRINT. ASSIGN is ignored by FORMAT, DISKCOPY, and DISKCOMP.

ATTRIB

The ATTRIB command is the command used to change the read/write and archive file attributes. When used with parameters, ATTRIB changes the attributes of a file. When used without the parameters, ATTRIB displays the attributes.

Format

[*D:Path*]ATTRIB [+ R¦ – R][+ A¦ – A][*FileSpec*][/S]

D:Path is the drive and path where the command file is located if it is not in the current directory.

+ R makes *FileSpec* read-only.

– R makes *FileSpec* read/write operations possible.

+ A sets the archive bit of *FileSpec*.

– A resets the archive bit of *FileSpec*.

FileSpec is an optional drive and path, plus the file name and extension, of the file that is the object of the command. Wild cards are allowed.

/S causes all files in the directory and its subdirectories to be modified.

Type

Transient.

BACKUP

This command performs a backup of your hard disk. Since many errors may occur on such a large volume of data, backing up is a must. BACKUP saves all of your current data, file by file, directory by directory, to diskettes.

Format

[D:Path]BACKUP SourceD:[FileSpec] DestD:
     [/S][/M][/A][/D:mm-dd-yy] [/T:hh:mm:ss][/F][/L[:LogFileSpec]]

D:Path is the drive and path where the command file is located if it is not in the current directory.

SourceD is the drive specification of the source drive to be backed up; this can be a diskette or a hard disk.

FileSpec is an optional drive and path, plus the file name and extension, of the file that is the object of the command. Wild cards are allowed.

DestD is where the backups will be stored (a diskette or a hard disk).

/S backs up files of the current specified directory.

/M backs up modified files.

Unless the /A parameter is used, BACKUP will erase all the files on *DestD*. The target disk will be formatted according to the capacity of the drive. Mismatches in capacity and formatting are not allowed.

/A appends the backup files to the files already on *DestD* instead of writing over them.

/D:*mm-dd-yy* works like /M, but the "modified since" date is specified by *mm-dd-yy*, not the last backup date.

/T:*hh:mm:ss* backs up files on or after the indicated time when /D is used.

/F causes BACKUP to format the destination disk if it has not already been formatted.

/L creates a log file.

LogFileSpec is an optional name for the log file (the default name is BACKUP.LOG).

Type
Transient.

Restrictions

You cannot back up files that you are sharing but do not currently have access to. Do not use BACKUP with JOIN, SUBST, APPEND, or ASSIGN. FORMAT must be available for use in the same directory as BACKUP, since it may be needed to format the target disk.

BREAK

This command makes programs easier to interrupt. Turning BREAK on makes DOS check more often for the Ctrl-Break key combination. For example, if you are compiling a long program and the compiler encounters an error and gets stuck in a loop, you will want to halt execution. Having BREAK set to ON will allow you to do this.

Format
BREAK [ON ¦ OFF]

ON enables Ctrl-Break.

OFF disables the Ctrl-Break function (this is the default).

Type
Resident.

—————— *BUFFERS* ——————

This command causes a certain number of file-transfer buffers to be set aside in memory. While most programs only require a few buffers, remember that every disk access requires one. It is recommended that you set BUFFERS equal to the appropriate number, as shown in Table 18.1. Note that a value of 3 buffers for system RAM of less than or equal to 128K is used only for high-capacity drives.

BUFFERS VALUE	SYSTEM RAM (K)
2 or 3	< =128
5	129–256
10	257–512
15	513 and up

Table 18.1: BUFFER settings per system RAM

Format
BUFFERS = x

x is the number of buffers to be set up. If this command is not specified, DOS 3.3 will determine the number of buffers automatically, based on the current system memory.

Type
Configuration.

CALL

CALL allows a true subroutine capability in DOS 3.3. When you are executing a batch file, it may sometimes be necessary to run a second batch file and then return to the first batch file at the place where the second file was called. In other words, you may want to run a second batch file without having to completely restart the first one. This can be done with the CALL command.

Format

CALL *FileSpec*

> *FileSpec* is the optional drive and path name, plus the file name, of the second batch file to be executed.

Type

Batch, resident.

Restrictions

CALL should not be used to pipe or redirect output. Recursive calls are allowed, but you are responsible for ensuring that the logic eventually ends.

CHCP

This command allows you to change the currently loaded code page for all eligible installed devices. The NLSFUNC command must be loaded prior to using CHCP. Although this command is internal, it may need to access the COUNTRY.SYS file. Should this be the case, and should the COUNTRY.SYS file not be on the default drive, DOS will display the message "File not found."

Format
CHCP [xxx]

   xxx is the code-page number.

Type
   Resident.

Restrictions
   The corresponding device drivers for the specified code page must be available. NLSFUNC must have been executed previous to this command.

CHDIR (CD)

When moving through the directory structure, you must change the directory you are in. CHDIR (or simply CD) is an easy way to do that. Executing CHDIR .. will put you in the immediate parent directory of the directory you are in. (The two-dot symbol denotes this particular parent directory.)

Format

C[H]D[IR] [*D:Path*]

D:Path is the optional drive and path specifying which directory you wish to make the default directory.

Type

Resident.

CHKDSK

A problem in the system area can prevent you from using your disk. The correctional facilities of CHKDSK will help you solve such a problem by resolving errors in the disk's file allocation table.

Format

[*D:Path*]CHKDSK [*FileSpec*][/F][/V]

D:Path is the drive and path where the command file is located if it is not in the current directory.

FileSpec is an optional drive and path, plus the file name and extension, of the file that is the object of the command. Wild cards are allowed.

/F allows corrections on the disk.

/V lists all files and their paths.

Type

Transient.

Restrictions

CHKDSK will not work on drives created by JOIN or SUBST, or on networked drives.

CLS

Sometimes the screen becomes cluttered, or you have a batch file that does many different things, and you no longer need to see everything put on the screen. To clear the screen, you can use the CLS command. After the screen erasure, the cursor is placed at the top left of the screen.

Format
CLS

Type
Resident.

COMMAND

The COMMAND.COM command processor, invoked when the computer is turned on, is the part of DOS that takes in, translates, and executes commands. Invoking a second command processor can give you the ability to execute DOS commands from inside a program and then return to that program. The COMMAND command also allows you to load a custom command processor that has special functions and abilities or altered command definitions.

Format

COMMAND [*D:Path*][/P][/C *String*][/E:*xxxxx*]

D:Path is the drive and path where the command file is located if it is not in the current directory.

/P makes the new processor the primary processor.

/C *String* executes the command represented by *String*.

/E:*xxxxx* sets the DOS environment size to *xxxxx* bytes.

Type

Resident.

COMP

This command compares the contents of two or more files to see if they are the same.

Format

[*D:Path*]COMP [*FileSpec1*] [*FileSpec2*]

D:Path is the drive and path where the command file is located if it is not in the current directory.

FileSpec1 is the optional drive and path, plus the file names and extensions, of the first set of files to be compared. Wild cards are allowed.

FileSpec2 is the optional drive and path, plus the file names and extensions, of the second set of files to be compared. Wild cards are allowed.

Type

Transient.

COPY

Copies of read-only files created with COPY will *not* be read-only.

The COPY command has three distinct uses. You can use it to duplicate files, to access devices, or to concatenate files.

Duplicating files with COPY, using the first format of this command, allows you versatility in moving files around the disk system. Whole directories can be copied and thus moved to another location or to another disk. Without COPY, you would never be able to transfer newly purchased programs from diskettes to your hard disk, or copy files to a diskette for another system.

The second format of COPY is especially useful for printing multiple files at once, which cannot be done with the TYPE command. It is also the only way for you to directly send information to a device from DOS.

The third format of the COPY command allows files to be concatenated; that is, ASCII-type files can be added to the end of one another to form one big file.

Format

COPY [/A][/B]*SourceFile* [[/A][/B][*DestFile*][/A][/B][/V]]

COPY [/A][/B]*Source* [/A][/B][*Dest*][/A][/B][/V]

COPY [/A][/B]*SourceFile1* + *SourceFile2*[/A][/B] + ...
       [*ConcatFile*][/A][/B][/V]

These switches will affect the file immediately preceding the place where the switch is used, as well as all files following it, until the next time the switch is used.

The /A switch is used with *SourceFile, Source,* or *SourceFile1, SourceFile2* to read data up to but not including the first Ctrl-Z (end-of-file) character; the file is treated as an ASCII file. This is the default when concatenating (format 3).

The /A switch is used with with *DestFile, Dest,* or *ConcatFile* to write a Ctrl-Z at the end of the file.

The /B switch—(the default for duplicating files (format 1))—is used with *SourceFile, Source,* or *SourceFile1, SourceFile2* to copy the entire file up to the last Ctrl-Z.

The /B switch is used with *DestFile, Dest,* or *ConcatFile* to make sure that no Ctrl-Z will be written at the end of the file.

/V causes DOS to check that all of the specified files were copied successfully.

SourceFile is the drive, path, file name, and extension of the file to be copied.

DestFile is the drive, path, file name, and extension of the file to which *SourceFile* will be copied.

Not specifying a destination file in the third format of the COPY command will result in all source files being appended to the end of the first source file.

Source and *Dest* can be either device or file specifications, although DOS only allows ASCII files to be read from a device.

SourceFile1 and *SourceFile2* are a list of files to be added together (*SourceFile2* to the end of *SourceFile1,* etc.).

ConcatFile is the file composed of the concatenation of the source files.

Type
Resident.

COUNTRY

Since the format of such things as the date and time may change from country to country, your computer must be able to recognize and adapt to these different formats. The COUNTRY command has provisions for up to 21 country codes, and it will also call up a specified code page.

Format

COUNTRY = xxx,[yyy] [,FileSpec]

xxx is the three-digit international code of each country.

yyy is the specified code page.

FileSpec is the location and name of the file containing the country information; the default is \COUNTRY.SYS.

Type

Configuration.

CTTY

If you have a special system configuration or another workstation connected through one of the auxiliary serial ports (AUX, COM1, COM2, COM3, or COM4), CTTY can change the current input and output device (which is usually the keyboard and screen) to something else. You could, for example, specify a teletype as a console.

Format

CTTY *Device*

> *Device* is a valid device name.

Type

Resident.

Restrictions

The keyboard and monitor will be reset as the main console when you use BASIC and other programs that do not use DOS function calls.

Specifying a non-input device such as LPT1 in a CTTY command will hang the system. The computer will try to input data from this port, which cannot be done.

DATE

This command changes the date. Use it either to update or to simply find out what day of the week a certain date is. DATE also resets a permanent clock's date, should one be installed.

Format

DATE [*mm-dd-yy* ¦ *dd-mm-yy* ¦ *yy-mm-dd*]

If the *mm-dd-yy* specification is left off, you will be prompted for it. The order of *mm-dd-yy* is dependent on the country you have selected.

mm is the month (01 to 12).

dd is the day (01 to 31).

yy is the year, either 80 to 99, or 1980 to 1999.

Type

Resident.

DEBUG

Although DEBUG
is not discussed in
the DOS 3.3 user's man-
ual, it *is* included on the
DOS 3.3 master disk.

DEBUG fixes and changes assembly-language programs. It provides a way to run and test any program in a controlled environment: you can change any part of the program and immediately execute the program without having to reassemble it. You can also run machine-language (object) files directly. Programmers often use this DOS tool to make quick program changes, to test variations, and to rapidly isolate errors in assembly-language code.

Format
[*D:Path*]DEBUG [*FileSpec*] [*Param1*] [*Param2*]

> *D:Path* is the drive and path where the command file is located if it is not in the current directory.

> *FileSpec* is an optional drive and path, plus the file name and extension, of the file that is the object of the command.

> *Param1* and *Param2* are any optional parameters that are needed by *FileSpec*.

Type
Transient.

━━━━━━━ *DEL* ━━━━━━━

This command removes a file from the directory. The file is still physically present on the disk and can be retrieved by using certain non-DOS disk utilities (such as the Norton Utilities), but it is not accessible using the directory structure.

Format
DEL *FileSpec*

FileSpec is an optional drive and path, plus the file name and extension, of each file to be deleted. Wild cards are allowed.

Type
Resident.

Restrictions
You cannot use DEL to delete read-only files or any subdirectory still containing files.

When issuing the command DEL *.*, which deletes all files in the current directory, DOS will issue the warning "Are you sure (Y/N)?" to verify that you really wish to take such a drastic action. Issuing the DEL command with a subdirectory as the *FileSpec* parameter deletes all of the files in that subdirectory, but not the subdirectory itself.

DEVICE

This command loads a device driver. A driver can be anything from a keyboard enhancement routine to a RAM disk specification. DEVICE can be used many times in the CONFIG.SYS file, limited only by how the drivers use the system's memory.

Format

DEVICE = *FileSpec[Switches]*

> *FileSpec* is the optional drive and path, plus the file name and extension, of the specified driver file.

> *Switches* are the switches corresponding to the specific driver files.

Type

Configuration.

DIR

The DIR command offers several ways to see what files you have. Without this command, it would be extremely difficult, if not impossible, to operate a computer system of any size.

Format

DIR [*FileSpec*][/P][/W]

All DIR parameters represented by *FileSpec* are completely independent from one another. They can be used in any combination, either alone or together, to narrow down the directory listing.

FileSpec is an optional drive and path, plus the file name and extension, of the file that is the object of the command.

/P causes the computer to prompt you to continue listing the directory entries if the listing is longer than one screen.

/W causes the listing to be displayed in wide format (without the size, date, and time, and in a horizontal listing).

Type

Resident.

Restrictions

Hidden files will not be shown when you use the DIR command.

DISKCOMP

Unlike the COMP command, which compares two sets of files, the DISKCOMP command compares two diskettes (not hard disks). It is usually used to verify a COPY or BACKUP operation.

Format

[*D:Path*]DISKCOMP [*D1*:[*D2*:]][/1][/8]

> *D:Path* is the drive and path where the command file is located if it is not in the current directory.

> *D1* and *D2* are the two drives to be compared.

> /1 forces the computer to compare the diskettes as if they were single-sided (no matter what they really are).

> /8 forces the computer to read and compare only the first eight sectors on each track, even if they are 9- or 15-sector diskettes.

Type

Transient.

Restrictions

DISKCOMP will not work on a hard disk or with the JOIN, ASSIGN, or SUBST commands.

━━━━━━━━━ *DISKCOPY* ━━━━━━━━━

This command gives you a quick way to copy a diskette with a lot of data on it that would otherwise take forever to copy with the COPY command. DISKCOPY copies the raw data of the diskette, so if the diskette is a system diskette, the new copy will also be a system diskette. If the source diskette is not a system diskette, then the copy will not be a system diskette either, even if the destination diskette originally was a system diskette. The second diskette will be an *exact* copy of the first. This command also formats a nonformatted destination diskette during the copying process.

Format
[*D:Path*]DISKCOPY [*SourceD:DestD:*][/1]

> *D:Path* is the drive and path where the command file is located if it is not in the current directory.
>
> *SourceD* is the source drive to be copied.
>
> *DestD* is the destination drive to be copied onto.
>
> /1 forces the computer to copy only the first side of the source diskette to the first side of the destination diskette, as if they were both single-sided, even if they are double-sided.

Type
Transient.

Restrictions
You cannot use this command with a hard disk; also, it does not recognize an assigned or substituted drive, and should not be used with JOIN. DISKCOPY cannot reliably read a double-sided disk formatted in a high-capacity drive, and it will not work with network drives.

ECHO

When you set up a batch file, there are times when you don't want the executing commands to be displayed on the screen. ECHO suppresses the screen's presentation of batch-file command execution.

ECHO can be used to send a line of text to the printer or a file; for example, ECHO Hello >LPT1 will cause "Hello" to be printed. To print a character that has some other function, enclose it in double quotation marks.

Format

ECHO [ON ¦ OFF ¦ *String*]

ON turns on the display of commands (the default).

OFF turns off echoing.

String is a message that is to be displayed regardless of whether ECHO is ON or OFF.

Type

Batch, resident (acceptable on a DOS command line).

EDLIN

EDLIN is the DOS line editor. Unlike many word processors, it is not a full-screen editor. EDLIN has no formatting commands, and you must change data a line at a time. It is good for modifying short ASCII files and for creating and modifying simple batch files.

Format

[*D:Path*]EDLIN *FileSpec*[/B]

D:Path is the drive and path where the command file is located if it is not in the current directory.

FileSpec is an optional drive and path, plus the file name and extension, of the file that is the object of the command.

/B causes EDLIN to load a file containing embedded Ctrl-Z codes.

Type

Transient.

ERASE

The ERASE command removes a file from the directory. The file is still physically present on the disk and can be gotten back by using a disk utility, but it is not accessible using the directory structure.

Format

ERASE *FileSpec*

> *FileSpec* is the optional drive, optional path, file name, and extension of each file to be erased. Wild cards are allowed.

Type

Resident.

Restrictions

You cannot use ERASE to delete read-only files or to remove a subdirectory.

When you enter the command ERASE *.*, which will erase all files in the current directory, DOS will issue the warning "Are you sure (Y/N)?" to ensure that you wish to take such drastic action. Issuing the command ERASE *FileSpec,* where *FileSpec* is the name of a subdirectory, deletes all files in the subdirectory but not the subdirectory itself.

EXE2BIN

This advanced command formally converts executable files to command files. A file with an .EXE extension is used as the source file, and a file with a .COM or .BIN extension is created.

Format

[D:Path]EXE2BIN SourceFile [DestFile]

The EXE2BIN command is not available with DOS 3.3.

D:Path is the drive and path where the command file is located if it is not in the current directory.

SourceFile is the drive, path, file name, and extension of the file to be converted; .EXE is the default for the extension.

DestFile is the drive, path, file name, and extension for the converted file; .BIN is the default for the extension. If this parameter is not included on the command line, the resultant file will have the same drive, path, and file name as the source file, but its extension will be .BIN.

Type

Transient.

Restrictions

SourceFile must be a programmer's object file created with the LINK program. The code and data of the file must be less than 64K.

FASTOPEN

DOS can take a long time to search for a file or directory, especially if it is located in subdirectories. The FASTOPEN command maintains a list of the most recently accessed directory and file locations on the disk. This means that when you repeatedly access a directory or file, all DOS has to do is check in memory where that directory or file is located and then access it, without having to check through the disk's directory tree. This process can save a good deal of time.

Format
[*D:Path*]FASTOPEN *D1*:[= *Size*]

> *D:Path* is the drive and path where the command file is located if it is not in the current directory.

> *D1* is the drive to which FASTOPEN will be attached (the command can be issued for each drive separately).

> *Size* is the number of directory or file entries that FASTOPEN will remember.

Type
Transient.

Restrictions
FASTOPEN will not work with JOIN, SUBST, or ASSIGN, or with network drives.

FCBS

On older-style DOS versions—specifically, version 1—files were accessed via file control blocks (FCBs). These are approximately 40-byte sections in memory that tell DOS the file's name and other attributes. The FCBS command allows you to access these.

Format

FCBS = *MaxNum,PermNum*

MaxNum is the number of FCBs that may be opened concurrently (the default is 4).

PermNum is the minimum number of FCBs that will remain open when DOS tries to close files automatically (the default is 0).

Restrictions

If *PermNum* is less than *MaxNum,* DOS can close an FCB without alerting the program that is using the FCB. This can cause major problems.

FDISK

Hard disks can be set up to have more than one type of operating system on them. For example, you can have DOS 3.3 managing one part of a disk and UNIX managing another. Each of these sections is called a *partition*. You can have from one to four partitions on a disk (see Appendix C).

Partitions must be set up before the disk is logically formatted. If your disk is already being used and you wish to make a partition, you will have to back up all of your data, run FDISK on the system diskette, and then reformat your disk.

All data on your hard disk will be destroyed when you create partitions with FDISK.

Two types of partitions can be set up for DOS: a primary partition and an extended partition. DOS only needs the primary partition, which can be as large as 32Mb. If you have more hard-disk space available than that on one hard disk, you will need to create an extended partition, which you assign the next logical drive letter. You can also subdivide the extended partition into more logical drives, up to the letter Z. Partitioning is done because DOS is limited to 32Mb per drive.

Format

[*D:Path*]FDISK

> *D:Path* is the drive and path where the command file is located if it is not in the current directory.

Type

Transient.

Restrictions

FDISK can only be used on hard-disk systems. A disk must be reformatted logically after being partitioned. FDISK will not work if another process is accessing the disk.

FILES

Just as the number of buffers to be used by DOS can be specified, so may the number of files open at any one time. The FILES command specifies the size of the file control area in which file control blocks are created.

Format

FILES = x

> *x* is a number between 8 and 255 (8 is the default) specifying the number of files that can remain open at one time.

Type

Configuration.

When you are using the FILES command, keep in mind that the size of DOS increases by 48 bytes for each file beyond the eight default files.

FIND

FIND allows you to search through a file to locate any particular string of text characters.

Format

[D:Path]FIND [/V][/C][/N]"String" [FileSpec...]

> *D:Path* is the drive and path where the command file is located if it is not in the current directory.

> /V causes FIND to display each line not containing *String*.

> /C counts the number of lines containing *String* and shows the total.

> /N shows the relative line number of each line containing *String*.

> *String* is the string of characters to be searched for.

> *FileSpec* is the drive, path, file name, and extension of each file to be searched. Multiple files should be separated by a space.

Type

Transient.

Restrictions

Wild cards not allowed with this command. FIND will end its search at the first Ctrl-Z encountered in a file.

FOR

FOR sets up a repeating loop in a batch file. This is useful for repeating an operation with a different parameter a specified number of times.

Format

FOR %%*Var* IN (*ComSet*) DO *Command*

Var is a variable name.

ComSet is the set of values to be used successively by *Command*.

Command is the command to be executed using %%*Var* as a varying parameter (which uses the values given in *ComSet*).

Type

Batch, resident.

Restrictions

The variable name used in a FOR command cannot be a DOS reserved word.

FORMAT

When you want to use a new disk with your system, it must be formatted. Certain markings must be placed on the disk to help the computer know where it is when it accesses the disk. The disk is not actually erased but is reset to a state in which nothing is on it.

The FORMAT command can create both a data disk, in which all storage space is available for use, and a system diskette, which is bootable and contains DOS's two hidden system files and the COMMAND.COM file. FORMAT will also check the disk for any areas that have gone bad and mark them accordingly, so that no data will be saved in those areas.

> The FORMAT command destroys the contents of a disk, so be careful. Write-protecting any disks in other drives during a format may help prevent errors.

Format
[D:Path]FORMAT D1:[/S][/1][/8][/V][/B][/4][/N:xx][/T:yy]

D:Path is the drive and path where the command file is located if it is not in the current directory.

D1: is the drive to be formatted.

/S causes a system disk to be made.

/1 formats only one side of the disk.

/8 formats the disk with 8 sectors instead of 9.

/V prompts for a volume label when formatting is complete.

/B formats the disk with 8 sectors and leaves room for the hidden system files, but does *not* transfer the system to the diskette. This allows for the use of the SYS command with any DOS version.

/4 causes a high-capacity drive to create a 360K, double-sided diskette.

/N:xx specifies that the disk be formatted with xx sectors per track.

/T:yy specifies that the disk be formatted with yy tracks.

Type
Transient.

Restrictions
FORMAT ignores assignments made with ASSIGN. /V cannot be used to format a diskette for DOS 1.1.

GOTO

During a batch file's execution, it may become necessary to skip over some commands and execute others in a file. Or it may be necessary to jump back to another point in a file, perhaps for some logical looping. GOTO allows you to transfer execution.

 Use descriptive labels in your GOTO commands.

Format
GOTO [:]*Label*

> *Label* is the line identifier used by the batch file to indicate the line to which GOTO will transfer control.

Type
Batch, resident.

GRAFTABL

It is nice to be able to display the full ASCII range of characters on the screen so that you can see exactly what you are dealing with. If you have a Color Graphics Adapter, this command will enable you to display the ASCII characters that have codes from 128 to 255.

Format

[*D:Path*]GRAFTABL [437¦860¦863¦865¦/STATUS]

D:Path is the drive and path where the command file is located if it is not in the current directory.

437 loads the U.S. code page.

860 loads the Portuguese code page.

863 loads the Canadian code page.

865 loads the Norwegian and Danish code page.

/STATUS shows the number of the code page currently in use.

Type

Transient.

GRAPHICS

This command allows you to transfer graphics screens to your printer using the Shift-PrtSc key combination. The printing time will depend on what graphics mode you are in.

Format

[*D:Path*]GRAPHICS [*PrinterType*] [/R][/B][/LCD]

D:Path is the drive and path where the command file is located if it is not in the current directory.

PrinterType is an optional printer-type specification. It can be COLOR1, COLOR4, COLOR8, COMPACT, GRAPHICS, or THERMAL.

/R prints a reverse-video image.

/B prints the background color when *PrinterType* is COLOR4 or COLOR8.

/LCD prints the image produced on a liquid crystal display.

Type

Transient.

IF

Conditional statements play an important role in any type of programming. A conditional statement simply says "Do one thing if a certain condition is true; otherwise, do another thing." This allows branching, or decision making, in your programs.

In most high-level programming languages, conditionals are defined with the IF command. IF A = B THEN GOTO :START is executed as "If A equals B, then transfer control to the line labeled :START; otherwise, just go on to the next instruction."

Format

IF [NOT] *Condition Command*

NOT inverts the truth of the condition. If NOT is included, a true condition would be regarded as false, and a false condition as true.

Condition is the criterion for the execution of *Command*. *Condition* can be in one of the following formats:

ERRORLEVEL *Code* is used to determine if the return code of the last program or command that was executed equals *Code* or is higher.

String1 = =*String2* specifies that *String1* must equal *String2* for the condition to be true.

EXIST *FileSpec* causes the condition to be true if the file defined by *FileSpec* resides in the specified directory.

Command is the action (usually a command) that is executed when *Condition* is true or not false.

Type

Batch, resident (acceptable on a DOS command line).

Restrictions

DOS is case-sensitive for *String* values.

JOIN

JOIN makes DOS treat a whole disk drive as if it were a subdirectory of another drive. The JOIN command has three main formats. The first displays all directory and disk names that have been joined; the second actually performs the joining; and the third disjoins a directory and disk.

Formats
[*D:Path*]JOIN
[*D:Path*]JOIN *Drive2 Drive1*
[*D:Path*]JOIN *Drive2* **/D**

D:Path is the drive and path where the command file is located if it is not in the current directory.

Drive2 is the drive to which a directory will be attached or released.

Drive1 is the drive and path of the directory to be joined.

/D causes any previous joining of *Drive2* to be unjoined.

Type
Transient.

Restrictions
Use JOIN only on multidrive systems. JOIN cannot be used to join a SUBST-created drive.

KEYB

This command is used to load a new keyboard translation table for a specific country. There are 21 country codes to choose from.

Format

[*D:Path*]KEYB [*xx*[,[*yyy*],[*FileSpec*]]]

D:Path is the drive and path where the command file is located if it is not in the current directory.

xx is a keyboard code representing a country.

yyy is the code page to be used.

FileSpec is the drive, path, file name, and extension of the keyboard definition file (the default is \KEYBOARD.SYS).

Type

Transient.

LABEL

LABEL allows you to give a disk a volume label electronically. You will then see your disk's name each time you call up a directory.

Format

[*D:Path*]LABEL [*D1*:][*String*]

D:Path is the drive and path where the command file is located if it is not in the current directory.

D1: is the drive containing the disk whose label is to be changed or displayed.

String, when specified, will become the label of the disk in *Drive2*.

Type

Transient.

LASTDRIVE

If you have more than five drives hooked up to your system, or if you are using the SUBST command often and need to declare a drive name beyond E, you need this command. LASTDRIVE configures the system so that you can access drives up to the specified drive, which may even be Z.

Format

LASTDRIVE = *D*

D is the last accessible drive; the default is E.

Type

Configuration.

Restrictions

If you specify a letter range that is not sufficient for the number of drives currently hooked up to the system, LASTDRIVE will not be accepted. For example, if you specify G as the final drive, and have eight drives hooked up to your system, LASTDRIVE will not work—you've only assigned seven letters to cover your eight drives.

MKDIR (MD)

The MKDIR command (or MD for short) creates a new directory, either in the current working directory or at the specified path location in an existing tree. This new directory will be empty of files initially, but it is usable immediately.

Format

M[K]D[IR] [*D:Path*]

D:Path is the optional drive and path specifying which directory you wish to create.

Type

Resident.

MODE

The MODE command controls and redirects output. There are ten formats for this useful command. The first selects various print modes on parallel printers, the second redirects output, and the third changes the parameters of the serial port. The fourth format changes the display type, and the fifth sets the video mode and, simultaneously, adjusts the horizontal alignment of the monitor.

The MODE command can also work with code pages. The sixth and seventh formats install code-page device drivers in the specified device. The eighth format selects the code page to be activated for the specified device. (You can have several code pages loaded into the device at once, but only one can be active at any one time.) The ninth format displays the active code page and then displays all of the code pages that can be activated for the specified device.

The tenth format reinstalls the currently active device driver in the specified device if it was erased. This comes in handy if for some reason you need to turn your printer off. Instead of using the first or second format to reload the driver, which in fact is already in computer memory anyway, you can use the tenth format to make another copy and place it into the device's memory.

Formats

[*D:Path*]MODE LPT*x*: [*CPL*][,[*LPI*][,P]]
[*D:Path*]MODE LPT*x*: = COM*y*
[*D:Path*]MODE COM*y*[:]*Baud*[,[*Parity*][,[*Bits*][,P]]
[*D:Path*]MODE *Type*
[*D:Path*]MODE [*Type*], *Shift* [,T]
[*D:Path*]MODE *Device* CODEPAGE PREPARE = ((*CP*)*FileSpec*)
[*D:Path*]MODE *Device* CODEPAGE PREPARE = ((*CPList*)*FileSpec*)
[*D:Path*]MODE *Device* CODEPAGE SELECT = *CP*
[*D:Path*]MODE *Device* CODEPAGE[/STATUS]
[*D:Path*]MODE *Device* CODEPAGE REFRESH

D:Path is the drive and path where the command file is located if it is not in the current directory.

x is a printer number.

CPL is the number of characters per line.

LPI is the number of lines per inch.

P causes the computer to continuously retry accessing the port during time-out errors.

y is a serial-port number.

Baud is a baud rate for the COM port (110, 150, 300, 600, 1200, 2400, 4800, 9600, or 19200).

Parity is a parity value for the COM port; it can be even, odd, or none (the default is even).

Bits is a combination of two parameters specifying the number of stop and data bits used.

Type is the display type being used. It is specified as 40, 80, BW40, BW80, CO40, CO80, or MONO.

Shift is the direction for a screen shift, either L or R.

T puts a test pattern on the screen for checking the screen alignment when shifting.

Device is a valid device name (CON, LPT1, and so on).

CP is a code-page number (437, 850, 860, 863, or 865).

CPList is a list of code-page numbers.

FileSpec is the file containing the code-page data. Its value is 4201.CPI for the IBM Proprinter; 5202.CPI for the IBM Quietwriter III Printer; EGA.CPI for EGA displays; or LCD.CPI for LCD displays.

/STATUS displays the active code page and the other available code pages for *Device*.

Type
Transient.

MORE

This command is similar to the DIR/P command, which pauses the directory listing after each screenful of data and asks you to press a key to continue. MORE is a filter—that is, data is sent to it, and MORE processes the data and sends it out in a new format. In this case, the filter simply prints the data a screenful at a time and prints " – MORE –" at the bottom of the screen until you press a key.

Format
[*D:Path*]MORE

> *D:Path* is the drive and path where the command file is located if it is not in the current directory.

Type
Transient.

NLSFUNC

NLSFUNC supports national-language features and code-page switching. It uses the new extended country information provided with DOS 3.3 to load the part of the keyboard translation table containing the country-specific information.

Format

[*D:Path*]NLSFUNC [*FileSpec*]

D:Path is the drive and path where the command file is located if it is not in the current directory.

FileSpec specifies the location and name of the country-specific code file (the default is \COUNTRY.SYS).

Type

Transient.

PATH

You often need to access a program in a directory other than the one you are in. The PATH command gives DOS a list of drives and directories to search through, in the order given, until it finds the requested program file. Beware of the order given, however: if there are two different files with the same name in different directories along the path, then the first one encountered will be used.

Format

PATH [D1:*Path1***][;D2:Path2...]**

[*D1:Path1*] is the first drive and directory searched.

[*D2:Path2*...] is the second drive and directory searched, and so on.

Type

Resident.

Restrictions

PATH will not work for data files, overlay files, or other non-executable files (see APPEND).

PAUSE

This command temporarily halts the execution of a batch file. A message will be printed on the screen telling you to strike a key when you are ready to continue.

Format

PAUSE [*String*]

> *String* prints a specified string (a message) on the screen before "Strike any key when ready."

Type

Batch, resident (acceptable on a DOS command line).

PRINT

The PRINT command invokes, modifies, and adds files to an internal software-based queue. Queues offer you a way to set up the computer to output multiple files in order automatically.

Format

[*D:Path*]PRINT [*Params*][/C][/T][/P][*FileSpec,*...]

D:Path is the drive and path where the command file is located if it is not in the current directory.

Params contains optional switches and parameters that redefine queue characteristics. They are as follows:

/D:*Device* specifies the output device.

/B:*BuffSize* specifies the output buffer's size in bytes.

/U:*BusyTicks* specifies how long the queue will wait each cycle if the printer is too busy to print new data.

/M:*MaxTicks* specifies how much time the queue has to send data to the printer.

/S:*TimeSlice* specifies the number of time slices.

/Q:*QueueSize* specifies the maximum number of entries in the queue.

/C cancels previous and following entries on the command line.

/T terminates the queue; everything is canceled and stopped.

/P adds previous and following entries on the command line to the queue.

FileSpec, ... is an optional list of the paths, names, and extensions of files to be queued for printing.

Type

Transient.

Restrictions

You cannot use a printer without the PRINT command while a queue is printing. PRINT cannot be used on a network. The disk where the files are located cannot be removed from the drive until the queue has completed printing.

PROMPT

This command changes the system prompt to whatever you like—
it can display the time, the date, or a simple message. This is useful
for finding out which directory you are in before you modify or delete
any files.

Format

PROMPT [*String*]

String is a string of characters that can contain special-purpose
entries. Possible values are shown in Table 18.2.

CHARACTERS	DESCRIPTION
$$	$ sign
$t	Time
$d	Date
$p	Current directory
$v	DOS version number
$n	Default drive identifier
$g	> symbol
$l	< symbol
$b	¦ symbol
$q	= symbol
$h	Erasing backspace
$e	Escape character
$_	Carriage return and line feed

Table 18.2: Special-purpose PROMPT codes (meta strings)

Type

Resident.

RECOVER

Sometimes a part of a disk goes bad—that is, the computer cannot read it, and access to the files in that area may be denied. The RECOVER command reads the file part by part, skipping over the bad data, and rewrites the file without the bad data, allowing the user access to what's left. RECOVER can be used to recover specific files or an entire disk.

Format

[*D:Path*]RECOVER [*D1*][*FileSpec*]

D:Path is the drive and path where the command file is located if it is not in the current directory.

D1 is the drive identifier for the disk to be recovered.

FileSpec is an optional drive and path, plus the file name and extension, of the file that is the object of the command. Wild cards are allowed.

Type

Transient.

Restrictions

RECOVER should not be used on a network disk.

REM

It is often helpful to place comments in your file code, so that if you come back to those files later, you can quickly and easily understand what they contain and how they work. In batch files, this is done with the REM command. The contents of a REM command line are not executed or displayed if ECHO is OFF, but they will be readable if you look at the file itself.

Format

REM *String*

String represents nonexecutable comments.

Type

Batch, resident (acceptable on a DOS command line).

Restrictions

Comments may be up to 123 characters long per REM statement. Enclose characters that have special meanings to DOS (such as ¦) in double quotation marks ("¦").

RENAME

The RENAME command (which can be shortened to REN) performs the very useful function of renaming a file.

Format

REN[AME] *OldFile NewFile*

OldFile is the optional drive and path, plus the file name and extension, of the file that will be renamed. Wild cards are allowed.

NewFile is a new file name and extension for *OldFile*. Wild cards are allowed. The *NewFile* parameter does not require or accept a prefixed drive and path.

Type

Resident.

Restrictions

You cannot use RENAME to give a subdirectory a new name.

REPLACE

The REPLACE command is an advanced, selective version of the COPY command. It is useful for changing versions of DOS when files need to be updated. It is also useful for selective backups of files without the BACKUP command. For example, if you work with a single-disk word processor, then a backup disk might only contain copies of the text files you've worked on. REPLACE would only replace the files on the backup disk that were changed on the original, or it would only make copies of newly created files—not older, unchanged files.

Format

[*D:Path*]REPLACE *SourceFile* [*Dest*][/A][/P][/R][/S][/W]

D:Path is the drive and path where the command file is located if it is not in the current directory.

SourceFile is the optional drive and path, plus the file name and an optional extension, of each file that will be a replacing file.

Dest is the optional drive and path of the files to be replaced.

/A adds files to those already present.

/P prompts you before replacing a file.

/R replaces both normal and read-only files on *Dest*.

/S replaces all files in the directory structure that have matching file names.

/W waits for you to insert a diskette.

Type

Transient.

─────── *RESTORE* ───────

This command is the reverse of BACKUP: it restores files to the disk and directory from which they were backed up.

Format

[*D:Path*]RESTORE *SourceD FileSpec*[/S][/P][/B:*mm-dd-yy*]
[/A:*mm-dd-yy*][/M][/N][/L:*hh-mm-ss*][/E:*hh-mm-ss*]

D:Path is the drive and path where the command file is located if it is not in the current directory.

SourceD is the drive containing the backed-up files to be restored.

FileSpec is the optional drive and path, plus the file names and extensions, of the files on *SourceD* to be restored. Wild cards are allowed.

/S restores files in subdirectories of the files specified in *FileSpec*.

/P prompts you before a file is restored if that file was modified since it was last backed up.

/B:*mm-dd-yy* causes all backed-up files that were last modified on or before *mm-dd-yy* to be restored.

/A:*mm-dd-yy* causes all backed-up files that were last modified on or after *mm-dd-yy* to be restored.

mm-dd-yy represents a date in months, days, and years.

/M compares the backed-up files and the files on the destination disk; it then restores the files that have been changed or erased since the last backup.

/N restores files that no longer exist on the destination disk.

/L:*hh-mm-ss* restores all files changed since the time specified by *hh-mm-ss*.

/E:*hh-mm-ss* restores all files changed prior to the time specified by *hh-mm-ss*.

hh-mm-ss represents time in hours, minutes, and seconds.

RESTORE will overwrite files with the same name if they are in the specified directory. Use the /P switch (or the REPLACE command) to avoid rewriting a file.

Type
Transient.

Restrictions

Only files created with BACKUP will be restored. Do not use RESTORE if SUBST, JOIN, or ASSIGN was invoked in a BACKUP operation.

RMDIR (RD)

You may find it necessary to delete or remove a directory. You must first delete all files or subdirectories in the directory, and then use the RMDIR command.

Format
R[M]D[IR] [D:*Path*]

D:*Path* is the drive and path of the directory to be removed.

Type
Resident.

SELECT

SELECT is an advanced version of the FORMAT command. It allows you to specify a new keyboard layout and country-specific date and time formats.

Format
[*D:Path*]SELECT [[A: ¦ B:]*DestD*:[*DestPath*]] *xxx yy*

> *D:Path* is an optional drive and path where the command file is located.

> A: or B: is the source drive that contains the command files and country information (A: is the default).

> *DestD:DestPath* is the drive and optional path of the disk to be formatted. The root directory is the default for an unspecified *DestPath*.

> *xxx* specifies the country code.

> *yy* specifies the keyboard code.

Type
Transient.

Restrictions

Drives A and B are the only source drives, and the destination drive must not be the same as the source drive. The U.S. keyboard file is resident in the computer's memory, so it does not need to be on the source disk. CONFIG.SYS and AUTOEXEC.BAT files are created on *DestD*. High-capacity diskettes must be used in high-capacity drives.

SELECT uses FORMAT, so anything on the destination disk will be destroyed after this command is used. SELECT may be used on a hard disk, so be careful.

SET

The SET command changes strings and definitions within the DOS environment of your computer. This area of memory set aside for special definitions and defaults can be used by the system and also can be changed by the user. With SET you can display the current DOS environment, erase the current definition of *Name,* create a new DOS environment string, or change one that already exists.

Format

SET [Name = [Param]]

Name is a user-specified string used in place of *Param.* It can also contain the DOS environment strings PROMPT, PATH, LASTDRIVE, or COMSPEC.

Param is what *Name* will represent, or it is the new setting for one of the DOS environment strings.

Type

Resident.

Restrictions

There are only 127 bytes of total available DOS environment by default. You can, however, change this with the SHELL command's /E switch.

SHARE

This command loads routines that enable file sharing and allows you to "lock" a disk or all or part of a file so that it cannot be used by another process on the same computer. SHARE does not prevent the use of a file by another computer when you are using networks; that kind of protection should be provided with your network software.

Format

[*D:Path*]SHARE [/F:*FileMem*][/L:*Locks*]

> *D:Path* is the drive and path where the command file is located if it is not in the current directory.

> /F:*FileMem* sets aside the memory to be used for keeping track of file sharing (the default is 2048 bytes).

> /L:*Locks* specifies the number of locks that can be in effect at once (the default is 20).

Restrictions

You may only load the SHARE command once. Subsequent attempts at loading will yield an error message. You must reboot to remove SHARE.

SHELL

If you are a system programmer or if you have your own command processor, this command is for you. When DOS loads, SHELL can specify and load your command processor instead of COMMAND.COM. You can also use SHELL with the /E switch to load in the standard COMMAND.COM file, but with an expanded DOS environment.

Format

SHELL = *ComFileSpec* **[/E:***xxxxx***][/P]**

ComFileSpec is the drive, path, and file name of the new command processor.

/E:*xxxxx* defines, in bytes, the size of the DOS environment.

/P keeps the specified command processor resident and causes AUTOEXEC.BAT to be executed after the processor has been loaded.

Type

Configuration.

SHIFT

Batch files often need information from the user—a drive identifier, a file name, a yes-or-no answer, and so on. These temporary values can be put into the variables %0 through %9 and be made available to the batch file when it is run. For those applications that require more than ten variables, Microsoft has developed the SHIFT command. This command simply shifts all of the variables down one number. For example, executing SHIFT would cause the new %1 to equal the old %2, the new %2 to equal the old %3, and so on. %9 could reference a formerly inaccessible eleventh parameter value.

Format
SHIFT

Type
Batch, resident (acceptable on a DOS command line).

SORT

SORT is another filter command. Data is sent in, and depending on the parameters, sorted and displayed, or routed to another file. Directories may be displayed in a sorted format, but the files will not be physically sorted on the disk.

Format
[*D:Path*]SORT [/R][/ + *Col*]

> *D:Path* is the drive and path where the command file is located if it is not in the current directory.
>
> /R sorts in reverse-alphabetical order.
>
> / + *Col* starts the sorting with column *Col* (the default is column 1).

Type
Transient.

STACKS

This command is intended for very advanced users. It allows you to change the stack resources that are normally defined for you. Stack frames are used for interrupt processing.

Format

STACKS = *n,s*

> *n* specifies the number of stack frames.
>
> *s* specifies the number of bytes in each frame.

Type

Configuration.

SUBST

The SUBST command is the opposite of the JOIN command. It creates a new disk drive corresponding to a directory. Starting with one directory structure, you can take a directory and all of its subdirectories and make that branch of the tree into the root directory of a new, fictitious drive. This new drive accesses all of its data from a physically existing drive, and thus cannot be considered a RAM disk.

Like the JOIN command, SUBST has three distinct formats for its use. The first displays all of the current substitutions, the second actually performs a substitution, and the third cancels out a substitution.

Formats
[*D:Path*]SUBST
[*D:Path*]SUBST *NewD Path2*
[*D:Path*]SUBST *NewD* /D

D:Path is the drive and path where the command file is located if it is not in the current directory.

NewD is the drive to be created or abolished.

Path2 is the drive and directory specification to be made into drive *NewD*.

/D abolishes an existing *NewD* substitution.

Type
Transient.

Restriction
The last available drive is drive E unless the LASTDRIVE command is used.

SYS

If you have made a data diskette and wish to make it into a system diskette, or if you wish to transfer a new version of DOS to an older-version DOS diskette, this command may be the answer. When FORMAT /S is used to format a disk, SYS is invoked automatically to transfer the system files. The SYS command does not transfer COMMAND.COM, but does transfer the two hidden BIOS and DOS files.

Format
[*D:Path*]SYS *DestD*:

> *D:Path* is the drive and path where the command file is located if it is not in the current directory.

> *DestD* is the drive the system files will be transferred to.

Type
Transient.

Restrictions

There must not be any files on the data diskette, since the two system files must be the first two files on the disk. SYS will not work on a network drive.

TIME

This command is used to set the system time. It may also be used to reset an internal clock. Setting the time comes in very handy when errors occur—you can tell exactly when a file was last written to or changed. It also provides a trail by which a programmer can trace the file-saving flow of a program. It is advisable to set the time and date every time you boot the system.

Format
TIME [*hh:mm*[*:ss*[*.xx*]]]

hh is the current hour, in 24-hour format. To translate from 12-hour to 24-hour if the time is between 1:00 P.M. and 12:00 A.M., add 12 to the hour (for example, 7:45 P.M. = 19:45).

mm is the current number of minutes.

ss is the current number of seconds.

xx is the current number of hundredths of seconds.

Type
Resident.

TREE

TREE displays a listing of all of your directories and subdirectories and the files in them. This is especially useful for identifying long directory specifications that should be cut down.

Format

[*D:Path*]TREE [*D2:*][/F]

D:Path is the drive and path where the command file is located if it is not in the current directory.

D2 is the drive identifier of another drive you want TREE to affect.

/F displays all paths and names of files in the directories.

Type

Transient.

TYPE

TYPE displays the contents of an ASCII file. ASCII files contain no control codes that would affect the screen display; they appear as straight listings of data.

Using TYPE on a non-ASCII file could have no effect, or it could display meaningless symbols on your screen. It could also lock up your system entirely. If this happens, you'll need to reboot.

Format
TYPE *FileSpec*

FileSpec is the optional drive and path, plus the file name and extension, of the file to be displayed.

Type
Resident.

VER

The VER command displays the current version of DOS in which you are working.

Format

VER

Type

Resident.

VERIFY

This command turns the global verify feature of DOS on or off. When it is on, everything written to a file will be checked buffer by buffer, to ensure the accuracy of the transmission. This is a useful feature, but your system will run more slowly. Use VERIFY ON when you must be completely sure of the validity of the file data being transferred—for example, during BACKUP operations.

Format

VERIFY [ON ¦ OFF]

ON turns the feature on.

OFF turns VERIFY off. This is the default.

Type

Resident.

Restrictions

VERIFY will not work with network disks.

VOL

The VOL command shows you the volume label of the disk contained in a specified drive.

Format

VOL [*D*:]

D is a specified drive, if different from the default drive.

Type

Resident.

XCOPY

XCOPY is a modified version of the COPY command. It does the same thing, only better. Instead of reading and writing files one at a time, XCOPY reads files into a buffer that is equal in size to available memory, and then writes out the contents of the buffer (this is usually several files). XCOPY can be used for a single file or for several different groups of files. You can combine its switches as well.

Format

[*D:Path*]XCOPY [*FileSpec1*][*FileSpec2*][/A][/D:*mm-dd-yy*] [/E][/M][/P][/S][/V][/W]

D:Path is the drive and path where the command file is located if it is not in the current directory.

FileSpec1 is the necessary drive, path, and file-name specifications for the files to be copied. Wild cards are allowed.

FileSpec2 is the necessary drive, path, and file-name specifications for the files to be written to. Wild cards are allowed.

/A copies only files with a set archive bit.

/D:*mm-dd-yy* copies only files created or modified on or after the specified date; the format depends on the COUNTRY specification.

/E creates corresponding subdirectories on *FileSpec2* before copying is done (even if *FileSpec1* contains no files to transfer).

/M copies files with a set archive bit and resets the archive bit on the source file.

/P prompts you before each file is copied.

/S also copies files from all subdirectories within the specified directory. Corresponding subdirectories will be created on *FileSpec2* for all *FileSpec1* directories that contain files.

/V turns VERIFY on during execution of this command only.

/W causes XCOPY to prompt you to insert different disks before it executes.

Type
Transient.

Restrictions
XCOPY will not copy to or from devices. It also will not copy hidden files from the source and will not overwrite read-only files on the destination.

XCOPY sourcedir destdir /s /e

↑   ↑

doesn't have to   include subdirs
already exist

APPENDICES

This appendix defines all of the important DOS-related terms used in this book. Although these terms are defined in the text when they are first introduced, the glossary presented here offers concise definitions that will refresh your memory when you read a chapter later in the book, or when you simply can't remember the meaning of a particular term.

active partition   The section of a hard disk containing the operating system to be used when the hardware powers up.

ANSI driver   A device driver, contained in the ANSI.SYS file, that loads additional support for advanced console features.

application program   A program that performs or replaces a manual function, such as balancing a checkbook or managing inventory.

Application Programming Interface (API)   The set of all OS/2 system service calls, accessible through the standard OS/2 call-return technique.

archive bit   A bit in a file specification used to indicate whether the file in question needs to be backed up.

ASCII   American Standard Code for Information Interchange; the coding scheme whereby every character the computer can access is assigned an integer code between 0 and 255.

assembly language   A symbolic form of computer language used to program computers at a fundamental level.

asynchronous communications   *See* serial communications.

AUTOEXEC.BAT   A batch file executed automatically whenever the computer is booted up.

background task   A second program running on your computer; usually, a printing operation that shares the CPU with your main foreground task.

base name   The portion of a file name to the left of the period separator; it can be up to eight characters long.

BASIC   Beginner's All-purpose Symbolic Instruction Code. A computer language similar to the English language.

batch file   An ASCII file containing a sequence of DOS commands that, when invoked, will assume control of the computer, executing the commands as if they were entered successively by a computer user.

baud rate   The speed of data transmission, usually in bits per second.

binary   A numbering system that uses powers of the number 2 to generate all other numbers.

bit   One-eighth of a byte. A bit is a binary digit, either 0 or 1.

bit mapping   The way a graphics screen is represented in the computer. Usually signifies point-to-point graphics.

booting up   *See* bootstrapping.

boot record   The section on a disk that contains the minimum information DOS needs to start the system.

bootstrapping   When the computer initially is turned on or is rebooted from the keyboard with Ctrl-Alt-Del, it "pulls itself up by its bootstraps." *See also* warm booting, cold booting.

branching   The transfer of control or execution to another statement in a batch file. *See also* decision making.

break key   The control-key combination that interrupts an executing program or command; activated by pressing the ScrollLock key while holding down the Ctrl key.

buffer   An area in memory set aside to speed up the transfer of data, allowing blocks of data to be transferred at once.

byte   The main unit of memory in a computer. A byte is an eight-bit binary-digit number. One character usually takes up one byte.

cache   A portion of memory reserved for the contents of recently referenced disk sectors. Facilitates faster reaccess of the same sectors.

case sensitivity   Distinguishing between capital letters and lower-case letters.

chaining   Passing the control of execution from one batch file to another. This represents an unconditional transfer of control.

character set A complete group of 256 characters that can be used by programs or system devices. Consists of letters, numbers, control codes, and special graphics or international symbols. *See also* code page.

cluster A group of contiguous sectors on a disk. This is the smallest unit of disk storage that DOS can manipulate.

COBOL A programming language usually used for business applications.

code page A character set that redefines the country and keyboard information for non-U.S. keyboards and systems.

cold booting When the computer's power is first turned on and DOS first boots up. *See* bootstrapping.

COMMAND.COM The command processor that comes with DOS.

command line The line on which a command is entered. This line contains the command and all of its associated parameters and switches. It may run to more than one screen line, but it is still one command line.

command processor The program that translates and acts on commands.

compressed print Printing that allows more than 80 characters on a line of output (usually 132 characters, but on newer printers up to 255 characters per line).

computer-aided design (CAD) program A sophisticated software package containing advanced graphics and drawing features. Used by engineers, architects, and designers for drawing and design applications.

concatenation The placing of two text files together in a series.

conditional statement A statement in a batch file that controls the next step to be executed in the batch file, based on the value of a logical test.

CONFIG.SYS An ASCII text file containing system configuration commands.

configuration An initial set of system values, such as the number of buffers DOS will use, the number of simultaneously open files it will allow, and the specific devices that will be supported.

console   The combination of your system's monitor and keyboard.

contiguity   The physical adjacency on a disk of the disk sectors used by a file.

control codes   ASCII codes that do not display a character but perform a function, such as ringing a bell or deleting a character.

copy protection   Special mechanisms contained in diskettes to inhibit the copying of them by conventional commands.

CPU   Central Processing Unit. The main chip that executes all individual computer instructions.

Ctrl-Z   The end-of-file marker.

cursor   The blinking line or highlighting box that indicates where the next keystroke will be displayed or what the next control code entered will affect.

cutting and pasting   Selecting text from one part of a document or visual display and moving it to another location.

cylinder   Two tracks that are in the same place on different sides of a double-sided disk. May be extended to include multiple platters. For example, Side 0 Track 30, Side 1 Track 30, Side 2 Track 30, and Side 3 Track 30 form a cylinder.

daisy-wheel printer   A printer that uses circular templates for producing letter-quality characters.

data area   The tracks on a disk that contain user data.

database   A collection of data organized into various categories. A phone book is one form of database.

database management system   A software program designed to allow the creation of specially organized files, as well as data entry, manipulation, removal, and reporting for those files.

data bits   The bits that represent data when the computer is communicating.

data disk   A disk that has been formatted without the /S switch. The disk can contain only data; no room has been reserved for system files.

data stream   The transmission of data between two components or computers.

dead key   A reserved key combination on international keyboards, which outputs nothing itself but allows the next keystroke to produce an accent mark above or below the keystroke's usual character.

debugging   The process of discovering what is wrong with a program, where the problem is located, and what the solution is.

decimal   A numbering system based on ten digits.

decision making   A point in a batch file at which execution can continue on at least two different paths, depending on the results of a program test. Also known as logical testing or branching.

default   The standard value of a variable or system parameter.

deferred execution   In a program or batch file, when execution is delayed until a value for some parameter is finally entered or computed.

delimiter   A special character, such as a comma or space, used to separate values or data entries.

destination   The targeted location for data, files, or other information generated or moved by a DOS command.

device   Any internal or external piece of peripheral hardware.

device driver   Also known as an interrupt handler. A special program that must be loaded to use a device. Adds extra capability to DOS.

device name   Logical name that DOS uses to refer to a device.

digital   A representation based on a collection of individual digits, such as 0's and 1's in the binary number system.

digitizer   A device with a movable arm that can take an image and break it up into small parts, which the computer translates into bits.

directory   A grouping of files on a disk. These files are displayed together and may include access to other directories (subdirectories).

directory tree   The treelike structure created when a root directory has several subdirectories, each of the subdirectories has subdirectories, and so on.

disk drive   A hardware device that accesses the data stored on a disk.

diskette   A flexible, oxide-coated disk used to store data. Also called a floppy diskette.

disk optimizer   A program that rearranges the location of files stored on a disk in order to make the data in those files quickly retrievable.

DOS   Disk Operating System. A disk manager and the program that allows computer/user interaction.

DOS environment   A part of memory set aside to hold the defaults needed in the current environment, such as COMSPEC, PATH, LASTDRIVE, and so on.

DOS prompt   Usually C> or A>. The visual indication that DOS is waiting for a command or prompting you for input.

dot-matrix printer   A printer that represents characters by means of tiny dots.

double-density diskette   A diskette on which magnetic storage material is arranged twice as densely as usual, allowing the storage of twice the usual amount of data. Generally refers to a 360K, 5¼" diskette.

drive identifier   A single letter assigned to represent a drive, such as drive A or drive B. Usually requires a colon after it, such as A:.

DRIVER.SYS   A file containing a device driver for an extra external disk drive. Used in the CONFIG.SYS file.

dual tasking   Causing two tasks or programming events to occur simultaneously.

echoing   Displaying on your video monitor the keystrokes you type in.

EDLIN   The DOS line editor.

end-of-file marker   A Ctrl-Z code that marks the logical end of a file.

environment   The context within which DOS interfaces with you and with your commands.

error level   A code, set by programs as they conclude processing, that tells DOS whether an error occurred, and if so, the severity of that error.

expansion cards   Add-on circuit boards through which hardware can increase the power of the system, such as adding extra memory or a modem.

expansion slots   Connectors inside the computer in which expansion cards are placed so that they tie in directly to the system.

extended ASCII codes   ASCII codes between 128 and 255, which usually differ from computer to computer.

extended DOS partition   A hard-disk partition used to exceed the 32Mb, single-disk barrier; it can be divided into logical disk drives.

extended memory   Additional physical memory beyond the DOS 1Mb addressing limit.

extension   The one to three characters after the period following the base name in a file specification.

external buffer   A device, connected to the computer and another device, that acts as a buffer.

Family Application Programming Interface (FAPI)   The suggested subset of OS/2 system service calls that enable a developed .EXE program to run under either DOS or OS/2.

file   A collection of bytes, representing a program or data, organized into records and stored as a named group on a disk.

file allocation table (FAT)   A table of sectors stored on a disk, which tells DOS whether a given sector is good, bad, continued, or the end of a chain of records.

file name   The name of a file on the disk. Usually refers to the base name, but can include the extension as well.

file version   A term that refers to which developmental copy of a software program is being used or referenced.

filter   A program that accepts data as input, processes it in some manner, and then outputs the data in a different form.

fixed disk   IBM's name for a hard disk.

floppy diskette   *See* diskette.

flow of control   The order of execution of batch-file commands; how the control flows from one command to another, even when the next command to be executed is not located sequentially in the file.

foreground task   The main program running on your computer, as opposed to the less visible background task (usually a printing job).

formatting   The placement of timing marks on a disk to arrange the tracks and sectors for subsequent reading and writing.

fragmentation   A condition in which many different files have been stored in noncontiguous sectors on a disk.

function keys   Special-purpose keys on a keyboard, which can be assigned unique tasks by DOS or by application programs.

gigabyte (Gb)   1024 megabytes.

global characters   *See* wild cards.

graphics mode   The mode in which all screen pixels on a monitor are addressable and can be used to generate detailed images. Contrasts with text mode, which usually allows only 24 lines of 80 characters.

hard disk   A rigid platter that stores data faster and at a higher density than a floppy diskette. Sealed in an airtight compartment to avoid contaminants that could damage or destroy the disk.

hardware   The physical components of a computer system.

hardware interrupt   A signal from a device to the computer, indicating that an event has taken place.

head   A disk-drive mechanism that reads data from and writes data to the disk.

head crash   Occurs when the head hits the disk platter on a hard disk, physically damaging the disk and the data on it.

help file   A file of textual information containing helpful explanations of commands, modes, and other on-screen tutorial information.

hexadecimal   A numbering system in base 16. A single eight-bit byte can be fully represented as two hexadecimal digits.

hidden files   Files whose names do not appear in a directory listing. Usually refers to DOS's internal system files, but can also refer to certain files used in copy-protection schemes.

high-capacity diskette   A 1.2Mb, 5¼" floppy diskette.

high-resolution mode   The mode on a video monitor in which all available pixels are used to provide the most detailed screen image possible. On a color monitor, this mode reduces the possible range of colors that can be output.

horizontal landscape   When output to a printer is not done in the usual format, but rather with the wider part of the paper laid out horizontally, as in a landscape picture.

hot key A key combination used to signal that a memory-resident program should begin operation.

housekeeping Making sure the directory stays intact and well organized, and that unnecessary files are deleted.

hub The center hole of a diskette.

IF A conditional statement in a batch file.

ink-jet printer A printer that forms characters by spraying ink in a dot pattern. *See* dot-matrix printer.

interface The boundary between two things, such as the computer and a peripheral.

interrupt A signal sent to the computer from a hardware device, indicating a request for service or support from the system.

keyboard translation table An internal table, contained in the keyboard driver, that converts hardware signals from the keyboard into the correct ASCII codes.

key combination When two or more keys are pressed simultaneously, as in Ctrl-ScrollLock or Ctrl-Alt-Del.

key redefinition Assigning a nonstandard value to a key.

kilobyte (K) 1024 bytes.

laser printer A printer that produces images (pictures or text) by shining a laser on a photostatic drum, which picks up toner and then transfers the image to paper.

LCD Liquid Crystal Display. A method of producing an image using electrically sensitive crystals suspended in a liquid medium.

letter-quality printer A printer that forms characters that are comparable to those of a typewriter.

line editor A program that can make textual changes to an ASCII file, but can only make changes to one line of the file at a time.

line feed When the cursor on a screen moves to the next line, or when the print head on a printer moves down the paper to the next line.

literal Something that is accepted exactly as it was submitted.

lockup Occurs when the computer will not accept any input and may have stopped processing. Requires that the computer be warm or cold booted to resume operating.

log file   A separate file, created with the BACKUP command, that keeps track of the names of all files written to the backup diskette(s).

logging on   Signing onto a remote system, such as a mainframe or telecommunications service.

logical   Something that is defined based on a decision, not by physical properties.

logical drives   Disk drives, created in an extended DOS partition, that do not physically exist, but DOS thinks they do. A means for DOS to access a physical disk that has more than 32Mb available.

logical testing   *See* decision making.

machine language   The most fundamental way to program a computer, using instructions made up entirely of strings of 0's and 1's.

macro   A set of commands, often memory-resident. When executed, they appear to the program executing them as if they were being entered by you.

medium-resolution mode   The mode on a Color Graphics Adapter in which only 320 × 200 pixels of resolution are allowed.

megabyte (Mb)   1024 kilobytes.

memory   The circuitry in a computer that stores information. *See also* RAM and ROM.

memory-resident   Located in physical memory, as opposed to being stored in a disk file.

menu   A set of choices displayed in tabular format.

meta symbols   Special single-character codes used by the PROMPT command to represent complex actions or sequences to be included in the DOS prompt.

microfloppy diskette   The 3½'' diskette format used in the new Personal System/2 and many other computers.

modem   A device that transmits digital data in tones over a phone line.

monitor   The device used to display images; a display screen.

monochrome   Using two colors only—the background and foreground.

mouse   A device that moves the screen cursor by means of a hand-held apparatus moved along a surface such as a desk. The computer can tell how far and in which direction the mouse is being moved.

multiprocessing *See* Multitasking.

multitasking When two or more computing applications are executing simultaneously.

multithreading Simultaneously running multiple independent code sequences (threads) within a single program (task).

national language-support operations The DOS 3.3 feature that supports displays and printers, using a new range of code and character groupings.

network Several computers, connected together, that can share common data files and peripheral devices.

nibble Four bits, or half a byte.

octal A numbering system in base 8.

OS/2 Operating System/2. The latest advanced operating system from Microsoft and IBM, which manages computer/user interaction, enhanced memory features, and multitasking.

operating system *See* DOS.

overlay files Files containing additional command and control information for sophisticated and complex programs. An overlay file is usually too large to fit into memory along with the main .EXE or .COM file.

overwriting Typing new data over what is already there.

parallel communications Data transmission in which several bits can be transferred or processed at one time.

parameter An extra bit of information, specified with a command, that determines how the command executes.

parity The bit, added to the end of a stream of data bits, that makes the total of the data bits and the parity bits odd or even.

partition The section of a hard disk that contains an operating system. There can be at most four partitions on one hard disk.

Pascal A programming language used mainly in computer science.

password A sequence of characters that allows entry into a restricted system or program.

path The list of disks and directories that DOS will search through to find a command file ending in .COM, .BAT, or .EXE.

peripheral   Any physical device connected to the computer.

piping   Redirecting the input or output of one program or command to another program or command.

pixel   The smallest unit of display on a video monitor—in short, a dot—which can be illuminated to create text or graphics images.

platter   The rigid disk used in a hard-disk drive.

plotter   A device that draws data on paper with a mechanical arm.

port   A doorway through which the computer can access external devices.

Presentation Manager   The windowing interface of OS/2's Version 1.1, which displays executing programs within separate screen windows on the same display monitor.

primary DOS partition   Up to the first 32Mb of a hard disk. Contains the boot record and other DOS information files.

printer   A device that outputs data onto paper using pins (dot matrix), a daisy wheel, ink jets, laser imaging, and so on.

process   *See* task

protected mode   The principal operating environment of OS/2 that supports multitasking, process protection, and advanced memory management.

public domain   Something not copyrighted or patented. Public domain software can be used and copied without infringing on anyone's rights.

queue   A series of files waiting in line to be printed.

RAM   Random Access Memory. The part of the computer's memory to which you have access; stores programs and data while the computer is on.

RAM disk   An area of RAM that acts as if it were a disk drive. All data in this area of memory is lost when the computer is turned off or warm booted. Also known as a virtual disk.

range   A contiguous series of values (minimum to maximum, first to last, and so on).

read-after-write verification   An extra level of validity checking, invoked with the VERIFY command or the /V switch. Rereads data after writing it to disk, comparing the written data to the original information.

read-only status   Indicates that a file cannot be updated but can be read.

read/write bit   The bit in a file specification that indicates whether a file can accept changes or deletions, or can only be accessed for reading.

real mode   The single tasking unprotected operating environment that runs old DOS programs under OS/2.

redirection   Causing output from one program or device to be routed to another program or device.

REM statement   A line in a BASIC program containing remarks or comments for program explanation or clarification.

reserved names   Specific words, in a programming language or operating system, which should not be used in any other application context.

resident commands   Commands located in random-access memory.

resource allocation   Making system facilities available to individual users or programs.

reverse video   Black letters on a white background.

ROM   Read-Only Memory. The section of memory that you can only read from. This contains the basic computer operating system and system routines.

root directory   The first directory on any disk.

scan code   The hardware code representing a key pressed on a keyboard. Converted by a keyboard driver into an ASCII code for use by DOS and application programs.

scrolling   What the screen does when you're at the bottom of it and press Return—all of the lines roll up.

secondary command processor   A second copy of COMMAND-.COM, invoked either to run a batch file or to provide a new context for subsequent DOS commands.

sector   A division of a disk track; usually, 512 bytes.

serial communications   Data transmission in which data is transferred and processed one bit at a time. Also known as asynchronous communications.

Session Manager The OS/2 program that presents a menu of choices enabling you to switch your video display between your DOS program and any of the active OS/2 protected mode programs.

shareware Public domain software. *See also* public domain.

snapshot program A program used in debugging to store the status of system or application program variables.

software The programs and instruction sets that operate the computer.

software interrupt A signal from a software program that calls up a routine that is resident in the computer's basic programming. Also, a software signal to the computer that the software program has finished, has a problem, and so on.

source The location containing the original data, files, or other information to be used in a DOS command.

spooling Simultaneous Peripheral Operations On-Line. Using a high-speed disk to store input to or output from low-speed peripheral devices while the CPU does other tasks.

spreadsheet program An electronic version of an accountant's spreadsheet; when one value changes, all other values based on that value are updated instantly.

start bit The bit sent at the beginning of a data stream to indicate that data bits follow.

stop bit The bit sent after the data bits, indicating that no more data bits follow.

string A series of characters.

subcommands Several special commands used only within batch files.

subdirectory A directory contained within another directory or subdirectory. Technically, all directories other than the root directory are subdirectories.

switch A parameter included in DOS commands, usually preceded by the slash (/) symbol, which clarifies or modifies the action of the command.

synchronization The coordination of a sending and receiving device, so that both simultaneously send and receive data at the same rate.

system disk   A disk containing the necessary DOS system files for system booting.

task   An OS/2 program and the set of system resources that it uses.

text mode   The mode in which standard characters can be displayed on a monitor.

thread   A logical sequence of code in an OS/2 program. This is the fundamental entity that is assigned CPU time in the OS/2 multitasking environment.

time slice   The smallest unit of time managed and assigned by the operating system to programs and other processing activities.

toggle   A switch or command that reverses a value from off to on, or from on to off.

track   A circular stream of data on the disk. Similar to a track on a record, only not spiraling.

transient command   A command whose procedures are read from the disk into memory, executed from memory, and then erased from memory when finished.

utility   A supplemental routine or program designed to carry out a specific operation, usually to modify the system environment or perform housekeeping tasks.

variable parameter   A named element, following a command, that acts as a placeholder; when you issue the command, you replace the variable parameter with the actual value you want to use.

verbose listing   A listing of all files and subdirectories contained on the disk and path specified in the command. Activated by the CHKDSK command with the /V switch.

vertical portrait   The conventional 8¼-by-11-inch output for printed information, with the long side of the paper positioned vertically.

virtual disk   *See* RAM disk.

volume label   A name, consisting of up to 11 characters, that can be assigned to any disk during a FORMAT operation or after formatting with the LABEL command.

warm booting   Resetting the computer using the Ctrl-Alt-Del key combination. *See* bootstrapping.

wide directory listing   An alternate output format that lists four columns of file names.

wild cards   Characters used to represent any other characters. In DOS, * and ? are the only wild-card symbols.

word processor   A computerized typewriter. Allows the correction and reformatting of documents before they are printed.

write-protection   Giving a disk read-only status by covering the write-protect notch.

APPENDIX B ASCII CODES

This appendix presents information on how ASCII codes are created, used, and manipulated in DOS. It discusses the different numbering systems used to create these codes, as well as how codes are grouped to form identifiable character sets. Using this information, you can both manage your DOS system more readily and manipulate file data for yourself.

CHARACTER SETS

Just as you use an alphabet and a decimal numbering system, the computer uses its own character and numbering system. DOS maintains, in memory, all of the characters of the English alphabet, including numbers and symbols, as well as some foreign symbols (such as accented vowels). This group of symbols is called a character set. By changing the symbols in this set, you can obtain completely new character sets. This is especially useful for people living in other countries, who have less daily need of U.S. standard characters and who would rather work with their own characters.

ASCII CODES

A character is any letter, number, punctuation symbol, or graphics symbol. In other words, it is anything that can be displayed on a video screen or printed on a printer.

Each character in a character set has a number assigned to it, which is how the computer refers to the various characters in the set.

For example, code 65 refers to a capital A, and code 97 refers to a lowercase a. These codes are called ASCII codes (pronounced "*ask-ee* codes"); ASCII stands for American Standard Code for Information Interchange.

Codes 0 through 31 are used as control codes. Displaying one of these codes will cause something to happen instead of causing a symbol to be displayed. For example, displaying code 7 will result in the computer's bell or beeper being sounded. Displaying code 13 will result in a carriage return.

Codes 32 through 127 are ASCII character codes for numbers, letters, and all punctuation marks and symbols. Codes 128 through 255, known as extended ASCII codes, vary from computer to computer. They usually comprise foreign characters, Greek and mathematical symbols, and graphics characters. (Graphics characters consist of small lines and curves that can be used to create geometric patterns.)

DOS 3.3 has several available ASCII tables, called code pages. The most common is the standard U.S. code page (see Table B.1); the next most common is the Multilingual code page (see Table B.2).

MAPPING ONE CHARACTER SET ONTO ANOTHER

Any device that displays characters has a device driver that literally drives, or controls, the device. When the computer tells a printer to print the letter A, DOS sends the code 65 to the printer driver, which converts the 65 into a series of control codes that will print the A.

For the sake of consistency, computers, printers, and displays all have the same character sets and coding system for ASCII codes 32 through 127. This ensures that when you press a key, the desired character will be displayed, and the same character will be printed by your printer.

The process of matching ASCII codes against characters in a character set is called *mapping.* The following section describes how you map a set of numbers onto a set of characters so that they correspond exactly to each other.

Hex Digits 1st / 2nd	0-	1-	2-	3-	4-	5-	6-	7-	8-	9-	A-	B-	C-	D-	E-	F-
0-		►		0	@	P	`	p	Ç	É	á	░	└	╨	α	≡
1-	☺	◄	!	1	A	Q	a	q	ü	æ	í	▒	┴	╤	β	±
2-	●	↕	"	2	B	R	b	r	é	Æ	ó	▓	┬	╥	Γ	≥
3-	♥	‼	#	3	C	S	c	s	â	ô	ú	│	├	╙	π	≤
4-	♦	¶	$	4	D	T	d	t	ä	ö	ñ	┤	─	╘	Σ	⌠
5-	♣	§	%	5	E	U	e	u	à	ò	Ñ	╡	┼	╒	σ	⌡
6-	♠	▬	&	6	F	V	f	v	å	û	ª	╢	╞	╓	µ	÷
7-	•	↨	'	7	G	W	g	w	ç	ù	º	╖	╟	╫	τ	≈
8-	◘	↑	(	8	H	X	h	x	ê	ÿ	¿	╕	╚	╪	Φ	°
9-	○	↓	)	9	I	Y	i	y	ë	Ö	⌐	╣	╔	┘	Θ	∙
A-	◎	→	*	:	J	Z	j	z	è	Ü	¬	║	╩	┌	Ω	·
B-	♂	←	+	;	K	[	k	{	ï	¢	½	╗	╦	█	δ	√
C-	♀	∟	,	<	L	\	l	|	î	£	¼	╝	╠	▄	∞	ⁿ
D-	♪	↔	-	=	M	]	m	}	ì	¥	¡	╜	═	▌	φ	²
E-	♫	▲	.	>	N	^	n	~	Ä	₧	«	╛	╬	▐	ε	■
F-	☼	▼	/	?	O	_	o	⌂	Å	ƒ	»	┐	╧	▬	∩	

Table B.1: U.S. ASCII table (code page 437)

Hex Digits 1st / 2nd	0-	1-	2-	3-	4-	5-	6-	7-	8-	9-	A-	B-	C-	D-	E-	F-
0-		►		0	@	P	`	p	Ç	É	á	░	└	ð	Ó	-
1-	☺	◄	!	1	A	Q	a	q	ü	æ	í	▒	┴	Ð	ß	±
2-	●	↕	"	2	B	R	b	r	é	Æ	ó	▓	┬	Ê	Ô	=
3-	♥	‼	#	3	C	S	c	s	â	ô	ú	│	├	Ë	Ò	¾
4-	♦	¶	$	4	D	T	d	t	ä	ö	ñ	┤	─	È	õ	¶
5-	♣	§	%	5	E	U	e	u	à	ò	Ñ	Á	┼	ı	Õ	§
6-	♠	▬	&	6	F	V	f	v	å	û	ª	Â	ã	Í	µ	÷
7-	•	↨	'	7	G	W	g	w	ç	ù	º	À	Ã	Î	þ	¸
8-	◘	↑	(	8	H	X	h	x	ê	ÿ	¿	©	╚	Ï	Þ	°
9-	○	↓	)	9	I	Y	i	y	ë	Ö	®	╣	╔	┘	Ú	¨
A-	◎	→	*	:	J	Z	j	z	è	Ü	¬	║	╩	┌	Û	·
B-	♂	←	+	;	K	[	k	{	ï	ø	½	╗	╦	█	Ù	¹
C-	♀	∟	,	<	L	\	l	|	î	£	¼	╝	╠	▄	ý	³
D-	♪	↔	-	=	M	]	m	}	ì	Ø	¡	¢	═	¦	Ý	²
E-	♫	▲	.	>	N	^	n	~	Ä	×	«	¥	╬	Ì	¯	■
F-	☼	▼	/	?	O	_	o	⌂	Å	ƒ	»	┐	¤	▀	´	

Table B.2: Multilingual ASCII table (code page 850)

NUMBERING SYSTEMS

Computers use a variety of numbering systems to operate. The most basic numbering system is the binary system, in which there are only two digits, 0 and 1. The digital circuitry used in computers operates by using small voltages that turn magnetic bits on or off. Therefore, 0 and 1 are used to represent the two states of off and on, respectively.

Counting in binary is not difficult, but it does require some adjustment from your standard decimal-numbering scheme. The progression of numbers and their matching decimal conversions are shown in Table B.3.

Chapter 8 contains a detailed explanation of the binary numbering system. The general rule for converting numbers from binary to decimal is to multiply the number in every binary number column by 2 raised to the column-number power. You count column numbers from the right, starting with 0. For the binary number 1101, for example, you would obtain

$$(1 \times 2^0) + (0 \times 2^1) + (1 \times 2^2) + (1 \times 2^3)$$

BINARY	DECIMAL
0	0
1	1
10	2
11	3
100	4
101	5
110	6
111	7
1000	8
1001	9
1010	10

Table B.3: Binary-to-decimal conversion

where any number to the 0 power (2^0 in this case) is defined as equal to 1. This is called *counting in base 2*.

The *decimal* system counts in base 10. Using the same method of converting binary numbers, you can see that breaking down the decimal number 2014 into its component parts works like this:

$$(4 \times 10^0) + (1 \times 10^1) + (0 \times 10^2) + (2 \times 10^3)$$
$$= 4 + 10 + 000 + 2000$$
$$= 2014$$

Another numbering system is called *octal*, or base 8. This system has only eight digits, 0–7. The octal number 701 is converted to base 10 (decimal) by the following computation:

$$(1 \times 8^0) + (0 \times 8^1) + (7 \times 8^2)$$
$$= 1 + 0 + 448$$
$$= 449$$

The last major numbering system in computers is called *hexadecimal*, which counts in base 16. This system has 16 digits in it: 0–9 and A–F, which form the counting sequence 0123456789ABCDEF. To count in this system, you use the same method you use for other numbering systems. The hexadecimal number BA7 translates to decimal as

$$(7 \times 16^0) + (A \times 16^1) + (B \times 16^2)$$

which is equal to

$$7 + (10 \times 16^1) + (11 \times 16^2)$$

which is also equal to

$$7 + 160 + 2816$$
$$= 2983$$

Hexadecimal notation is convenient for byte values because a hexadecimal digit is equivalent to 4 ($2^4 = 16$) binary digits (called a *nibble*) and there are 8 bits ($2^8 = 256$-character set) in a byte. A byte can therefore be represented by two hexadecimal digits.

Table B.4 demonstrates how to count in hexadecimal.

HEXADECIMAL	DECIMAL
0	0
.	.
.	.
9	9
A	10
B	11
.	.
.	.
F	15
10	16
.	.
.	.
1A	26

Table B.4: Hexadecimal-to-decimal conversion

Hard disks are usually so large that they can contain more than one type of operating system. For example, you can have DOS 3.3 manage one part of a disk and UNIX manage another. Each of these sections is called a *partition*. You can have from one to four partitions on a disk.

Partitions are used to make the hard disk, especially a very large one, a more economical investment. They allow you to effectively have up to four completely different computer systems resident in one set of hardware. However, since they do not share a common software environment, they cannot share data directly.

Two types of partitions can be set up for DOS: a *primary DOS partition* and an *extended DOS partition*. The primary DOS partition is the partition that contains DOS and is the first partition on the disk. This is the only partition that must be on the disk if your disk is no larger than 32Mb. The extended DOS partition is a separate partition that cannot be used for booting, but can be divided into separate logical drives.

If you have more than 32Mb available on one hard disk, you will need to create an extended DOS partition, which is assigned the next logical drive letter. For example, if you had a 60Mb hard-disk drive, and wanted access to all of it, you would create a 32Mb primary partition and a 28Mb extended partition. The primary partition could be accessed as drive C, while the extended partition would be called drive D. You could also subdivide the extended partition into more logical drives (up to the letter Z).

You must create partitions before using a hard-disk drive. You will probably take the easiest route by simply making the entire disk into

APP. C

If your disk is already being used and you wish to make a new partition, you will have to first back up all of your data and then run FDISK from a system diskette. Finally, you'll need to reformat your disk before restoring your files to it.

one primary partition. The FDISK program presented here, however, is necessary in several more advanced situations. For example, you may plan on using multiple operating systems from the same disk. FDISK will let you set up unique partitions for each system. (Each of these would be a primary partition, but only one could be designated the active partition, the one that will gain control at boot up.) Then again, you may be using one of the large hard disks (40–70Mb) that are increasingly common. Since DOS can only access a logical drive of 32Mb or less, you'll need to partition a larger physical drive into multiple logical drives. Only in this way can you store and retrieve information on the larger hard disk.

CONFIGURING A DOS PARTITION

In this section, you will see exactly how to use the FDISK command. This procedure is very important, and it can have serious consequences if done incorrectly. However, it can also make your system more efficient, when done properly. FDISK is only usable on hard-disk systems.

Invoking the FDISK command is as simple as typing

FDISK

and pressing Return. (Remember to have your path set properly to include the directory containing the FDISK command file.) After this command creates the appropriate partition(s), you must then logically format the disk.

When you first execute FDISK, the screen will clear and the FDISK Options screen will appear. This contains the menu used to get around in FDISK (see Figure C.1).

All data on your disk will be destroyed when you create partitions with FDISK.

As you can see, there are four choices. If you have a system with more than one hard-disk drive, the number in the "Current Fixed Disk Drive: 1" line would be changed to the number of drives in your system. Also, a fifth option, "Select Next Fixed Disk Drive," would be displayed on the screen. You can only work on one hard-disk drive at a time, but you can switch from the drive you are working on to another drive. For now, let's assume you have one hard-disk drive and that the screen in Figure C.1 is what you see.

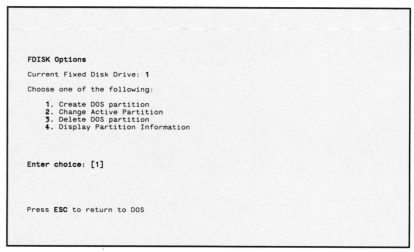

```
FDISK Options

Current Fixed Disk Drive: 1

Choose one of the following:

    1. Create DOS partition
    2. Change Active Partition
    3. Delete DOS partition
    4. Display Partition Information


Enter choice: [1]



Press ESC to return to DOS
```

Figure C.1: The FDISK Options menu

CREATING A PARTITION

If you plan to use your hard disk to support another operating system, do not partition the whole disk. Leave some room so that another system can be loaded onto the disk.

The first option on the FDISK Options menu is to create a DOS partition. Since you are using DOS, and not another operating system like UNIX, you can only create DOS partitions. Should you wish to put another operating system onto the disk, that system would have its own version of FDISK and could then create its own partitions next to DOS's.

Choosing the first option to create a DOS partition results in Figure C.2. If you select option 2 at this point, intending to create an extended DOS partition *before* creating a primary partition, DOS will display a message indicating that you cannot do so, and will suggest that you press Esc to return to the main FDISK Options menu. Assuming you are starting from scratch, you would select choice 1 to create the primary DOS partition. You will then see the screen shown in Figure C.3.

If you want to use the whole disk for DOS, then you answer Y on this screen. The computer will allocate the entire disk, and then come back with the message

System will now restart

Insert DOS diskette in drive A:
Press any key when ready . . .

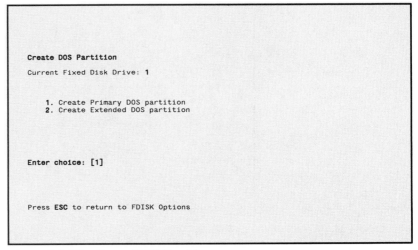

Figure C.2: The Create DOS Partition menu

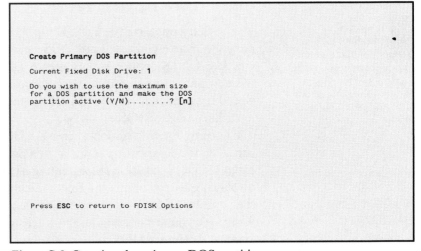

Figure C.3: Creating the primary DOS partition

Since you just created the partition, there is still nothing on the hard disk. The system must be rebooted from the disk drive. You can now format the entire hard disk just as you would a floppy diskette.

If you answer N, as shown in Figure C.3, you have the opportunity to create a smaller partition, as shown in Figure C.4. As you can see, there are 305 *cylinders* available on the total disk. A hard disk consists of several platters, similar to a diskette; each platter consists of a

```
Create Primary DOS Partition

Current Fixed Disk Drive: 1




Total disk space is  305 cylinders.
Maximum space available for partition
is  305 cylinders.

Enter partition size...........: [ 200]


No partitions defined

Press ESC to return to FDISK Options
```

Figure C.4: Defining the primary DOS partition's size

series of concentric tracks made up of sectors. Each platter lies above another and is read by a different disk head. Viewed vertically, a series of tracks (with the same track number, but on different platters) located one above the other constitute a cylinder. The brackets in the screen shown in Figure C.4 indicate the place where you may enter a number for cylinders that is less than the default maximum (305 on this disk).

Notice that the second-to-last line on the screen tells you that no partitions have been defined yet. If you are using your disk for DOS alone, you should accept the default maximum cylinder value. All disk space will then be available for DOS and your DOS files. If you plan on splitting up your disk between DOS and another operating system, however, you'll have to decide for yourself what percentage of total disk space is needed for the other operating system. In this example, you intend to create an extended DOS partition, so 200 was entered for the number of cylinders in the primary DOS partition.

Entering 200 results in the screen shown in Figure C.5. This screen tells you that the first partition on drive C is a primary DOS partition (PRI DOS) that starts at cylinder 0 and ends at cylinder 199, constituting a total of 200 cylinders. Pressing Esc at this point returns you to the FDISK Options menu. If you again try to create a primary partition, DOS will show the following message on your

```
Create Primary DOS Partition

Current Fixed Disk Drive: 1

Partition Status   Type  Start  End Size
   C: 1            PRI DOS    Ø   199 2ØØ




Primary DOS partition created

Press ESC to return to FDISK Options
```

Figure C.5: Primary DOS partition screen

There can only be
one primary DOS
partition. When DOS
boots up, the system files
from this partition are
loaded into memory for
your operations.

screen:

Primary DOS partition already exists.
Press ESC to return to FDISK Options

In this example, you have only used 200 cylinders out of a possible 305, so you can make an extended DOS partition. To do so, you select choice 1 on the FDISK Options menu (see Figure C.1) and then select choice 2 on the Create DOS Partition menu (see Figure C.2).

The resulting screen, shown in Figure C.6, allows you to create an extended DOS partition. This screen tells you the current partition information—that is, that there are 305 total cylinders available for use—and also tells you that 105 cylinders remain unused. The 105 value is used as the default entry at this stage. You only need to type in a number over the 105 to override the default. In Figure C.6, 55 was entered for the desired extended DOS partition, leaving 50 cylinders unused on the disk for another operating system.

The screen will now clear, redisplay the partition information (including that on the new extended DOS partition), and print the message

Extended DOS Partition created
Press ESC to return to FDISK Options

```
Create Extended DOS Partition

Current Fixed Disk Drive: 1

Partition Status   Type  Start  End  Size
  C: 1             PRI DOS   Ø   199  2ØØ


Total disk space is  3Ø5 cylinders.
Maximum space available for partition
is  1Ø5 cylinders.

Enter partition size...........: [  55]




Press ESC to return to FDISK Options
```

Figure C.6: Creating an extended DOS partition

near the bottom of the screen. Pressing Esc will result in the next step of the process (see Figure C.7).

Since you have just created an extended DOS partition, DOS wants to know if you want to create logical drives within this new partition. It tells you the total available cylinders in the partition and asks you to enter a size for the logical drive. In this example, you enter 45. The resulting screen will contain the logical drive information (drive name, starting cylinder, ending cylinder, and total cylinders used).

Suppose you wanted to create another logical drive, E, using the remaining ten cylinders. You could again choose option 1 on the FDISK Options menu. You would go again to the Create DOS Partition menu, but there would be one new choice displayed:

3. Create logical DOS drive(s) in the Extended DOS partition

This would bring you back to the screen for defining logical drives, where you could then enter the information for drive E. Going through this same sequence again in order to use the remaining ten cylinders will result in Figure C.8. Notice that the cylinder numbers are within the bounds of the extended DOS partition. You are told that DOS created two logical drives, D and E, with sizes of 45 and 10 cylinders. Furthermore, you're reminded that no more space remains for any other logical drives. Press Esc, and you will once again be back at the FDISK Options menu.

If you try to create another extended partition, you will get a partition information screen and the message

Extended DOS partition already exists.
Press ESC to return to FDISK Options

```
    Create Logical DOS Drive(s)




    No logical drives defined


    Total partition size is   55 cylinders.
    Maximum space available for logical
    drive is   55 cylinders.
    Enter logical drive size........: [  45]


    Press ESC to return to FDISK Options
```

Figure C.7: Defining logical drives

```
    Create Logical DOS Drive(s)

    Drv Start End  Size
     D:  200  244    45
     E:  245  254    10











    All available space in the Extended DOS
    partition is assigned to logical drives.

    Logical DOS drive created, drive letters
    changed or added
    Press ESC to return to FDISK Options ▪
```

Figure C.8: Logical drive summary screen

CHANGING THE ACTIVE PARTITION

The *active* partition is the partition that is used to boot the system. It is the default partition. Choosing option 2 on the main FDISK Options menu leads you to a menu like that shown in Figure C.9, in which the partition information is displayed along with the total number of cylinders available on the disk. FDISK now wants to know the number of the partition that you wish to make active.

If you enter the number 2, as shown in the figure, DOS will inform you that only the primary DOS partition (1) may be made active. Type the number 1 so that the primary DOS partition will have control when the system comes up. Pressing Return will result in the adjusted partition information display seen in Figure C.10.

Notice the letter A on the first line of this display. An A under "Status" tells you that partition 1 is the active partition. Pressing Esc takes you back to the FDISK Options menu.

DISPLAYING PARTITION INFORMATION

Option 4 on the FDISK Options menu is used to display information about the partitions. This is useful because no extra functions will be executed at the same time; you can simply look at the information. Choosing option 4 yields the screen shown in Figure C.11.

```
Change Active Partition

Current Fixed Disk Drive: 1

Partition Status   Type   Start  End  Size
   C: 1             PRI DOS    0   199  200
      2             EXT DOS  200   254   55


Total disk space is  305 cylinders.

Enter the number of the partition you
want to make active...............: [2]



Partition selected (2) is not bootable,
.active partition not changed.
Press ESC to return to FDISK Options
```

Figure C.9: The Change Active Partition menu

The information at the top of the screen is familiar by now. But what if you want to see information about the logical drives that have been defined? Look at the bottom half of the screen, where you are asked if you want to see this information. Replying with Y results in a display of information about these logical drives (see Figure C.12). Pressing Esc at this point will return you to the FDISK Options menu.

```
Change Active Partition

Current Fixed Disk Drive: 1

Partition Status   Type  Start  End Size
  C: 1        A    PRI DOS    Ø   199  2ØØ
     2             EXT DOS  2ØØ   254   55


Total disk space is 3Ø5 cylinders.




Partition 1 made active

Press ESC to return to FDISK Options ▪
```

Figure C.10: Display of the active partition

```
Display Partition Information

Current Fixed Disk Drive: 1

Partition Status   Type  Start  End Size
  C: 1        A    PRI DOS    Ø   199  2ØØ
     2             EXT DOS  2ØØ   254   55


Total disk space is 3Ø5 cylinders.


The Extended DOS partition contains
logical DOS drives. Do you want to
display logical drive information?  [Y]


Press ESC to return to FDISK Options
```

Figure C.11: Displaying partition information

DELETING DOS PARTITIONS

As with most things, what DOS giveth, DOS can taketh away—with a little prodding from you. Selecting choice 3 on the FDISK Options menu produces the Delete DOS Partition menu, shown in Figure C.13.

```
Display Logical DOS Drive Information

Drv Start End  Size
 D:  200  244    45
 E:  245  254    10












Press ESC to return to FDISK Options ▪
```

Figure C.12: Logical drive information

```
Delete DOS Partition

Current Fixed Disk Drive: 1

Choose one of the following:

    1.  Delete Primary DOS partition
    2.  Delete Extended DOS partition
    3.  Delete logical DOS drive(s) in
        the Extended DOS Partition


Enter choice: [ ]



Press ESC to return to FDISK Options ▪
```

Figure C.13: The Delete DOS Partition menu

Using this menu, you can delete any of the information you've already set up. You may want to expand or contract other partitions, or you may no longer want to use a partition in the manner you originally designed. In any case, you can only make changes in a certain order. You cannot delete the primary DOS partition without first deleting the extended DOS partition. If you try, DOS will give you this message:

**Cannot delete Primary DOS partition on
drive 1 when Extended partition exists**

Press ESC to return to FDISK Options

In addition, you cannot delete an extended DOS partition without first "undefining" (deleting) the logical drives in that partition. Trying to delete the extended DOS partition before deleting the drives in it will simply display the current partition information with the patient message

**Cannot delete Extended DOS partition
while logical drives exist.
Press ESC to return to FDISK options**

Choice 3 in the Delete DOS Partition menu is probably the first selection you will need to make; you work your way backwards through the order in which you created things. (Actually, you will find that this is a fairly natural process.) Selecting choice 3 produces the screen shown in Figure C.14, which contains the logical drive information and the size of the extended DOS partition the drives are in. You are also warned that any data contained in the logical disk drive to be deleted will also be deleted.

If you still want to delete the drive, simply enter the drive identifier. You will then be asked to confirm this step. In Figure C.14, you have selected drive E to delete first, and confirmed the choice by typing Y. If you had entered N, you would have been returned to the FDISK Options menu.

Once FDISK deletes the logical drive, it updates the display at the top of the screen and asks for another drive to delete. If you wanted to regain all the space used by this partition, you would then enter drive D, confirm your entry, and end up with the screen shown in Figure

C.15. Pressing Esc twice at this point will bring you back up through the menu screens to the main FDISK Options menu.

Now that the logical drives are gone, you can delete the extended DOS partition itself if you choose to do so. Choosing option 2 on the Delete DOS Partition menu results in the familiar form of an FDISK screen (see Figure C.16). Again, you are shown the partition infor-

```
Delete Logical DOS Drive

Drv Start End  Size
 D:  2ØØ   244   45
 E:  245   254   1Ø




Total partition size is   55 cylinders.

Warning! Data in the logical DOS drive
will be lost. What drive do you wish
to delete........................? [e]

Are you sure.....................? [y]


Press ESC to return to FDISK Options
```

Figure C.14: Deleting a logical drive

```
Delete Logical DOS Drive

Drv Start End  Size
 D: drive deleted
 E: drive deleted




Total partition size is   55 cylinders.
All logical drives deleted in the
Extended DOS partition



Press ESC to return to FDISK Options ▪
```

Figure C.15: Summary of logical drive deletions

```
Delete Extended DOS Partition

Current Fixed Disk Drive: 1

Partition Status   Type  Start  End Size
   C: 1       A    PRI DOS    0   199  200
      2            * EXT DOS  200  254   55




Warning! Data in the Extended DOS
partition will be lost. Do you wish
to continue......................? [y]


Press ESC to return to FDISK Options
```

Figure C.16: Deleting the extended DOS partition

mation display (as in Figure C.11), warned that data will be lost, and asked if you really want to delete the extended DOS partition. If you reply Y, the screen will be updated to show only the primary DOS partition and the message

> **Extended DOS partition deleted**

> **Press ESC to return to FDISK Options**

Press Esc to return once again to the FDISK Options menu.

INDEX

video, reverse, 156, 235, 237, 641
Video Graphics Array (VGA), 154
virtual disk, 228. *See also* RAM disk
virtual memory, 531
VOL command, 625
volume labels, 82–84, 643
VOPT utility, 427–428

W

warm booting, 351, 643
White Crane Systems, 436
wide directory listing, 54–55, 644
wild-card characters
in copying multiple files, 159
described, 644
in directory display requests, 58
testing effects of using, 62
Windows
calculations with, 470–472
changing default disk drive in, 465
Clipboard access in, 506–509
clock display in, 505
configuring, 499–504
Control menu of, 462–464
database management Cardfile program
in, 479–489

described, 445–448
directories listings in, 465, 467–469
and EMS, 511, 524
exiting, 469–470
file control in, 465–467
file editing and note making with Notepad
program in, 492–499
hardware required by, 448
installing, 448–459
Reversi game in, 504–505
running, 461–463
spooling output from, 489–492
starting, 459–461
using DOS commands in, 469–470
using MS-DOS Executive in, 464–470
.WK1 file extension, 55
.WKS file extension, 55
word processors, 114–117, 435–438, 534,
644
write-protection, 644

X

XCOPY command, 67–73, 626–627
XenoCopy-PC utility, 437
XenoSoft, 437
XTREE program, 395

Selections from
The SYBEX Library

SPREADSHEETS AND INTEGRATED SOFTWARE

The ABC's of 1-2-3 (Second Edition)
Chris Gilbert/Laurie Williams
245pp. Ref. 355-4

Online Today recommends it as "an easy and comfortable way to get started with the program." An essential tutorial for novices, it will remain on your desk as a valuable source of ongoing reference and support. For Release 2.

Mastering 1-2-3 (Second Edition)
Carolyn Jorgensen
500pp. Ref. 528-X

Get the most from 1-2-3 Release 2 with this step-by-step guide emphasizing advanced features and practical uses. Topics include data sharing, macros, spreadsheet security, expanded memory, and graphics enhancements.

Lotus 1-2-3 Desktop Companion (SYBEX Ready Reference Series)
Greg Harvey
976pp. Ref. 501-8

A full-time consultant, right on your desk. Hundreds of self-contained entries cover every 1-2-3 feature, organized by topic, indexed and cross-referenced, and supplemented by tips, macros and working examples. For Release 2.

Power User's Guide to Lotus 1-2-3
Peter Antoniak/E. Michael Lunsford
368pp. Ref. 421-6

This guide for experienced users focuses on advanced functions, and techniques for designing menu-driven applications using macros and the Release 2 command language. Interfacing techniques and add-on products are also considered.

Lotus 1-2-3 Instant Reference SYBEX Prompter Series
Greg Harvey/Kay Yarborough Nelson
296pp. Ref. 475-5; 4 3/4x8

Organized information at a glance. When you don't have time to hunt through hundreds of pages of manuals, turn here for a quick reminder: the right key sequence, a brief explanation of a command, or the correct syntax for a specialized function.

Mastering Lotus HAL
Mary V. Campbell
342pp. Ref. 422-4

A complete guide to using HAL "natural language" requests to communicate with 1-2-3—for new and experienced users. Covers all the basics, plus advanced HAL features such as worksheet linking and auditing, macro recording, and more.

Simpson's 1-2-3 Macro Library
Alan Simpson
298pp. Ref. 314-7

Increase productivity instantly with macros for custom menus, graphics, consolidating worksheets, interfacing with mainframes and more. With a tutorial on macro creation and details on Release 2 commands.

Mastering Symphony (Fourth Edition)
Douglas Cobb
875pp. Ref. 494-1

Thoroughly revised to cover all aspects of the major upgrade of Symphony Version 2, this Fourth Edition of Doug Cobb's classic is still "the Symphony bible" to this complex but even more powerful package. All the new features are discussed and placed in context with prior versions so that both new and previous users will benefit from Cobb's insights.

Focus on Symphony Macros
Alan Simpson
239pp. Ref. 351-1
An in-depth tutorial guide to creating, using, and debugging Symphony macros, including developing custom menus and automated systems, with an extensive library of useful ready-made macros for every Symphony module.

Focus on Symphony Databases
Alan Simpson/Donna M. Mosich
398pp. Ref. 336-8
Master every feature of this complex system by building real-life applications from the ground up—for mailing lists, inventory and accounts receivable. Everything from creating a first database to reporting, macros, and custom menus.

Better Symphony Spreadsheets
Carl Townsend
287pp. Ref. 339-2
Complete, in-depth treatment of the Symphony spreadsheet, stressing maximum power and efficiency. Topics include installation, worksheet design, data entry, formatting and printing, graphics, windows, and macros.

Mastering Quattro
Alan Simpson
400pp. Ref. 514-X
This tutorial covers not only all of Quattro's classic spreadsheet features, but also its added capabilities including extended graphing, modifiable menus, and the macro debugging environment. Simpson brings out how to use all of Quattro's new-generation-spreadsheet capabilities.

Mastering Framework II
Douglas Hergert/Jonathan Kamin
509pp. Ref. 390-2
This business-minded tutorial includes a complete introduction to idea processing, "frames," and software integration, along with its comprehensive treatment of word

processing, spreadsheet, and database management with Framework.

Advanced Techniques in Framework: Programming in FRED
Alan Simpson
320pp. Ref. 246-9
This introduction to the FRED programming language is for experienced Framework users who need to expand their word processing, spreadsheet, graphics, and database management skills.

Mastering Excel on the IBM PC
Carl Townsend
550pp. Ref. 403-8
A complete Excel handbook with step-by-step tutorials, sample applications and an extensive reference section. Topics include worksheet fundamentals, formulas and windows, graphics, database techniques, special features, macros and more.

Mastering Enable
Keith D. Bishop
350pp. Ref. 440-2
A comprehensive, practical, hands-on guide to Enable 2.0—integrated word processing, spreadsheet, database management, graphics, and communications—from basic concepts to custom menus, macros and the Enable Procedural Language.

Mastering Q & A
Greg Harvey
399pp. Ref. 356-2
This hands-on tutorial explores the Q & A Write, File, and Report modules, and the Intelligent Assistant. English-language command processor, macro creation, interfacing with other software, and more, using practical business examples.

Mastering SuperCalc 4
Greg Harvey
311pp. Ref. 419-4
A guided tour of this spreadsheet, database and graphics package shows how and why it adds up to a powerful business planning tool. Step-by-step lessons and real-life examples cover every aspect of the program.

Understanding Javelin PLUS
John R. Levine
Margaret Levine Young
Jordan M. Young
558pp. Ref. 358-9
This detailed guide to Javelin's latest release includes a concise introduction to business modeling, from profit-and-loss analysis to manufacturing studies. Readers build sample models and produce multiple reports and graphs, to master Javelin's unique features.

DATABASE MANAGEMENT

Mastering Paradox (Third Edition)
Alan Simpson
600pp. Ref. 490-9
Paradox is given authoritative, comprehensive explanation in Simpson's up-to-date new edition which goes from database basics to command-file programming with PAL. Topics include multiuser networking, the Personal Programmer Application Generator, the Data-Entry Toolkit, and more.

Mastering Reflex
Robert Ericson/Ann Moskol
336pp. Ref. 348-1
A complete introduction to Reflex: The Analyst, with hands-on tutorials and sample applications for management, finance, and technical uses. Special emphasis on its unique capabilities for crosstabbing, graphics, reporting, and more.

dBASE III PLUS Programmer's Reference Guide (SYBEX Ready Reference Series)
Alan Simpson
1056pp. Ref. 508-5
Programmers will save untold hours and effort using this comprehensive, well-organized dBASE encyclopedia. Complete technical details on commands and functions, plus scores of often-needed algorithms

The ABC's of dBASE III PLUS
Robert Cowart
264pp. Ref. 379-1
The most efficient way to get beginners up and running with dBASE. Every 'how' and 'why' of database management is demonstrated through tutorials and practical dBASE III PLUS applications.

Mastering dBASE III PLUS: A Structured Approach
Carl Townsend
342pp. Ref. 372-4
In-depth treatment of structured programming for custom dBASE solutions. An ideal study and reference guide for applications developers, new and experienced users with an interest in efficient programming.

Also:
Mastering dBASE III: A Structured Approach
Carl Townsend
338pp. Ref. 301-5

Understanding dBASE III PLUS
Alan Simpson
415pp. Ref. 349-X
A solid sourcebook of training and ongoing support. Everything from creating a first database to command file programming is presented in working examples, with tips and techniques you won't find anywhere else.

Also:
Understanding dBASE III
Alan Simpson
300pp. Ref. 267-1

Understanding dBASE II
Alan Simpson
260pp. Ref. 147-0

UNDERSTANDING DOS 3.3   The Companion Diskette ($19.95)

If you have found *Understanding DOS 3.3* to be useful, you will be glad to learn that every one of the batch files in this book is contained in a companion diskette. Save time, energy, and money—and avoid the drudgery of typing these excellent programs—by ordering the *Understanding DOS 3.3* Companion diskette now.

An excellent introductory training guide to DOS is also available in audio cassette form. Two cassettes and an accompanying Professional Learning Manual can be your personal aid to quick and easy understanding of DOS.

Use the order form below to order any of the fine products produced by Judd Robbins. Mail today, with complete payment, to Computer Options, P.O. Box 9656, Berkeley, CA 94709-9656.

_____

_____ copies of *Understanding DOS 3.3* Companion Diskette,

at $19.95 each _____

_____ copies of *ReComm*, the DOS Command Reissuing Utility,

at $19.95 each _____

_____ copies of *Introduction to DOS* Audio Cassette Training,

at $19.95 each _____

_____ Shipping and handling (add $2.50 per item)

_____ California sales tax (please add appropriate amount

for your city/county) _____

TOTAL ORDER: _____

_____
Name

_____
Address

_____
City   State   Zip

_____
Phone

TO JOIN THE SYBEX MAILING LIST OR ORDER BOOKS
PLEASE COMPLETE THIS FORM

NAME _____ COMPANY _____

STREET _____ CITY _____

STATE _____ ZIP _____

☐ PLEASE MAIL ME MORE INFORMATION ABOUT **SYBEX** TITLES

ORDER FORM (There is no obligation to order)

PLEASE SEND ME THE FOLLOWING:

TITLE	QTY	PRICE
_____	___	___
_____	___	___
_____	___	___
_____	___	___

TOTAL BOOK ORDER _____ $_____

CUSTOMER SIGNATURE _____

SHIPPING AND HANDLING PLEASE ADD $2.00 PER BOOK VIA UPS _____

FOR OVERSEAS SURFACE ADD $5.25 PER BOOK PLUS $4.40 REGISTRATION FEE _____

FOR OVERSEAS AIRMAIL ADD $18.25 PER BOOK PLUS $4.40 REGISTRATION FEE _____

CALIFORNIA RESIDENTS PLEASE ADD APPLICABLE SALES TAX _____

TOTAL AMOUNT PAYABLE _____

☐ CHECK ENCLOSED ☐ VISA
☐ MASTERCARD ☐ AMERICAN EXPRESS

ACCOUNT NUMBER _____

EXPIR. DATE _____ DAYTIME PHONE _____

CHECK AREA OF COMPUTER INTEREST:

☐ BUSINESS SOFTWARE

☐ TECHNICAL PROGRAMMING

☐ OTHER: _____

THE FACTOR THAT WAS MOST IMPORTANT IN YOUR SELECTION:

☐ THE SYBEX NAME

☐ QUALITY

☐ PRICE

☐ EXTRA FEATURES

☐ COMPREHENSIVENESS

☐ CLEAR WRITING

☐ OTHER _____

OTHER COMPUTER TITLES YOU WOULD LIKE TO SEE IN PRINT:

_____

_____

OCCUPATION

☐ PROGRAMMER ☐ TEACHER

☐ SENIOR EXECUTIVE ☐ HOMEMAKER

☐ COMPUTER CONSULTANT ☐ RETIRED

☐ SUPERVISOR ☐ STUDENT

☐ MIDDLE MANAGEMENT ☐ OTHER:

☐ ENGINEER/TECHNICAL _____

☐ CLERICAL/SERVICE

☐ BUSINESS OWNER/SELF EMPLOYED

CHECK YOUR LEVEL OF COMPUTER USE

☐ NEW TO COMPUTERS

☐ INFREQUENT COMPUTER USER

☐ FREQUENT USER OF ONE SOFTWARE

   PACKAGE:

   NAME _____

☐ FREQUENT USER OF MANY SOFTWARE

   PACKAGES

☐ PROFESSIONAL PROGRAMMER

OTHER COMMENTS:

_____

_____

_____

_____

_____

_____

_____

PLEASE FOLD, SEAL, AND MAIL TO SYBEX

SYBEX, INC.
2021 CHALLENGER DR. #100
ALAMEDA, CALIFORNIA USA
                94501

SEAL

SYBEX Computer Books are different.

Here is why . . .

At SYBEX, each book is designed with you in mind. Every manuscript is carefully selected and supervised by our editors, who are themselves computer experts. We publish the best authors, whose technical expertise is matched by an ability to write clearly and to communicate effectively. Programs are thoroughly tested for accuracy by our technical staff. Our computerized production department goes to great lengths to make sure that each book is well-designed.

In the pursuit of timeliness, SYBEX has achieved many publishing firsts. SYBEX was among the first to integrate personal computers used by authors and staff into the publishing process. SYBEX was the first to publish books on the CP/M operating system, microprocessor interfacing techniques, word processing, and many more topics.

Expertise in computers and dedication to the highest quality product have made SYBEX a world leader in computer book publishing. Translated into fourteen languages, SYBEX books have helped millions of people around the world to get the most from their computers. We hope we have helped you, too.

For a complete catalog of our publications:

SYBEX, Inc. 2021 Challenger Drive, #100, Alameda, CA 94501
Tel: (415) 523-8233/(800) 227-2346   Telex: 336311
Fax: (415) 523-2373

SUMMARY OF DOS COMMANDS*

COMMAND	DESCRIPTION	FORMAT	PAGE
KEYB	Loads in new keyboard translation table and code page	[*D:Path*]KEYB [*xx*[,[*yyy*],[*FileSpec*]]]	592
LABEL	Defines or changes existing volume label	[*D:Path*]LABEL [*D1:*][*String*]	593
MKDIR (MD)	Creates a new subdirectory	MD [*D:*]*Path*	595

MODE	Defines attributes for all ports and code pages	[*D:Path*]MODE LPT*x*: [*CPL*][,[*LPI*][,P]]
		[*D:Path*]MODE LPT*x*: = COM*y*
		[*D:Path*]MODE COM*y*[:]*Baud*[,[*Parity*] [,[*Bits*][,P]
		[*D:Path*]MODE *Type*
		[*D:Path*]MODE [*Type*], *Shift* [,T]
		[*D:Path*]MODE *Device* CODEPAGE
		   PREPARE = ((*CP*) *FileSpec*)
		[*D:Path*]MODE *Device* CODEPAGE
		   PREPARE = ((*CPList*) *FileSpec*)
		[*D:Path*]MODE *Device* CODEPAGE SELECT = *CP*
		[*D:Path*]MODE *Device* CODEPAGE[/STATUS]
		[*D:Path*]MODE *Device* CODEPAGE REFRESH
			596

MORE	Pauses the display of long files	[*D:Path*]MORE	598
NLSFUNC	Loads in routines for code pages and the CHCP command	[*D:Path*]NLSFUNC [*FileSpec*]	599
PATH	Defines search list for .EXE, .COM, and .BAT files	PATH [*D1:Path1*][;*D2:Path2*...]	600
PRINT	Queues files for printing	[*D:Path*]PRINT [/D:*Device*][/B:*BuffSize*][/U:*BusyTicks*] [/M:*MaxTicks*][/S:*TimeSlice*][/Q:*QueueSize*][/C][/T] [/P][*FileSpec*,...]	602
PROMPT	Changes the system prompt	PROMPT [*String*]	603
RECOVER	Rescues damaged files	[*D:Path*]RECOVER[*D1*][*FileSpec*]	604
RENAME (REN)	Changes the name of a file	REN *OldFile NewFile*	606

*See Part 6, ''DOS Command Reference,'' for a complete description of subcommands and their parameters.

SOFTWARE & HARDWARE CENTER
11386 SW Burton-Hillsdale Hwy
Beaverton   OR   97005
(503)626-0696

****
**   Sales Invoice   **
**   0100894104   **
** 09/15/89 12:23:23   **
****
Served by: Kip Triplett
Paid by:
   CASH   24.95

Qty Description	Tx	Price
1 UNDERSTANDING DOS 3.3N		24.95

                  SALE TOTAL   24.95

              Amt Tendered   24.95

	SUMMARY OF DOS COMMANDS*		
COMMAND	**DESCRIPTION**	**FORMAT**	**PAGE**
REPLACE	Copies, adds, and updates programs	[*D:Path*]REPLACE *SourceFile* [*Dest*][/A][/P][/R][/S][/W]	607
RESTORE	Reads backup file back onto disk	[*D:Path*]RESTORE *SourceD FileSpec* [/S][/P][/B:*mm-dd-yy*] [/A:*mm-dd-yy*][/M][/N][/L:*hh-mm-ss*][/E:*hh-mm-ss*]	608
RMDIR (RD)	Deletes empty directories	RD [*D:Path*]	610
SELECT	Creates a system disk with country information	[*D:Path*]SELECT [[A: ¦ B:][*DestD*:[*DestPath*]] *xxx yy*	611
SET	Changes defaults and definitions in DOS environment	SET [*Name* = [*Param*]]	612
SHARE	Loads network lock-out routines	[*D:Path*]SHARE [/F:*FileMem*][/L:*Locks*]	613
SORT	Sorts data by column	[*D:Path*]SORT [/R][/ + *Col*]	616
SUBST	Makes DOS think a directory is a disk drive	[*D:Path*]SUBST [*D:Path*]SUBST *NewD*[*Path2* [*D:Path*]SUBST *NewD* /D	618
SYS	Transfers hidden system files to another disk	[*D:Path*]SYS *DestD*:	619
TIME	Sets the system time	TIME [*hh*:*mm*[:*ss*[.*xx*]]]	620
TREE	Lists all directories, subdirectories, and files on a disk	[*D:Path*]TREE [*D2*:][/F]	621
TYPE	Displays the contents of an ASCII file	TYPE *FileSpec*	622
VER	Displays the current version of DOS	VER	623
VERIFY	Causes DOS to verify everything that is written to disk	VERIFY [ON ¦ OFF]	624

*See Part 6, "DOS Command Reference," for a complete description of subcommands and their parameters.

SUMMARY OF DOS COMMANDS*			
COMMAND	**DESCRIPTION**	**FORMAT**	**PAGE**
VOL	Displays volume label of drive	VOL [*D:*]	625
XCOPY	Copies complete directories, subdirectories, and files	[*D:Path*]XCOPY[*FileSpec1*][*FileSpec2*][/A][/D:*mm-dd-yy*] [/E][/M][/P][/S][/V][/W]	626

*See Part 6, ''DOS Command Reference,'' for a complete description of subcommands and their parameters.

CONFIGURATION FILE COMMANDS*			
COMMAND	**DESCRIPTION**	**FORMAT**	**PAGE**
BREAK	Determines when DOS checks for a Ctrl-Break	BREAK = [ON ¦ OFF]	557
BUFFERS	Sets number of buffers	BUFFERS = *x*	558
COUNTRY	Specifies date and time formats	COUNTRY = *xxx*,[*yyy*] [,*FileSpec*]	568
DEVICE	Loads device drivers into memory	DEVICE = *FileSpec*[*Switches*]	573
FCBS	Defines how many file control blocks can be used at once	FCBS = *MaxNum,PermNum*	582
FILES	Specifies how many files can be accessed at once	FILES = *x*	584
LASTDRIVE	Specifies the highest drive letter	LASTDRIVE = *D*	594
SHELL	Specifies location of a different command processor	SHELL = *ComFileSpec* [/E:*xxxxx*][/P]	614
STACKS	Specifies new stack resources	STACKS = *n,s*	617

*See Part 6, ''DOS Command Reference,'' for a complete description of commands and their parameters.